Critical Acclaim for *Not Every Spirit*

I have used several different introductory theology texts for teaching my basic courses, and Morse's book is by a good margin the most thoughtful and provocative. Although regularly invoking (in a way that feels neither authoritarian nor antiquarian) an impressive range of traditional voices, what is most impressive about this text is the way in which Morse manages to communicate a powerful and contemporary theological vision of his own without failing to give the reader a sense of the broad range of possible approaches to any given theological problem.

— **Paul DeHart,** Associate Professor of Theology, Vanderbilt University Divinity School

Written during postliberalism's height and first published a decade prior to current philosophies and theologies of "the event," Morse's *Not Every Spirit* expertly delivers a concise, yet comprehensive, Christian dogmatics predicated on the notion of grace as event. For Morse, the Gospel is not a narrative in search of supplementation by human performance; it is something that *happens,* first and foremost. Accordingly, this book functions as a call to the church to stop acting and start witnessing — and for systematic theologians to put away the scripts and pick up the seismographs. It has fundamentally changed the way I think about, and do, Christian theology.

— **Trevor Eppehimer,** Associate Professor of Systematic Theology, Hood Theological Seminary

Someone once said that most thinkers are either "clumpers" or "splitters," people who can think imaginatively and paint in bold strokes, or people who can think very precisely and analyze. Christopher Morse is among those unusual people who can do both. He understands the grand sweep of the gospel, of God's love poured out on a creation that groans in travail, and he knows how to help Christians think rigorously about what they believe — and what they disbelieve. Not every spirit is Christ's Spirit; sometimes the Church must say "no." It is part of Morse's gift to place such nay-saying in the service of God's truth.

— **Joseph L. Mangina,** Associate Professor of Systematic Theology, Wycliffe College, Toronto

There is no introduction to Christian doctrine that does a better job of equipping students to ask the questions that the church needs to ask about its faith and practice. By understanding doctrine as a reflection of what Christians *refuse* to believe about God, Christ, and the world around them, Christopher Morse offers a genuinely novel approach to systematic theology that is deeply rooted in Scripture and the life of the church. Neither trendy nor traditionalist, this book exemplifies a generous orthodoxy that provides unparalleled resources for disciplined yet charitable dialogue across even the most seemingly intractable confessional divisions.

—**Ian A. McFarland,** Associate Professor of Systematic Theology,
Candler School of Theology, Emory University

This is the finest one-volume dogmatics available in English today.

—**Kendall Soulen,** Professor of Systematic Theology
at Wesley Theological Seminary

For the many Christians who have a nearly allergic reaction to systematic theology, equating it with being authoritarian and closed-minded, this boldly subtitled *A Dogmatics of Christian Disbelief* can be a cure. Indeed, with faith comes many disbeliefs — such as a mistrust of authorities and an aversion to closed-mindedness. This book clears the ground of disbeliefs in order to expose those things we do believe, and treasure. My students, many of them experienced pastors and from a wide spectrum of denominations, typically approach this book with reluctance (it's thick and about dogma!), then reach its final chapters with real gratitude for the new trails in their theological imaginations it has helped them to discover, trails first cleared by our ancestors in the faith, as well as trails as yet untraversed.

—**Kelton Cobb,** Professor of Theology and Ethics,
Hartford Seminary, Hartford, Connecticut

Christopher Morse's *Not Every Spirit* is a most distinctive apology for Christian faith, a postmodern update of Aquinas, superbly combining the dogmatic tasks of Systematics with Ethics (the science of moral reasoning) for a changed and changing world. As a liberation theologian, committed to finding and publishing good news for the poor, I am pleased to have such a richly profound resource that recognizes Christianity's historic abuses yet allows me to explore its potential and actual role in establishing human worth and freedom on personal and collective levels, in devotional, private dimensions, and institutional, liturgical forms. One cannot help but be deepened by an encounter with the honest and honorable Spirit in *Not Every Spirit*. That Professor Morse's text is intellectually rigorous yet is readable and sensible makes his a model method for doing theology in the twenty-first century and beyond.

—**JoAnne Marie Terrell,** Associate Professor of Ethics and Theology, Chicago Theological Seminary

The signal merit of this book, as studied as it is readable, is Morse's ability to draw readers into the innermost workings of Christian doctrines, displaying the connections and dynamics which enliven them. By engaging contemporary objections and clarifying those disbeliefs which positive Christian faith enjoins, Morse demonstrates afresh how the Christian gospel itself exposes Christian teaching to the most salutary criticism. That our faith requires theology, and that theology requires argument within, around, and for the sake of a better faithfulness — of these truths Morse is the most expert of teachers. And I can think of no textbook that so convincingly shows how dogmatics, by pursuing that better faithfulness, thereby serves the better righteousness for which Christians both hope and labor.

—**Philip G. Ziegler,** Lecturer in Systematic Theology, University of Aberdeen

Praise for *Not Every Spirit,* first edition

Professor Morse's meticulous scholarship in this book convinces Christians to examine not only what they believe but also to give attention to what they are called to disbelieve. In today's world of turmoil, distrust, and violence, Morse's work challenges Christians to reflect seriously on what they are to believe and what they are to do.

—**Delores S. Williams,** Union Theological Seminary

Every chapter . . . displays Morse's profound competence as a theologian. . . . This has already proved to be a valuable text for courses in systematic theology.

—**Charles M. Wood,** Perkins School of Theology, Southern Methodist University

This is a really distinctive voice in current theology with an important fresh approach. Exploring the *disbeliefs* that lie at the heart of Christian faith in accessible, concise, and original ways, Morse proves the truth of his own maxim that a good dogmatics is the best antidote to dogmatism about both faith and morals.

—**David H. Kelsey,** Yale University Divinity School

Not Every Spirit is an outstanding introduction to Christian Theology. Christopher Morse creatively illuminates a wide range of crucial contemporary issues. Arguing that the Christian faith entails not only beliefs, but also disbeliefs, Morse shows the theoretical and practical significance of these disbeliefs in a provocative and insightful way. The result is a theology that is both critical and affirmative.

—**Francis Schüssler Fiorenza,**
Harvard University, The Divinity School

NOT EVERY SPIRIT

NOT EVERY SPIRIT

A Dogmatics of Christian Disbelief

SECOND EDITION

Christopher Morse

NEW YORK • LONDON

Second edition 2009

The Continuum International Publishing Group Inc
80 Maiden Lane, New York, NY 10038

The Continuum International Publishing Group Ltd
The Tower Building, 11 York Road, London SE1 7NX

www.continuumbooks.com

T & T Clark is an imprint of The Continuum International Publishing Group

A catalog record of this book is available from the Library of Congress.

Printed in the United States of America

ISBN 978-0-567-02743-6

To
Craig C. Berggren

CONTENTS

PREFACE TO THE SECOND EDITION

I am grateful for the responses received since 1994 to the initial publication of *Not Every Spirit* and am glad for the opportunity this second edition affords to introduce in a new preface for prospective readers the aim and rationale of this text. Changes in the course of events during these intervening years have brought new manifestations of what the Psalmist calls "the terror of the night... and the destruction that wastes at noonday" (Ps. 91:5–6). Yet the call to hearers of the gospel message not to believe every spirit but to "test the spirits to see whether they are from God" remains as timely today as ever (1 John 4:1).

I foreground this call out of a particular background. Early in my beginning years on the Union Seminary faculty I co-taught a course on the Christian doctrine of God with a very engaging senior colleague, the late Dorothee Sölle. Some wondered at this joint effort, given our differences in perspective. But in addition to our mutual regard and friendship we shared a common delight in the vocation of theology and its pertinence for the church and society, and we were united in our determination to help students experience its vitality. At each class session we took turns presenting some aspect of church doctrine, to which the other would then give a response and invite class discussion. What we soon came to recognize was that our responses to each other, though always good natured, had unintentionally begun to follow a similar pattern. When I made the presentation, Professor Sölle, who was always and rightly intent to combat the most oppressive features as she saw them in much traditional theism, would tend in effect to reply, "If what you say is indeed traditional Christian teaching, I could accept it, but that is not what traditional Christian teaching is." Conversely, I, who admittedly had grown up blissfully free of the heavy hand of dogma and instead had discovered the history of doctrine when I came upon it as a student to be full of energizing insights and surprises, would in turn instinctively find myself prompted to respond, "Well, if what we have just heard is a description of traditional Christian teaching no one would believe it, but that is not what traditional Christian teaching is." The seeds of what later now becomes the approach of this book were at least in part planted in this class. Coupled with this academic context was a lingering impact from my previous parish days outside the classroom when as a new struggling preacher in the social upheavals of the sixties I had confronted in 1 John 4:1 a sermon text that both baffled and continued to intrigue me as to what its possible import for the present day might be. Contrary to one very mistaken reviewer, who supposed that a secularized indifference to the presence of the Spirit reflective of earlier death-of-God theologies had been the impetus behind my later work, it was instead precisely the gospel testimony to the gift of God's own Spirit as that which calls us to differentiate and not simply celebrate spiritual claims that elicited my curiosity and impressed itself upon me. It still does.

I mention this academic and church background of ferment especially for new readers, some of whom may be approaching the extraordinary subject called "dogmatics" for the first time. My hope is that they will find the time spent with the content of this volume, though demanding of their own reflection as the subject requires, not forbidding or without its companionable pleasures along the way.

The delight to be found in the calling to do theology and the experience of its current vitality awaits the interested student of the twenty-first century no less than previously. Nor has the intrigue lessened in moving beyond conventional prejudices and stereotypes, though these may change, in rethinking the question of what significance dogmatics as an undertaking can have today as a faithful testing of the spirits. I gratefully acknowledge the early conflictual yet invigorating influence of such Union associates in systematic theology as Dorothee Sölle, along with the other colleagues whom I reference by name at various places in these pages. They each have contributed to shaping the trajectory of my own thought, especially when it takes paths different from their own.

In arguing that the truth of the "good news" to which Christian theology attends is ever timely, and never timeless, the task of discerning what is presently and most urgently in our midst becomes one that is ever renewing and ongoing. The so-called "deposit of faith" that is said to be once for all entrusted to the saints (Jude 1:3, 2 Tim. 1:14) is not a buried treasure but one conveyed in earthen vessels that are alive to their specific times and places and not apparent all at once. Such living truth as somehow "once for all" but not "all at once" — living Truth that in the gospel message of Jesus Christ refuses the deadening containment of folded grave clothes and has yet many things to say (John 16:12) —

may best be realized as the Psalmist's *hesed*, or steadfast love, that both "endures forever" (Ps. 106:1) and yet like daily bread from heaven or manna in the wilderness (Ps. 78:24) endures only by currently coming forth as new every morning (Exod. 16:21) to be praised by singing unto the Lord "a new song" (Ps. 96:1, 98:1, 149:1). Thus the approach to dogmatics within the one volume constraints of this text seeks to heed both that which is remembered as *once-for-all* and enduring forever in biblical traditions of testimony as these are attested in the ongoing life of the church and, inseparably from this, that which is promised as *not all-at-once* but new every morning and having yet many things to say by the Spirit's leading into further truth.

In such an approach the main intent of dogmatics is neither to be defensive nor apologetic with regard to Christian faith claims but rather to propose and deploy a creditably accountable way for adjudicating their trustworthiness. This focus upon adjudication rather than indoctrination means that the aim is not to establish or enforce belief but rather to inquire into its current profession. Chapters 1–5 seek to spell out a possible way of accountable adjudication in a day when major theological appeals to authority used in previous centuries no longer have creditable currency. Chapters 6–14 seek to illustrate this way's deployment in the case of nine major areas of Christian doctrine. One need not adopt the rhetoric of postmodernism to acknowledge how questionable certain premises formerly held to be prerequisites for doing theology have now become. In past generations these necessary conditions have been thought to include, as in earliest times, a commonly acknowledged creed or rule of faith, a *regula fidei*; a commonly acknowledged teaching authority, be it a catholic magisterium, or simply an agreed upon way of regarding the Bible; a common religious experience or faith consciousness; or, at the minimum, a common rationality or structure of reasoning. Now with today's multicultural diversity across denominational lines and beyond them our only commonly acknowledged starting points in coming together to engage in Christian theology may simply be that (1) we have all heard of "God"; (2) we do not believe everything we have heard; (3) yet something in what we have heard matters enough to us that we are here. So be it; it is enough to begin.

This book is for readers of whatever persuasion who may object to much that is being represented today as the Christian faith and yet, in part for this very reason, find themselves motivated, perhaps surprisingly, to give the claims of this faith a further hearing. Such readers may or may not themselves profess to be Christians, but they are sufficiently intrigued by the subject of what such profession entails. For them God talk is not a matter of indifference. It has practical as well as theoretical ramifications, whether for good or ill in life today, that extend beyond the conventional categories usually associated with what we may think of as religion. While the topics covered in this text will be more familiar to some than to others — more like a native language than a foreign language — I have written the book, though necessarily compact in keeping to one volume, to be understandable and of value both for those approaching the study of dogmatic theology for the first time, as well as for those with prior background and knowledge of the issues who will read it in comparison with other treatments. The additional comments in the endnotes have been provided with both groups in mind.

The responses from scholarly reviews of the first edition, from letters of pastors and other interested readers and from students and teaching assistants who have worked with this book as a course text, have been generous in their assessments. Where points of criticism have been raised they are deserving of consideration. One reviewer has characterized the work methodologically as a "theology of due process." I find this to be a fair description, but only if it is not taken to imply a judicious neutrality that simply weighs pros and cons without committing to a verdict. That would overlook my emphasis upon the proscriptive and not simply descriptive responsibility of dogmatics. My calling to mind of the steps of medieval dialectic and disputation is an example of what I mean by such responsible proscription. In insisting upon providing a fair hearing of disputed questions of faith that have plausible alternative answers, and the current objections these pose, the dogmatic purpose is always to arrive at a judgment, a *responsio*, for which in turn an accountable explanation, introduced by the word "hence," the *ergo*, must be given. The ability to conduct such due process was a requirement for all those seeking master's degrees in theology in the medieval universities, and I think it holds significant value for theological students today. Such training goes to the heart of what it takes to bear faithful and not false witness. Unless one is able to recognize and state views opposite to one's own accurately enough so that those holding them will allow that their positions have been fairly represented, no creditable testing of the spirits can occur, and one is left merely with unaccountable charges and countercharges of bearing false witness — the so-called *rabies theologorum* of an earlier age, or the political smear campaigns of today's media attack ads. Ironically, the media age of the Internet has made the age of medieval disputation suddenly more interesting. Testing the spirits, in the sense of adjudicating claims made in the name of God, requires not only that inquiry be made into how the statements of such claims function as language games on their own native playing field, but how the game is now being played rhetorically, i.e., how disputed issues are currently being posed or framed. The steps as I have adapted them from the form of Thomistic disputation noted in this book are included with explanatory notes in Appendix A of this second edition.

Another reviewer, writing in 1996, applauded the fact that, while the most formative creedal confessions of Christianity characteristically do indeed affirm the faith in light of its rejections, no other contemporary dogmatic text to his knowledge was so in keeping with this classical interpretive procedure. Yet for this very reason he then expresses all the more disappointment that in his judgment I simply succumb to a liberal zeitgeist in addressing what he denotes as feminist, gay/lesbian, and pluralist issues. The three examples given are that I am merely being "politically correct" in contending (1) that destructive consequences for both the church and society follow when generic meanings of "father" and "son" and of masculine pronouns are either explicitly or implicitly attributed to God's triunity, (2) that the covenant fidelity of a homosexual couple is congruent with scripture and as a gift of God's grace is not to be dishonored, and (3) that, as I state, "one may confess the reality of Jesus Christ without ever having heard or ever being aware of the words Jesus Christ, or intending a Christian witness." How much more courageous, indeed "dogmatic," this reviewer concludes, it would have been had I directed my faithful disbeliefs against, instead of in support of, such positions and thereby shown a rejection of the prevailing zeitgeist. In a similar vein another otherwise complimentary reviewer questions whether my claim that "using the Bible to predict destruction of people other than your own kind has led in the past to attempts to justify the extermination of Jews, the burning of dissenters, the institutions of racial slavery and segregation, and the dehumanizing of all who are viewed as outsiders and different, whatever the cultural form this discrimination may take" is not a case of simply "playing to the gallery."

Within this same period, however, still another reviewer, who likewise commends the book's scholarship and clarity, faults it on opposite grounds precisely for not attending enough to the current zeitgeist with more appreciative regard for its New Age spirituality. The emerging trends, so he writes in 1994, show evidence of a culture that is less prone to thinking of the "spirits" of 1 John 4:1 in terms of their political significance. Or, in the words of still a further reviewer's question to me in 1996, why should we think that culturally this is a time when false spirits are especially prevalent? This reviewer criticizes my testing for being so thoroughly controlled by scriptural and christological considerations as to be unable to recognize liberative, ecological, and religiously plural stirrings of the Spirit.

What these contrasting comments illustrate is that within the generally commendatory reviews of this text the criticisms of its approach have tended to fault it either for being too beholden to what is current to be properly dogmatic, or too beholden to enduring scriptural and christological traditions to be properly current. No doubt there are points to take account of on both sides, and future readers may judge for themselves. But I dissent from any suggestion that applying the tests of continuity with apostolic tradition and congruence with scripture somehow violates the tests of cruciality and coherence, or vice versa, as set forth in chapter 4. These reviewers are correct in noting that the focus of *Not Every Spirit* is neither upon finding validation in a dogmatic past nor in constructing a theory of contemporary culture. But neither, as I explain in chapter 2, do I equate the current cultural significance of dogmatics as a testing of the spirits with what Ernst Troeltsch called the construction of a "cultural synthesis."

As to other critical suggestions that more could be said in interpreting this or that point of doctrine, I can only concur. I also appreciate the observation that the page limits of the book require that its discussions in places are necessarily condensed and compact. On this point I offer not a defense but a further introductory reminder of the book's intended plan and purpose. By design I have tried to produce a work limited to one volume that would be accountably creditable in the current state of theological scholarship as a "dogmatics" and at the same time also considerate of the reader and accessible, especially for inquiring students. In writing each section my fourfold aim, however successful, has been to be accurate, clear, and pertinent, but also as concise as possible. The reason is that as a teacher I am aware of how the sheer multivolume length of many dogmatic works can discourage at the outset the otherwise interested student. As a teaching text *Not Every Spirit* obviously does not pretend to cover all aspects of the commonly held teachings of the ecumenical church but is meant to engage the reader in actually doing dogmatics in a way that matters and invites further exploration. The goal is to assist the reader's own ability to "test the spirits" by developing an accountable stance with regard for disputed points. With this end in mind reference is made to an ecumenical range of issues and to selective readings from classical and contemporary sources.

As explained in the beginning chapters, merely the term "dogmatics" is generally freighted with such an unpopular connotation today, whether in church, academic, or secular circles, that first the conventional associations that call to mind an authoritarian and not to be questioned dogmatism must explicitly be rejected. Such dogmatisms in their various social, political, and religious guises are by no means limited today to theology. I contend that dogmatics as the critical discipline here outlined is the antidote of dogmatism.

Also in the title, the term "Christian disbelief,"or "faithful disbelief," may strike some as an oxymoron, but only if it is mistakenly confused with faithless unbelief. A distinction between faithful disbelief and faithless unbelief finds no self-evident expression in English usage. Nor is this distinction adequately expressed, for example, in German translation as *christlichen Unglaube*. This became apparent in 1994 upon this book's first printing when a copy was presented to a distinguished delegation of German contributors to the newly endowed Dietrich Bonhoeffer Chair in Theology and Ethics at Union upon their arrival for that chair's installation. Concern upon seeing the book's title led to questions as to whether I, as the one to be inaugurated as the first recipient of this chair, had in fact authored a text opposing Christian faith. It took several German friends and colleagues at a hastily called meeting to give assurance of Morse's "piety" before the installation ceremonies began! My inaugural address, taken from chapter 1, thankfully removed the initial misunderstanding of the title. There is, as I am intent to show, a faithful refusal intrinsic to biblical testimonies regarding faith in God, a refusal to credit what is not worthy of trust precisely because of God's confessed trustworthiness. When this intrinsic refusal of faith goes unrecognized, then faithfulness, whatever its religious and spiritual pretensions, in such a context of testimony cannot be said to exist. The enduring pertinence of such a context of usage is that it continues to call both present-day credulity with its false hopes and cynicism with its hopelessness into question. Here the prophetic promise of hope for the future to the biblical figure of Rachel in her "refusal to be consoled" serves as the iconic leitmotif of the book (Jer. 32:16–17). This is not a hope ever divorced from what the Apostle Paul calls "the sufferings of this present time" (Rom. 8:18).

I have underscored this refusal intrinsic to biblical testimony to faith in God by seeking to uncover in commonly held church doctrines what I call the disbeliefs that they enjoin and entail at the present time. For this reason the expression "I disbelieve that . . . " — or better, since church testing is a communal undertaking, "We disbelieve that . . . " — is to be read as simply "I (or we) refuse to believe that . . . " This clarification at the start hopefully will eliminate any confusion in trying to follow the proposed faithful disbeliefs that may be caused by the apparent expression in places, as one reviewer has pointed out, of the awkward double negative. These faithful disbeliefs become enfleshed on location in the concreteness of changing situations. Thus the lists given in this book are offered as illustrative proposals, not graven images, which themselves remain open to further testing and specification in coming contexts that cannot be predescribed or predetermined. But, though these proposed faithful disbeliefs are inconclusive in that they represent no foreclosure of the future and its coming judgments, the call to dogmatic testing, so understood, is never inconsequential or loses its urgency for any community en route in the life of faith. As such it remains a never outdated summons to one way of delighting in the ever forthcoming *hesed* of God. My hope is that this second edition will serve to convey to new readers at least something of the wonder of this gospel summons.

I gladly reaffirm the acknowledgments in the original Preface, and particularly the book's dedication to Craig C. Berggren for the reasons there stated that apply no less to this second edition. My additional thanks go to the students, from varied contexts ranging from university and seminary classrooms to the remarkable theological studies program at Sing Sing Correctional Facility under Professor Mark L. Chapman of Fordham, who have worked with this text. For assistance in updating references in this second edition I thank Jennifer Heckart, Ph.D. candidate at Union. For so ably steering this second edition through to its publication I thank the editor at T. & T. Clark/Continuum, Burke Gerstenschläger, and the editorial staff.

PREFACE TO THE FIRST EDITION

During the years of my teaching at Union I have shared the seminary's commitment that the right to speak in a community respectful of difference carries with it the responsibility to listen and try to hear as well. Without this matrix of opposition to stereotyping and the bearing of false witness my work, at least in the form here presented, would not have developed. It is offered primarily for the kind of students of theology I have been privileged to know, and others equally interested, who read theological texts not as an indoctrination to which they are expected to conform, but as an invitation to think through the issues of Christian faith for themselves with regard to the communities of which they are part.

My own particularity as a United Methodist minister and seminary teacher includes the unmistakable Virginia Methodism of my roots, but with it the ecumenical contexts of my academic theological education, as well as of my regular participation at different times during my years in Manhattan in worshiping congregations of more than one confessional tradition, Roman Catholic as well as Protestant.

This publication coincides with the endowment of a Dietrich Bonhoeffer Chair in Theology and Ethics that has been made possible by the generosity of contributors both in this country and in Germany. The endowment is designed to insure that the critical study of church doctrines and of dogmatics as a discipline remains alongside the other disciplines in the Union curriculum. There is a certain irony in associating the Bonhoeffer chair at Union with a contemporary rethinking of the role of dogmatics in communities of Christian faith. Upon his arrival for a year of study at Union in 1930 Bonhoeffer expressed his initial dismay at what he saw to be a "naive dogmatism" in which "the students . . . have not the faintest notion what dogmatic theology is about."[1] Not all who have played a part in Union's history have been persuaded that dogmatic theology is what Union should be about, but the reopening of the question of what is meant by that term, and how the task of dogmatics at the present time may actually confront the "naive dogmatism" of both credulity on the one hand and cynicism on the other, is what this volume is about.

Preliminary outlines for some of these chapters were worked on during brief academic sabbatical residencies, first over a decade ago at the Episcopal Divinity School in Cambridge, Massachusetts, and later at St. Faith's parish in London, and at Pusey House and Library at Oxford University. I remain most appreciative of the gracious hospitality extended to me by my hosts in each instance. Further opportunities to pursue certain ideas in this manuscript were afforded by invitations to deliver the Brown Lectures at my alma mater, Randolph-Macon College, to lecture in Perth, Western Australia, at the Anglican Summer School (in a beautiful January setting, despite the 105 degrees Fahrenheit!), and to take part in local church forums, parish weekends, and clergy conferences. From the exchanges on these occasions I was helped in revising and continuing my work.

But always I have come back to the classrooms of students, who in a variety of theological courses through the years have not hesitated to let me know where things made sense and where they didn't, where the points mattered or held no interest. There is scarcely a page of this book that does not recall to me some student question, disagreement, or remark that provoked me to try and see more clearly why those, including myself, who indeed hear the gospel as good news, so often find the very church doctrines intended to convey this news presented as tiresome, sometimes hateful, and even harmful.

A number of friends and colleagues, both faculty and students, have kindly responded to my queries on particular points and references relating to their own areas of specialization, and I sincerely thank them. Delores Williams offered the time to read and share with me her reflections. My thanks are also expressed to Agneta Enermalm-Ogawa for her expertise in Greek, to Jae-Bum Hwang for his prompt research assistance, to Leah Robinson for the subject index, to the staff of the Walter Burke Library at Union, to Norman A. Hjelm, then a publisher, who supported my early ideas for this book, and to Harold W. Rast and the editorial staff of Trinity Press International for bringing it to publication.

As each chapter has been written several readers, from differing standpoints, have continued to offer me their observations and helpful suggestions. I am very indebted to Mitchell J. Wood for his perceptive comments for improvements, especially as this project was getting underway, and to Dorothy Martyn, J. Louis Martyn, Daniel Spencer, and Robert Weatherford. James F. Kay gave me the benefit of his criticisms with a characteristic thoroughness and attention to detail matched only by the depth of his supportive theological interest. He also worked with me in drawing up the name and scriptural indexes.

From the time of his own student days at Union in the early eighties, Craig C. Berggren has provided insight, encouragement, and friendship essential to the completion of these pages. To him this book is dedicated.

Part 1

Christian Faith as Disbelief

Chapter 1

THE CALL TO FAITHFUL DISBELIEF

To believe in God is not to believe everything. In fact, it is hard to imagine what believing everything would mean. Perhaps insofar as "believing" can be defined as "trusting," one might say that in the dependency of earliest childhood we come closest to an indiscriminate trust. So it was once fashionable for some psychologists of religion to argue, thereby giving rise to many bad sermons on the theme "except ye become as a little child" (see Matt. 18:3).

Surely a tendency to trust everything without awareness of what is untrustworthy is not the faith in God to which we have been called by the gospel. But are there some things that Christian faith refuses to believe? And if so, how do we come to recognize what they are? These are the questions that the following pages will attempt to address. They have to do with the issue of determining what is untrustworthy from the standpoint of Christian faith.

"Do Not Believe Every Spirit"

Running through the traditions of scripture within the Bible there is what may be termed a call to "faithful disbelief." A key instance of this is most simply expressed in words of the First Epistle of John: "Beloved, do not believe every spirit, but test the spirits to see whether they are from God; for many false prophets have gone out into the world" (4:1). This charge not to believe every spirit is addressed to a community seeking to be faithful to God, a community that apparently recognizes itself when addressed as "Beloved." For this reason I refer to the charge as a call to *faithful* disbelief. In a biblical understanding of faith in God what is the role of this call not to believe every spirit? What disbeliefs does faithfulness require of us and of Christian communities in our time? These are questions posed by the statement in 1 John.

Similar questions are posed by various other writings of scripture. Elsewhere in the New Testament, for example, in the synoptic Gospels of Matthew, Mark, and Luke, we read, "And if anyone says to you at that time, 'Look! Here is the Christ!' or 'Look! There he is!' — do not believe it. False Christs and false prophets will arise and produce signs and omens, to lead astray, if possible, the elect" (Mark 13:21–22; see also Matt. 24:23–24 and Luke 17:23). To the Thessalonians it is written, "Not all have faith" (2 Thess. 3:2). To the Romans, "Not all have obeyed the gospel" (Rom. 10:16). In the Letter to the Galatians Paul's words are, "Formerly, when you did not know God, you were enslaved to beings that by nature are not gods. Now, however, that you have come to know God, or rather to be known by God, how can you turn back again to the weak and beggarly elemental spirits [*stoicheia*]? How can you want to be enslaved to them again?" (Gal. 4:8–9).

This call not to credit or give credence to that which is not of God is given repeated assertion in the Old Testament injunctions against idols: "Do not turn to idols or make cast images for yourselves: I am the Lord your God" (Lev. 19:4). In the Hebrew scriptures the blessing of God is seen to include the cursing and rejection of that which is not of God. We see this understanding carried over into the New Testament where the Greek word for "cursed" is *anathema.* Paul, to cite one instance, writes to the Galatians, "If anyone proclaims to you a gospel contrary to what you received, let that one be accursed [*anathema*]" (Gal. 1:9). We shall return to the application of the anathema and its implications for theology in chapter 3.

What is plain at the outset is that in a variety of biblical passages we encounter a persistent theme — that having faith in God means that some things are to be refused credence and trust. This is the case even in that familiar text of 1 Corinthians 13:7, which reads in English translation, "Love bears all things, believes all things, hopes all things, endures all things." Taken in the context of Paul's teaching, the phrase "believes all things [*panta pisteuei*]" does not assert that with love anything and everything is trusted, accepted, given credence and assent. What is meant is that "love *is faithful* in all things."

Yet ordinarily we do not associate disbelief with faithfulness toward God. It is far more customary to speak of beliefs of the Christian faith than of disbeliefs of the Christian faith. By standard dictionary definition a disbeliever, in a theological sense, is said to be someone who lacks faith in God and is an active unbeliever in God. The older term derived from the Latin for a disbeliever is *infidel.* As such, the idea of "disbelieving" has generally carried an unfavorable connotation in

Christian thinking, one that is not as disgraceful as "infidelity," perhaps, but close.

Apologists for religion as a universal human capacity have sometimes sought to make the case that the mere act of believing in itself is part of the essential goodness of human nature. Writing in the first half of this century on "the present condition of belief," one author begins, "I wish to show that it is better to believe than to disbelieve, and by 'better' I mean both more rational and more profitable."[1] He also meant more faithful, speaking as a Christian, for in the account offered no positive significance is given to disbelief as an aspect of faith in God. The notion that there is something better about believing as such, than about disbelieving, may be deeply ingrained in those of us who grew up to the lilting words of the revival song, "Only believe, only believe. All things are possible, only believe."[2]

Unlike some other languages, including the language of the New Testament itself, English vocabulary has no verbal form of the noun *faith*. We can speak of "having faith" or "being faithful," but to use a verb we must say, "We believe." Wherever in the New Testament Greek the word *faith* (*pistis*) is used as a verb (*pisteuein*), in English this is most often translated by the verb *to believe*. Faith comes to equal believing, trusting, and assent.

Yet when we look at what human faithfulness involves in many biblical accounts, this limitation in our way of speaking becomes apparent. We are at a loss to find an exact word to express the sort of active refusal that occurs not apart from but within the worship and service of God. To love God, in the sense of placing trust and hope in the One identified in scriptural traditions and attested in the ongoing life of the church as the Lord, is at the same time to refuse to trust and hope in what the writers of scripture in their distinctive ways refer to as idols, false gods, false prophets, unclean spirits, or even as the Antichrist. Scripturally this refusal to give allegiance to that which is not of God is presented as a faithful act. To believe in God is at once to disbelieve what is not of God. Faith in God, we are led to conclude, is not only believing; it is a disbelieving as well. The disbelieving that arises in response to the biblical call to faith in God is what these chapters will seek to explore.

Faithful disbelief, as a focus of inquiry, is distinguishable from both doubt and skepticism. The refusal to assent to that which is ungodly is not to be confused with existential doubt, an important theological subject in its own right, but a different one. The familiar lines of Tennyson come to mind:

> There lives more faith in honest doubt,
> Believe me, than in half the creeds.[3]

In twentieth-century theology the words of Paul Tillich on this subject have been the most influential: "Existential doubt and faith are poles of the same reality, the state of ultimate concern."[4] Those taking a contrary view have delighted in the response of Karl Barth, "There is certainly a justification for the doubter. But there is no justification for doubt itself (and I wish someone would whisper that in Paul Tillich's ear)."[5] Whatever the merits of this dispute, the attempt to map faithful disbelief introduces us to another set of issues. The subject before us is not the distrust of God that remains present even within our struggles to be faithful, but rather the recognition of what our struggles to be faithful, with all their doubts, call us to distrust as not being of God.

Nor is our topic simply to be equated with that of skepticism, although points of affinity readily come to mind. The skeptical philosophies of Greco-Roman antiquity reemerged with new vigor during the fifteenth century; shortly thereafter Europe began to feel the cultural impact of the Reformation.[6] Their influence was evident in Christian theology even before the Enlightenment, in which such figures as Descartes, Locke, Hume, and Kant permanently affected the future accounting of Christian faith claims by their critical analyses of the justification of belief. Just as disbelief of that which is not of God may be said to be the act of a faith commitment, so skepticism has generally portrayed itself as an act of moral commitment. According to its major theorists, to believe or give assent without sufficient evidence is immoral as well as irrational.[7] On what counts as sufficient evidence in matters of belief, however, skeptical philosophers have not always agreed. But they have agreed on the premise that credulity, in the sense of belief without adequate justification, is the enemy to be opposed.

There clearly is a kinship between elements of skepticism as we find them developed in Western philosophy and the call to the disbelief of idols that appears throughout the Bible. This is a kinship too often unrecognized by those who tend to view critical thinking in Christian theology as an alien imposition of so-called hellenization or the Enlightenment. But differences as well prevent us from proceeding theologically as if the issues of faithful disbelief were simply the same as those prescribed by the traditional agenda of critical philosophy. They are not.

The biblical call not to believe every spirit raises questions other than those commonly dealt with in a general theory of human perception. Faithful disbelief as a subject of theological analysis presents problems other than the uncovering of the limits of knowledge. Its exploration assumes no philosophical commitments to what has come to be called and debated as foundationalism, the effort, following Descartes, to ground all knowledge claims in some fundamental certitude that cannot except by self-contradiction be doubted. What is at stake is not so much what

Locke (and later John Henry Newman for quite different reasons) pursued as a grammar of *assent* to propositions of Christian belief; it is more a logic or grammar of *dissent* to propositions and practices disallowed by faithful refusals to believe.[8] The focus is not on the apologetic task of justifying Christian belief in God but on the polemical and dogmatic (in a sense to be explained) task of uncovering what Christian belief in God rejects as unworthy of credence. While the skeptical attitude has traditionally been seen to involve a suspension or withholding of judgment, an attitude overcome by faith, biblical disbelief may be seen to involve an exercise of judgment in refusing appeals for allegiance, an exercise engendered by faith. Christian faith, if we follow this route of inquiry, is not "the willing suspension of disbelief" (Coleridge), but rather its willing commencement.[9] In each of these respects there is a difference to be noted between an investigation of the role of disbelief in Christian faith and the agenda most characteristic of skeptical philosophy.

The impetus and starting point in this project for thinking of disbelief as a call of faith is scriptural rather than philosophical, although in all readings of texts as scripture, in all hermeneutics, philosophical presuppositions and influences of some sort inevitably play a part in the midrash or exegesis.

In 1 John 4:1 the charge not to believe every spirit is immediately preceded by the statement, "And by this we know that he [God] abides in us, by the Spirit that he has given us" (1 John 3:24b).[10] The givenness of God's Spirit is here the premise for the call to faithful disbelief. This premise is characteristic of the other scriptural references as well. That the Johannine call to disbelief is issued with the Old Testament background of testing for true and false prophesy in mind is clear from the clause that follows: "For many false prophets have gone out into the world" (1 John 4:1b). The testing of spirits to distinguish the spirit that God has given from the spirit opposed to the will and way of God's gift involves the testing of prophecy or teaching, that is, of what is being said and otherwise signified within the community. In this instance we are not led to think of spirits as the popular imagination might tend to picture ghosts or goblins. Nor are spirits only to be associated with what today would most likely be classified as psychic phenomena or the occult.[11] In the view of the author of 1 John, the spirits to be tested are exemplified by true and false prophets and the confessions they represent.

The Apostle Paul as well understands love toward God to involve a testing of spirits. "And this is my prayer, that your love may overflow more and more, with knowledge and full insight to help you determine [test] what is best" (Phil. 1:9–10). "Do not quench the Spirit. Do not despise the words of prophets, but test everything; hold fast what is good, abstain from every form of evil" (1 Thess. 5:19–22). Paul extends the call for "testing" not only to distinguish between every spirit that is from God and every spirit that is not from God, as in 1 John 4:1, but also to discern among the differing gifts of God's own Spirit. Raymond Brown in his commentary analysis of 1 John cautions against equating the Johannine and Pauline references to testing the spirits in this respect.[12] It is necessary to recognize that in 1 John the spirit that finds expression in the "secessionists" from the community, as Brown designates those whom the Johannine author is opposing as false prophets, is considered not to be from God. In Paul's usage, by contrast, the spirits to be distinguished are often all viewed as various manifestations of God's one Spirit (1 Cor. 14:12). The testing in these Pauline instances, unlike in 1 John 4:1, is among "gifts that differ according to the grace given to us" (Rom. 12:2, 6). Yet in Paul's writings it is still the case that even when all gifts are of God's Spirit, what God may give to someone may not be given, and thus will not be right — in this sense at least not be "of God" — for another. The one Spirit who activates all in the community of faith for the common good "allots to each one individually" (1 Cor. 12:11).

Recognizing the significant dissimilarities, where the Johannine and Pauline references to testing the spirits do agree is that in both traditions a refusal is called for as an expression of faith. "Prophets" in both the Johannine and Pauline writings are those who pronounce a claim upon us, upon our attention and our allegiance. To know oneself claimed by God is at the same time to know oneself called to test all claims in this light and to refuse those that are contrary and seek to usurp it. Because of the correlation between false prophecy and false spirits that one finds throughout the scriptures, we may speak today of "spirits" as — whatever else may be involved — *claimants*, either legitimate or illegitimate, for our attention and allegiance. The Christian faith in acknowledging the sovereign claiming of human life by God refuses to acknowledge any claim upon human life which violates that of God. Such refusal is the disbelief of Christian faith.

Nowhere do we see this refusal more graphically portrayed in the Bible than when the issue of false hope is at stake. It is the false prophet who is said to treat the wound of the people carelessly, "saying, 'Peace, peace,' when there is no peace" (Jer. 8:11). We are told as well of Job and his defiant resistance to the false comforters who try to "make night into day," asking them, "Who will see my hope?" (Job 17:12, 15). But there is another, less well-known figure in the scriptures who as a focus of meditation personifies how deeply the gospel may be said to honor the witness of faithful disbelief. Her name is Rachel, and with her portrayal a further dimension of our subject is introduced.[13]

Rachel's Refusal

Of this Rachel, we are told, her suffering was such that she refused all consolation. As the Gospel of Matthew puts it, quoting the words of Jeremiah, "A voice was heard in Ramah, wailing and loud lamentation, Rachel weeping for her children; she refused to be consoled, because they were no more" (Matt. 2:18, Jer. 31:15).

In its hearing of the story of Christmas the church is confronted with Rachel's refusal. The voice of Rachel is part of the chorus that proclaims Christ's birth. Along with the sound of wise men and shepherds, of the angels and all the heavenly host praising God and singing, there is this other sound — the sound of "a voice heard in Ramah, wailing and loud lamentation, Rachel weeping for her children." With a voice so out of pitch and out of season for what is anticipated as a time of joyful celebration Rachel comes before us.

Matthew's account of the Nativity refers to Rachel weeping for her children in telling of King Herod's slaughter of Bethlehem's children. Herod the King orders the wise men to bring him word where Jesus is to be found. "When Herod saw that he had been tricked by the wise men, he was infuriated, and he sent and killed all the children in and around Bethlehem who were two years old or under" (Matt. 2:16). The prophecy of Jeremiah is then recalled. It is Jeremiah, 500 years before the birth of Jesus, who first speaks of Rachel weeping when the people of Israel were being taken into exile. And the Rachel to whom Jeremiah refers first appears in the pages of Genesis, a setting some 1,000 years and more before the time of Jeremiah. In Genesis, Rachel is identified as the mother of Joseph and Benjamin, from whom the northern tribes of Israel were descended. We are dealing here with ancient Hebrew traditions most likely known to those to whom Matthew's Gospel is written.

In the setting of the earliest references in Genesis 35:16–20 Rachel is depicted as a woman who dies in childbirth. She is remembered as someone in great pain; in "travail and hard labor" reads the blunt text. As her son Benjamin is being born, Rachel with her dying breath calls the baby, "Son of my sorrow." When Rachel died she was buried, according to some traditions, "on the way" to Bethlehem (Gen. 35:19).[14] Her husband Jacob, we are told, "set up a pillar at her grave; it is the pillar of Rachel's tomb, which is there to this day" (Gen. 35:20).

In a second reference, this time in the prophecy of Jeremiah, the figure of Rachel represents the suffering, not of one who dies in the pain of childbirth, or in what could be called a tragedy of nature, but of those who are deprived of their freedom by an oppressive power in history. When Israel was conquered and many of its people were carried off into exile, the long march of captives passed down the road by Rachel's tomb. It was a road of bitter grief. Jeremiah reports the Lord saying in this situation, "A voice is heard in Ramah . . . Rachel is weeping for her children; she refuses to be comforted" (Jer. 31:15). What is noteworthy in this second reference is that Jeremiah hears a word of the Lord coming to Rachel and to those who suffer within the sound of her voice. "Thus says the Lord: 'Keep your voice from weeping, and your eyes from tears; . . . there is hope for your future' " (Jer. 31:16–17). Perhaps there is a clue in this word which Jeremiah hears coming to Rachel that may explain why the early Christians spoke of Rachel when they told of Jesus' birth.

As biblically viewed, there are situations in which only God may speak of hope. There is a hope that only God can give. Who can give hope to a slave or exile and make that captive "see freedom in the air" when there is none on the ground?[15] Who can give hope when innocent children become the victims of the evils of nature and history? For anyone to speak cheaply and glibly about hope in the midst of such evil is certainly to utter blasphemy. Rachel *refuses* all consolation. This the biblical testimonies recognize and respect. Rachel "*refuses* to be comforted." Yet the word comes to her in her refusal: "There is hope for your future." The word comes through Jeremiah, suggesting there must be a God of Rachel somewhere.

As Matthew's Gospel presents it, that somewhere is Bethlehem, where in a night of treachery Rachel's tomb and the Christ Child's birthplace are brought together. With the advent of the Christ the Herods of this world are yet provoked to their destruction of the innocent, thereby recapitulating the very voice of refusal entombed on the way to Bethlehem. Rachel in Genesis is referred to in relation to the pain and suffering of childbirth. Rachel in Jeremiah is referred to in relation to victims of exile and oppression. Rachel in Matthew, presumably with these ancient traditions in mind, combines both of them in recounting Herod's slaughter of innocent children on the occasion of Jesus' birth. In each of these three instances the figure of Rachel personifies the human encounter with whatever in nature and history seeks to destroy the hope of the world.

It should be observed that no explanation is given in these scriptures to the question of why, despite all her resistance, such suffering, injustice, and oppression afflict Rachel in places on this earth, no answer to why evil lays claim to innocent children. What Rachel does is refuse all false comfort and facile explanation. She refuses to be consoled.[16] And by her inclusion this refusal is honored in the Gospel as a faithful testimony. That is the point I find so striking. In the darkness surrounding Rachel, just as much as in the light surrounding the natal star, the birthplace of the Christ is revealed. At the Nativity a manger somehow adjoins her tomb. Of this her disbelief of all consolation not of God becomes the faithful witness. Her voice, so Jeremiah tells us, is the one God hears.

In pondering these texts Martin Luther saw in Rachel the gospel's link between the Nativity and Good Friday.[17] In the godforsakenness of God's own Son on the Cross (Matt. 27:46) the promised hope for Rachel is embodied. By not believing any consolation short of God's own descent into hell in Christ, the refusal of Rachel becomes a faithful witness pointing to the Resurrection. From the perspective of Resurrection faith, both the credulity that seeks comfort in false hope, and the cynicism that says there is no hope that can be trusted in the manger adjoining Rachel's tomb, are revealed as *not* to be believed.

Wherever we find today the credulity willing to believe anything comfortable that passes itself off as spirituality or God-talk, and wherever we find today the cynicism that says there is no hope or faith worth trusting, Rachel's refusal becomes a most timely witness to a Resurrection faith.

An example of such refusal appears in the following excerpts from a letter written to me, upon the announcement of my appointment to teach theology in the 1970s, by a Roman Catholic missionary friend in a troubled region of South America:

> When the official churches of this God are at best silent or choose to ignore the torture and violation of the people, when they often cooperate with the evil powers that govern us, blessing their weapons, cars, houses, and their social lives in the name of God, when they use that very same name of God to silence the cries of suffering and agony of the people, what could I or should I do?
>
> By profession I belong to the organized church and as such participate in its sin, no matter how much I protest . . . I am part of the machinery as a Christian and as a priest, and in the eyes of many here as a white man. Yet my heart is on the other side, and I try to work where my heart is, trying, if possible, to limit the suffering, to restrain the lust of the torturer. Still my question remains. What has God to do in this world of torture, suffering, abuse, humiliation, violation, in this world where because of this misery, the poverty, surviving, simply surviving is a daily achievement? Because the farmer lives at the subsistence level, the factory worker (barely) keeps his family alive, and the miner never reaches your age — because of all that can we say, "Praise the Lord"?
>
> No. Here God is an article that can only be sold, like all the other imported goods, to the North American–oriented upper class. If I have to choose, I will choose the world where there is no God because this is the real one, the one where the Hope is. I do hope you will be a man of faith during all this year.

To the extent that Rachel's refusal is heard in this letter as faithful disbelief and not as faithless unbelief we are reminded of a Good Friday witness to the God whose name refuses to be spoken unless God speaks it through the silenced one.

The Truth that Harbors a Lie

In the late nineteenth century, Leo Tolstoy, already an accomplished novelist, undertook to write a work that he titled *An Investigation of Dogmatic Theology.* Only the introduction was first published and, as far as is known, much circulated. But in this introduction he tells what led him to take up theology. In words not unlike those of the priest in South America Tolstoy writes that when he turned his attention to what is done in the name of religion he was horrified and at once resolved to withdraw from the Orthodox Church entirely.

> During this time [1877–78] Russia was at war. And in the name of Christian love Russians were killing their brothers. There was no way to avoid thinking about this. There was no way to ignore the fact that murder was evil and contrary to the most fundamental tenets of any faith. Nonetheless, in the churches they were praying for the success of our weapons, and the teachers of faith looked upon this murder as the outcome of faith. . . . At one time I would have said that all of it was a lie; but now it was impossible to say this . . . I have no doubt that there is truth in the doctrine; but there can be no doubt that it harbors a lie; and I must find the truth and the lie so I can tell them apart.[18]

Today, if one thinks of the church internationally and ecumenically, we hear many voices raised from various quarters essentially repeating the words of Tolstoy. "I have no doubt that there is truth in the doctrine; but there can also be no doubt that it harbors a lie; and I must find the truth and the lie so I can tell them apart." A teaching that may be true when heard in one context with one understanding can be false when heard in another context with another understanding, even though the words may remain exactly the same. And, like Tolstoy, the people whose voices are being raised most often are those who have experienced an intolerable contradiction between the life to which the gospel calls them and what they see in specific instances being done in the name of Christianity. Their witness is to say "No." They join Rachel in her refusal to be consoled.

This presence of faithful disbelief in the church, I am suggesting, gives the church's teaching and practice its timeliness in every cultural situation. This witness of refusal gives church theology (when faithfully carried out) an almost impertinent social pertinence.

If to believe in God is at the same time to disbelieve that which is not of God, every Christian confession of faith may be seen not only as affirming belief in God, but as entailing disbelief of what this faith in God refuses. At crucial historical junctures in the life of the church these refusals have been made explicit. Ordinarily they remain merely implicit in our confessions, "virtual" truths they are sometimes called, or the net effects that are not explicitly stated.

One of the plainest examples of this is provided by what may be the earliest of Christian confessions, "Jesus Christ is Lord." The words are familiar to many Christians today as an almost platitudinous expression of ritual and piety. Probably for most they seem quite removed in meaning from anything currently political. But the term "Lord" had a secular denotation in the Roman world. Only Caesar preeminently could be Lord. The loyalty oath, the pledge of allegiance, throughout the empire was expressed in the words *"Kyrios Kaisar"* ("Caesar is Lord").[19] Baptism in such a social environment was in part a radically political act, for the confession "Jesus Christ is Lord" represented a subversive claim. Entailed in the faith that Jesus was Lord was the disbelief of Caesar as Lord. The disbelief is what gave the confession concrete meaning and timeliness in that social context. The earliest Christians were persecuted not for what they professed to believe, but for their disbeliefs. Their refusal to worship at the imperial shrines is what identified them to the governing authorities.[20]

My thesis is that the truth in Christian doctrine harbors a lie whenever the faithful disbeliefs these doctrines entail go unrecognized. Therefore, the task of theology in our present situation is to determine what disbeliefs are enjoined and entailed today by our faith affirmations.

There are some things that Christian faith refuses to believe. But how do we come to recognize what they are? To this question we will turn in the following chapters.

Chapter 2

THEOLOGY AS THE TASK OF FAITHFUL DISBELIEF

The biblical call not to believe every spirit brings with it a commission to test the spirits. How this task develops and comes to be understood within Christianity as a theological discipline called dogmatics is the subject to which we now turn. The aim of this chapter is to situate the inquiry into faithful disbelief within a historical spectrum of viewpoints regarding what makes Christian dogmatic theology a creditable undertaking. This spectrum will not presume to cover the full range of opinion.[1] Rather, it represents one reading of influential elements from the history of theology which pertain to the subject of dogmatics as a discipline. These elements provide points of reference that are necessary for understanding theology as the task of faithful disbelief.

The Suspicion of Theology

As an exercise of critical judgment, Christian theology is born of both the church and the academy and is constantly suspected by each of being illegitimate. The suspicion in Tertullian's question from around 200 C.E. remains to this day: "What has Athens to do with Jerusalem? What has the academy to do with the *ekklēsia?*"[2] The orientation of every Christian seminary, divinity school, or university department of religious studies reflects its answer to this question. Tertullian's remark has often been used to introduce theological disputes about the relation between reason and faith, or between nature and grace. My use at this point is more limited. I cite Tertullian's words here as a way of asking how the critical dimension of Christian theology — the assessment of claims purporting to be of God — has been characterized historically with respect to both academia and the church. Conceptions of the academy and the *ekklēsia* vary throughout history, but despite this variance they remain two points of reference by which Christian theology defines itself.

From Athens the church gets the term *theology*. Christianity does not invent it. Among the ancient Greeks *theologia* carries two meanings. One is simply "sayings about the gods." The other involves analysis of such sayings and may best be defined as "the logic of ultimate reality." Aristotle, for example, provides an illustration of these two uses. In his *Metaphysics* he refers to Hesiod and the other poets who tell stories of the gods as theologians.[3] Yet Aristotle also labels as theology the knowledge of ultimate or irreducible premises that are necessary for understanding reality. In this second sense, Aristotle characterizes theology as a science that is logically prior to such other sciences as physics and mathematics in that it supplies their most basic presuppositions.[4]

From Jerusalem, on the other hand, academia receives a new subject matter for the term *theology* in both of these meanings; scholarly research is not the origin of it. This content of the sayings and their logic (*logia*) about God and ultimate matters (*theos*) is derived instead from a preaching called "the gospel." This preaching speaks of things, as Luke the evangelist puts it, "which have been accomplished among us" (Luke 1:1). These are things that are said to have culminated in Jerusalem.

For his part, Augustine was persuaded that some of the ancient philosophers had themselves anticipated the wisdom of Christianity by a recognition of the distinction between the world and God, with this proviso: What is true in any philosophy, Augustine held, is the wisdom that concurs with the understanding that comes from faith in the one Mediator of God and humanity, Jesus Christ. Only in this mediation is the knowing of what is of God and what is not of God unmistakable.[5] It is this christological proviso, announced in terms of the "things which have been accomplished among us" in Jerusalem, that marks the emergence in the academic arena of a distinctively Christian testimony regarding the testing of spirits. The wisdom of such testimony, in the view of the Apostle Paul, appears to be sheer foolishness to those whose thinking does not stem from the call of faith that arises from this gospel (1 Cor. 1:18–25).

For several centuries before the birth of Jesus the Athenian academics and their later Roman counterparts had indeed recognized that sayings and their logic (*logia*) about gods and ultimate matters (*theos*) were of critical consequence for a society. Such *theologia*, whatever their content, were understood to shape for good or ill not only the dramatic imaginations and folklore of a people, but their patriotic loyalties and the premises of their reasoning as well. To be a true lover of wisdom, or a philosopher, required that one not simply speak of the gods but ponder the deeper import of such sayings and exercise an ability to assess the art of their literary construction, the craft (and craftiness!) of politicians in appealing to them, and the principles for understanding the natural world that they, often indirectly, represented.[6] Assessment of what is said and done in the name of deity required, from the standpoint of Athens as well as of Jerusalem, that one learn when to say No in matters of God-talk. How a community of faith properly learns to do this becomes a continuing theological issue.

We see an example of this in the influence of Platonism, or more exactly of Neoplatonism, upon traditions of Christian thinking that adopt the principle of the so-called *via negativa*, or the *via remotionis*. The mystical writings of the Pseudo-Dionysius (c. 500 C.E.) reflect this influence, but the way of negation receives its clearest doctrinal application in John of Damascus (c. 675–c. 749), and later in Thomas Aquinas.

There is a formal sense in which the inquiry into faithful refusal may be said to exemplify a *via negativa*, or "way of negation." There are instances in which faithfulness leads a community to confess that something is not godly even when in that same instance the community cannot adequately express what godliness is. For John of Damascus this occurs specifically in the characterization of God's being. To say that deity is incorporeal, unbegotten, without beginning, changeless, and imperishable is to say that God is not subject to creaturely corporeality, to coming into being, to temporal categories, to inconstancy, and to decay. Such expressions, considered to be in keeping with the gospel by John of Damascus, do not indicate what God essentially is, but what God is not.[7] As Thomas Aquinas states it, "For, by its immensity, the divine substance surpasses every form that our intellect reaches. Thus we are unable to apprehend it by knowing *what it is*. Yet we are able to have some knowledge of it by knowing *what it is not*."[8] An importance of the inquiry into faithful disbelief is the exploration of what Thomas here calls "some knowledge" of what is not of God.

But in another respect, that having to do more with content than with form, the *via negativa* and faithful refusal are not to be equated. This is the case when the way of negation is pursued according to what is labeled the rule of remotion, the *via remotionis*. This latter rule is explained in Thomas's statement that "we approach nearer to a knowledge of God according as through our intellect we are able to remove more and more things from Him."[9] John of Damascus makes the point in a more objectionable way with the statement, "It is more in accordance with the nature of the case rather to discourse of Him in the way of abstracting from Him all that belongs to us." [10] Understood in this manner, the Neoplatonic origins of the principle tend to undermine the conclusion of Augustine that all true philosophy is subject to the Word made flesh in the mediation of Jesus Christ.[11] Rather, the incarnational reality of God enfleshed in those things concerning Christ the Mediator "which have been accomplished among us" in Jerusalem is not a removal or an abstraction from "all that belongs," in the sense of "pertains," to us. Nor can our human corporeality be rightly understood as a removal or an abstraction from "all that belongs" to this incarnate Christ. Thus, while the inquiry into faithful disbelief bears some theological affinity in form to the principle of the *via negativa*, it is not consistent with this approach when the content of negation is interpreted Neoplatonically as a *via remotionis.*[12]

Another factor of tension arousing suspicion in theology's joint parentage as a critical discipline has to do with the idea of dogma. This term also derives from Athens and develops a history within Christianity of conflicting connotations. The philosophical schools of antiquity came to be identified and distinguished from one another by their particular teachings or *dogmata.* These dogmas served as dividing lines or norms according to which some claims were ruled acceptable and others unacceptable by the community. One finds the Greek word *dogma* used for both a teaching and a decree. In Luke 2:1, for example, we read, "In those days a decree [*dogma*] went out from Emperor Augustus that all the world should be registered." These uses coalesce in the development of Christian theology. Dogma comes to mean *decreed teaching.*

Not all branches of the Christian church have continued to use the word *dogma* or to be explicit about decreeing which of their principles of thought and action identify the faith of their community. But even traditions opposed to creeds and formulations, as well as those open to the greatest diversity of convictions, exhibit at least implicitly some sort of confessional standards, norms, and, in the broadest sense, distinguishing marks that are the functional equivalents of dogma. The insistence upon openness in effect becomes a dogma tacitly decreed by members of the community. Dogmas are those teachings deemed to be essential to the community's identity. While the distinguishing marks of the Christian communions and the explicitness with which these marks are formulated differs, Protestantism, even in its most noncreedal manifestations, is in these respects no less dogmatic than Roman Catholicism or Eastern Orthodoxy.

When the call not to believe every spirit leads communities to confront questions about where dividing lines of identification are to be drawn between faithful and unfaithful confession of God, theology in practice becomes "dogmatic," whether or not the term itself is used. Since the seventeenth century the study of what the church has decreed and should decree as being of God and as not being of God has generally come to be known in the curriculum of theological disciplines as dogmatic theology, or dogmatics.

While dogmatic inquiry is not limited to negative statements, Christian confessional affirmations historically have resulted from the responsibility of faith in specific situations to clarify its refusals. As Karl Barth expressed this responsibility just prior to World War II, at a time when all his writings were being declared illegal in Nazi Germany, "If the Yes does not in some way contain the No, it will not be the Yes of a confession."[13] "If we have not the confidence . . . to say *damnamus* [what we refuse], then we might as well omit the *credimus* [what we believe]."[14]

From its origins Christian theology exemplifies the fact that a No is contained in the confessional Yes of faith. The Apostles' Creed as it gradually emerged from a baptismal confession used in Rome in the latter part of the second century refutes false teaching in each of its tenets and does not address aspects of the gospel that were uncontested at the time.[15] The concern for a *rule* or a *canon* of faith during this same period to distinguish true from false testimony involved, in the language of the title of Irenaeus's major work, the struggle *Against Heresies*.[16] The formation of orthodoxy in the developments of the ecumenical councils of Asia Minor in the fourth and fifth centuries shows as well a similar tendency to articulate the Yes of faith through recognition of the No.

To our modern ears, however, the word *dogmatic* rightly raises suspicions because of the connotation of dogmatism as an authoritarian mentality that prohibits free inquiry. Such an association of the word's meaning with uncritical acquiescence to official decree represents just the opposite of the original usage. According to an account in Acts, Paul and his followers were accused in Thessalonica of "turning the world upside down" by "acting contrary to the decrees [*ton dogmaton*] of the Emperor, saying that there is another king named Jesus" (Acts 17:6–7). In contrast, it is reported of Paul and Timothy in the chapter preceding that "as they went from town to town, they delivered to them for observance the decisions [*ta dogmata*] that had been reached by the apostles and elders who were in Jerusalem" (Acts 16:4). In these texts from Acts the apostolic dogmas of Jerusalem are thus contrasted with the emperor's dogmas.

By the fourth century, however, with the changes that occurred under Constantine, the contrast between apostolic and imperial decree became less clear. Now no longer outlawed by Caesar but officially summoned by imperial edict, the Greek-speaking church councils of Nicaea (325), Constantinople (381), Ephesus (431), and Chalcedon (451), and others that followed into the eighth century,[17] declared the lines of apostolic dogma under the auspices of the Byzantine emperors. This is not to say that the emperors, or those clerics who sided with them, always got their way. Unlike New Testament times, however, nonconformity to church teaching in some instances now became tantamount to a civil crime. Ecclesiastical decree carried the enforcement provisions of canon law. The term *dogmatic* thus takes on historically the connotations of an imperial mindset that tolerates no disagreement, losing what Paul Tillich called its "genuine meaning."[18]

Thus at the turn of the twentieth century when the liberal Protestant scholar Adolf von Harnack published his *History of Dogma*, he characterized dogma (and by implication dogmatic theology) as an imposition of "the Greek spirit on the soil of the Gospel."[19] Harnack underscored the inevitable tension, as he saw it, between this alien "Greek spirit" with its dividing lines of orthodoxy and what he perceived to be the Galilean spirit of Jesus with its emphasis upon the love of God and neighbor. Yet Harnack in his day was no less insistent about theological dividing lines of identification, "lest we exchange the real Christ for one we have imagined." Only now "the basis for a reliable and common knowledge of this person" was said to come "through critical historical study." In effect, critical historical method as pursued in the academy became the decreed rule, or governing dogma, for identifying which God-talk among Christians qualifies as legitimate theology and which does not. Harnack directed his own academic scorn against those who confused the pulpit with the scholar's lectern and in so doing showed themselves to be "contemptuous of scientific [*wissenschaftliche*] theology."[20]

There are important reasons for reclaiming the term *dogmatic theology* today from the connotation of an uncritical dogmatism. When dogmatics is understood theologically as the testing of "decreed teaching," it may be seen as one of the most radically critical of all disciplines, involving the requirement of continual self-criticism and ideological critique as well. The reason is that in the church's self-understanding from earliest times only the call of God constitutes a Christian community's true identity as the *ekklēsia* (the "called forth"). Therefore, dogma ultimately can only be that which God decrees to be taught. What God decrees stands over, and in judgment of, everything that human societies may decree. Anything in what the church, the academy, or the larger civil society explicitly or implicitly decrees that is contrary to what God decrees does not, according to the church's own understanding of its calling, qualify as Christian dogma.[21]

When understood in this sense, the term *dogmatic theology* most aptly serves to indicate the parameters of criticism that must be recognized if a testing of the spirits is to be faithful. To treat the present-day meaning of Christian faith in the unity of its parts — the systematic task of theology — requires judgments that are not only historical but dogmatic as well. As the task of faithful disbelief, Christian theology is thus more than a descriptive discipline; it is *proscriptive* as well. The historical account of what has occurred in the church's past, and the empirical or phenomenological accounting of what currently is occurring in the churches and their cultural contexts, are necessary analytic ingredients for dogmatic testing.[22] But for Christian faith what has occurred and what is occurring have always to be viewed in light of what God decrees to occur. Theology as the task of faithful disbelief is inevitably a dogmatic undertaking in that it does not simply catalogue varieties of religious experience, of ritual and doctrinal formulations, or of available patterns of spirituality. It asks what faithfulness refuses as false claimants for our attention and allegiance in these areas as well as in all others.

Whether such inquiry, in going beyond the description of phenomena and becoming proscriptive, is said to qualify as an acceptable enterprise in the eyes of the academy and the church depends upon the standards that each holds regarding theology's accountability. The case for legitimacy has been variously made.

Theology's Academic and Ecclesial Referents: Three Views of Their Relationship

With regard to the legitimacy of Christian theology as a critical task, there are three primary differences in the way that the relationship between academia and the church has been viewed historically. One follows from the view that the faith perspective given by God's grace *completes* the perspective afforded by natural reason. It exceeds the capacities of natural reason and is thus *supra* natural. But it is complementary and not *contra* natural because all nature as God's own creation is good. A second position follows from the view that the faith perspective of grace *contradicts* that of natural reason as far as knowing the things of God is concerned. It is indeed *contra* natural because in the light of grace nature is shown now to be fallen and in opposition to its own created good. Still a third position follows from the view that the faith perspective of grace rightly *conforms* to that of natural reason. If it does not do so it amounts to nothing more than superstition, fanaticism, and blind subservience to authority. These differences are best characterized as tendencies of thought illustrated in, but not limited to, the example of Thomas Aquinas in the thirteenth century, of Martin Luther in the sixteenth century, and of Immanuel Kant and similar Enlightenment figures in the eighteenth century. Subsequent theologies tend to incorporate one or another of these three tendencies, or, more typically, some adaptation of several of them.

In the medieval synthesis of faith and culture, as exemplified in the thirteenth-century *Summas* of Thomas Aquinas, ecclesial and academic standards for judging the validity of theological inquiry are not held to be in essential conflict. What may be said to be creditable as the task of holy teaching (*sacra doctrina*) according to the canons of the church may also be said to be creditable as a proper academic discipline according to the canons of science in the university. It is not that the same premises are said to apply for both the doing of natural philosophy and the doing of sacred theology. But for Thomas the mode of inquiry carried out by theology as *sacra doctrina* is as legitimate by the academy's own standards as it is by the standards of the church.[23] Both standpoints can allow for the recognition that such sacred teaching qualifies as a valid science in that it develops the implications of a way of knowing derived from a tradition of basic premises taken to be revealed to faith. Every science brings its particular perspective to focus upon the created nature of things, and theology is not unlike any other academic discipline in this regard. Moreover, as a science theology excels all others insofar as the certainty of its perspective is derived from what God has revealed rather than from the fallibility of human vision. Its subject matter in this case is of greater worth since it alone provides the ultimate frame of reference for bringing the knowledge of the world gained from all other sciences into the proper relationship for a complete and coherent unity. And its practical purpose is superior to any other because its aim is nothing less than eternal blessedness. Tertullian's question is thus answered in Thomas's reckoning by saying that nothing intrinsic either to the requirements of the academy or to the requirements of the church prevents either from being able in principle to acknowledge that this is so.

With the coming of the Reformation this situation changes. No longer are Athens and Jerusalem said to be capable in principle of a common understanding about what constitutes Christian theology's legitimacy and warrant. When true to the gospel, ecclesial standards for assessment now are seen intrinsically to be such as to require the rejection of the academy's standards for evaluating God-talk. We find this view expressed in an early writing from Martin Luther.[24] "No one is worth calling a theologian," Luther argues, "who seeks to interpret the invisible things of God on the basis of the things that have been created." Such is the approach of those scholastics who, under the sway of Aristotle, decide according to their own definitions of the highest good what is glorious and then attempt to conceive of deity in conformity to their notion of glory. Rather, God has "determined . . . to be known from sufferings." Indeed, "God is not to be found except in sufferings and in the cross." Thus the theology of the cross, that is, Jerusalem, is not the complement but the radical reversal of the theology of glory, that is, Athens. At the Cross *deity* is defined from its "backside," as it were (Exod. 33:21–23), by the humanity of One crucified. What *ultimate strength* means is defined by weakness. What *wisdom* means is, in the Cross, defined by foolishness. "For the foolishness of God is wiser than human beings, and the weakness of God is stronger than human beings" (1 Cor. 1:25).

In the *Heidelberg Disputation* of 1518, from which these references are taken, Luther writes, "The theologian of glory says bad is good and good is bad. The theologian of the cross calls things by their proper name." That is the point. As long as one does not know the Christ crucified of the gospel one does not know the character of the reality in which all creatures live and move and have their being. Ultimate reality, God, is hidden in what, according to the ruling scholastic presuppositions stemming from Aristotle, is the opposite of the highest good, namely, in suffering. For Aristotle it is a contradiction in terms to say that the highest good suffers. In Luther's view grace may only be said to be known *sub contrario*, beneath its opposite.

This is not an argument, as it is sometimes erroneously portrayed, of faith versus reason. The disagreement has to do with the capacity to recognize the premises of reasoning intrinsic to faith. It should not be supposed that Luther's view in this instance espouses an irrationalism. The same is definitely true for John Calvin and other Reformers as well. What is rejected is the scholastic assumption derived from Aristotle that a logic which is universally demonstrable with respect to things as they presently appear in this world can lead one to a true recognition of ultimate reality. In the Cross the so-called wisdom of this world as to the meaning of God is reduced to nonsense.

If it is the case that in this tendency of Reformation thinking ecclesial standards for recognizing theology's legitimacy require the rejection of the academy's standards, the reverse position may be said to characterize the Enlightenment. Like the Reformation two centuries earlier, the Enlightenment of the late seventeenth and eighteenth centuries is not reducible to a single, uniform movement. What distinguishes it in comparison is that academic standards are now given primacy, and these are seen to require the rejection of church standards in determining what talk of God, if any, qualifies as creditable scholarship.

One recalls the motto of the Enlightenment as expressed by Immanuel Kant, "*Sapere aude*. Have the courage to use your own understanding."[25] Dare to think for yourself without accepting any so-called authority uncritically. It is a failure of nerve which refuses to criticize, to test, to demand evidence. Any authority requiring unquestioned belief in its putative sacred doctrine is an authority seeking to impose its power through superstition.

When Thomas Jefferson wrote the initial draft of the Declaration of Independence, it contained the words, "We hold these truths to be sacred and undeniable that all men are created equal." The final draft has the words "sacred and undeniable" crossed out, and "self-evident" is written in their place. That is the Enlightenment. Appeals to the "sacred" were no longer accepted as "undeniable." Only accounts of what was self-evident (or thought to be!) to experience were considered creditable.

Kant himself attempted, not too convincingly, to distinguish between what he called the public and private uses of reason.[26] Privately a pastor of a congregation is bound to teach the catechism to the young and to preach within the approved limits of church doctrine. But insofar as the pastor is also a scholar such an individual is free to inform the scholarly public of "carefully tested and well meaning thoughts" — even about elements that may be discovered to be erroneous in church teaching. The scholarly use of public reason takes priority over the private requirements of church teaching in determining the legitimacy of theology. Only academic standards include freedom of inquiry, and hence they require the rejection of church standards wherein such freedom is necessarily curtailed.

Thus if we apply Tertullian's question of the relationship of Athens and Jerusalem in recognizing the legitimacy of the critical dogmatic role of theology within Christianity, these three main answers may be said to find expression in the history of theology:

1. The academy and the church can in principle acknowledge the same criteria for validating theology's distinctive legitimacy, a position we see articulated in the medieval *Summas* of Thomas Aquinas.

2. With the Reformation the distinctively Christian criteria are held to be incompatible with the academic premises of scholasticism. Rationality is not rejected, but it is grounded in a scandalous *ratio dei*, a comprehension of things that is given only in the crucified Christ. From the standpoint of the cross and resurrection any academic criteria used to judge theology that are based upon a universally demonstrable logic are found wanting.

3. With the Enlightenment the academic criteria for establishing the warrant of theology as a critical discipline are separated from the ecclesial requirements because of the latter's alleged authoritarianism. Appeals to the self-evidence of human experience as something common to all become the basis for judgments about what makes theology creditable.

The Disputed Legitimacy of Dogmatic Theology Following the Enlightenment

In the nineteenth century the dogmatics of Friedrich Schleiermacher displays the influence of each of these three perspectives and the logical difficulties of attempting to reconcile them. Schleiermacher explicitly holds to the first, or Thomistic, position with respect to a common academic and ecclesial recognition in principle of the status of dogmatics as a discipline. The scientific character of Christian theology can be established as a "positive" science (*Wissenschaft*) without violating either church or academic requirements.[27] Nevertheless, Schleiermacher's way of explaining this reflects the tendencies of both the Lutheran and the Enlightenment positions.

It is Lutheran, in the sense of the second position, in that what is posited within Christianity for theology to examine is said to be a particular communal consciousness of "the redeeming influence of Jesus of Nazareth." This is a special consciousness in which the antithesis between sin (what we are redeemed from) and grace (the redemptive power itself) is transmitted solely from the preaching of the gospel, beginning with Jesus' own self-proclamation of his God-consciousness. The requirement for theology as a "positive science" is first to uncover what constitutes the essential identity of a community's self-consciousness by examining what is posited in that community's actual history, and then to detect all corruptions of this identity which occur within the ongoing life of the community in light of this essence.

Where this perspective becomes more like the third, or Enlightenment, position can be seen in Schleiermacher's view that while "the redeeming influence of Jesus of Nazareth" is a given subject matter for theology that is unique to a Christian community, it is also to be understood as only one form (*Gestaltung*) of a universal "feeling of absolute dependence," an experience allegedly common to all.

Whether Schleiermacher's theology succeeds in maintaining the Thomistic view that theology is in principle capable of being accredited as a positive science both by the church and by the academy depends upon how the particular experience of "the redeeming influence of Jesus" is understood to cohere with the common universal experience of "the feeling of absolute dependence." Are the axioms of reasoning in Christian faith universally recognizable in principle, or are these axioms distinctive to the context of the gospel? On the one hand, Schleiermacher holds that the universal feeling of absolute dependence which is common to all human existence as such is "immediate" (*unmittelbar*). Such feeling is instinctive and not a product of reflective intellectual inference. On the other hand, he argues that this universal feeling is never unmediated. It is only present in some particular formation of piety within historical existence. It is conveyed by the environmental media — speech, gesture, music, for example — essential to all communal life. The universal experience is thus present solely through some historically particular formation and is denotable only as its "presupposition."[28]

If the conclusion to be drawn from Schleiermacher is that the particular consciousness of the redeeming influence of Jesus is but one among a number of formations of a universally recognizable human experience of absolute contingency, it obviously conflicts with the distinctiveness principle of the second position, that of Luther's theology of the Cross. But if the proper conclusion is rather that the universal human experience of absolute contingency is not accessible to theological analysis except by way of the particular redeeming influence of Jesus of Nazareth, such a position comes closer to that of Luther than to that either of Thomas or of Kant and the Enlightenment.[29]

With this configuration of earlier tendencies within the dogmatics of Schleiermacher, we mark the beginning, it is often said, of the modern, or post-Enlightenment, period in Christian dogmatic theology. The contradictions posed by the three ways that we have noted of accrediting the testing of spirits as a legitimate theological task become acute following Schleiermacher in the early years of the twentieth century in the theologies of Ernst Troeltsch and Karl Barth.[30]

In 1908 Troeltsch, who was then professor of systematic theology at Heidelberg, wrote an assessment of the theological scene in his native Germany during the previous half century.[31] The "chief characteristic" of that period was, as he put it, "the decline of the church's voice in the whole of public life, above all in the interests and intellectual horizons of educated Germany and across the whole spectrum of academic work." What the churches were teaching, he observed, was no longer a matter of public debate. "Ordinary academic and literary activity passes them by, and gets on with its own problems and tasks quite independently." Church teaching had become mainly "personal, subjective convictions of a confessional sort," and attempts were being made simply to make these conform with traditional statements of doctrine.

At the same time, Troeltsch noted, academic theology had "become far more indifferent to the problems of the church." Indeed, "the educated and liberal world perceives with naive astonishment" that the churches, which they largely have disregarded, still exercised "some quite considerable political influence" of a strongly conservative character. Credulity thus was manifest on both sides. What is disastrous for a culture, Troeltsch argued, is any attempt to separate what he called "religious faith" from "scientific work." Rather, "the different sources of knowledge must somehow coincide and harmonize." Here "scholars and professors must lead the way."[32] Such a harmony becomes possible when it is commonly recognized that the claims of faith have their meaning and truth not in some supernatural revelation apart from history, but in relation to the one historical world of which all human knowledge is part. Theology is dependent, therefore, upon the proper use of the same historical-critical methods employed by any other academic discipline whose object of inquiry is accessible only in historical form. While dogmatics as a proscriptive task is itself not a science, it is legitimate as a discipline when it is based upon accurate description that is carried out according to academically recognized scientific methods.

Troeltsch's position involves two basic premises that he contended are essential for any theological work in the modern world.[33] The first is that theology's object of study is religion. What the church has traditionally appealed to as "revealed knowledge," and assumed to be supernatural and as such off limits to academic scrutiny, is more accurately to be interpreted as religious power, that is, power that is manifested by a religion. The second premise is that religion is never abstract or ahistorical; it exists only in historical cults or forms that are relative to its surrounding culture and are neither changeless nor absolute. Thus the subject matter with which contemporary theology must deal cannot be simply the Bible or the creeds. Instead, the whole relativistic cultural configuration of the Christian religion in the world as it develops in history provides the data for theology.

As Troeltsch recognized, if these two premises are accepted — that revelation occurs only in religion, and that religion occurs only in historically relative forms — then theology faces an acute problem with the traditional claim of the church that Jesus Christ is the one and only Lord and Savior, not only for Christianity, but for the whole world. Troeltsch's own answer to this problem was to say that, once one begins to investigate the syncretistic origins of Christianity in history, one is forced to acknowledge that "Christianity is by no means the product of Jesus alone" and that it is impossible to call "the Christian community the eternal absolute center of salvation for the whole span of humanity."[34] For Christianity to attempt to remain christocentric in a world of many increasingly intermingling religions and diverse cultures would be similar to cosmology in the twentieth century attempting to remain geocentric. Planet Earth is not the center of the universe, although it is our home.

Viewed historically, the constant in Christianity, Troeltsch concluded, is not Jesus Christ, for although these words designate the primary symbol of our religion, that symbol is interpreted variously in different times and places. We cannot say that the Christian community and cult will, as Troeltsch put it, "remain bound to the historical personality of Jesus."[35] The constant in Christianity, and what is essential for it and thus for theology, is that "the historical Christian religion" contains within itself a "productive power . . . to create new interpretations and new adaptations — a power which lies deeper than any historical formulation which it may have produced."[36] "Thus," Troeltsch writes, "we are thrust back again to history itself and to the necessity of constructing from this history a religious world of ideas which shall be normative for us."[37] For Troeltsch, in sum, what credits or discredits theological work is the adequacy or inadequacy of the cultural synthesis that it constructs to meet the religious needs of the time.

Karl Barth was a young pastor, fresh from his academic training in the best historical-critical theology of his day, when he heard Troeltsch lecture in 1910. He later wrote that, after listening to Troeltsch, he had "the dark foreboding that it had become impossible to advance any farther in the dead-end street where [theologians] were strolling in relative comfort."[38] (To be fair to Troeltsch, we should remember that he did not have an equal chance to know and respond to Barth.)[39] "Is it possible," Barth asked, "for a historian as such to do justice to Christianity?"[40] Barth, whose long career as a professor of dogmatic theology was just beginning in the final years of Troeltsch's life, also rejected, as did Troeltsch, the attempt to separate academic theology from the life of the church. But for Barth this rejection first emerges from the context of the church, from his efforts as a pastor and not as a professor. What makes the separation intolerable for Barth is not that church teaching fails to understand the historically relative character of its symbols and constructs. He agrees that it must do so. Rather, the theology at the universities fails to understand that no human method, historical-critical or otherwise, no matter how academically scientific, can uncover or construct *God.*

Barth came to this position from two very ordinary difficulties in the life of a pastor, both of which put his academic theological training to the test. The first was the sermon. He found that it was humanly impossible to preach God's word. That is to say, he discovered the terrible fact that no preacher can make God real to anyone no matter how hard he or she tries. The call of the church is to signify the gospel, but the church is powerless in itself to make the gospel significant. We simply cannot determine when in our words and actions God will choose to confront us and others through, and in spite of, what we say or do. The preacher can no more conjure up the Spirit or produce God's grace for others than one human being can produce faith within another, or hope, or love. Falling in love is something that finally no human being can compel. In this recognition Barth is close to Augustine's view that "to delight in the law of the Lord" (Ps. 1:2) is not subject to our control, for whatever power resides in the human will, it cannot make us delight in something. "Theology is the description of an embarrassment," Barth later wrote, in that we are called by the gospel to *speak* God's word and are unable to speak *God's* word.[41]

The second crisis in Barth's early ministry was the struggle for social justice. As a young pastor he had supported a strike of factory workers and identified with their cause even though the owner of the factory and his family were members and leading benefactors of the local church.[42] In doing so Barth discovered what to him was the equally terrible fact that no human agent or group of agents can by their own power sustain the social movement for justice or prevent its self-deception. The self-styled religious socialists in this regard were even more vulnerable than the secular socialists. When his own teachers, the most prominent critical theologians in Germany, joined in applauding Kaiser Wilhelm II's war policies in 1914, one month after the outbreak of World War I, Barth wrote that their action was for him like "the twilight of the gods." All their religious talk of truth and scholarship was transformed overnight into "intellectual 42 centimeter cannons."[43]

Thus, for Barth, disillusioned by the religion of both the church and the university, the problem ultimately became a struggle for hope. "We are Christians? Our nation is a Christian nation?" he wrote in 1916, "What a wonderful illusion . . . what a self-deception. We should above all be honest and ask ourselves far more frankly what we really gain from religion. . . . Are we hoping that something may happen?"[44] Unlike Troeltsch, for whom credulity was the enemy to combat in the tradition of the Enlightenment, the young Barth's temptation was cynicism, and to combat this he found himself drawn closer to the *sub contrario* principle of the Reformers and to the theology of the crucified Christ.

What Barth came to affirm and explicate throughout all his later work in his *Church Dogmatics* is that something ultimate does happen when the gospel of Jesus Christ is preached and signified as parable in the social conflicts of the present age. This happening is finally not adequately identifiable in terms of world history, or of religious phenomena, or of moral values — though, to be sure, in a secondary sense each of these categories of explanation may be said to be applicable. What occurs is expressed in the words of the Apostle: "God decided, through the foolishness of our proclamation, to save those who believe" (1 Cor. 1:21). If this saving reality is ultimately what is at stake, then no method as such — historical-critical, or any other — has the capacity to grasp it. The most scientific historian can no more demonstrate than anyone else when in human words and actions and the events of this world *God* acts to save.

In the strange "new world" within the Bible, as Barth called it, when it is not seen as some world other than the one we live in, but as this very world in its true reality, what is impossible with humans becomes possible, indeed actual, with God.[45] If this were not so, then nothing the church could say or do would really matter, all our best efforts at morality and religion notwithstanding. Because in the gospel of Jesus Christ faith is given to know of what God is doing in the world, there is hope for this world in Christ that is not dependent upon, or reducible to, any religion or culture.

Hence for Barth, in his early thought and continuing on through all his later work as well, the only genuine accreditation a theology can have resides in the event of its conformity to what God speaks to us of Jesus Christ in, and in spite of, ordinary creaturely words and acts.[46] But this kind of creditability only God can demonstrate, as when God spoke through Balaam's jackass (Num. 22:28–30), and then not as something that any theology or jackass can claim as its possession. In theological work God alone credits and thereby makes credible whatever true witness there is to Jesus Christ. Such witness is not confined to the church, to Christianity, or to religion.[47] The promise that a just and gracious God tests all human testing sets the theologian free to get on with the task commissioned by the call to faithful disbelief. In conforming its methods to the proper subject matter of God's own eventful self-witness, dogmatics has as much right as any other scholarly discipline to be considered a science. As such, it is reminded of its limits as a human work not to be confused with the ultimate truth of dogma that only God can decree. Any other claims that theology makes for its own legitimacy, in Barth's view, are spurious and are to be exposed as such.

While there are certainly other formative influences as well, most of the disputes over what constitutes a valid Christian theology in the twenty-first century continue to reflect in some form or another at least the tendencies most sharply represented by the dogmatic approaches of Ernst Troeltsch and of Karl Barth.

The theologies of liberation after 1960 provide an interesting case in point. These are not simply derivative of what has gone before but introduce a new chapter of testing the spirits in the history of Christian dogmatics.[48] Again we are not looking at a uniform school of thought but at a family resemblance among certain African American, Latin American, feminist, queer studies, so-called Third World (and increasingly other) works that seek to give primary regard to those that hitherto have suffered from official disregard. Despite the diversity of the forms of oppression considered, a distinguishing characteristic of this perspective is the emphasis that no theology is creditable either as an ecclesial or an academic discipline unless it is accountable with ecological awareness to the situation of people whose humanity or environment is currently in jeopardy.

When the contention between the perspectives of Troeltsch and of Barth is viewed with consideration for this liberationist requirement of accountability, two conclusions may be drawn. One is that the strength of Troeltsch's position appears in the stress that is placed upon the earthly, historical character of theology's subject matter. What is given in Christianity as data for theology comes enfleshed in specific historical contexts out of which power for new social constructions emerges. Liberation theologies support the call for theology's indigenization and cultural contextualization in parts of the world where imported missionary theologies have been dominant. The confession of a docetic Christ in disregard of the flesh of human history is exposed as a lie.

The second conclusion is that the strength of Barth's position appears in the stress that is placed upon the identity of Jesus Christ. Any confession of some immanent power enfleshed and contextualized in human history that disregards the differentiating identification of good and evil powers that is given in the biblical testimony to the life, death, and destiny of Jesus Christ is exposed as equally false. The kind of christocentrism Troeltsch rejects should be rejected, for it amounts to saying that Christianity itself, or the Christian religion, is Lord and Savior of all peoples and all other religions. But if the Jesus Christ attested in the gospel is not synonymous with any religion, including historical Christianity, but is the identification of both the oppression to be overcome and the power that overcomes it, as Barth argues, then christocentrism has a very different significance. A genuine theology of freedom in a world where religions themselves are often the causes of oppression cannot allow any religious zeitgeist to masquerade as liberator with its identity undetermined. In this connection, the decision of the World Alliance of Reformed Churches in Ottawa in 1982 declaring South Africa's apartheid doctrine to be a "theological heresy" is in keeping with the Barmen Declaration by Germany's Confessing Church against Nazi religion almost a half century earlier.[49] With the arrival of the twenty-first century's "global war on terror," the detonation of bombs by all sides has seen proponents claiming warrant in the name of God and their different religions.

Conclusions

Within the current spectrum of theological thinking that declares its intention to be both academic and ecclesial, any notion that Christian theological claims have a privileged status unaccountable in the arena of public reasoning has largely been abandoned.[50] Here the tradition of the Enlightenment and of Troeltsch has proved decisive. At the same time there is considerable recognition that accountability does not mean a conformity to, or a harmonization with, the prevailing culture. What is stressed in this recognition is the particular integrity and logic of Christian faith, its own grammar and textuality, as some refer to it.[51] This stress is coupled with the first insistence that theology cannot simply posit its claims in giving an account of Christian faith but must explain how these claims relate to the knowledge claims of other academic disciplines.[52] Thus, on the question of determining whether or when dogmatic theological criticism has legitimacy today, an interplay still continues of those tendencies that we have noted in the perspectives of Luther and Barth with those of the Enlightenment and of Troeltsch.

In one respect this interplay of insistence upon the particularity and integrity of Christian faith and, at the same time, the public accountability demanded of theology as a scholarly discipline, suggests that we are once again at a sort of Thomistic juncture. That is to say, it is now generally granted that the legitimacy of theology as a discipline of criticism must in principle be accessible to determination both by the church and by the academy, as it was in the instance of Thomas Aquinas. In another respect we obviously are at a very different place from that of Thomas. As the liberation theologies make clear, with their insistence upon a more primary accountability and consideration for the concreteness of historical struggles in specific contexts of suffering and oppression, our present fractured time is not one like that of Thomas of constructing all encompassing summas of theology, or even what Troeltsch called a harmonizing "cultural synthesis."

If the call not to believe every spirit is to be heeded today in faithful regard not only of the disharmony of increasing cultural diversity but of intolerable social inequity, the necessary requirement of dogmatics is a current investigation of Christian disbeliefs — that is, of those refusals of belief that are at the present time enjoined and entailed in traditional Christian professions of faith.

In this chapter I have attempted to outline something of the history of how the call not to believe every spirit has given rise in Christian communities to the task of recognizing what is not of God. If we apply the label of "dogmatics" to this particular task, then dogmatic theology by definition is not creditable merely as a descriptive discipline; it must be *proscriptive* as well. But can a proscriptive discipline that presumes to speak of "what God decrees" and of "what faithfulness refuses" be credited today with knowing what it is talking about? There are those in both the church and the academy who do not think so. They remain suspicious of theology's dogmatic legitimacy. Testing the spirits is obviously not an exact science, and some would say it is no longer feasible even as a discerning art. But neither, it can be argued, is it as a properly limited theological task merely an arbitrary exercise unaccountable for its claims in the arena of public reasoning. In the next two chapters we shall turn first to an account of these limits and then consider the tests that are required to determine doctrinal faithfulness.

Chapter 3

TESTING THE SPIRITS TODAY

In 1933 the young German pastor and theologian Dietrich Bonhoeffer wrote a short statement entitled, "What Should The Student of Theology Do Today?" He answered that the student should prepare, through studies, to test the spirits in the church of Christ.[1] In associating the testing of spirits with the doing of theology, Bonhoeffer's announcement, as the previous chapter has shown, cannot be said to have been unusually remarkable. The time of its issuance, nevertheless, was. The "today" was 1933, the year that Adolf Hitler came to power in Germany. The relevance of this circumstance for our topic is worth considering. We shall return to it in a moment.

The first chapter concluded with the thesis, alluding to words of Tolstoy, that the truth in Christian doctrine harbors a lie whenever the faithful disbeliefs these doctrines entail go unrecognized. The second chapter proposed that a requisite task of Christian dogmatic theology is to determine the disbeliefs that are enjoined and entailed in the present situation by the church's faith affirmations. The word *enjoined* carries two definitions, both of which are consciously intended here. It can mean either those disbeliefs and refusals that are "mandated," or it can mean those disbeliefs and refusals that are "prohibited" and "disallowed" by faith. The word *entailed* conveys a meaning similar to *mandated*, but in the specific sense of "being logically implied." But even if such a task is still acknowledged to be a creditable undertaking, within what limits may it be said to be feasible today?

Tolerance and the Intolerable

At the present time there are good reasons for resisting too confident a designation of what is "not of God." For example, we may hear in the term *dogmatic inquiry*, understandably so, the possible introduction of an inquisition-like mentality leading to an intolerant orthodoxy. Talk of the intolerable triggers thoughts of an intolerance inconsistent with the gospel. The rise of any fundamentalism that seems all too eager to say what is not of God, and who is not of God, is a major source of concern in the contemporary world, not only for religious communities but for our entire global civilization as well. We read of the horrors perpetrated in the church and by the church in the Middle Ages in the attempt to inquire into the beliefs of others so as to compel conformity to the prevailing orthodoxy.[2] We rightly resist any inquiry into testing the spirits and disbelieving that which is not of God if it leads in the direction of a renewed inquisitorial attitude. Historically a preoccupation with heresy hunting has often resulted in fanaticism and bigotry, the repression of nonconformists, and even death to dissenters and to those of faithful disbelief.

Today, in the academic study of religion, pluralism rather than idolatry is the theme more often addressed. A growing number of contemporary theological texts emphasize religious and cultural pluralism as the central problem for interpretations of Christianity. To raise the question of idolatry, on the other hand, appears to harken back to a vanishing cultural past in which Christianity, or more exactly some particular form of Christianity, was culturally dominant to the exclusion of other vital traditions. With the breakdown of Christendom, it is argued, the most pressing problems for theology have become the valuing of the varieties of religious experience and the relativity of their cultural manifestations.

There is most of all the vexing issue of authority. By what right does contemporary theology rule out any claims purporting to be of God as intolerable? How is such intolerant proscription justifiable as anything other than merely an arbitrarily unaccountable and capricious act?

These objections have to be taken into account in any theology that seeks to be faithful to the gospel. It is equally plain that, whatever importance is to be attached to the fact of religious pluralism, its significance for Christian theology cannot be determined by bracketing the question of idolatry.[3] Unless one takes a position that everything is God, the question of what is not God and not of God remains unavoidable. If the call not to believe every spirit is integral to biblical faith, testing the spirits is as necessary in a context of presumed cultural tolerance and pluralism as in situations of cultural intolerance that exhibit rejections that cannot be said to arise from Christian faith. The question is how such testing for that which is truly intolerable to faith is to be done.

The freedom to differ requires not that one forego the exercise of judgment, but exactly the opposite. What must be safeguarded is the right to the exercise of judgment on the part of all affected. In no area of life do we assume that all judgments in all contexts are equally valid. Pilots and passengers, surgeons and patients have different responsibilities.

Who finally adjudicates differences of judgment in matters of communal faith is a question every church body must determine, and historically in varying ways each denomination has done so. The responsibility of theology as a critical discipline of dogmatics is to assist communities of faith in their exercise of judgment as to what is rightly to be rejected as intolerable. As such, dogmatics does not itself speak for the church, but always to the churches, and to those outside the churches who are affected and who may be interested. This sort of theology is not a program to be imposed but a task to be pursued. Dogmatics is the antidote of dogmatism.

With regard to assessing beliefs and disbeliefs for their faithfulness, three "rights" must always be distinguished. One is the right to hold a conviction. Another is the right to authorize a conviction within a community as constitutive of that community, to say that this is what identifies us as the people we are. Third is the rightness of the conviction itself, whether it is right, the question of the conviction's truth. Fanaticism and bigotry represent, at the level of judgment, a confusion of the right of authorization with the rightness or truth of a conviction. What is of God is what has been officially authorized as such, no questions may be asked. The consequence is that the right to dissent or to hold any other conviction is denied. When tolerance or acceptance, on the other hand, becomes indifference, what happens at the level of judgment is a confusion of the right to hold a conviction with the rightness of the conviction itself. What is of God is whatever anyone happens to believe; believing makes it so. The result in this instance is that the right to authorize a conviction within a community as normative or constitutive of that community is denied.

As a creditable academic and ecclesial discipline, dogmatic theology itself has no right of authorization. Its assessments are offered only as an appeal for consideration and are themselves always subject to continuing communal testing. Its dogmatic responsibility is to evaluate the rightness of convictions and what they entail. In this endeavor the right to hold differing convictions is methodologically assumed and essential.

The German Church Struggle Following 1933

One of the most widely cited instances of testing the spirits in the twentieth century occurred in the events in Germany in the years 1933 and following. It is pertinent, especially for those not familiar with the story, to recall briefly something of the climate of that time.

With the triumph of Hitler and the Nazi movement in 1933 a number of church persons, including some of the leading theologians, believed that a new manifestation of God's Spirit was emerging within the German people. A newly formed organization of politically conservative Protestants calling themselves "German Christians" issued a manifesto. In it they made such statements as the following: "We stand on the basis of positive Christianity. Ours is an affirmative, truly national faith in Christ, in the Germanic spirit of Luther and of heroic piety." "We want a Protestant church rooted in our own culture. . . . We want to overcome degenerate phenomena . . . by faith in our nation's God-given mission." "As long as Jews have the right to citizenship . . . there is . . . a danger of bastardisation and an obscuring of racial differences."[4] Twenty thousand people in Berlin applauded and shouted their approval when the leader of this group called for a second Reformation that would result in a national church based upon, in his words, "a racially attuned experience of God."[5]

The results of this call can be seen in the following paragraphs from a Christian sermon preached in Berlin in 1936:

> Christmas is the feast of light of our ancestors, the ancient Germans, and so is several thousand years old. In the height of the winter solstice between 23–25 of the Yule month (December), the various members of each family came together under the leadership of the head of the family and met under a tree in the woods. The Winter man, Old Ruprecht, as the representative of the old dying year, appeared and gave out gifts. Burning torches were lit up by the burning flames of the Christmas tree. With wide open eyes, young and old stood around the tree. The deepest darkness of the longest night could not take away from them the hope of seeing again the light of the sun, which their God would give them in the coming year. And this is why we still give gifts around the Christmas tree.
>
> And just as our ancestors did not lose their faith in the coming light and the sun despite the ice and cold of the longest night, yes, indeed even celebrated the festival of light, so we took stand today in the light after long darkness.
>
> Germany, after the Great War, was threatened with collapse. But then he came who, despite the great darkness in so many German hearts, spoke of light and showed them the way to the light. His appeal found an echo in thousands and hundreds of thousands of German souls, who carried the appeal further. It swelled out like a sweeping cloud and then happened the greatest miracle: Germany awoke and followed the sign of light, the Swastika.
>
> The darkness is now conquered, now suffering is over, which

> so long gripped our people. The Sun is rising ever higher, with our ancient German symbol, the Swastika, and its warmth surrounds the whole German people, melts our hearts together into one great community. No one is left out, no one needs to hunger or freeze, despite the deep night and snow and ice because the warmth from the hearts of the whole people pours out, in the emblems of the National Socialist Welfare programme and the Winter Help work and carries the German Christmas into the most forsaken German heart.
>
> In this hour, Adolf Hitler is our benefactor, who has overcome the winter night with its terrors for the whole people and has led us under the Swastika to a new light and a new day.[6]

These "German Christians," as they were called, never represented the majority of Protestants within Germany, but neither did the so-called Confessing Church, in which Bonhoeffer and Barth participated, which opposed them.

Officially the Roman Catholic leaders, for their part, also declared their opposition to the "German Christians," yet the instructions of one archbishop to his priests indicated the climate prevailing in 1933. He wrote that in all their preaching and religious instruction in the parishes priests are to stress those teachings that further "the consolidation of state authority." He warned against saying or doing anything that "could be construed as criticism of the leading personalities in state and community or of the political views they represent."[7] Seen in this social context, Bonhoeffer's call to prepare oneself to "test the spirits in the Church of Christ" cannot be dismissed as simply empty rhetoric.

The following year, in May 1934, the Synod of the Confessing Church assembled in Barmen and issued an urgent call to "test the spirits" that has become the most widely known declaration of faithful refusals, or anathemas, in our century.[8] It announced:

> In view of the errors of the "German Christians" of the present Reich Church government which are devastating the Church and are also thereby breaking up the unity of the German Evangelical Church, we confess the following evangelical truths: . . . Jesus Christ, as he is attested for us in Holy Scripture, is the one Word of God which we have to hear and which we have to trust and obey in life and death.[9]

Following each of its affirmations the Barmen Declaration stated an ensuing disbelief:

> We reject the false doctrine, as though the Church could and would have to acknowledge as a source of its proclamation, apart from and besides this one Word of God, still other events and powers,

> figures and truths, as God's revelation.... We reject the false doctrine, as though there were areas of our life in which we would not belong to Jesus Christ.... We reject the false doctrine, as though the Church were permitted to abandon the form of its message and order to its own pleasure or to changes in prevailing ideological and political convictions....

and so on. Barmen provides an example of how the disbeliefs on that occasion made the faith affirmations concrete and timely in their particular cultural situation.

Today Barmen also merits criticism. In subsequent years the churches of Germany acknowledged Barmen's failure to disclaim theologically the anti-Semitic racism of the time. Debate currently continues, both in Germany and elsewhere, over whether Barmen's christological concentration upon Jesus Christ as "the one Word of God" proscribes all anti-Semitic views and practices, or tacitly fuels them. Both in what it did and failed to do Barmen illustrates the point that the truth in Christian doctrine harbors a lie whenever the faithful disbeliefs these doctrines currently enjoin and entail go unrecognized.

More recent examples come to mind when faith required the clear witness of what called for refusal and rejection. For the churches of the United States "the axial moment" occurred with the tormented struggle over desegregation in the sixties as it culminated in the assassination of Martin Luther King, Jr.[10] Church and state, reaping the whirlwind of generations of intolerable self-contradiction, finally had to say No to their policies of officially sanctioned racial segregation. Yet many self-contradictions on this matter within Christian communities in the United States still remain. In yet another instance, in 1982, at its meeting in Ottawa, Canada, the World Alliance of Reformed Churches pronounced the following with regard to South Africa: "We declare with Black Reformed Christians of South Africa that apartheid is a sin, and that the moral and theological justification of it is a travesty of the Gospel, and in its persistent disobedience to the Word of God, a theological heresy."[11] How are such judgments reached? Clearly many factors are involved. Theological examination is but one of them. Social consequences of the spirits in question become impossible any longer to reconcile with the gospel to which Christian communities are committed. Resistance to injustice erupts, forcing the church to declare itself by word and deed on matters previously evaded or ignored. The point is well expressed in words from John Henry Newman:

> And so generally: great truths, practical or ethical, float on the surface of society, admitted by all, valued by few, exemplifying the poet's adage, "Probitas laudatur et alget," until changed circumstances, accident, or the continual pressure of their advocates,

> force them upon its attention. The iniquity, for instance, of the slave-trade ought to have been acknowledged by all men from the first; it was acknowledged by many, but it needed an organized agitation, with tracts and speeches innumerable, so to affect the imagination of men as to make their acknowledgment of that iniquitousness operative.[12]

Nevertheless, it is one thing to say that in faith we are not to believe every spirit, not, that is, to be tolerant of the intolerable by crediting or giving credence to every claimant for our attention and allegiance purporting to be of God. It is quite another thing to say how testing for false prophecy and for that which is to be disbelieved as not of God is to be done. From the question of the academic and ecclesial legitimacy of testing the spirits today, and its social importance, we return to the question of feasibility. Within what constraints may such a task be understood to be faithfully doable?

1 John 4:2

One way to begin to get our bearings on this subject is by taking some soundings with regard to the passage in 1 John. How does a community of faith such as the author of this epistle is addressing "test the spirits to see whether they are of God"? To this question the passage gives a very straightforward answer. "By this you know the Spirit of God: every spirit that confesses that Jesus Christ has come in the flesh [*en sarki*] is from God" (1 John 4:2). But what does it mean to confess that Jesus Christ has come "in the flesh"?

One of the major disputes in the early church had to do with the actual fleshliness of Jesus. Did Jesus really live in a body that could feel pain, forsakenness, and abuse, or did he only appear to do so? Those views which held that Jesus as the Christ was too godly, too divine, to have entered actually unto death in the flesh and blood sufferings of human life came to be disbelieved and rejected.[13] Thus we read, "Every spirit that confesses that Jesus Christ has come *in the flesh* is from God." The author of 1 John in this instance does not oppose spirit and flesh as two separate kinds of phenomena, such as, for example, the psychical and the physical. In this particular text no opposition between spirit and flesh is indicated. Rather, the only spirit that is said to be identifiably of God is one of flesh, the flesh of Jesus Christ.

This insistence upon the coming in the flesh was more than a mere acknowledgment that Jesus Christ once lived historically as a human being. Raymond Brown writes, "The epistolary author seems concerned with the salvific importance of the flesh and the death of Jesus, not with a defense of the reality of Jesus' humanity."[14] If this is a correct reading, then the flesh of Jesus must be understood in some decisive sense to be involved in, or to incorporate, the flesh and blood sufferings of every present time. Otherwise, talk of salvific importance for today would be vacuous.

Ignatius of Antioch in the second century makes precisely this point. According to Ignatius, all who say that the passion of Jesus was only an illusion in so doing become an illusion.[15] The early Christian confession of Jesus Christ's coming *in the flesh* is not understandable as merely an assertion of presumed historical fact. It is not simply a statement about the past. In Ignatius's words, "Whoever does not confess that my Lord was clothed in the flesh . . . is clothed with a corpse."[16]

Confession of Jesus Christ *en sarki*, therefore, is not reducible to stating the words, "I believe that Jesus of Nazareth once lived as a historical person." Simply stating words, no matter how correct, does not constitute what this epistle calls a "confession." This is borne out by other biblical passages as well. To confess the name of Jesus is not merely to engage in "Lord, Lord" talk.[17] To confess is to show forth the saving power of Jesus Christ now coming into the actual flesh and blood sufferings that present themselves to us and around us wherever we are located in space and time.[18] That, according to the dogmatic import of the passage in 1 John 4:2, would appear to be the most basic criterion for testing all spirits. If this sounding is accurate, it provides a sensibility from which all other tests for doctrinal faithfulness may be understood to gain their theological bearings.

We see the early patristic theme of Ignatius reaffirmed by the Reformers. Commenting upon this passage in 1 John, Martin Luther observes, "Whoever denies the power and efficacy of Christ's coming denies that Christ came in the flesh . . . I too have seen some spirits who indeed confessed Christ by name but actually denied Him."[19] Similarly, John Calvin writes, "Granted [there are those] that confess Christ to be both God and man, yet they certainly do not retain the confession of which the apostle demands, for they rob Christ of His power." "By saying that [Christ] came we must note the cause of His coming; for the Father did not send Him for nothing."[20]

From this reading of 1 John we may conclude the following: the test of every spirit is whether the power of Jesus Christ, that for which Jesus Christ was sent, is being evidenced in connection with specific flesh and blood sufferings that are contemporaneous with that spirit's confession. If this be the test, then the Spirit of God is as much a reality of politics and economics as of religion, of the so-called profane world as of the sacred. Any form of ideology, or of religion, including Christianity, whether considered profane or sacred, whether found inside the churches or out, that does not evidence the power of Jesus Christ amid the actual sufferings of its present environment is to be disbelieved. Such spirits, as claimants for our allegiance, no matter how orthodox their articulation or pious their pretension, are not from God. They do not confess the decisive salvific coming of Jesus Christ "in the flesh."[21]

It is important for contemporary readers, conditioned as we have become by both the church and the academy to think of the gospel as a species under the broader genus of religion, to notice that in this instance nothing whatever is said to the effect that Christianity, as a world religion, is to be considered the good and true spirit, and that all other religions of the world are to be considered false spirits not of God. How quickly in reading "the spirit of Jesus Christ" do we jump to the conclusion that this means "the spirit of Christianity." Christianity as such, or even religions as we tend to think of them historically in the modern sense, did not exist within the purview of this Johannine epistle. Confessing Jesus Christ cannot be equated with confessing a religion, including the Christian religion. That would plainly represent an anachronistic way of thinking. It is mistaken to suppose that the epistle's references to Jesus Christ are synonymous with references to Christianity. On this point Karl Barth objects, rightly in my judgment, to Ernst Troeltsch. The confession of Jesus Christ in the flesh is not condensable into something historically definable as a religious phenomenon.[22] Otherwise, the epistle's message would be that every spirit that confesses Christianity is of God and every spirit that does not confess Christianity is not of God. But this the epistle, or for that matter the entire New Testament, nowhere says. We shall return to the problems that result from confusing references to Jesus Christ with references to Christianity when we come to the doctrinal chapters of part 2.

The Anathema

This brings us back to the word *anathema* introduced in chapter 1. The abuse of this concept in the history of the church has justifiably led to the idea of a punitive and prejudicial intolerance toward dissent.[23] The concept itself stems from ancient Israel's view that what is blessed of God is to be separated apart from what is not of God. The blessing of God involves the cursing of all that is antithetical to God. "And you shall not bring an abominable thing into your house, and become accursed like it; you shall utterly detest and abhor it; for it is an accursed thing" (Deut. 7:26).

The Greek word of the New Testament for "cursed," *anathema*, denotes what is refused and rejected. Many historic confessional statements of the church in their original formulations contain a list of anathemas. In Latin the anathema is also expressed as a *damnatio* or *damnamus*, literally, "this we damn." In the Middle Ages such censure became highly developed. There was even the concept of *damnatio in globo*, which meant a total rejection of everything someone represented. Luther received a *damnatio in globo* by the church authorities of his time. But this did not dissuade him from the view that faithfulness requires every Christian, both as a right and a duty, "to separate one teaching from another and say, 'God has said this, [God] has not said that! Again, 'this comes from God, that comes from the devil.' "[24] Whatever its later abuses, the application of the anathema within the New Testament, mainly in the writings of Paul, is strikingly consistent with the test given in 1 John 4:2 for recognizing false prophets and the spirits that are not of God. To the Corinthians Paul writes, "Let anyone be anathema who has no love for the Lord. Our Lord, come!" (1 Cor. 16:22). Wherever the love of the Lord is not evidenced let this be rejected — and only this be rejected — by the coming of the Lord.

If the disciple Peter is thought of as the first general pastor or pope of the church, then it is equally striking to observe that the first papal anathema was in effect self-directed. We are told in the Gospel of Mark that when Peter was accused in the courtyard at Jesus' trial of being one of the followers of Jesus, "he began to curse [*anathematizein*, 'to anathematize']" in denying the truth of who he actually was by swearing, "I do not know this man you are talking about" (Mark 14:71). He thus anathematized himself as a denier of having been with Jesus.

From these and other New Testament references to the anathema we may conclude that it is the false denial of the presence, the power, and the love of Christ in the midst of the flesh and blood trials of the world that is to receive the anathema. We may also conclude from the import of these New Testament references that nothing except this denial is to receive the anathema.

Ultimately, as we have noted in chapter 1, no testing of the spirits is possible or actual unless God grants God's own Spirit. This both the scripture and the teaching of the church consistently affirm. Immediately preceding the charge not to believe every spirit but to test them in 1 John 4:1 are these words: "And by this we know that he [God] abides in us, by the Spirit that he has given us" (1 John 3:24). Again the point is repeated: "By this we know that we abide in him [God] and he in us, because he has given us of his Spirit" (1 John 4:13).

It is also affirmed in both the scriptures and the teaching of the church that we must be careful how we profess this, for the gift of God's presence is never a cause for smugness, and no individual or community can ever claim it in ownership as its possession. No human power can produce God's Spirit. The Holy Spirit does not come through human manipulation, by turning down the lights or turning up the music. This coming does not depend upon whether we feel inspired or not, or on how religious or irreligious we imagine ourselves to be. Most particularly, theological reasoning as pursued in dogmatics only serves to recognize false prophecy and ungodliness insofar as it serves the gift of God's Spirit. We will consider these matters having to do with the Holy Spirit further in chapter 9.

Not Peddlers but Stewards: The Pauline Images

In the writings of Paul we also find the emphasis that ultimately all human testing or judgment is subject to the gift of God's Spirit. The following verses from the Corinthian correspondence show Paul's distinctive way of making this point:

> Think of us in this way, as servants of Christ and stewards of God's mysteries. Moreover, it is required of stewards that they be found trustworthy. But with me it is a very small thing that I should be judged by you or by any human court. I do not even judge myself. I am not aware of anything against myself, but I am not thereby acquitted. It is the Lord who judges me. Therefore do not pronounce judgment before the time, before the Lord comes, who will bring to light the things now hidden in darkness and will disclose the purposes of the heart. Then each one will receive commendation from God. (1 Cor. 4:1–5)

The word "stewards" in this passage, *oikonomous*, is no longer common in ordinary English speech. A possible alternative here is "caretakers," but that tends to suggest "curators," as if the mysteries of God were museum artifacts that Christ's servants are called to stand guard over as one guards relics from the past. The context makes it clear that Paul is not thinking of "stewards of God's mysteries" as curators in this sense, for he writes that stewards are to be found trustworthy, not by any human courts presently sitting in session, but by a Lord who is coming to bring to light things now hidden in darkness. The mysteries of God, therefore, have to do with a Lord that is coming, that is presently at hand but not in our possession, not in hand. They are not relics to be conserved and preserved as grave clothes preserve a dead body in a tomb.

Another possible translation of *oikonomous* is "housekeepers" or, more literally still, "home economists."[25] But again, this is not housekeeping in the sense of merely keeping everything well dusted and in place. It is housekeeping, rather, in the sense that one actively expects the owner to arrive momentarily. One constantly waits on the Lord. "Trustees" is sometimes used, but it suggests the management of investment and does not adequately convey the idea, not of managing, but of waiting upon the mysteries, of being on watch for the ways of God's coming home to us.

Nearest in meaning to the context is the English word *attendants.* What Paul appears to have in mind is that the vocation of servants of Christ is to be regarded as that of attendants of the mysteries of God, in the sense of being attentive to these inbreaking mysteries. The Lord who is at hand calls apostles to be on hand. In all human testing and judgment, in Paul's view, Christ's servants are under the constraint of the mysteries of God, a constraint that they cannot manipulate. Any attempt to understand the dogmatic task of testing for doctrinal faithfulness today that seeks to be ecclesial cannot ignore the orientation provided by this Corinthian text.

Appeal to mystery is often made in contemporary theology to end further testing and judgment. "It is all a mystery anyhow, so who knows whether any position is right or wrong, true or false?" Such thinking does not reflect biblical usage. In the New Testament scriptures the "mysteries of God" are not viewed as unknowable but as known in the life of faith. To cite examples: in Ephesians we read, "With all wisdom and insight he [God] has made known to us the mystery [*mystērion*] of his will" (Eph. 1:8–9); according to the Gospel of Matthew, Jesus says to the disciples, "To you it has been given to know the secrets [*mystēria*] of the kingdom of heaven" (Matt. 13:11). By referring to mysteries Paul is not suggesting some sort of divine unidentifiable flying objects — things eerie, confusing, and esoteric. Rather the mysteries of God are the ways of God in getting through to us, in opening our eyes to face reality, in bringing us to faith, and hope, and love. They are what the older theologies did not hesitate to call "the economy [*oikonomia*] of God."[26] In Paul's account such mysteries are neither static nor inert. They confront us, come to meet us, and give evidence to faith in breaking in upon the affairs of this world. The discipline of theology as such does not provide us with some privileged access to these mysteries of grace. It knows, as Augustine observed, nothing that the most humble, unlettered person of faith does not know of God. It waits as a housekeeper upon an arriving God to possess and inhabit what is God's own. We can neither claim nor master these mysteries. They can only claim and master us.

That is why those who are called to test the spirits are constantly faced with a great temptation. It is hard to wait upon the mysteries and abide by their constraints in season and out of season. It is hard to be attentive to a gift and not be able to produce the arrival of God on our terms, or to program and deliver faith, and hope, and love through our skill and scholarship. The temptation, as Paul sees it, is to take another course completely and to settle for what the market will reward, for what we can deliver, for some counterfeit word that is subject to our management, promotion, and technique. The temptation of every apostle is to give up attending the mysteries and become "peddlers [*kapēleuontes*] of God's word" (2 Cor. 2:17). Paul's metaphor here of "peddlers," when taken in context, suggests an attempt to work a deal with what he calls "God's word," to presume to determine an exchange rate for it and manipulate the terms of its sale. Peddlers of God's word, that is, are those who entice others to think that they can get from them what only God can give. As such they stand in sharp metaphorical contrast to stewards of the mysteries of God.

These scriptural soundings from Pauline as well as Johannine and other testimonies require no forced harmonization or denial of their distinctiveness to impress upon us the constraints and limits of an ecclesial theological response to the call not to believe every spirit. They provide an orientation and shape a sensibility for the contemporary work of dogmatic analysis.

Academic Limits

Along with the constraints of an ecclesial orientation there are also the academic and scholarly limits to be observed in pursuing this dogmatic proposal. These will further be addressed in chapter 5. The analysis of "spirits" to be undertaken in part 2 will be confined to faith claims that appear in commonly held doctrines, or teachings, of the ecumenical church. To inquire as to the disbeliefs that these claims enjoin and entail it will be necessary in each instance to give an interpretive account of the doctrine. Selectivity and partiality obviously are inevitable in setting forth such accounts, but the intent is to be both concise and accurate in summarizing certain basic faith affirmations found in the teaching of most Christian churches. The guiding question throughout will be, What implicit refusals of belief do these doctrines as faith confessions contain?

Before turning to part 2 and the contents of Christian doctrines, there still remains for consideration the issue of the criteria to be used in making dogmatic assessments. We shall next look at tests that are required for a creditable dogmatic accountability.

Chapter 4

TESTS OF DOCTRINAL FAITHFULNESS

With the biblical witness as confirmed in the ongoing community of faith providing the orientation for their theological task of testing, Christian churches ask specific questions in seeking to recognize when faithfulness requires that some spirit of the times be disbelieved. Is the claim being made continuous with what is apostolic in the tradition? Is it congruent with what the Word of God in scripture is speaking? Is it consistent with the community's prayer and worship? Is it truly catholic, that is, true for the church everywhere and not just in one place? Is it consonant with experience; that is, does it ring true to life in faith? Is it in keeping with a good conscience? What are the effects or consequences? Is the spirit that is being advocated pertinent to, or an evasion of, what is crucial, what matters most, in the situation at hand? Is it coherent in relation to contemporary modes of thought? How comprehensive is the particular teaching with respect to the full range of Christian confession?

Which of these tests actually are applied, and which either explicitly or implicitly tend to be given the greater priority in accounting for the doctrines of a community, are matters that vary according to the practices and policies of the different ecclesiastical communions. As such these practices and policies themselves may be said to comprise a community's procedural doctrines regarding its faith doctrines, what it teaches about how its teachings are to be evaluated.[1] They are rules of faith, *regulae fidei*, regulating communal confessions of the content of faith, *substantia fidei*. Each of the tests to be applied raises problems today that a theology to be creditable must recognize and address.

I am not suggesting that as individuals any of us simply goes through daily life with a handy slide-rule of ten questions by which we calculate on the spot what we shall refuse to believe. Our strongest beliefs and disbeliefs are seldom, if ever, arrived at by calculation. But when we do confess what they are we do use such terms as tradition, scripture, prayer, the holy catholic church, experience, conscience, fruitful consequences, what matters most crucially, is most coherent, and most adequately comprehends both the heritage of faith and its current significance. The continual testing for faithfulness on the part of each individual of the church in daily life is but brought together, pursued, and made more explicit in the ecclesial and academic discipline of dogmatics.

Let us now consider individually the questions listed above. They make up the ten most commonly applied tests for doctrinal faithfulness. There are problems raised by appealing to each of these tests that require our asking how their application is best to be understood today. We shall see that whether singly or combined these tests do not provide an automatic calculus for establishing faithful teaching. What they do provide are rubrics of accountability within which dogmatic assessments under the constraint of God's Spirit and the mysteries of God's coming are made.

For shorthand purposes I will label these tests as the "Ten Cs." They are:

1. Continuity with apostolic tradition
2. Congruence with scripture
3. Consistency with worship
4. Catholicity
5. Consonance with experience
6. Conformity with conscience
7. Consequence
8. Cruciality
9. Coherence
10. Comprehensiveness.

1. Continuity with Apostolic Tradition

In *The Longer Catechism of the Eastern Church* promulgated in Moscow in 1839 this first test is presented as follows: "What does the Church teach us, when it calls the Church Apostolic? It teaches us to hold fast the Apostolical doctrine and tradition, and eschew such doctrine and such teachers as are not warranted by the doctrine of the Apostles."[2] We may take this as a typical statement of the appeal to apostolic tradition. It is one of the most ancient appeals in the testing of Christian doctrine.

This test is most clearly reflected in those New Testament scriptures that explicitly acknowledge an oral tradition prior to the written canon. In the New Testament the term *tradition* (*paradosis*), like the term *gospel* (*euangelion*), is in the first instance used as a verb and only secondarily as a noun.[3] The meaning of "traditioning" in the New Testament is that of "delivering something" in the sense of "handing on" or "handing over." Thus in addressing the Corinthians Paul writes, "For I handed on [*paredōka*, 'traditioned'] to you as of first importance what I in turn had received: that Christ died for our sins . . . , that he was buried . . . , that he was raised . . . , and that he appeared" (1 Cor. 15:1–8). What has been traditioned is here characterized to the Corinthians by Paul not as mere information that may or may not prove to be of value but as that "through which also you are being saved" (1 Cor. 15:2). There is a salvific, or saving, tradition of apostolic witness that Paul in this instance identifies with gospeling. The events constituting the salvific flesh and blood coming of Jesus Christ involve a "handing over," a *paradosis*, a *traditio*.

The prologue to the Gospel of Luke also provides us with an example of "traditioning" used as a verb. "Since many have undertaken to set down an orderly account of the events that have been fulfilled among us, just as they were handed on [*paredosan*, 'traditioned'] to us by those who from the beginning were eyewitnesses and servants of the word, I too decided . . . to write an orderly account" (Luke 1:1–3).

In these two texts from two different authors we see a New Testament sense of traditioning as handing on the gospel, as conveying the word and power of Jesus Christ by which humanity is set free and saved. We see what may be called a *paradosis* of freedom.

But there is a second sense in which the term *paradosis*, or tradition, appears in the New Testament. In the passion narratives of the betrayal of Jesus it is said that Judas "traditioned" Jesus into the hands of sinners (Matt. 26:45, Mark 14:41).[4] Pontius Pilate is reported to have "traditioned" Jesus to crucifixion (Mark 15:15). Those who criticize the disciples for breaking with tradition are, in Matthew 15:6, given a rebuke by Jesus: "So, for the sake of your traditions [*paradosin*] you make void the word of God." In addition to the tradition that conveys the gospel of freedom, there is thus also a tradition that betrays and crucifies Christ. In the gospel narratives Judas and Pilate, to be sure, have their place in the drama of salvation, and God brings forth victory from faithless betrayal, crucifixion, and death. But the apostles of Christ are never called to the tradition of betrayal. The *paradosis* that betrays the freedom of Christ is never apostolic tradition.

"Tradition" in the New Testament contexts either may be apostolic, and gospel-conveying, or it may be Judas-like, and a betrayal of the gospel. From this it must be concluded that apostolic tradition, contrary to a widespread assumption, is not necessarily whatever is historically ancient or entrenched by long-standing ecclesiastical custom. To be continuous with the apostolate is to be discontinuous with Judas tradition — discontinuous in the sense that a break with some custom or convention of betrayal is made. Opposing traditions confront communities of faith in every age requiring that the community distinguish between them. According to New Testament usage, the fact that a teaching or practice is ancient does not make it the apostolic gospel. "You abandon the commandment of God and hold to human tradition [*paradosin tōn anthrōpōn*]" (Mark 7:8). The betrayal represented by Judas also is ancient, long-standing, and continuing tradition. Thus, apostolic continuity is never merely historical continuity, nor is apostolic succession merely historical succession.[5]

In applying the test of continuity with apostolic tradition a case must be made to account for whether the doctrinal claim in question is judged to represent a "virtual" truth — that is, an authentic unfolding expression of the apostolic mission — or whether it witnesses to a different spirit altogether. If continuity with what is apostolic in traditioning involves discontinuity with what represents betrayal of the apostolate in traditioning, then this test clearly is not a means simply for perpetuating whatever is old and conserving whatever is the status quo. Those who say that nothing can be apostolic unless it has already become customary or conventional are obligated to explain how their appeal to tradition is continuous with the gospel's *paradosis* of freedom and how it differs from a Judas *paradosis* of betrayal. If apostolic traditioning confesses that Jesus Christ has come in the flesh, and if it attends to the mysteries of God by being attentive to a coming Lord, then it includes witness to the future of Christ as well as to Christ's past. The apostolate witnesses as much to the new that is promised in Christ as to the old, to the Omega as well as to the Alpha.[6] The two cannot be separated in the gospel's *paradosis* of freedom. Memory and hope, story and promise, occur inseparably together in apostolic tradition. To keep the memory from blocking the hope (the temptation of conservatives), and to keep the hope from severing itself from the memory (the temptation of liberals), is the task of all dogmatics that seeks to be attentive to apostolic tradition.

While historically there has been a difference of teaching within Roman Catholic and Protestant communions regarding whether or not apostolic tradition in the church provides a supplement to what is contained in the written scripture, there has been no difference in the common ecumenical teaching that such tradition cannot conflict with scripture when each is rightly understood. The words of the Second Helvetic Confession of 1566 represent, in their historical context, a Reformed polemic against Rome, but no branch of Christendom does not in substance subscribe to them: "It would be wicked [*impium*] to assert that the apostles by a living voice [*viva voce*] delivered anything contrary to their writings [*contraria scriptis suis tradidisse*]."[7] This leads us to a second test, the appeal to scripture.

2. Congruence with Scripture

No test is more widely applied by churches in accounting for doctrinal faithfulness than the appeal to scripture. And the application of no test is more disputed. In the Lutheran Formula of Concord of 1584 this appeal is stated at the very beginning as the rule and norm: "Holy Scripture alone [*sola Sacra Scriptura*] is acknowledged as the [only] judge, norm, and rule, according to which as by the [only] touchstone, all doctrines are to be examined and judged, as to whether they be godly or ungodly, true or false."[8] Whatever the historical importance of the slogan *sola scriptura* in Reformation polemics against the authority of Rome, no Reformer ever taught that scripture could be understood apart from God's Spirit and the workings of God's grace. But the Reformers did assume a "clarity" within scripture with regard to the essential message of salvation, an assumption that has its theological critics today.[9]

For the New Testament authors, of course, congruence with scripture meant congruence with the Hebrew scriptures. Such congruence was understood to involve the interpretation of the Hebrew scriptures in light of their future culmination in the events concerning Jesus Christ. This exegesis would not pass muster with those whose interpretation is done in some other light.

The use of the Old Testament by the New Testament authors helps us to see how complex and multifaceted the appeal to scripture is. Every appeal to scripture involves presuppositions regarding scripture. Some doctrine about scripture is implied in every use of the Bible. In this respect the varieties of contemporary historical and sociological textual critics and philosophers of hermeneutical theory are no different from their New Testament forebears. For Christian faith the primary assumption is that the canonical scriptures convey a true witness of God. The Bible as such is not God and becomes an idol when so treated. But God is believed to have elected to speak as God wills through these scriptures, enabling them when this occurs to become — not as a static thing, but as an occurrence of communication — God's Word. We shall look further at the implications of this belief concerning the Word of God in chapter 6.

In simplest terms, to apply the test of congruence with scripture today in dogmatics is to ask about the *import of the canonical witness for faith*. Because the form and content of this import and witness are rightly subjects of continuing scrutiny and debate within the discipline of dogmatic theology, the appeal to scripture today also requires that an exegetical case be made, an account given. Such an account will always be subject to further critical evaluation, correction, and possible rejection, but no contemporary dogmatics is creditable as an ecclesial and academic discipline if it evades this exegetical responsibility.

Congruence with scripture in doctrine has historically been understood not to mean the mere repetition of the actual words of biblical proof texts. Congruence has been sought with the full import of the words, with that which not only is explicit but implicit in scripture as well. Not only what can be "read therein [*in ea legitur*]," as the Thirty-nine Articles of the Church of England stated it in the sixteenth century, but what can be "proved thereby [*inde probari potest*]," constitutes the content of holy scripture's sufficiency for salvation.[10] Or, in the language of the Westminster Confession of Faith of 1647, "The whole counsel of God, concerning all things necessary for his own glory, and human salvation, faith, and life, is either expressly set down in Scripture, or by good and necessary consequence may be deduced from Scripture [*aut consequentia bona et necessaria derivari potest a Scriptura*]."[11]

It is not only a modern hermeneutical insight that the import of the canonical scriptures for faith involves a study of their contexts. Again, the words of the Second Helvetic Confession make this point clearly:

> We hold that interpretation of the Scripture to be orthodox and genuine which is gleaned from the Scriptures themselves (from the nature of the language in which they were written, likewise according to the circumstances in which they were set down, and expounded in the light of like and unlike passages and of many and clearer passages) and which agrees with the rule of faith and love, and contributes much to the glory of God and human salvation.[12]

Academic exegesis today tends to give more attention to what this Confession calls "the circumstances in which they were written" than it does to what the Confession calls exposition "in the light . . . of clearer passages, and which agrees with the rule of faith and love [*cum regula fidei et caritatis congruit*]."[13] This latter principle, sometimes also referred to as the principle of the analogy of faith (*analogia fidei*), stipulates that obscure passages are to be interpreted in light of plain ones and that individual texts are to be interpreted in light of the fullness of the canonical context as apprehended in faith that evidences God's love.[14]

With regard to the contextual question, there are at least three contexts involved with every appeal to scriptural congruence which must be taken into account: (1) the original context (or contexts) of writing and redaction by which the text as now received came into existence, (2) the canonical context in which the text now has its place in relation to other more or less different texts within the one Bible in the community of worship that reads, preaches, teaches, and listens for word of the same one God in them all, and (3) the current cultural context, or listening environment, in which the text is presently heard.

A simple illustration, such as most of us could duplicate, shows the importance of environmental contexts in determining what words mean. During the late autumn a sign at a hotel desk in Virginia Beach read, "Winter rates now in effect." Since the tourist season on the Virginia coast had largely ended this meant that the fees were now lower. On the same date the identical sign was posted at a hotel desk in Miami Beach. But in south Florida the main tourist season was just getting underway. Winter rates meant that the fees were now higher. The very same words had exactly the opposite import for the pocketbook depending upon the location.

In addition to the locale in which a scripture is read and heard, the receptivity of the reader and hearer must be factored into account. Adolf von Harnack once remarked that some of Karl Barth's early biblical interpretation was "speculation for which I have no antenna."[15] Contemporary hermeneutical discussions emphasize the multiple factors that condition our human antennas for hearing — factors of culture, ethnicity, class, sex, economic privilege or deprivation, and interest. How a scripture is heard in another context may be quite different from what its human author originally intended.

A different hearing from the one originally intended does not necessarily mean that what is heard is false. Thomas Aquinas argued that the literal sense of a text was indeed, as the common view held, what the author intended, but in the case of sacred scripture the ultimate author is God.[16] Therefore, the meaning of a text in its future contexts of hearing and reception extends beyond the conceivable knowledge of any original human author. Every text must be viewed with regard to its *tendency* as well as to its human author's *intention.* The gospel writers' reading of Hebrew messianic prophecies, for example, interprets them as pointing to the nativity of Jesus Christ. If this were not the intent of the original human authors of these prophecies, does that fact make the gospel interpretation false? Not in principle, it may be argued, in the sense that the tendency of these texts may convey nevertheless a faithful witness to the coming of Jesus as the Messiah.

It is equally the case that the scriptures may be heard in certain contexts as having tendencies that promote false prophecy and Judas tradition. We find this recognition in the New Testament itself. In the wilderness temptation of Jesus it is the Devil who quotes the scripture of Psalm 91:11–12 to Jesus in order to get him to leap from the pinnacle of the temple, saying, "Throw yourself down; for it is written, 'He will command his angels concerning you,' and 'On their hands they will bear you up, so that you will not dash your foot against a stone' " (Matt. 4:6). According to Matthew, Jesus disbelieved the Devil and rejected the use of scripture for one's self-destruction. Appeals to scripture have been used historically to perpetuate such human destructiveness as racial slavery, ethnic warfare, anti-Semitism, and social practices injurious to women and sexual minorities. In testing doctrinal faithfulness by congruence with the import of the canonical witness for faith, a case must be made that is mindful of these issues of context.

3. Consistency with Worship

Is the doctrine consistent with the prayer and praise of our worship of God? This ecumenically recognized test is especially honored in Anglicanism and Eastern Orthodoxy, and in those communions that give priority to liturgical life, including its creedal traditions, over the framing of confessional pronouncements. *Lex orandi* (*or supplicandi*) *est lex credendi et agendi*, "the rule of prayer is the rule of belief and action." The formulation of this test is attributed to Prosper of Aquitaine and Pope Celestine I in the fifth century.[17]

In keeping with this principle, dogmatic statements are often said to be "doxological," in that if they truly are teachings decreed by God they praise God and do not simply state information about God.[18] How the logic of a doxological statement differs from and may relate to that of an ontological statement or of a historical statement (i.e., to the logic of a statement purporting to make an accountable reality claim or reference) is an important question of theological discussion and debate. For instance, assuming that both are to be characterized as doxological, is the statement that Jesus Christ was crucified under Pontius Pilate any different logically from the statement that Jesus Christ ascended into heaven and sits at the right hand of the Almighty?

The appeal to consistency with worship will obviously have different meanings according to different understandings of what constitutes Christian worship. Is worship to be defined by the order of the Mass with clear guidelines governing the administration of Word and Sacrament? Does Christian devotion within its rich variety of expression involve a definite and specifiable structure of prayer, the same anatomy, as it were, of faithful response, such as adoration, confession of sin, thanksgiving, and supplication, without which such devotion would not be faithful worship? Are there certain forms of address essential to true prayer?

It is not hard to understand why in the history of Christianity all major controversies over true and false doctrine have been integrally related to issues pertaining to worship. While centuries-old disputes over icons, or over theories of eucharistic presence, may strike the present-day student of theology as inordinate, no disagreements currently in the churches are likely to occasion more acrimony and conflict than those having to do with the revision of prayer books and hymnals. Free church worship, without its explicit creeds or prayer books, also knows its own rigidities of implicit ritual if the extemporaneous preacher steps too far out of line.

The Reformers' denunciation of what they viewed to be the excesses of the Roman Mass led, as would be expected, to the counter charge by Rome that the Protestant doctrines violated the *Lex orandi, lex credendi* principle. A rejoinder to this accusation appears in the Second Helvetic Confession where reference is made to the church historian Socrates of Constantinople (c. 380–450). "Socrates, in his history, says, 'In all regions of the world you will not find two churches which wholly agree in prayer' (*Hist. ecclesiast.* 5.22, 57)."[19] "Socrates says: 'It would be impossible to put together in writing all the rites of the churches throughout cities and countries. No religion observes the same rites, even though it embraces the same doctrine concerning them. For those who are of the same faith disagree among themselves about rites' (*Hist. ecclesiast.* V.22, 30, 62)."[20] Yet the Reformers for their part also affirmed the test of consistency with worship by identifying the true church as being, in the words of Calvin, "where we see the Word of God purely preached and heard, and the sacraments administered according to Christ's institution."[21]

Despite the obvious historical diversity of ritual and rite within the churches, and the lack of unanimity regarding what is true preaching and properly administered sacrament, this third test of doctrinal faithfulness requires that dogmatic analysis answer certain questions that otherwise would be ignored. Consider, for example, the colloquialism familiar in some Christian circles that a theological position is false if "it won't preach." In one respect such a complaint could be dismissed as a misunderstanding about the relation of theology to preaching. No theology itself is to be preached; the gospel is to be preached, and theology as a secondary critical discipline is reflection upon this prior testimony. But in another respect the point raised by this statement is pertinent to this third test. For example, the most problematic teaching of John Calvin is also the one that, considering the attention he devotes to the matter in the *Institutes*, is for him the most problematic to preach, the doctrine of the eternal predestination of the lost. According to Calvin, who here follows Augustine, the doctrine of the double decree should be preached, but in such a "fitting" way that no one is ever viewed as rejected and that nothing is ever preached that would deprive anyone of hope.[22] Clearly the difficulties in this position troubled Calvin, who had a more profound sense of what they were than most of his critics and did not hesitate to speak of the secret election of some to damnation as a "horrible decree [*decretum horribile*]."[23] "But I say: we ought to embrace the whole human race without exception in a single feeling of love; here there is no distinction between barbarian and Greek, worthy and unworthy, friend and enemy, since all should be contemplated in God, not in themselves."[24]

Does Calvin's teaching meet a resistance in the proclamation of the gospel in Christian worship and, if so, should this resistance be taken into account in testing the faithfulness of the teaching? Does the doctrine that some individuals are designated for everlasting damnation prior to creation conflict with the rule of *Lex orandi, lex credendi et agendi?*

Consider, as a more contemporary example, this question: are church teachings currently taking sufficient account of the content of the gratitude to God expressed in the prayers of those whose life together such teachings may condemn? We shall have occasion to return to this largely ignored question in examining some present-day problems with church teachings regarding sexuality in chapter 12. Again, what is being tested is the consistency of the teachings with worship.

Recognition of the liturgical diversity within Christian worship leads to the consideration of a fourth test for faithfulness, that of the universal oneness or catholicity of the church and its doctrine.

4. Catholicity

"Wherever Jesus Christ is, there is the universal [*katholike*] church": so writes Ignatius of Antioch, most likely toward the end of the first century.[25] In this earliest reference to the church as catholic the contrast is drawn with the church as a local congregation: "Wherever the bishop . . . the congregation; just as wherever Jesus Christ . . . the church universal." Gradually the term *catholic*, while not appearing in the New Testament itself, comes to be used as a designation for the church and its teaching insofar as they are true to the apostolic faith. In the words of the Apostles' Creed used in both Roman Catholic and Protestant churches, faith is affirmed in "the holy catholic church." Similarly, the ecumenically held Nicene Creed from the fourth-century councils of Nicaea and Constantinople speaks of "one, holy, catholic, and apostolic church."

By the fifth century the identification of catholic teaching with true or orthodox teaching finds its classic formulation in the canon of Vincent of Lerins: "What is held everywhere, always, and by all is what is to be believed [*quod ubique, quod semper, quod ab omnibus creditum est*]."[26] This threefold test of doctrine assesses its universality, antiquity, and consent.

It is easy to see why this fourth test was the one most frequently leveled in accusations against the Protestant Reformers. The earliest confessional documents of the Reformation in response take pains to insist upon their true catholicity. The Confession addressed to the emperor Charles V at the Diet of Augsburg in 1530 states that nothing in the Reformers' teaching bears a discrepancy with the Church Catholic. Where, following Luther, objection to ecclesiastical practice arises, it is only over "abuses, which without any certain authority have crept into the churches."[27] "These, because they could not with good conscience [*bona conscientia*] be approved, have to some extent been corrected." (Note in this instance how "conscience" is introduced as a test of catholicity. We shall return to this further appeal in a moment.)

Similarly, and even more emphatically, the Latin text of the Formula of Concord issued in 1584 contains the following:

> And inasmuch as immediately after the times of the Apostles, nay, even while they were yet alive [*superstites essent*, literally "while the Apostles were still standing by"], false teachers and heretics arose, against whom in the primitive Church symbols were composed, that is to say, brief and explicit confessions, which contained the unanimous consent of the Catholic Christian faith, and the confession of the orthodox and true Church (such as are the *Apostles*, the *Nicene*, and the *Athanasian Creeds*): we publicly profess that we embrace them, and reject all heresies and all dogmas which have ever been brought into the Church of God contrary to their decision.[28]

The next paragraph of the Formula of Concord directs its attention to what is referred to as "the idolatrous rites and superstitions" of the papacy and the sects at the present time, and it pronounces that the teachings of Martin Luther's Catechisms and the Lutheran confessional documents provide "the unanimous consent and declaration of our Christian faith" against them. The appeal to catholicity thus remains, but it now is turned back against Rome.

The identification of catholicity with the threefold Vicentian Canon of ecumenicity, antiquity, and consent is challenged in the Second Helvetic Confession of 1566:

> Wherefore we do not permit ourselves, in controversies about religion or matters of faith, to urge our case with only the opinions of

> the fathers or decrees of councils, much less by received customs, or by the large number of those who share the same opinion, or by the prescription of a long time. Therefore, we do not admit any other judge than God himself, who proclaims by the Holy Scriptures, what is true, what is false, what is to be followed, or what is to be avoided.[29]

To understand the significance of this test it is helpful to see how the appeal to that which is believed "everywhere, always, and by all" is *not* meant to be taken. Obviously, it is not to be interpreted as an empirical statement, and no doubt was not originally proposed as such. Even among the earliest Christians, as we see from the four canonical Gospels themselves (not to mention the numerous noncanonical writings that appeared), not everything was held to be exactly the same by everyone at the time, much less by everyone in all times and in all locations. What the rule does (the reason it retains an importance) is lead dogmatics to ask whether a teaching may rightly be judged to constitute the *sine qua non* of Christian identity — that without which no community would be identifiably Christian — or whether it is a nonessential matter that nevertheless may acceptably contribute to the well-being of some particular Christian communities at some particular times but is not necessary for the faithfulness of all. This is the distinction often recognized in ecumenical dialogues between the *esse* and the *bene esse* in Christian rites and doctrines. If the less than essential, less than the *esse*, is nevertheless not thought to be a false spirit, or ungodly, it is said to be a matter that may, but need not, be accepted by a Christian community, and as such is part of the *adiaphora* (practices not enjoined, either as mandated or as prohibited) contributing to the *bene esse*, or well-being, of the church.

The appeal to catholicity in testing the spirits to recognize faithful disbeliefs is not determined statistically by census, or historically by research. If the gospel is truly of God, its claim extends everywhere, always, and upon all. The rule of *quod ubique, quod semper, quod ab omnibus creditum est*, as the writings of Vincent of Lerins themselves emphasize, seeks only to establish that which is essential to the gospel. But can a doctrine be essential at one time and place and nonessential at another time and place? John Henry Newman thought not, and his words "once true always true" in the nineteenth century spoke, and no doubt still speak, for many.[30] But dogmatic inquiry has never been exempt from probing the truth question in relation both to its intrinsic sources and to contemporary modes of thought, a further standard we must consider under the rubric of "coherence." Newman himself did this as well as anyone of his time, distinguishing in effect in his theory of doctrinal development between practical necessity, even for falsehood in church teaching, and essential unchanging truth.[31] Dogmatic analysis of the question today, however, cannot rest with this conclusion.

5. Consonance with Experience

The test to which we now turn has become a characteristic of much post-Enlightenment theology where it is often given priority. This is the case not only in the more liberal theological traditions, both Protestant and Roman Catholic, once called "modernism," that have been formatively influenced by Kant, but in those less academically oriented faith movements as well which in various ways place stock in the evidences of the Spirit as found in religious experience.

We may appropriately refer to "consonance" in appealing to experience as a test of doctrine in that what is suggested by this term carries the musical connotation of "ringing true" and "being in tune with" experience. Grounds of authority are here shifted from external norms to norms in some sense intrinsic to human selfhood. But the specification of what that sense of normative experience is remains one of the most disputed problems associated with this fifth test.

The word *experience* itself is subject to such a broad range of definition that any appeal regarding it must be clearly specified if the test is to have meaning. Following are questions that must be answered in dogmatic theology by those attempting to justify a position with such a test. Merely to list them is to offer a roll call of influential thinkers that we can only name in passing here:

1. Is the experience to which appeal is being made for justification of the doctrine to be understood as influence limited to forms of consciousness, as in the case of Schleiermacher, or does it also include the influence of the unconscious as well, as with Freudians and others?

2. Is experience by definition limited to that which is distinctively human, as in the case of existentialist theologies influenced by Martin Heidegger's analysis of the uniquely human self-awareness of being (*Dasein*), or is the term applicable not only to human subjectivity, in both its conscious and unconscious dimensions, but more broadly to other than human and even inanimate reality also, as in the case of Alfred North Whitehead and those empirical theologies of reality as organic process influenced by him?

3. Is experience best conceived as the interaction of any organism with its environment, as some naturalistic metaphysics maintains; or, is human intentionality an essential aspect of the concept, as the

so-called phenomenological philosophies and theologies following Edmund Husserl insist?

4. By appealing to experience is the idea that of sense experience, and are these senses limited to the common impressions of seeing, hearing, smelling, tasting, and feeling, or are there additional "senses" of perception and apprehension to be taken into account?

5. Increasingly in contemporary thought the idea of universal, culturally invariant human experience is questioned. Are there, as Kant taught, *a priori* conditions of human subjectivity irrespective of social context, or is human selfhood more radically disparate depending upon contextual factors of race, gender, income, and class?

6. Is there an experience of Christian faith that is universal among all Christians; for example, some fundamental awareness of salvation or, even more minimally, of what Augustine called the "restless heart," that *cor inquietum* which, created by God, is never satisfied until it rests in God?[32]

The liberation theologies have been especially intent upon emphasizing the distinctiveness of experience among particular groups, and upon recovering vital experiences of those who previously have been disregarded and ignored by the dominant ethos. Black consciousness, feminist consciousness, Third World consciousness, gay and lesbian consciousness, have become familiar themes in Christian theology since the 1960s, with roots often hitherto unrecognized going back generations earlier. Reference is made to "the hermeneutical privilege of the oppressed."[33] All of this raises two additional questions about using experience as a communal test:

7. Whose experience is being taken into consideration?

8. Within what communal boundaries is the appeal relevant?

Twentieth-century empirical theologies in North America have primarily been shaped, not only by British and European traditions of empiricism stemming mostly from Locke, Hume, Kant, and their successors, but by the distinctive empiricisms of William James, John Dewey, Alfred North Whitehead, Charles Hartshorne, and others less well known with affinities to them.[34] Characteristic of these theologies are the generative motifs of developing organism and ongoing process. In Whitehead the most comprehensive view is reached. The "key notion" to be drawn from our experience by which to comprehend reality, Whitehead wrote in 1938, is that "the energetic activity considered in physics is the emotional intensity entertained in life."[35] With this key notion at its base, process theologies most indebted to Whitehead seek to provide an empirical description of nature in both its physical and mystical aspects. The most characteristically North American theologies and philosophies of religion through the twentieth century may be said to share empiricist assumptions.

More recently the appeal to experience has come under mounting criticism on both philosophical and scriptural grounds. Philosophically, questions mostly have to do with the relation of language to experience and of factors other than received sense data in perception and discovery. Widely challenged today is the premise of René Descartes that all certainty is grounded in an ineradicable self-consciousness, a position usually labeled "foundationalism," and the premise of John Locke that the human mind as a blank tablet is positioned so as to mirror in formally specifiable ways actualities that lie beyond it.[36] The influence of the later philosophy of Ludwig Wittgenstein in acknowledging the formative role of language in shaping experience may be seen in theological arguments that in effect propose the reversal of Schleiermacher's thesis that Christian faith statements are accounts of prior Christian feelings of piety (*Frömmigkeit*) set forth in speech. Rather than such statements articulating prior faith experience, it is maintained, they are more aptly understood as the condition for faith experience, just as a grammar is the condition for speech.[37] Once-sacrosanct assumptions regarding empirical methods are now discounted in contemporary philosophies of science, while those thinkers concerned with distinctively personal ways of knowing also question empiricism as a method.[38]

From the side of biblical theology the concentration upon eschatological and apocalyptic scriptural traditions since the 1950s has led to further issues regarding the appeal to experience. Jürgen Moltmann's influential text *Theology of Hope*, first published in German in 1964 and widely translated shortly thereafter, provides the best known example of the application of these newer apocalyptic insights to theology.[39] If revelatory language is considered from the perspective of scriptural apocalyptic as the taking place of that which is future and coming, its relation to present experience is not one of conformity and confirmation. Instead, such language is performative in that it calls into question present experience and initiates new experience.

Criticisms such as these do not invalidate the test of consonance with experience. They show that the application of this test, like the others, is by no means self-evident. Historically, the pejorative charge of "enthusiasts" has been leveled against those who were thought to put too much stake in this appeal. So it was that some of the more sober-minded Anglican divines criticized the eighteenth-century followers of John Wesley. Wesley's strong objections to the charge of enthusiasm bear noting here because they reveal the several tests which he emphasized in advocating what he called "heart religion" in a "catholic spirit."

In a letter to one of his most excoriating critics, the bishop of Exeter, who had authored several pamphlets under the title "The Enthusiasm of Methodists and Papists Compared," Wesley writes:

> From those words, "Beloved, believe not every spirit, but try the spirits, whether they be of God," I told them they were not to judge of the spirit whereby any one spoke, either by appearances, or by common report, or by their own inward feelings; no, nor by any dreams, visions, or revelations, supposed to be made to their souls, any more than by their tears, or any involuntary effects wrought upon their bodies. I warned them, all these were in themselves of a doubtful, disputable nature; they might be from God, and they might not; and were therefore not simply to be relied on, any more than simply to be condemned, but to be tried by a farther rule; to be brought to the only certain test, the law and the testimony.[40]

In addition to this appeal to scripture, to "the law and the testimony," Wesley adds the following tests in his sermon "The Nature of Enthusiasm." In this sermon he writes, "Though there is a real influence of the Spirit of God, there is also an imaginary one: and many there are who mistake the one for the other."[41] "Trust not in visions or dreams; in sudden impressions, or strong impulses of any kind. Remember, it is not by these you are to know what is the will of God on any particular occasion; but by applying the plain scripture rule, with the help of experience and reason, and the ordinary assistance of the Spirit of God."[42] To these further tests of "experience and reason, and the ordinary assistance of the Spirit of God" Wesley adds that the question of fruitfulness should be raised. In seeking to discern God's direction for one's life when confronted by a choice of options the question to be asked is, "In which of these states can I be most holy, and do the most good?"[43]

This latter test of fruitfulness was emphasized by Wesley in his sermon, "Beware of False Prophets":

> Our blessed Lord saw how needful it was for all men to know false prophets, however disguised.... He therefore gives us a short and plain rule, easy to be understood by men of the meanest capacities, and easy to be applied upon all occasions: "Ye shall know them by their fruits." ...First, what are the fruits of their doctrine as to themselves? What effect has it had upon their lives? ...Secondly, what are the fruits of their doctrine as to those that hear them;— in many, at least, though not in all; for the Apostles did not convert all that heard them. Have these the mind that was in Christ? And do they walk as He also walked?[44]

No one in Christian history has placed more emphasis upon "the witness of the Spirit" and the doctrine of "assurance" than did John Wesley. But his equally characteristic, even though far less equally celebrated, admonition remains, "Receive nothing untried."[45]

We shall look at the appeal to fruitful effects or consequences, but before doing so there is a test of doctrinal faithfulness belonging here that is sometimes included within the appeal to experience, yet which because of its importance merits a separate designation. This is the appeal to conscience.

6. Conformity with Conscience

In considering the test of catholicity we noted the words of the Augsburg Confession, among the earliest of Reformation confessional documents, that define Roman "abuses" as those that cannot be approved with *bona conscientia*. Lacking this approval of "good conscience," these particular rites, doctrines, and practices are said to have no catholic authority.[46]

The appeal to conformity with conscience finds expression in Reformation discussions of Christian liberty. The Westminster Confession of Faith of 1647 sums up the matter characteristically as follows:

> God alone is Lord of the conscience, and hath left it free from the doctrines and commandments of men which are in any thing contrary to his Word, or beside it in matters of faith or worship. So that to believe such doctrines, or to obey such commands out of conscience, is to betray true liberty of conscience; and the requiring of an implicit faith, and an absolute and blind obedience, is to destroy liberty of conscience, and reason also.[47]

What is fascinating in this appeal is that historically it has been interpreted to involve two claims that would on the surface appear to be contradictory. The one we see expressed in the statement above: conformity with conscience never leads to anything that is contrary to God's Word. The other is that freedom of conscience must be guaranteed to all as an inalienable right of creation, including those who do not acknowledge what the church proclaims as God's Word. These two claims, however, are not incompatible. The Presbyterian (USA) *Book of Order*, for example, in citing this section of the Westminster Confession under its "Preliminary Principles," states:

> Therefore we consider the rights of private judgment, in all matters that respect religion, as universal and unalienable: We do not even wish to see any religious constitution aided by the civil power,

> further than may be necessary for protection and security [a further tenet by no means shared historically by all the branches of Christendom that would otherwise hold to what is said regarding conscience] and at the same time, be equal and common to all others.[48]

The appeal to conscience is most definitely not only a Protestant test. Roman Catholic teaching finds clear articulation in the declaration of Vatican II entitled *Dignitatis Humanae* (1965): "In religious matters no one is to be forced to act against his conscience, or is, within just limits, to be hindered from acting in conformity with his conscience, whether privately or publicly, whether alone or in association with others."[49] A strong affirmation also is given in the pastoral constitution *Gaudium Et Spes* (1965): "In the depths of his conscience man detects a law which he does not make for himself but which he must obey. Its voice always summons him to love and to do what is good and to shun what is evil. . . . His dignity lies in obeying it; and according to this law he will be judged."[50]

The abiding value of this test lies in its protection of human integrity and in its defense of faithful disbelief. In and of itself, however, the appeal to conscience does not, except in principle, establish the content of communal doctrine. In principle, a "good conscience" is said to arrive at that which is faithful to God's Word, but in fact conflicting opinions regarding such faithfulness have and continue to be supported on all sides by this same appeal. The Society of Friends is most notable among religious bodies for its practice of waiting in silence for the Spirit to prompt a consensus of conscience. Majority views, however, are not held to represent necessarily such a consent to God's Spirit. Ecumenically and historically in some areas of the church's life such a consensus in the Holy Spirit has not been reached. The Rachels of this world refuse their consent to be consoled. Thus against the imposition of all authoritarian strictures the rule of conformity to conscience is recognized as an inviolate human freedom. No doctrine of the church can bind the human conscience against itself.

The problem with this test is evident in the acknowledgment that not all appeals to conscience represent what the words from the Augsburg Confession cited above refer to as "good conscience." In Christian moral teaching conscience may be said to be errant, even when sincere, as well as false and fallen, although never entirely destroyed. As *Gaudium Et Spes* puts this point, "However, it often happens that conscience errs through invincible ignorance; yet it does not on that score lose its dignity. This, however, cannot be said when a man cares little to seek for what is true and good, and when through a habit of sin, his conscience little by little becomes practically blind."[51]

This is not the place to pursue all the relevant issues treated in moral theology and philosophy respecting the nature of human conscience. The extent to which conscience is a universally experienced faculty capable of distinguishing between right and wrong, and one that whatever its fallen state and practical blindness may yet in some crucial respect serve as an appeal for communal doctrinal faithfulness, is a highly controverted subject. The thicket here for dogmatics is tangled but not without instructive paths.[52] This test remains irreplaceable, however, because of what in the jargon of common parlance today must be called "the bottom line" in all this discussion of conscience, namely, the refusal to believe that what is of God's Spirit ever violates the integrity of the human spirit.

7. Consequence

We come back now to the test of effects or consequences mentioned earlier. "You will know them by their fruits," are words of Jesus as reported in Matthew's Gospel (Matt. 7:16). The American pragmatist William James emphasized this appeal as the hallmark of pragmatic assessment with the phrase "fruits not roots," a criterion which he found admirably exemplified in Jonathan Edwards's 1746 *Treatise Concerning Religious Affections.*[53] James's interests were in the psychology of what he called "religious propensities," but his influence in American theology has been pervasive. There is an adage that says that as every German thinker is dialectical by nature, so every American is pragmatic. How does it matter, and what difference does it make? How does it work? These questions come most naturally to us. The test of consequence might even be said to be instinctual.

While this appeal would seem to follow most readily from the reputed self-evidence of common sense, when applied to the evaluation of doctrinal faithfulness it also is not without its problems. Most simply the question is, how long does it take to see the consequences? At what point in the future are the effects sufficient for a judgment?

In some applications the point is almost immediate. For instance, in *The Didache*, a second-century manual of church instruction, prophets are defined as false if they stay for more than two days, or if they ask for money![54] On a more serious note, if acute pain is being inflicted one is conscious immediately when it ceases. The Black Theology of James H. Cone provides an astringent antidote to those political and religious doctrines and their exponents that take refuge in evasive ambiguity to avoid concrete instances of social oppression.[55] The righteous God of biblical faith is not impartial with regard to what is right and not right in a society; this God is a partisan on the side of those for whom the right is currently being denied. The test of consequence requires dogmatics to give attention to the effect of what the church is saying and doing for harm or benefit upon all, but it can only do this for all by concentrating its focus upon those specific victims currently regarded in the situation at hand as being "the least" (Matt. 25:40 and 45).

Many results of evil, to be sure, are not immediately obvious, even to the most victimized themselves. Historical consequences are fraught with ambiguity, and long-term effects may prove quite different from first results. The liberators in one time and place may themselves become the oppressors in another. All human judgments remain subject to the final judgment of God. Scripture abounds with such testimony.

The application of this test requires a future. For this reason William James thought that it would be rejected in dogmatic thinking. "Dogmatic philosophies have sought for tests for truth which might dispense us from appealing to the future.... The history of dogmatic opinion shows that origin has always been a favorite test."[56] But James is incorrect as far as a dogmatics informed by biblical prophecy and eschatology is concerned. We see a characteristic biblical illustration of this appeal to the future in the words of Deuteronomy 18:21–22: "You may say to yourself, 'How can we recognize a word that the Lord has not spoken?' If a prophet speaks in the name of the Lord but the thing does not take place or prove true, it is a word that the Lord has not spoken." Yet the Hebrew scriptures know that the Word of the Lord comes to pass in God's own time, and that the faithful watch and wait for it.

As general guidelines for determining consequences, such questions as the following have been asked theologically as key ones. Does the spirit increase love? Does it produce what the prophets called true peace, or *shalom*? Does it further God's righteous justice? Does it provide liberation? Does it upbuild the community (not to be confused with mere earthly success)?

Critics of some liberation theologies object that faithfulness is not reducible to whatever presently helps you overcome your oppressions and repressions.[57] But if apostolic tradition is a *paradosis* of freedom, in Paul's words, "through which you are being saved" (1 Cor. 15:2), is there no connection? The test of fruitful effect, however, did not originate with pragmatic philosophy or with twentieth-century developments in liberation theology. Once again, this test yields no automatic conclusion, and a theological case must be made. But if historical ambiguity should not be naively underestimated, neither can it be allowed to prevent concrete dogmatic judgments in the here and now. "See, now is the acceptable time" accompanies the biblical theme of watching and waiting; "See, now is the day of salvation" (2 Cor. 6:2). "Choose this day whom you will serve" (Josh. 24:15). The factor of timeliness indicated by this call suggests that yet a further test is necessary in determining doctrinal faithfulness. We may think of it as the test of cruciality.

8. Cruciality

The purpose of this test may be briefly stated. Is the doctrine in question, what the community is saying and doing, pertinent to, or an evasion of, what is crucial, what matters most in the present situation? Such a question does not rule out the consideration of long-term consequences. What is most crucial for faith may not be the immediate gratification of desire, but it may not be, as well, the deferral of desire in the name of "pie in the sky bye and bye." If the desire is for what God wills in the present situation, the spirit cautioning deferral is not of God.

An illustration of the problem from the civil rights movement of the 1960s is instructive here. When Martin Luther King, Jr., was arrested in Birmingham, Alabama, in April 1963 for leading demonstrations against the segregation laws, he was condemned by leading white religious leaders of the area, Protestant, Roman Catholic, and Jewish, for actions that they called "unwise and untimely." His *Letter from Birmingham City Jail* focuses upon this charge and addresses it in a remarkable manner. King's words to his fellow clergy include the following statement: "In the midst of blatant injustices inflicted upon the Negro, I have watched white churches stand on the sideline and merely mouth pious irrelevancies and sanctimonious trivialities."[58] Opponents of the demonstrations, on the other hand, vigorously contended that in the crisis of that situation the more responsible act was to call for "law and order and common sense."[59] When, then, does "law and order and common sense" become "pious irrelevancy and sanctimonious triviality"? When do acceptable teachings under ordinary circumstances become unacceptable teachings in other circumstances? That most simply put is an issue dogmatic testing has sometimes ignored. According to the rule of cruciality, the answer is when the spirit being confessed in these teachings serves to evade "weightier matters of the law."

The words come from the Gospel of Matthew's account of Jesus' rebuke of the scribes and Pharisees. "Woe to you, scribes and Pharisees, hypocrites! For you tithe mint, dill, and cummin, and have neglected the weightier matters of the law: justice and mercy and faith. It is these you ought to have practiced without neglecting the others. You blind guides! You strain out a gnat but swallow a camel!" (Matt. 23:23–24). The pertinence of a church pronouncement or policy to what matters most in a current crisis, to what in the specific situation represents for that time and place "weightier matters of the law," is a question for dogmatics requiring a determination. Here again, there will be conflicting opinions, but a dogmatic assessment cannot avoid making this sort of determination along with its other tests.

Despite the difficulties of applying the rule of cruciality in trying to assess the comparative importance among communal doctrines and practices, this test as no other serves the further function of reminding dogmatics of the timeliness of the mysteries of God. Dogmas attentive to such mysteries cannot be viewed as timeless abstractions; they are to be seen as timely witnesses. A biblical faith, however, is not sanguine about the human capacity for telling time. On his entry into Jerusalem Jesus weeps over the city, we are told, because it did not recognize "the time" of God's "visitation" (Luke 19:44). And to the multitudes who can see a cloud rising in the west and say at once that a shower is coming, or can see the south wind blowing and say that there will be scorching heat, these words of Jesus are given: "You know how to interpret the appearance of earth and sky, but why do you not know how to interpret the present time?" (Luke 12:54–56). From this we may conclude that a test of every spirit is whether that spirit is telling the right time of God.

The biblical posture of watching and waiting involves this attention to what is timely and crucial. The Gospel of Luke recounts Jesus reading in the synagogue from the scroll of Isaiah: "The Spirit of the Lord is upon me." How is one to know? How is one to recognize that Spirit? "Because he has anointed me to bring good news to the poor. He has sent me to proclaim release to the captives and recovery of sight to the blind, to let the oppressed go free, to proclaim the year [the right time] of the Lord's favor" (Luke 4:14–21). It would appear from this text that to watch for the Lord is to watch out for the needs of those whose lives at present are in jeopardy. To wait upon the Lord is to wait upon the current needs of those whose oppression the Lord comes to free. To tell the year of the Lord's favor, the right time of this Lord, is not to turn away from the hour at hand into some supposedly more spiritual never-never realm of contemplation. It is to watch and wait for what is timely in the conveying of life where we are.

9. Coherence

The final two tests may seem to reflect more the academy's concerns than those of the church, but they are ecclesial as well. By "coherence" I mean to suggest the sorts of appeals usually indicated under the rubric of reason. *Reason* is too general a term in that each of the ten appeals we are considering involves reasoning in the particular sense of making a case or providing an account of the conclusion rendered.

Coherence is a more significant term theologically in that it calls to mind the basic Christian affirmation that in the reality of Jesus Christ "all things cohere." As the Epistle to the Colossians puts it, "All things have been created through him and for him. He himself is before all things, and in him all things hold together [*synestēken*, 'cohere']" (Col. 1:16–17). As we observed in the discussion of Luther's references to the "theology of the cross" in chapter 2, the issue is not faith versus reason, but the premises of reasoning in faith. The call to test the spirits is a call to reasoning in responding to the coherence enfleshed in Jesus Christ.

The term *coherence* for this test also serves to remind dogmatics that to be a creditable discipline both what may be called internal coherence and external coherence are aspects of church doctrine to be examined. By *internal coherence* I mean the self-consistency of the community's doctrines with each other. Does the particular doctrine under examination contradict other doctrines held by the community? Does it involve a self-contradiction? The application of this criterion does not rule out the place of paradox or dialectic in doctrinal interpretation. For example, to say that all things are at once impossible and possible is not a contradiction when placed within the context of Jesus' statement, "For mortals it is impossible, but with God all things are possible" (Matt. 19:26).[60] Statements of paradox and dialectic, as any other, may be examined for their consistency as well as for their inconsistency.

The fact that coherence is understood christologically enables theological reasoning to take into account the reality of that which is new. A coming Lord involves a future as well as a past. Not only, as the Colossian Epistle puts it, are all things to be understood "through him," but also "for him." Internal coherence as self-consistency must not be viewed as a self-enclosed system preventing new insight.[61]

The issue of external coherence is more debated in Christian theology. What is often referred to as a Kierkegaardian "fideism" is a position reputed to hold that in matters of faith only internal coherence is to be regarded. What the weight of ecumenical church teaching has held, however, is that the very internal coherence of the gospel and its teachings requires that the external coherence of the gospel's claims be accounted for. By this it is usually meant that a dogmatic interpretation is creditable only when it explains how the variety of knowledge claims made in faith relate to the current state of knowledge claims being made in other contemporary disciplines. In some instances the relation may be one of correspondence. The affirmation, for example, that Jesus was crucified under Pontius Pilate corresponds in character to a historical statement. In other instances a categorical distinction is involved, as, for example, when it is argued that the references to creation in the Book of Genesis are of a different category of discourse from the accounts of natural science. The test of coherence does not legislate *how* the knowledge claims of faith are to be interpreted in relation to the present state of scientific inquiry, and in this matter theologies differ. What it requires of every theology is that an account of the relation be offered for assessment. If all things are believed to have coherence in Christ, the demand for this external as well as internal coherence may be said to be as ecclesial as it is academic.

The term *systematic theology* as another label for dogmatics points especially to this test of coherence. To say that Christian theology is systematic means that the theology referred to considers its elements as a unity of parts. A "system" is a unity of parts, and the variety of testimonies in scripture and the ongoing life of the church does not have to do with the worship of many deities but of the one and only God. A proper systematic interpretation of Christian faith does not seek to impose an alien system of thought upon this variety of witness. Rather, it seeks to uncover point by point how the variety attests to the One God. This is the uncovering of faith's intrinsic coherence.

We can see that the rule of coherence has particular importance for theology as a scholarly discipline of thought, but the ramifications for faithful disbelief are intensely personal as well. To cite an example, should one believe any church teaching that does not in some sense make sense to that individual? We noted this question in raising the issue of the similarity between skepticism and faithful disbelief in chapter 1. Here there is a historical division of viewpoint among the churches. Some would say Yes, to unite with the community is to assent implicitly to what the community affirms even though some members of the community are obviously not yet at the same level of understanding as others. To take this position, as John Henry Newman observed, logically requires some sort of doctrine of ecclesial infallibility. What one implicitly trusts without making sense of can be, as it were, guaranteed to be trustworthy. Others would say No, the idea of implicit faith is not faith in any biblical or Christian sense at all, but a capitulation to superstition and heteronomous authority. It is wrong to assent to a faith the Holy Spirit has not witnessed in one's own spirit. Or, to recall Wesley's words, "Receive nothing untried." The issues are complex, but it is not difficult to see that the way in which the test of coherence is treated in assessing current church teachings and practices affects the approach taken to faithful disbelief.

10. Comprehensiveness

Our tenth test follows from the consideration of coherence, but it adds one further question important for the testing of doctrinal faithfulness. Does the teaching take into account the broadest possible range of relevant data?

To apply this test one must make a judgment as to what data are or are not to be deemed relevant. That judgment in itself must be open to continuing dogmatic evaluation and critique.

To what extent may a church teaching be said to be true if it contains scientific presuppositions that are false? The question is of particular importance today in matters of social ethics. Does the church have an obligation to point out cosmological or biological assumptions in its traditions that are no longer scientifically acceptable? For example, is the "demythologization" of biblical cosmological assumptions in the scriptures an obedient response to the call of faith conveyed through these scriptures, as Rudolf Bultmann so impressively taught in the first half of the twentieth century, or is that task a matter of betrayal, or at least of indifference, to faith?[62] Are false medieval assumptions about the physiology of gestation residual in some church teachings in sufficient degree to invalidate the pronouncements made therein about women's bodies and fetal life?[63] The appeal to comprehensiveness requires that such questions as these be asked.

A second line of inquiry is also part of the applicability of this test. By emphasizing certain points and ignoring others does a sufficient misrepresentation occur in the doctrine to disqualify it as an acceptable communal teaching? We shall have occasion to return to this question when we come to the contemporary problem of language regarding the being of God in chapter 7. A function of the interpretive principle known since Augustine as the analogy, or rule, of faith has been to see that the parts of scripture be interpreted in light of the whole.[64] Extended to apply to communal doctrines this principle supports the test of comprehensiveness. A practice or pronouncement that may not necessarily be incoherent with respect to the community's other practices or pronouncements, may still be criticized for comprehending too few of the issues relevant to the subject. Such a doctrine distorts the faith by what it omits.

Conclusion

We have now looked at ten criteria for evaluating the faithfulness of church teachings and in conclusion need to ask what has and has not been claimed by their review.

What do these so-called tests amount to? Is it not merely the rationalization of preference? Can they not be used to justify anything and everything? Is not the history of doctrine merely the history of the assertions and counter-assertions of arbitrary power? Insofar as the implied answer to these questions is Yes, there is admittedly some truth in it — except for the word "merely." And this is where the perspective of what in these pages is being referred to as faithful disbelief comes back into the picture.

The primary value of these tests is procedural. They serve not to vindicate Christian faith in God but to identify the grounds of appeal by which such faith testifies to its beliefs and disbeliefs and is brought to trial. They are the rules of communal dogmatic deliberation by which open account is rendered to all affected, both in the community and beyond, of "the lie," as Tolstoy put it, harbored by the truth of the doctrine. They provide publicly accountable appeals for the unmasking of false prophecy's pretension of piety. They are one means, not the only one to be sure, but not an insignificant one either, of keeping faith with Rachel in her refusal.

Part 2

Disbeliefs of the Christian Faith

Chapter 5

EXPLORING DOCTRINES: PREAMBLE TO PART 2

The theme of these pages thus far has been that in a biblical understanding one way in which faith in God is expressed is through the refusal to believe what is not of God. Theology as a critical academic discipline is not alien to the church's faith insofar as it represents a necessary response to the call not to believe every spirit but to test the spirits to see whether they are of God. We have further considered the constraints within which such a theological testing may be said to be both a creditable and a feasible undertaking for the church and the academy today.

We have now to ask what difference the argument of part 1 makes in the assessment of specific church doctrines. From focusing upon what it means to think of Christian faith as disbelief we now direct our attention to the uncovering of what may be called disbeliefs of the Christian faith.

But how shall we do this? To recall again the words of Tolstoy cited in chapter 1, "I have no doubt that there is truth in the doctrine; but there can be no doubt that it harbors a lie; and I must find the truth and the lie so I can tell them apart."[1] I have taken as my thesis that the truth in Christian doctrine harbors a lie whenever the faithful disbeliefs these doctrines entail go unrecognized. The question is how best to proceed toward this recognition. Should we begin by attempting to set forth the positive affirmations of a doctrine and then ask what negations are implied in them, or should we look first at negations that may be raised in objecting to a doctrine and then ask what positive affirmations these objections presuppose?

There are historical precedents in Christian theology for both these ways of proceeding. In some instances of doctrinal development the beliefs are recognized before the disbeliefs. Only later do unanticipated tendencies come to light that show themselves to be inimical to the original intent of the affirmations. In other instances the disbeliefs are recognized first; the lie is initially clearer than the truth. We see this especially in the formative history of Christian dogma leading up to the fourth- and fifth-century conciliar decisions of Nicaea (325), Constantinople (381), Ephesus (431), and Chalcedon (451). Before turning to the contents of individual doctrines a preamble is necessary about the issues posed when one tries to think of exploring doctrines as confessions of Christian faith.

The Tracing of Doctrines

In order to rethink church doctrines by inquiring into the disbeliefs that they enjoin and entail one approach would be to attempt first a general summary of what these doctrines essentially affirm as truth and then to ask what such core affirmations in effect deny. Another approach would be to begin with specific objections prompted by what the doctrines appear, at least to some, to be affirming that is inimical to faithfulness, and then to ask which of these objections to apparent lies are warranted. Friedrich Schleiermacher provides an example of the first way of proceeding, and Thomas Aquinas, the second. Let us look at each in turn.

1. *Begin by identifying what is essential:* Friedrich Schleiermacher

First determine from a study of a community's faith the elements that are essential to it, Schleiermacher advised, and then by this standard distinguish between those factors in the continuing life of that community that are true to this essence and those that represent corruptions of it. "Since the Christian Church, like every historical phenomenon, is subject to change, it must also be demonstrated how the unity of its essence is nevertheless not endangered by such modifications as it undergoes."[2]

In treating the doctrine of salvation, for example, Schleiermacher points out four entailed disbeliefs — he called them "natural heresies" — that this doctrine requires its adherents to recognize. To affirm as true that Jesus Christ is the sole Savior of humanity, if this is essential to a community's faith, is for that community to refuse to believe (1) that human beings do not need salvation, (2) that humans are not salvageable, (3) that Jesus Christ is too like other humans to be able uniquely to save, (4) and that Jesus Christ is too unlike other humans to have sufficient access to them to save.[3] The point being, as Schleiermacher himself expressed it, that such a community is faithful in refusing all heresies that define human nature in such a way that "a redemption in the strict sense cannot be accomplished," or that define the Redeemer in such a way "that He cannot accomplish redemption."[4] Every conceivable corruption that may in fact arise historically with regard to the Christian doctrine of salvation, Schleiermacher thought, will logically prove to be a consequence of at least one or more of these four heresies.

To follow this approach to the uncovering of faithful disbeliefs dogmatic inquiry begins with a summary of what is for the most part communally taken to be the essential truth of a doctrine. On the basis of this essence it then asks about what Tolstoy calls the "lie," and Schleiermacher the "natural heresy," that this doctrine harbors. The effort of summarizing the essentials of a community's fidelity as far as its doctrines are concerned becomes a matter of tracing the elements that remain most constant in that community's teaching. The attempt is then made to deduce from these constant elements the antithetical positions that logically fall outside the boundaries. An image that comes to mind for this approach to exploring doctrine is that of mapping land masses, acknowledging established territorial claims, and settling boundary disputes.

Of the ten criteria just discussed in chapter 4, primary weight in this dogmatic procedure is centered around the test of catholicity. The appeal to what is essential to Christian faith "everywhere, always, and by all" — even if made applicable only within the limits of a relatively small community — becomes the decisive test. Appeals to other criteria are then construed from this standpoint.

Schleiermacher himself argued that the determination of a faith community's distinguishable essence can only be undertaken with any definitiveness within such communities as are already sufficiently characterizable by a common form of spirituality or piety [*Frömmigkeit*]. Otherwise, as Troeltsch would later acknowledge, the only definitive "essence" that may be said to endure within the relativities of a community's history is the power within that communal history to generate new syntheses of cultural change. While in Schleiermacher's situation the emergent union of Lutheran and Reformed traditions in Prussia from 1814 to 1829 permitted the attempt at a common dogmatics, such was not possible, he held, between the still too dissimilar pieties of Protestants and Roman Catholics.

In today's more ecumenical and less denominationally defined context, by contrast, differences are often more pronounced within individual denominations and confessional bodies of Christianity than they are between them. It is equally the case that some similarities across confessional lines between certain voices within one community and kindred voices within another are far greater than those of anyone's own household. There is an ecumenicity that arises out of shared disbelief. This is what we are searching for.

To trace the essentials of doctrine accurately within concise limits is not easy. There is much variety of interpretation in the rich history of these doctrines, and any condensation will inevitably reflect bias and omission. The attempt to uncover faithful disbeliefs from this first perspective, however, requires at least a telescopic overview, a sort of aerial surveillance, of the primary contours of Christian teaching and their connecting links. Granting some inevitable degree of distortion within such a necessarily broad picture, a first step, nevertheless, in this approach to the chapters of part 2 would be to bring into as clear focus as possible characteristic affirmations of belief ecumenically acknowledged by most Christian churches.

But to speak of commonly recognized doctrinal contours or boundaries to be brought into view for the purposes of mapping immediately raises a further possibility of misdirection. To approach faithful disbeliefs by first determining what are the essential beliefs may suggest that issues of what constitutes faithful refusal are restricted to matters of the periphery. The doctrinal boundaries themselves may be visualized as static and fixed demarcations exempt from being questioned or even, if deemed necessary, redrawn. Within these set bounds of orthodoxy the content of Christian doctrines may be assumed to be viewable and traceable like permanent land masses. The enclosed interiors, as it were, the main territories of these primary land masses themselves, thus become off-limits to dogmatic questioning. But if the only disbeliefs permitted for consideration are those relating to the periphery, the task of testing the spirits accordingly becomes peripheral. To envision the tracing of doctrines as the mapping of land masses, or as a mirror imaging of an essentially fixed turf, is to confront the possibility of this misdirection.

Yet whether one speaks of a faith community's "essence [*das Wesen*]," as did Schleiermacher, or uses the term *identity* that is more in vogue today, the matter of a doctrine's distinguishing characteristics cannot be avoided. It is the case that some affirmations historically have had, and continue to have, a constancy of direction in Christian teaching. Better descriptions of the tracing of this constancy than the mapping of land masses would perhaps be the plotting of wind currents, or the charting of sea channels. Each of these metaphors merits reflection.

The nautical images of wind and sea for God's will and way are supported by such scriptural passages as "The wind [*pneuma*] blows where it chooses, and you hear the sound of it, but you do not know where it comes from or where it goes. So it is with everyone who is born of the Spirit [*pneumatos*]" (John 3:8); and "Deep calls to deep at the thunder of your cataracts; all your waves and your billows have gone over me" (Ps. 42:7). Even the more solid geological images of mountains and valleys, rough places and plains are not viewed as fixed and immovable terrain before the coming of the Lord: "Every valley shall be lifted up, and every mountain and hill be made low; the uneven ground shall become level, and the rough places a plain" (Isa. 40:4).

On the other hand, the richly metaphorical Letter of Jude shows how the more dynamic images of wind and sea can also be applied to the inconstancy of the "ungodly [*asēbeis*]" (Jude 1:4): "waterless clouds carried along by winds [*anemōn*]; autumn trees without fruit, twice dead, uprooted; wild waves of the sea, casting up the foam of their own shame; wandering stars for whom the deepest darkness has been reserved forever" (Jude 1:12–13). Against such inconstancy the writer of Jude appeals to the "beloved," to whom the letter is addressed, "to contend for the faith that was once for all entrusted [*hapax paradotheisē*, 'once for all traditioned'] to the saints" (Jude 1:3). This seemingly more fixed sense of *hapax* ("once for all") tradition is akin to the idea of something constant definitely "entrusted," or "put in trust," in 1 Timothy 6:20–21: "Timothy, guard what has been entrusted [*parathēkēn*] to you. Avoid the profane chatter and contradictions of what is falsely called knowledge; by professing it some have missed the mark as regards the faith." (See also 2 Tim. 1:12 and 1:14.) In Latin translation this charge to "guard what has been entrusted" becomes *"depositum custodi."* The translation of the Greek *parathēkē* into the Latin *depositum* leads to the expression "deposit of faith" in later church teaching, especially in Roman Catholicism. In such a deposit a definite once for all delineation of dogma is assumed, and from this perspective it appears that we are back again with fixed and static boundaries and a solid terrain.

Such need not be the conclusion if the etymological connotation of "deposit" in the Epistles to Timothy is read as fiscal rather than geological.[5] In the case of financial deposits a trust fund, though it may be constant in the sense of enduring, is not static. The deposit as principal over time accrues new interest. Roman Catholic teaching itself allows that the dogmatic formulations which it considers part of a permanent *deposit of faith* also may lend themselves to "new expressions" as long as these come to be officially approved as presenting "more clearly or more completely the same meaning."[6]

Across the ecumenical spectrum of the church there is constancy within the diversity of doctrine, to be sure, in some cases much more than in others, but nonetheless traceable. For all their divisions Christian churches are more united in most of the major doctrinal areas than divergent. Thus we may refer to mapping doctrinal contours. But to think of such constancy more in terms of wind currents or sea channels instead of fixed land masses helps us to see these commonly recognized doctrinal trajectories as dynamic locations (the older theologies called them *loci*) of living issues to which every new attempt to rethink the doctrine must pay some attention. The cartography required in this case is more of the order of a navigational guide than of a geodetic survey.

The Latin title for collections of core points of doctrines, *Loci Communes*, designates common pausing places for consideration.[7] It does not signify that all the issues cease to exist at these places or that they are already completely settled and solidified by what has been thought before. But it is equally important to see that the major Christian affirmations do have a continuing history and that, despite the different lines of interpretation within this history, a constancy of common pausing places remains identifiable.

If we think in terms of a more nautical metaphor, these pausing places are like the buoys that mark the channels of the deep. They neither contain nor confine the depths, but they point out their direction by warning of the shallows.[8] Their placement and location are subject to continuing communal decision. If communal doctrines, or dogmas, are thought of as buoy markers of the mysteries of God known to faith, then theological dogmatics may be understood as buoy tending. Ongoing debate, conversation, and new insight regarding the faith expressed in these doctrines cannot bypass these loci, these buoy markers, without forfeiting the doctrine's distinguishable channels, ending up off course or in the shallows, and thereby missing the subject.

For Schleiermacher, the essence of a Christian community is to be found in its piety, not its doctrines. Its doctrines derive from this piety and are to be understood as didactic expressions articulating a more primal faith experience. Yet Schleiermacher is also remarkable for his emphasis upon the communal context in which Christian piety itself is shaped. Doctrines play a part in this ongoing historical and cultural context that gives Christian experience its distinctive modification.

The question of whether doctrines as such are the products of discernment, articulating a more primal faith experience, or whether they are themselves facilitators of discernment, allowing for faith experience not possible without them, presents theology with a false alternative. Some elements of doctrine do serve to mirror the faith experiences of members within a community, and others serve more to enable experiences of faith that otherwise would not arise. But these elements may not be the same for all. Schleiermacher's own attempt to trace the primal conditions of human consciousness essential to the identification of Protestant piety, and to see doctrines as derivatives of that piety, had the effect of relegating to the periphery of consideration certain doctrines regarded as nonexperiential, the most important example being the doctrine of the Trinity.[9] Although our concern is with the exploration of doctrines and not with forms of pious consciousness, Schleiermacher's example is instructive in reminding us that the judgment one makes regarding what is essential relegates at the outset to the periphery certain objections thereby assumed to be beyond the bounds and nonessential to Christian faith.

2. *Begin with the objections:* Thomas Aquinas

An alternative approach would be to begin not with what is settled but with what is questionable, to start with particular objections, specific challenges raised to certain church teachings, and then to ask if these objections point to previously unrecognized currents and depths of Christian faith, or if instead they are off course. In this second instance attention is focused initially upon perceived blocks to faithfulness. One approaches dogmatics from the standpoint of a traffic jam, looking for those intersections within doctrines where the witness of the community is momentarily stalled or in collision. The goal of testing the spirits from this perspective is not to establish parking spaces reserved for the church, but to alleviate gridlock.

Of the ten criteria that have been discussed, primary weight in this second approach falls on the two tests of consequence and of cruciality, with such other tests, as for example apostolicity and congruence with scripture, interpreted chiefly with reference to these. Yet here as well the aim of testing is not simply to further mobility as such. It is to trace the routes that enable Christian fidelity toward God to move on in freedom. Not every route does so. A sense of direction and some awareness of bearings are thus presupposed, but in this case they come to recognition in the light of specific objections.

One example of this way of proceeding is to be found in the form of questioning that enlivened the scholastic disputations of the Middle Ages. If the *loci communes* are indeed locations of living issues, the determination of their true significance can best be brought to light by examining their plausible alternative interpretations. One begins, as does Thomas Aquinas in the *Summa Theologiae*, by introducing each doctrinal subject as a question for faith prompting alternative answers. Reflection generally follows five steps, usually indicated by Thomas with the words *utrum, videtur, sed contra, responsio*, and *ergo*. [10]

The *utrum* ["whether"] introduces the plausible options by asking of each point of sacred doctrine "whether it is the case that..." I emphasize "plausible" for if it is obvious from the start that there is only one answer, or that the only conceivable alternative is clearly wrong and lacks all plausibility, the conditions for disputation have not been met. No real issue has been posed. The *videtur* ["it would appear"] follows and presents what would at first glance clearly seem to be the answer, stating "it would appear to be that..." Upon further reflection, however, this apparent answer is found to be inadequate. What is remarkable at this point in Thomas's procedure is the suggested ideal of a fair hearing for opposing views, especially for views that may be judged finally to be unacceptable.[11] This has not been an ideal honored in dogmatic theology throughout much of its history. What appears to be the answer is given the full weight of plausibility; no straw cases are concocted merely for easy refutation. In presenting the *videtur*, Thomas is presenting points necessary for understanding what he will find to be the adequate determination of the issue. The *sed contra* next states a counter position, "on the other hand. . . . " Then Thomas offers his answer, his *responsio*, concluding with the *ergo* ["hence"] in which he elucidates his answer to the question by explaining what in the views set forth in the *videtur* he did not find adequate.

Working within the canons of dogma and worship in his time, Thomas obviously does not begin without a sense of direction or some awareness of his bearings within what in the Nicene Creed is affirmed as "the one, holy, catholic, and apostolic church." Most of his arguments depend upon citations of sources he treats as authorities, and in this respect they reveal a clear difference between what would most likely be considered persuasive in the thirteenth century and today. Yet what is striking is the way the exploration of *sacra doctrina* in his major work proceeds from questions, and from plausible objections posed to such doctrine, toward the uncovering and recognition, at least according to his determination, of what Christian faith refuses to believe. Bringing Thomas into a discussion of Schleiermacher's four "natural heresies" provides an interesting contrast. Beginning with the essential conviction that Jesus Christ is the sole Savior of humanity, that, in Schleiermacher's words, the redeeming influence is "mediated through him alone" [*nur durch ihn vermittelt ist*],[12] leads Schleiermacher to the recognition of four disbeliefs entailed in this conviction. It is inconceivable, in Schleiermacher's view, that there are any plausible objections that may be said to be faithful that are not already in some way implicit in the refusals to believe that human beings either do not need to be or cannot be saved, and that Christ either is too like us or not enough like us to save. But what of confessions that may affirm Christ as *a* unique Savior but not necessarily as *the* Savior? Do the four "natural heresies" address them, or on essentialist terms would such claims simply be ignored as nonessential for a Christian community?

The disputed question of whether, in acknowledging Jesus Christ as Savior, Jesus Christ must then be confessed as the *only* Savior, or whether redemption by Christ is only faithfully confessed as mediated through him *alone* [Schleiermacher's German word here is *nur*], falls outside the parameters of what has first been identified as the essence of Christian faith.

Yet this is precisely the issue Thomas raises. In question 26, article 1, of the *Summa Theologiae* 3a., he asks "whether it is the case that Christ is the sole mediator of God and humanity [*utrum esse mediatorem Dei et hominum sit proprium Christo*]." After setting forth plausible reasons in the *videtur* section for arguing why Christ apparently is not the sole mediator of salvation, Thomas then responds, to the contrary, with the judgment that Christ is. Redemption comes through the reconciling death of *solus Christus*. By first raising the objections, however, Thomas is now in a position to say what this claim of faith does *not* mean. "This does not exclude others being named subordinate mediators between God and humanity should they co-operate in uniting humans with God, either as preparing the way or as ministers."[13] Thomas offers as examples of "subordinate mediators" those who prefigured Christ and those who subsequently are given to share in his continuing ministry of reconciliation. While both Schleiermacher and Thomas affirm that Christ alone is Savior, Thomas's approach in effect leads to the explicit recognition of an additional disbelief. In confessing solely Jesus Christ as the Savior, Christian faith also refuses to believe that this saving by Christ alone excludes mediation by secondary means. At a number of intersections in church doctrines this disbelief provides a way for the stalled traffic of Christian confession to move on. It in turn leads to further questions and objections. We shall see how this is so not only in connection with the doctrine of salvation, but with the doctrines of the Word of God, the person of Jesus Christ, God's providence for creation, and of ecclesiology as well.

Further support for pursuing the recognition of faithful disbeliefs by way of raising objections to established teachings can be found in the unlikely instance of John Henry Newman. As previously noted in chapter 3, Newman, while a defender of Catholic dogma as "once true, always true," argues that some "great truths, practical or ethical, float on the surface of society . . . until changed circumstances, accident, or the continual pressure of their advocates, force them upon its attention."[14] Such truths may require an "organized agitation," in Newman's words, "to make their acknowledgement . . . operative." An illustration is "the iniquity . . . of the slave trade" that "ought to have been acknowledged by all men from the first," but was not until objections were mounted.

Following this line of thinking, it is as if the full *principal* of the deposit of faith cannot be known except in terms of its *interest* accrued through the questioning of future generations. The essence, to use this term, of a Christian dogmatic principle is precisely the deposit of apostolic *principal* whose truth values only become "operative" through the continual raising of objections as questions regarding faith's *interest*.

Careful readers will notice that Newman himself refers here only to what he calls "great truths, practical or ethical"; the quotation does not explicitly include "dogmatic" truths. In testing the spirits of doctrinal content, however, dogmatic elements cannot be divorced from elements that are practical and ethical. They are in fact inseparable.

This last point is vigorously maintained in contemporary liberation theologies, where it is argued that the primary characteristic of faithful objections is expressly the fact that they represent a way of seeing what Bonhoeffer called "the great events of world history from below, from the perspective of the outcast, the suspects, the maltreated, the powerless, the oppressed, the reviled — in short, from the perspective of those who suffer."[15] To those on the ground of disputed territory who are prevented from moving freely the picture looks quite different from the view provided from the heights of aerial surveillance. It is precisely the assumption of liberalism, writes Carter Heyward, that "God is simply above the fray."[16] "This, more than any other, is the grievance of Latin American, African American, Asian American, and feminist liberation theologians against the so-called objectivity espoused by liberal theological scholars."

When the values of partisan solidarity and intersubjectivity replace values of impartial objectivity, the task of accurately identifying "the fray" still remains. For its part the liberationist impetus in Christian theology recognizes this task by its insistence upon the inclusion of social analysis. The complaint against "so-called objectivity" is not to be dismissed as an argument for either myopia or inconstancy. It is, as Heyward's statement indicates, a refusal of those spirits of detachment that exercise a protective custody in claiming to represent "God."

Even the most radical objections presuppose something like — call them what we will — crucial buoy markers, acknowledged demarcation lines, current sonar charts — within disputed areas. Every attempt to trace what faith refuses as false and intolerable discloses some indicators of where a faithful confession of God is presumed to go off course. Any testing of objections, that is, also implies a view of what is deemed essential.

Conclusions

Looking only at their formal ways of proceeding, and leaving aside the contents of their dogmatics, one might be led to conclude that Schleiermacher's approach is being portrayed as in fact the more catholic, at least as Vincent of Lerins defined the term, while Thomas's approach, at least potentially, is thought to allow for more protest, and in this sense at any rate turns out to be more protestant! And what shall we make of John Henry Newman being cast, no less, in the role of a liberation theologian? (Surely an example of the falsity of so-called liberal objectivity could hardly be more blatant!)

I actually do think that the descriptions are correct, and that they help us to see something true that needs to be taken quite seriously. In testing for faithful disbeliefs today conventional stereotypes regarding authority within Christian theology quickly become passé. The more familiar ideological battle lines no longer are the scene of the action; they have shifted and may be expected to continue to shift. Dogmatics by slogan is neither creditable nor feasible. Polemic by libel can make for exciting fiction, but it is not the radical testing of spirits to which the call to faithful disbelief in the twenty-first century summons. The notion that within Christian faith the protestants are never catholic, or that the catholics never protest, that traditionalists cannot be liberationists, or that liberationists are never traditional, is soon dispelled when theology and its practitioners try to face the real corruptions and collisions of "the fray." This is by no means to deny differences or conflicts; it is to say that the real differences and conflicts are not illuminated by the stereotypes.

This observation is borne out when we ask of the two approaches which of the ten criteria for the testing of what faith refuses are the most operative in each.

Consider again the first approach. In attempting to begin with an identification of what is essential to the faith of a community, the formal test necessarily becomes that of catholicity. What is the *sine qua non* that is posited in the actual life of this community? Along with this goes the test that has been labeled comprehensiveness. That is, the accurate identification of what is essential stipulates that the broadest possible range of relevant data be taken into account in making the determination, and that no misrepresentation occur in emphasizing certain points and ignoring others on the map, as it were, of what is posited within the faith community. Where this first approach measures lowest on the scale is on the points of testing for consequence and for cruciality. The question is not whether the content of a particular theology following this line of thinking comes to be viewed as relevant. Schleiermacher's own theology clearly was so viewed by many whom he addressed as the "cultured despisers" of religion.[17] Rather, what is at issue is whether objections appealing to consequence and cruciality are liable to be dismissed without a ruling because the boundaries defining faithful jurisdiction have already been set.

Consider now the second approach. Despite the fact that Thomas himself worked within what he acknowledged to be the parameters of apostolic tradition, catholicity, and holy scripture, the test of consequence most shapes his formal procedure. What effects follow from objections to taking one plausible position in contrast to that of another? As this approach moves on beyond Thomas's own use of it to questions of what Newman called "operative truths," and then further to the grievances and protests addressed today in liberation theologies, the appeal most favored of the ten tests becomes that of cruciality. Where this second approach measures lowest on the scale is on the points of catholicity and comprehensiveness. This may sound surprising when one thinks of the unexcelled comprehensiveness of a medieval *summa*. Thomas obviously extended the procedure of disputation with its raising of plausible objections to nearly every conceivable topic of catholic teaching. But, apart from Thomas, the procedure itself of beginning with questions and objections, especially when the particular questions and objections are viewed as addressing "the weightier matters of the law," allows for less attention than the first to the question of whether the account given of Christian faith omits essential matters that are not currently being contested.

Not surprisingly perhaps, we are led to conclude that the uncovering of faithful disbeliefs demands that we try to think from both of these directions, checking results from one approach against the other. A brief survey of doctrinal *loci* requires some overview of commonly held affirmations, but the false spirits that they harbor can only be spotted on the ground where the actual impasses to faith are confronted. Some topics are less contested than others, and the accounts of the doctrines will vary accordingly as to which approach is emphasized. But a similar format will be used in the following chapters, and it will include these steps.

First, each chapter will begin with a brief introduction to what the doctrine is about.

Then several initial objections that come to mind with respect to the doctrine will be posed. What will be highlighted are those points where the communal doctrine as perceived is not persuasive to some within the community, where it may be charged with lacking concrete meaning, ignoring social consequences, contributing to rejections that do not arise out of Christian faith, and where it runs into intolerable conflict and contradiction with other Christian teachings. In trying to stake out conceivable and plausible objections the aim will be to keep the focus directed upon these areas. Reflection upon these initial objections will not proceed with the governing assumption that they, like Thomas's *videtur* positions, necessarily represent misperceptions that will be found to be inadequate. Some will later be determined so, some will not. Rather the aim will be to follow the ideal Thomas sets for stating each objection as fairly and plausibly as possible, not just to refute it, but to examine how it illumines faithful disbeliefs. The commitment to a fair hearing, with its repudiation of the bearing of false witness, is not a presumption of judicious neutrality. It is a requirement of due process for any creditable dogmatic testing.

Third, the major section of each chapter will be given to an interpretation of the doctrine's content which takes into account the initial objections that have been raised and makes determinations according to the ten tests discussed in chapter 4 about what the doctrine essentially rejects.

Each chapter will then conclude with a summary listing of all the faithful disbeliefs that have been proposed for recognition in the interpretation of the doctrine's content, and with a final response in light of these proposed disbeliefs to each of the initial objections that was presented at the start.

Chapter 6

THE WORD OF GOD

Introduction

God's otherness is one of communion. This statement comes as close perhaps as any single sentence can to saying what the Christian doctrine of the Word of God is essentially about. The doctrine is the elucidation of this basic conviction.

Under the rubric of the Word of God, theology confronts a cluster of wide-ranging issues regarding faith in God as One who is *self-communicating*. How God is believed to be self-communicating for purposes of human knowing leads theology to the use of the word *revelation*. The doctrine of the Word of God is thus sometimes referred to in dogmatic texts as the doctrine of the knowledge of God and sometimes as the doctrine of revelation.

Scriptural testimony to the conviction that God is not "we ourselves" (Ps. 100:3) is abundant.[1] The "I AM" of Exodus 3:14 who sends Moses to address the people of Israel is, in the words of the prophet Hosea, "God and no mortal, the Holy One in your midst" (Hos. 11:9). And, of this One, Isaiah prophesies, "For my thoughts are not your thoughts, nor are your ways my ways, says the Lord" (Isa. 55:8). The Holy One is other to ourselves, but other precisely, as Hosea expresses it, in our midst. Or, following Isaiah, the One whose ways are as high above our ways as the heavens are higher than the earth, is higher only as the One who is near and may be found. Just as rain and snow feed the earth, making it bring forth and sprout, so, in Isaiah's testimony, does the *word* of this One go forth (Isa. 55:6–11). The otherness of the One that comes to be identified by calling faith into being is precisely that, an otherness that calls, that communicates, and that establishes communion.

One way of providing a synopsis is to take note of the elements of this doctrinal area as it later develops which are prefigured *in nuce* in the following verse from Paul's Second Letter to the Corinthians: "For it is the God who said, 'Let light shine out of darkness,' who has shone in our hearts to give the light of the knowledge of the glory of God in the face of Jesus Christ" (2 Cor. 4:6). If we simply follow the words of this one verse, not as any sort of prooftext but as an illustration and outline of topics that subsequently come to be much discussed, we find here some of the main pausing places indicated for a consideration of this doctrinal subject.

We may observe at the outset six of these *loci.*

First, in Paul's statement God is depicted as saying something; God speaks.

Second, what God is depicted as saying is expressed through words of scripture; the quoted words "Let light shine out of darkness" are an allusion to the account of creation in Genesis 1:1–4.[2]

Third, as shown by this allusion to creation, God's words are presented by Paul as acts that accomplish something. What God says brings forth creation, calls into being a new state of affairs. The words "Let there be light" are followed in the Genesis text with the statement, "and there was light" (Gen. 1:3). This refrain of "Let there be" followed by "and there was" is repeated throughout the account in Genesis 1.

Fourth, the God who speaks through words of scripture and acts to accomplish what is spoken is also said to shine in our hearts. The external words are confirmed by an internal illumination. Later doctrines will speak of the external witness of the Word in scripture illumined by the internal witness of the Holy Spirit. There is a personal awareness of what God speaks at the deepest levels of our own being.

Fifth, this speaking and acting of God, as attested through scripture, and this shining of God in our own hearts, confirm one another in providing what Paul calls "the light of the knowledge of the glory of God," that is, in providing what doctrinally comes to be treated under the heading of "revelation."

Sixth, this knowledge is said to be focused "in the face of Jesus Christ."

Here in this brief list of topics we are introduced to a table of contents, as it were, of primary pausing places that come to be reckoned with continually in dogmatic theology under the heading of the Word of God.

Initial Objections

If we ask whether for Christian faith God's otherness is one of communion, we immediately confront initial objections. With conceivable objections on any topic obviously no limits can be set, but many if not most raised in connection with the doctrine of the Word of God fall into four overlapping groups. We may categorize them as objections having to do with (1) authority, (2) reification — that is, turning the Word of God into a tangible object or phenomenal entity, (3) exclusivity, and (4) mediation, or the way God's Word becomes known.

1. *It would seem that Christian teaching concerning the Word of God demeans human responsibility by imposing an external authority over human beings.*

Appeals to obey the Word of God have been used historically to maintain the rule of masters over servants and to stifle the rebellion of victims against unjust treatment by dominant forces. To have unquestioning obedience commanded by an external authority is to have human beings reduced to a state of abject dependency. Such a dependency is the denial of human maturity. To be human is to exercise responsibility as much as possible for one's actions within a society of mutual obligations, to think for oneself in open dialogue with others, and to act cooperatively for a common good, not in blind subservience to authoritarian decree but with creative initiative in accordance with one's full capacities of self-determination. It is, in the words of Immanuel Kant, to be released from "self-incurred tutelage."[3]

The idea of deity as the sheer arbitrariness of external power to which the creature must acquiesce in unquestioning submission is challenged by traditions within scripture itself. The God who establishes covenant and pledges to maintain righteousness and justice in faithfulness is questioned with regard to these commitments. For example, when the wholesale destruction of Sodom is threatened, a tradition within Genesis depicts Abraham as protesting before the Lord, "Far be it from you to do such a thing, to slay the righteous with the wicked, so that the righteous fare as the wicked! Far be that from you! Shall not the Judge of all the earth do what is just?" (Gen. 18:25).[4] The Psalmist's cry repeated by Jesus from the Cross, "My God, my God why hast thou forsaken me?," may be heard not as the self-pitying weeping of a passive victim, but as the "loud" voiced call upon God to keep God's commitment to vindicate righteousness (Ps. 22:1; Matt. 27:46).

A theological preoccupation with God's otherness, with God as not being "we ourselves," disguises the fact that there are also significant portions of scriptural testimony that stress God's intention that humanity become "as God is." "For I am the Lord who brought you up from the land of Egypt, to be your God; you shall be holy, for I am holy" (Lev. 11:45). Or, in the words of Jesus to his disciples in his teaching on the mountain, "Be perfect, therefore, as your heavenly Father is perfect" (Matt. 5:48). And from the passage in the Gospel of John traditionally referred to as the "high priestly" prayer of Jesus for all disciples both present and future: "The glory that you have given me I have given them, so that they may be one as we are one" (John 17:22). The One "who searches the heart," writes the Apostle Paul to the Romans, "knows what is the mind of the Spirit," in that this Spirit of God intercedes for us internally "with sighs too deep for words" (Rom. 8:26–27). The distance between God and humanity seems far less pronounced than the closeness in such scriptural statements as these. Likeness seems to be stressed over unlikeness.

These points address a perceived authoritarian character in Christian teaching regarding God's Word and the human subservience that is commanded. They comprise a first category of conceivable objections.

2. *It would seem that Christian teaching concerning the Word of God in effect attempts to turn God into a tangible object or a phenomenal entity.*

If the Word of God is held to be a proposition or a formulated statement, then it is held to be something that can be grasped as a tangible object is grasped. If the Word of God is held to be an issued order that can be stipulated as a law stating God's will, then it is held to be an objective datum. If the Word of God, on the other hand, is said to be a phenomenon of human subjectivity, or a state of consciousness, it is still being represented as a datum susceptible to discovery given the proper methods of analysis and research. All of these are efforts to reify God's Spirit and may be seen as attempts at gaining access to the human management or control of the ways of God.

Most particularly this reification is apparent in teachings that tend to equate the Bible with the Word of God. Belief in the inerrancy of God's Word becomes extended to claims of inerrancy for canonical documents. A similar argument can be made with reference to Roman Catholic dogma regarding papal infallibility. Belief in the infallibility of God's Word is extended to claims of infallibility for the *ex cathedra* definitions of the Roman pontiff's teaching concerning the faith or morals to be held by the universal church. In each case the Word tends to become equated with human words. God's living Spirit becomes a formulated text. The current investment of academic theology in various theories of hermeneutics, while disowning all claims for biblical inerrancy or papal infallibility, nevertheless exhibits a similar tendency to reduce the Word of God to the words of a text.

3. *It would seem that Christian teaching concerning the Word of God makes God exclusive to Christianity and denies that God can be known elsewhere.*

If God's Word is professed to be embodied only in Jesus Christ as the sole incarnate Word, and if the one body of this Christ is then said to be the Christian church, it clearly appears that such doctrine excludes from contact with God's Word all religions, traditions, and peoples that are not Christian. To assume that God is not present outside of Christianity is to foster attitudes of disregard, if not contempt, toward present-day Judaism and other so-called heathen religions and cultures. Such attitudes are totally irreconcilable with the message of neighbor love, if nothing else, in biblical faith.

The exclusivity carries over to the forms in which the Word of God is said to occur. These, following cultural patterns of the times in which the scriptures were formulated, for the most part are male and patriarchal. God, although consistently affirmed to be other than human in the sense of beyond the sexual differentiations of creatures, is nevertheless denoted in church teaching and liturgy almost entirely by male references and pronouns of masculine gender. If the Word of God becomes incarnate in the male figure of Jesus then, it has been taught, this Word can only be represented in certain acts of Christian eucharistic worship by male figures. Plainly an exclusivism that rules not only against those outside the church, but is directed against its own women members within it, has been the intolerable result.

The idea that God would exclude the vast majority of the human race from any communication with God makes a mockery of any doctrine that says God's otherness is one of communion. What emerges with such a doctrine is instead the idolatrous chauvinism of a male tribal deity. The consequences of such idolatry may be seen in the imperialistic tendencies of missionary expansion that accompany colonialism.

4. *It would seem that Christian teaching concerning the Word of God presupposes that God is known apart from ordinary media required for human communication.*

Objections in this fourth category reflect a line of questioning that runs counter to that of the second. Here the issue is not whether God's Word is being confused with some object, but whether this Word is being represented as so ethereal and disembodied that whatever awareness faith has requires no tangible means.

It appears that communion with this Word is presumed to occur as an immediacy of awareness. Call this mysticism, supernaturalism, or fideism, the result is the same. God's Word, if unmediated, is known apart from the ways required for all other human knowing. The ordinary channels of communication in this one instance are bypassed. Yet unless such so-called knowledge of God's Word remains totally private to the recipient and noncommunicable, it can only be confessed and expressed by human means of signification. The nature of the gospel is not to retain but to proclaim the Word of God. Thus whatever faith affirms to be revealed or disclosed by this Word must be revealed or disclosed through some sort of media. The treasure comes in "clay jars" (2 Cor. 4:7).

Any idea that revelation is formless and bypasses all normal channels of human knowing compels one to postulate an awareness apart from language, history, culture, time, and space — a putative reality, that is, that would require us to be other than human. Whatever the expression "the eyes of faith" rightly means, it cannot mean this. But the incoherence of such a position is not simply epistemological. The point is that a presumption of privileged and unaccountable knowledge devoid of all media of transmission violates other Christian teachings about human creaturehood, about biblical prophecy, and about the Incarnation.

With these four types of objections in mind let us now turn back to the outline suggested in the introduction and reflect on the contents of this doctrine.

Interpretation

1. God Says Something; God Speaks

The most basic element of faith affirmed in church doctrines of the Word of God is that God as self-communicating has spoken and continues to speak with human beings. Ultimate Reality confronts us in such a way that we are addressed. By being addressed we encounter One who is other to ourselves, but the otherness disclosed in this manner is one of communion and not separation. All spirits or teachings that either deny God's otherness or that interpret God's otherness as noncommunicative are hereby disallowed as faithful confessions.

The first question of a creature, the tempting serpent, in the Book of Genesis begins, "Did God say . . . ?" (Gen. 3:1). God is portrayed as questioning the human creature: "Where are you?," "Who told you that you were naked?," "Have you eaten from the tree of which I commanded you not to eat?," "What is this that you have done?" (Gen. 3:9–13). There is a calling out, an address, to which creation responds.

Also, among the Hebrew prophets we find the characteristic emphasis, "Now the word of the Lord came to me saying . . . " (Jer. 1:4). The Word of God is understood as coming to the prophet and enabling prophetic action and utterance. This Hebraic understanding is carried over into the New Testament. The Letter to the Hebrews, for example, begins, "Long ago God spoke to our ancestors in many and various ways by the prophets, but in these last days he has spoken to us by a Son" (Heb. 1:1–2).

Theology must deal with the problems of understanding and interpreting today the significance of these claims. Not only prophets and saints, but also the psychotic and the drugged, report hearing voices from God. The objection to any literal or nonsymbolic understanding of the Hebraic idea that God "speaks" is raised by Paul Tillich. He labels such a mistaken literalistic tendency to reduce the Word to talk, "the Protestant pitfall." (Tillich no doubt had in mind too many long-winded sermons.) In contrast to what he sees as a reduction of the *Logos* to rhetoric, of the Word to words, Tillich advocates what he takes to be a less verbal Greek notion of the Word, or *Logos*, as divine self-manifestation.[5] His interpretation seeks to take account of the sort of objections initially raised above in category 2. Karl Barth, on the other hand, strongly disagrees. For his part, Barth takes greater exception to what he sees as idealistic and nonincarnational tendencies of interpretation that in effect reduce the Word of God to forms of consciousness. In Barth's judgment, Tillich's existential ontology falsely "spiritualizes" the claim that God speaks, and treats it as merely a simile, having too little to do with actual, ordinary speech.[6] Barth's interpretation shows more alliance with the initial objections raised above in category 4. Such disagreement in interpretation is only one illustration of the fact that, while the belief that God communicates and addresses creation in God's Word is a constant current in Christian doctrine, how God's "speaking" is to be understood has been variously explained. Any proposed understanding today will require us to ask what a faithful affirmation that God speaks does *not* mean. To do this the other affirmations must also be brought into view.

2. God Speaks through Scripture

The opening words of the Second Helvetic Confession of 1566 express the affirmation, "We believe and confess the canonical Scriptures of the holy prophets and apostles of both Testaments to be the true Word of God, and to have sufficient authority of themselves, not of men." While the word "sufficient" here would be interpreted differently by some Protestants and Roman Catholics or Eastern Orthodox, this statement otherwise would find ecumenical agreement. It continues by affirming that the God who "spoke to the fathers, prophets, apostles . . . still speaks to us through the Holy Scriptures [*per Scripturas Sanctas*]."[7]

To many Christians the mention of the Word of God will most likely call to mind the Bible. Yet the Bible as a collection of writings may be said to be the Word of God only inasmuch and insofar as the God who "spoke to the fathers, prophets, and apostles" still speaks *through* it. The Word of God occurs *as* "Holy Scriptures" only in the sense that this Word occurs *per Scripturas Sanctas*. All teachings that tend to equate the Word of God with some object, including the Bible, and thus turn God into a thing, are marked for disbelief in biblical faith.

The Reformers emphasized this dynamic character of holy scripture by insisting that the Word occurs through it as it is preached and not simply quoted. Such a Word is not an artifact. Roman Catholic and Orthodox doctrine has made the point of stressing this dynamic character by holding that the Word is conveyed through scripture in the ecclesial context of apostolic tradition wherein this Word is preached, preserved, explained, and promulgated.[8]

The doctrine that the Bible is the Word of God inasmuch and insofar as God still speaks through these particular writings to author faith, hope, and love raises the question of whether *only* these writings are to be considered holy scripture. Is the present canon of scripture, which was generally recognized by the end of the fourth century, but remained disputed with respect to several of its contents at the time of Luther, still open or now closed?[9] Can anything now be added or deleted? Here the initial objections regarding exclusivity must be heard.

Three elements of Christian disbelief come into play at this point. One is the refusal of any claim that God from the beginning has withheld from the church truth that is essential to saving faith. Apostolic tradition as oral witness to God's self-communication through the gospel is prior to all apostolic writings. The New Testament writings are those texts that, it came to be believed, convey this apostolate, in distinction from other writings purporting to do so that came to be rejected as not conveying the apostolate. But a second disbelief coupled with this one is the refusal of any claim that God's Word can be confined and is not now free to speak wherever and as God chooses. The third disbelief is the refusal of any claim asserting that God has no new things to say through the continuing proclamation of the canonical scripture as God's living voice.

In one sense the question of canonical addition or deletion becomes moot if preaching and sacred tradition are held to be the continuing dynamic context in which the Word that God presently speaks *per Scripturas Sanctas* is said to occur. Proclamation as current witness and mission is not the mere repetition or quotation of Bible verses. As commissioned address to a specific time and place it necessarily involves a process of reciprocal interrogation between what has been handed down and what is new in the immediate situation. Such reciprocal interrogation is what preaching is all about. Faith in the Word of God, therefore, proscribes the reification of God's communication in the words of any text. On their surface many texts convey apparent meanings that violate the meaning that comes to be attested to faith in the continuing life of communal Christian worship. Against them, objections are to be raised. Preaching, by actions as well as words, questions the canonical scriptures in light of the present and questions the present in light of the canonical scriptures. In this crucial respect the canon is always open. *Only when the canon ceases to be preached does it become closed*, for then false assumptions and implications are presumed to go unchallenged by the Word speaking through the words. No addition or deletion of books would alter this fact. On the other hand, no controls can be placed on the freedom of God's Word in matters of canon selection, as in any other matters.

In discussing the test of "congruence with scripture" in chapter 4 it was argued that what this criterion amounts to is that a defensible exegetical case be made regarding the *import of the canonical witness for faith*. This is another way of saying that what the church finds to be authoritative in the Bible is only that scripture within it through which God continues to speak currently in commissioning the church to hear and follow God's Word. Otherwise the authority asserted regarding scripture fails to meet the test of consistency with worship. The eternal Word is always the timely Word, borne and delivered, as the scriptures themselves repeatedly testify, when the time comes.

3. God's Word Acts to Accomplish Something

In the account in Genesis 1, as has been mentioned, God creates by saying, "Let there be . . . " The pronouncement is presented as that which brings into being a new state of affairs. It does not describe some state of affairs that already exists. In the terminology of the linguistic philosophers it is "performative" and not simply informative utterance.[10] In the New Testament the incarnate Word of God is also linked with the act of creating. "All things came into being through him, and without him not one thing came into being" (John 1:3). Jesus Christ is said to be the one "through whom he [God] also created the worlds" (Heb. 1:2).

Similarly the Word of God is said to perform not only creation but also judgment. It is a righteous Word, the measure of what is right, that lays claim upon its recipients. We see this verdictive character of God's Word expressed by the Psalmist:

> Praise the Lord, O Jerusalem! Praise your God, O Zion! . . . He sends out his command to the earth; his word runs swiftly. He gives snow like wool; he scatters frost like ashes. He hurls down hail like crumbs — who can stand before his cold? He sends out his word and melts them. . . . He declares his word to Jacob, his statutes and ordinances to Israel. (Ps. 147:12–19)

Along with creation and judgment goes salvation as well. The Word of God acts to save. "Remember your word to your servant," prays the Psalmist, "in which you have made me hope. This is my comfort in my distress; that your promise gives me life" (Ps. 119:49–50). Paul refers to the gospel not only as God's message of good news concerning Christ but as "the power of God for salvation" (Rom. 1:16).

In these three respects the Word of God as creating, judging, and saving is affirmed in Christian doctrine as God's activity. God's Word is not only linguistic, either as speech or as written texts. As such, and in addition, it is also professed to be God's action and accomplishment. "For he spoke, and it came to be; he commanded, and it stood firm" (Ps. 33:9). The prophecy of Isaiah on this point expresses a consistent message of both the Old and the New Testaments:

> So shall my word be that goes out from my mouth;
> it shall not return to me empty,
> but it shall accomplish that which I purpose,
> and succeed in the thing for which I sent it.
> Isa. 55:11

What it means to affirm the active character of God's Word as God *doing* justice, in the sense of righteousness, is widely debated in Christian theology. How is such so-called action to be understood?[11] Only insurance laws, it would seem, are able to be very definite about the meaning of the term *act of God* today, and by this legal definition such acts regrettably are limited to calamities to life and property for which no one can be held liable.

At this point are we not forced to concede the objection that Christian doctrine, if it designates anything as God's action, tends to reduce God to a phenomenal entity? To say that God's Word in some respects occurs through human words but acts to accomplish creation, judgment, and salvation, is to acknowledge that there is indeed an earthly, natural medium of such acts whatever their other-than-earthly or supernatural significance.[12] There is, so most Christian teaching has held, a sacramental reality to God's Word. Christian faith proscribes all notions of an unmediated knowledge of a disembodied Word of God. But what of this other-than-earthly significance? Can it be spoken of without self-contradiction at all, and if so how is it to be understood? Here theological interpreters today face a number of questions. For some, "supernaturalism" is still considered an appropriate label; for others it is not. Is a supernatural act to be defined in the way that Augustine in the fifth century defined a marvel or "portent," that is, as a happening not "contrary to nature [*contra naturam*]," but one "contrary to what is known of nature [*contra quam est nota natura*]"?[13] Is it the attributing of extraordinary significance to what is otherwise, that is, apart from faith, explainable in ordinary terms? Is it, as the objections to perceived authoritarianism (and the insurance industry) imply, a manner of speech used to avoid responsibility (or liability)?

Today's liberation theologies raise the problem more from the standpoint of historical change than of natural order. It is not whether God's acts contravene the course of nature as presently known — the problem that exercised post-Enlightenment Protestant liberalism — but whether God acts to contravene the course of historical injustices in any definite and materially efficacious way. The questionableness of a suprahistoricalism rather than a supernaturalism is more the issue. But can God's Word as liberating action be identified unambiguously with any actual events in social history, or must such testimony to what God is doing remain general and ahistorical to avoid idolatrous reification?

Here we find no agreement of belief in contemporary theological interpretation. The usual answers tend to favor appeals to paradox or dialectic at this point, asserting that God acts through events that historians may recognize as historical but that God's acts through these events can never be recognized by historical methods. We are left with the recognition of two virtual disbeliefs implicit in the commonly held affirmation of faith in God's Word as God's act. First, such faith refuses to believe that God's Word occurs for earthly human knowing without the mediation of ordinary historical means necessary for communication. Even mystical insight, vision, and inspiration, insofar as these are avenues of God's Word, are no exception. Second, such faith refuses to believe that any ordinary historical means necessary for communication can cause God's Word to occur for earthly human knowing. That is to say, the means of signification have no power to make God's Word significant. By remaining mindful of these two disbeliefs, dogmatics may attempt to steer a course through the tides of conflicting theological opinion over how best to render account of the active agency of God's Word.[14]

An important consequence of recognizing these two disbeliefs is that theology as a discipline is set free to examine its subject matter without defensiveness in the face of science or fear of intruding upon the sacred. No methods of criticism can either prevent God from speaking or cause such a Word to occur. But such criticism — historical, literary, social, psychological, or whatever — serves the dogmatic cause of a faithful iconoclasm by helping to expose the idolatrous fetishism and attendant human disabling of deifying the means by which God's acts are communicated.

4. God's Word Shines in the Heart

God's illumination of the human heart as a way of God's self-communication is usually attributed in Christian doctrine to the agency of the Holy Spirit. As God's Word is spoken and enacted, the external witness of audible and "visible" words — the latter being Augustine's name for the sacraments[15] — finds confirmation in an internal witness. What comes by hearing to author faith has its resonating counterpart within.

This affirmation has its scriptural precedent in the various claims that resistance to God's Word represents a hardening of the heart. To hear God's Word, on the other hand, is to delight in this testimony in one's inmost being and to ponder it in one's heart. With respect to what God says and does, the church has traditionally disbelieved that there can be an essential contradiction in faith between what is congruent with scripture and what is consonant with experience. Any claim that the Word of God in scripture violates the internal witness of God's Word in the heart is proscribed. Any claim that the internal witness of God's Word in the heart denies the Word of God in scripture is proscribed. From the standpoint of Christian faith both claims represent false spirits that are not of God.

This is not to deny either that false spirits may and do speak with the words of scripture, as in the instance Matthew records of the devil quoting Psalm 91 in the temptation of Jesus (Matt. 4:5–6), or that false spirits may and do speak in the heart. But wherever and whenever an apparent conflict or contradiction arises between the external and internal witness of God's Word such scriptural congruence and experiential consonance are judged in Christian faith not to have been truly recognized.

The consensus of church teaching is that there is no Word of God from without that is not confirmed from within by the Holy Spirit. The disagreements historically have arisen over whether conversely there can be an internal illumination of the Word apart from its external proclamation. The Augsburg Confession of 1530 condemns all "Anabaptists and others, who imagine that the Holy Spirit is given to human beings without the outward word [*sine verbo externo*]."[16] But the Second Helvetic Confession of 1566 expresses the more widely embraced view: while the usual way of God's instruction is through the preaching of the Word and the illumination of the Holy Spirit, "at the same time we recognize that God can illuminate whom and when he will, even without the external ministry [*sine externo ministerio*], for that is in his power."[17]

This issue raises the subject of the knowledge of God and of church teachings regarding revelation.

5. God's Word Provides Knowledge of God

In Christian doctrine God is said to be *revealed* to human knowing in what God says and does. Every theology as a human attempt to speak of

God and of matters of ultimate importance presupposes some doctrine of revelation. How is God known? The sort of knowledge that we have of God determines whatever is to be said about God, about how God is to be addressed and expressed.

All church doctrines begin with the premise that there is some knowledge of Ultimate Reality, knowledge of God. The form this knowledge takes and the content of this knowledge are questions that any account of the Word of God must seek to address. Aspects of the doctrine of revelation have been vigorously disputed in the history of theology, but perennial issues arise whenever the topic of the knowledge of God is discussed.

We have already discussed the faith affirmation that God speaks through scripture. Let us now look at the issue of God's revelation, first through scripture, and then apart from scripture. That God is revealed through scripture is universally affirmed in church teachings, although how such revelation is to be understood in reference to current modes of thought remains a subject of continuing debate. With regard to revelation apart from scripture, there is less of a dogmatic consensus, but alternative currents of tradition can be distinguished.

Revelation through Scripture

There is a sense in which every text may be said to "reveal" something, whether it be facts, assumptions, omissions, errors, or perhaps the prejudices and interests, the insight and ignorance, of its author. So the Bible as well may be said to reveal such matters about its human authors. By reading biblical texts as testimony to the Word of God, however, the church affirms its faith that through these human authors with all their human limitations God has chosen to author a community with whom to be in communion. Christian doctrine holds that only God attests to God, but that this self-attestation becomes operative in a life story. It is the life story of God's Word with a particular people, Israel, as it culminates in accounts of what happens with a particular Jesus of Nazareth. There is great disagreement among interpreters over the continuities in this life story, but no disagreement in Christian faith that in some sense God's own eternal life is here being communicated.

The New Testament basis for saying that God is made known in the gospel is clear. The first four books are designated as accounts of this gospel "according to" Matthew, Mark, Luke, and John. And the Apostle Paul, whose earliest writings predate any others in the New Testament, writes, "For I am not ashamed of the gospel: it is the power of God for salvation to everyone who has faith, to the Jew first and also to the Greek. For in it the righteousness of God is *revealed* [*apokalyptetai*, 'apocalypsed'] through faith for faith" (Rom. 1:16–17). To say that

God is revealed in the gospel is to express the belief that God in speaking and acting through certain human affairs communicates "power for salvation," that is, power not subject to defeat by any opposition, which brings release from bondage.

The point has already been underscored that revelation through human words and actions, as well as through any other creaturely media, is understood in the New Testament, as in the Old, to be at God's choosing. This distinguishes such revelation through gospel proclamation from any sense of a mechanical incantation capable in itself of somehow producing divine presence. This revelation — Paul's word is *apokalypsis* — is referred to as something that happens and takes place *via* human means on the human scene in an eventfulness that is not subject to human control. God "deigns," writes John Calvin, to consecrate human mouths and tongues for service, "in order that his own voice may resound in them."[18] We are to attend to these means to hear God's Word, all the while remembering that "God's power is not bound" externally by any such means or human words.

To account for the type of knowing that is believed to be afforded by such revelation through scriptural testimony, attention must be paid to examining the forms such testimony takes. These are multiple, but an indispensable aspect of such revelatory testimony when viewed canonically is narrative. In some instances this story form is more explicit, in others it is presupposed. It is more apparent in the Four Gospels than in the Pauline epistles, although even there some narrative sequence is held to be "of first importance" (1 Cor. 15:3).[19] The church in its worship reads and signifies the gospel as an ongoing enactment of a story that in the New Testament understanding has its origins in the beginning with God and is not ended.

More recent theology has found in "narrative" a less problematic term for the revelatory witness of scripture than "history." The Bible is not a history book of continuous chapters in unbroken harmony and sequence. But story is the form required for history to become known to us. The story of the gospel, like the story of God's Word throughout the Bible, contains references to events in this world's history as well as references to events that do not fall within the limits of such history. Narration is the form in which Israel's cultic memory finds expression: "For it is the Lord our God who brought us and our ancestors up from the land of Egypt, out of the house of slavery, and who did those great signs in our sight" (Josh. 24:17). In the distinct traditions of Hebrew scripture God's presence is said to be manifested in sundry ways.[20] Yet all these manifestations presuppose in their canonical context a story of deliverance with respect to the time and space of this world's history. Biblical revelation is not simply an internal wisdom of the soul or a transcendental course of sacred affairs abstracted from the time and space of earthly history. The arena is the human scene in all its dimensions and embodiments.

Equally in the New Testament God is proclaimed as known in reference to narrated events of deliverance that cannot be divorced from world history any more than they can be subsumed in it. Here as well revelatory events find expression in narration. The story of God's activity in the Old Testament is brought into relation, though not in identical ways, to what happens with Jesus of Nazareth, "under Pontius Pilate," as the early creeds put it. The phrase *sub Pontio Pilato* in the church's creed and doctrine anchors the revelation of God through the gospel in events that are not simply reducible to matters of the inner life.

What happens concerning Jesus is that a particular human being is born, lives, and is put to death in a particular time and place. And of this One, and no other, it is announced, in the words of Peter's address on the day of Pentecost: "This Jesus God raised up . . . God has made him both Lord and Messiah, this Jesus whom you crucified" (Acts 2:32, 36). The particular sequence of events, therefore, is given an all-encompassing universal reference. To the One named here, as Paul writes, "every knee should bend, . . . and every tongue should confess" to the glory of God (Phil. 2:10–11).

This kind of revelation commonly has been said to be a matter of knowledge in the sense in which one knows and trusts a promise. Such a knowing of God is not held to be that of demonstrable fact or information. God's Word cannot be historically documented or empirically verified as reality; rather, as *God's* action this Word instead verifies and vindicates reality. Christian faith involves the hearing of the canonical story of the events concerning God's dealings with Israel and with Jesus of Nazareth as God's first-person promise to us today. In this way — in the hearing of that story as a promise — God attests to who God is.

Revelation of God through the scripture involves at some level, whether explicitly or implicitly, a particular narrative which is heard as a universal promise. We see this indispensable form of promissory narration not only in the gospel testimonies but also in the Hebrew writings: "The nations shall know that I am the Lord, says the Lord God, when through you I display my holiness before their eyes. I will take you from the nations, and gather you from all the countries, and bring you into your own land" (Ezek. 36:23–24). The past that is narrated in such scriptural testimony to God's faithfulness is understood by those communities that trust in its remembrance as a "memory of the future."[21]

Thus doctrinal accounts of revelation through scripture traditionally affirm both a historical dimension, a looking back that has to do with particular people, times, and places, and an eschatological or forward-looking dimension that has to do with the universal, all-inclusive future, the judgment and hope of every people, of all times, and all places. Faith exists wherever this narration concerning a particular past is heard as God's promise concerning a universal future. This trajectory from narrative particularity to promissory universality is stressed in the New Testament and emphasized throughout the history of doctrine in a diversity of ways. In recounting Peter's speech at Pentecost Luke writes, "For the promise is for you, for your children, and for all who are far away, everyone whom the Lord our God calls to him" (Acts 2:39). *"Fides et promissio sunt relativa"* ("faith and promise are related"), writes Martin Luther in his commentary on Romans. "If the promise ceases, faith also ceases; and if the promise is taken away, faith too is taken away, and conversely."[22] Christ comes to us "vested in his promises" as John Calvin puts it;[23] faith properly "begins, continues, and ends" with promise.[24] Words from Melanchthon aptly state the matter: "Faith does not mean merely knowing the story of Christ... [it] includes not only the story but also the promises and the fruit of the promise."[25]

In some doctrines the promise is interpreted primarily with reference to the forgiveness of sins while in others the reference is more explicitly to the ultimate revelation of God's coming glory. Yet because Jesus Christ is narrated and confessed as both the particular, historical One crucified *sub Pontio Pilato*, and the universal, eschatological One resurrected, the promise of the forgiveness of sins is equally affirmed as inseparable from the promise of God's ultimate and coming triumph over every power of sin and death.

We may sum up these more formal aspects of revelation through scripture by noting that God's self-communication is confessed in faith as a movement from particularity to universality involving both history and eschatology, both narration and promise. All doctrines of revelation through scripture in some way acknowledge these indispensable elements. Faithful disbelief is directed toward all conservative positions that appeal to the past and to the particular narrated memory of scripture in such a way as to rob the present and the future of the scripture's promissory hope for God's making "all things new" (Rev. 21:5), and it is equally directed toward all liberal positions that appeal to the scripture's promissory hope for the new in a way that severs it from the scripture's particular narrated memory.

The theology of the Latin American liberation theologian Juan Luis Segundo, S.J., provides a case in point of these two faithful disbeliefs. First Segundo elaborates the crucial importance of hermeneutical suspicion in continually uncovering oppressive ideological components of prevailing interpretations of scripture. The scriptural memory of God's Word cannot be used to block the hope. Next, Segundo warns against the tendency of many liberal Protestants in the United States who are rightly involved with matters of liberation "to question the necessity of returning to the sources or fonts of *Christian* revelation."[26] Once recognizing and naming corrupt interpretations, "one can," Segundo writes, "certainly move on to a new theology or a different tradition of 'revelation.' What seems odd to me is that any such new theology would continue to call itself 'Christian,' as they often do." The scriptural hope of God's Word cannot be severed from the memory.

The content of revelation through scripture, *what* is revealed, is in the first instance God's keeping of God's promise in every new situation. The name "God" is only applicable to the One who proves to be trustworthy in all things. To recall once again Paul's reference to the Gospel, "In it the righteousness of God [*dikaiosynē theou*] is revealed" (Rom. 1:17). This righteousness is the faithfulness of God — that is, *who* God is as trustworthy keeper of the commitment to make all things right and to vindicate the right in all things. In much of the most influential twentieth-century theology up until the 1960s one finds a tendency to use the term "*self*-revelation" to emphasize that what is revealed through the scriptures is not propositional information to which one must subscribe, not "revealed truths" in this sense, but a personal, committed Self who becomes known not as some*thing* but as Some*one* who keeps faith with us. Here the disbelief in all objectifications of revelation as artifact or entity is stoutly maintained.

By midcentury, however, theological ideas of self-revelation were themselves criticized for their excessive personalism in failing to account adequately for the biblical perspective that the apocalypse of God's faithfulness and glory involves not only the revelation of God's transcendent selfhood but of God's coming kingdom or realm as well.[27]

From yet another angle some contemporary theologians have questioned the coherence of the term *revelation* altogether as an appropriate concept for what the Christian faith affirms. The fact is that in the past Christian teaching generally has not only referred to God's revealed selfhood but to revealed truths, revealed dogmas, and revealed laws. It has contrasted these with all so-called natural truths, teachings, and laws that can be known by unaided reason apart from faith. Today a more adequate interpretation, the critics propose, is to say that the functional role of the biblical texts is not unlike that of other texts in the interpretation of human existence. Biblical writings simply are believed by Christians to do this more adequately. With respect to the subject of God, it is argued, as with any other subject, knowledge is a constructive hermeneutical act requiring the ordering and construal of accepted data by the use of the imagination.[28] There is from this standpoint only questionable validity to the older traditional distinctions between natural and revealed knowledge of God. All such knowing in Christian faith is held to be more aptly accounted for as natural.

Yet, whatever the revelation of God through scripture, there remain depths of God's mystery which classically have been said to lie beyond all human capacities for knowledge in this life. As we have noted earlier, however, the "mysteries of God" are referred to as "known" in the New Testament. In this perspective revelation may be said to make known (in the sense of identify the character of) the unknown (in the sense of the humanly unfathomable) fullness of God. For example, Thomas Aquinas writes, "Although in this life revelation does not tell us what God is, and thus joins us to him as to an unknown, nevertheless it helps us to know him better in that we are shown more and greater works of his and are taught certain things about him that we could never have known through natural reason."[29]

Knowledge of God apart from Scripture

Is there a knowing of God apart from the scriptures? Christian teaching has traditionally said Yes. The way in which this Yes is to be interpreted, however, has been viewed differently.

It has often been held in the history of Christian doctrine that a knowledge of God, in some sense, is a natural capacity of human existence, even apart from the telling of the sequence of events that is called biblical testimony and the gospel. This has commonly been referred to as a "natural" knowledge in distinction from a specifically "revealed" knowledge, a knowing sometimes described as according to the light of nature, rather than the light of grace, or the heavenly light of glory.[30] What is often claimed is that some awareness of God is intrinsic to human rationality.

We may note four distinguishable, although not entirely separable, positions that have been taken with regard to the issue of this so-called natural knowledge of God apart from scripture.

One view is that it is appropriate to speak of such a natural knowledge only in the sense of an innate human awareness that at least raises the question of God to which revelation through scripture speaks and gives answer. This is the idea of the *cor inquietum*, the "restless heart," to which Augustine refers in the opening lines of the *Confessions*. Being made for God, the human heart is restless until it rests in God. According to this view, human beings are by nature in quest of God. To be human is in this respect to be religious, to be *homo religiosus*, even though this questing takes disguised forms of which we are not fully conscious. In this connection Tillich's use of the term *preparatory revelation* appropriates a long-standing tradition.[31]

In a second instance an unaided knowledge of God is said to have the capacity for establishing *that* God is, but it cannot tell us *who* God is. This position is similar to the first, yet it claims more in asserting the rational demonstrability of the actuality of deity apart from scriptural testimony. That the one God exists is a truth "proved demonstratively by the philosophers," writes Thomas Aquinas, "guided by the light of the natural reason."[32]

Yet a third position holds that the so-called natural knowledge denotes a universal human propensity to fabricate objects of worship. An original religious tendency of human creaturehood is acknowledged in this view, but it is said to have become so distorted by sin as to result only in idolatry. Natural religion at best represents only a "suppressed" awareness of the truth (Rom. 1:18). As a suppressed knowledge it turns out to be not a true knowing of God in any saving sense but a fetish fixation that attempts to worship some aspect of creation, some creature, as if it were the Creator. No human religiosity, as fallen, represents a good in and of itself, and the church is not commissioned to proclaim natural religion. There is a "sense of deity" in all human beings, writes Calvin, but this universal religiosity, this propensity for the divine, has so confused the creature with the Creator that a universal idolatry has become the consequence.[33]

In the background of this third position are Paul's words in Romans 1:20–25:

> Ever since the creation of the world his (God's) eternal power and divine nature, invisible though they are, have been understood and seen through the things he has made. So they are without excuse; for though they knew God, they did not honor him as God or give thanks to him, but they became futile in their thinking, and their senseless minds were darkened.

A fourth line of interpretation holds that the knowing of God is never accurately to be attributed to a universal religious capacity of human nature, but that God also is never without self-witness anywhere in creation. Creation as such, either as nature or as history, does not of itself make this divine witness known. All witness of God apart from the scriptural witness, this fourth position teaches, reflects the light of Jesus Christ as the Word made flesh who is proclaimed in scripture. Such reflections of Christ, however, are not limited to Christianity, to the church, or even to what are usually thought of as religions and religious experiences. But they are true reflections — in Barth's terms, God's "lesser lights" — of the one Light of Life of whom the scriptures attest.[34] This interpretation does not acknowledge any knowing of God as a natural human capacity, something, that is, of which human nature in and of itself is capable. There is true witness beyond the particular promissory narration of the one Word that the church is commissioned to proclaim. But this extrabiblical witness, while not part of Christianity, is nonetheless still part of God's one active self-communicating Word. In this respect, all knowing of God is revealed knowing, but objection is registered against any claim that would make such knowing, or the activity of God's self-communicating Word, exclusive to Christianity or to Christians.

Each of these four lines of interpretation, while addressing different aspects of the issue and remaining distinguishable from the others, concurs in a fundamental disbelief of claims that would limit the knowledge of God to revelation through biblical testimony. The extent to which such extrabiblical knowledge may be said to be efficacious or operative is evaluated differently. The clear consensus of ecumenical doctrine is that one is to know God through the means that God grants. These means are not the same in all times and places. Yet Christian faith concurs in a disbelief of any claim suggesting that God, when truly known apart from scripture, is of a different identity from that of God revealed through scripture.

6. God's Word Provides Knowledge of God in the Face of Christ

Theological disputes over whether Christian faith should be understood as theocentric or christocentric miss the basic point if they fail to consider that all faith centered in God in the Christian context is focused upon Jesus Christ. Such faith may more aptly be described as christomorphic. What is at issue is not whether the particular events of the first-century Jesus occurred at the midpoint of world history, either in some linear sense or as an equidistant hub in some cyclical sense. At stake is the New Testament testimony that the Word of God became flesh in Jesus Christ. The verse of John 1:14, "And the Word became flesh and lived among us . . . full of grace and truth," has been called "the most influential New Testament text in the history of dogma."[35]

How this focus upon Christ is presented varies with the New Testament authors, but it is maintained by all. New Testament theology is essentially christology. In the Pauline text that we have been following as an outline the reference is to "the light of the knowledge of the glory of God in the face of Jesus Christ" (2 Cor. 4:6). Taken in its canonical setting, by which I mean bearing in mind the other scriptural accounts that comprise along with this text the church's one Bible, the theological import of the expression "the face of Christ" must be said to include the direction in which Christ, as Luke puts it, "set his face" (Luke 9:51). The self-communication of God instantiates and embodies what happens regarding Jesus Christ, not as an unidentified cipher with neither life, nor story, nor direction, but as the one who "set his face to go to Jerusalem" (Luke 9:51). Whatever else the doctrine of the incarnation of the Word seeks to affirm, this claim remains basic. The revelation of God thus may be designated as the *morphē* of Christ. To convey better the active rather than the static character of this revelation, we should translate the Greek noun *morphē* as a "forming" or a "shaping," rather than as a "form" or a "shape." Our sentence then reads, the revelation of God is the shaping of human affairs in relation to Jesus Christ. In this respect, church doctrines of the incarnate Word may appropriately be characterized as christomorphic.[36] Revelation is not simply a noetic concept or a matter of human self-consciousness. Biblically interpreted, it is also the vindication, or the taking form, of God's righteousness in all the earth.

Two further points in this connection raise special problems for dogmatics today. These problems as such are not new. Both are more properly dealt with under the locus of christology, and we shall return to them in chapter 8, but they should be introduced here because they are germane to the objections about exclusivity.

The first has to do with what it means to affirm that the incarnate Word of God in Jesus Christ is "only begotten," as the classical creeds so confess, following the Johannine reference to God's glory beheld as of "a father's only son [*monogenous*], full of grace and truth" (John 1:14). Is the face of Jesus Christ the only face of God? Is the only *morphē*, or revelatory shaping of events, that which bears relation to this Christ? Traditionally the church ecumenically has answered Yes. The only Word of God incarnate is Jesus Christ. But what is the content of such an affirmation? To consider this we must ask what interpretations of this belief are to be proscribed as false witness; what does confession of the Word of God as Jesus Christ *not* mean? A basis for answering this question has already been indicated in chapter 3. There, in reflecting upon the present theological implications of 1 John 4:2–3, it was argued that confession of Jesus Christ *en sarki* is not to be confused with the mere repetition of the words "Jesus Christ":

> Not everyone who says to me, "Lord, Lord," will enter the kingdom of heaven, but only the one who does the will of my Father in heaven. On that day many will say to me, "Lord, Lord, did we not prophesy in your name, and cast out demons in your name, and do many deeds of power in your name?" Then I will declare to them, "I never knew you; go away from me, you evildoers." (Matt. 7:21–23)

To confess today "that Jesus Christ has come in the flesh," it was observed, is to show forth the saving power of Jesus now coming into the actual flesh and blood sufferings that present themselves to us and around us wherever we are located in space and time. Support for such a reading of this text was cited in Ignatius, Luther, and Calvin, and their views are consistent with much of Christian interpretation.

While in this instance theological debates continue over the proper interpretation of Jesus Christ as the one and only incarnate Word of

God, two proscribed claims are clear. Christian faith refuses to believe that there is any Word of God that does not bear witness to the way, the truth, and the life revealed in Jesus Christ. Christian faith also disbelieves that witness to Jesus Christ is restricted to explicit use of the words "Jesus Christ," or to the speech, scriptures, and traditions of Christianity.

For Christian faith the ignoring of either of these disbeliefs amounts to a defacement of God's Word. There is no true confession of the Word of God which is not the confession of Jesus Christ, but one may confess the reality of Jesus Christ without ever having heard or ever being aware of the words "Jesus Christ," or intending a "Christian" witness.

The second, and closely related, question asks about the reality of the Word of God apart from the one Incarnation. In dogmatic theology this subject is sometimes addressed under the label of the *logos asarkos*, the "fleshless logos." The Johannine testimony that "the true light, which enlightens every one, was coming into the world" leads to this inquiry (John 1:9). Is the omnipresence of the Word of God somehow restricted by the one Incarnation of Jesus Christ's "coming into the world"? The issue is raised in second-century Christianity by Justin Martyr.[37] John Calvin's teaching on this point is not novel but consistent with earlier doctrines, although it has come to bear his name. The so-called *extra calvinisticum* holds that God's Word did not cease to share in the fullness of God's heavenly reality in becoming incarnate on earth in Jesus Christ. Calvin expresses this "extra" dimension of the Word as follows:

> For even if the Word in his immeasurable essence united with the nature of man into one person, we do not imagine that he was confined therein. Here is something marvelous: the Son of God descended from heaven in such a way that, without leaving heaven, he willed to be borne in the virgin's womb, to go about the earth, and to hang upon the cross; yet he continuously filled the world even as he had done from the beginning![38]

The problems arise in faithfully accounting for the exclusivity and inclusivity of the Word of God in light of the Word's particularity and universality. We shall address the problem of inclusive and exclusive God-talk in the next chapter when we consider the being of God. There is stronger disagreement to be found on these matters in the church and theology of the late twentieth century than ever before. It is crucial to note in navigating here that the two disbeliefs just mentioned with regard to the "only begotten" issue are applicable in this second instance as well: Christian faith entails a refusal to believe that there is any Word of God that does not bear witness to Jesus Christ, but it also entails an equal refusal to believe that such witness is restricted to the explicit use of the words "Jesus Christ" or to Christianity. These disbeliefs provide the markers in view of which current dogmatic inquiry may seek to account for the christological focus of church doctrine concerning the Word of God.

There now remains to be addressed the question of the place of human agency in the communication with God. If, as Christian doctrines of the Word of God affirm, God is revealed to human knowing by establishing communion, there is in revelation not only a giving on the part of God, but a participation on the part of the creature. How is this involvement of the creature to be understood in light of the initial objections raised against totalitarian notions of obedience and the passivity that such notions foster?

In this instance as well there are different emphases to be found in Christian tradition. Not all interpretations agree, and conflicting theological opinions remain. Yet two disbeliefs come to the fore as markers of faithful witness. The first claim which is refused is that faithful encounter with the Word of God is a result of human agency. The second claim which is refused is that faithful response to the Word of God as God's gift occurs apart from, or in violation of, human agency. By these two disbeliefs confession is made that the living Word of God exercises no authority that violates the integrity and free response in the life of its creaturely participants. And the faithful individual or community only "takes responsibility for" the Word of God by becoming enabled of this Word to respond freely.

A commonly reiterated theme in Christian doctrine is that the ability to respond appropriately to God is not a capacity subject to human possession. Whether we or anyone knows God or not is finally not a matter of any human accomplishment. Faith in the first instance is something that God does by granting, and not something that we have by nature. Faith, or better, faithfulness, is the biblical name for the response that revelation creates within the life of the creature. Why it is that some during their earthly lifetime come to hear the gospel story as the promise of God's caring spoken directly to them, while others do not, we do not know. What we do know in faith is that we have no warrant for setting ourselves up as judges of the destiny of those who may not share this faith.

Even though the human response of faith in the self-revealing of God is God's gift, and not our accomplishment, the human creature in this response is never a passive robot merely being acted upon. This point can be found in church doctrines from the beginning. Luther's use of the term *passive righteousness* to underscore the giftedness of saving faith to sinners should not be interpreted as implying any hesitation on his part to affirming that grace activates nature as God created it.[39] It is the unique action of God's grace that this action does not deny human freedom but institutes it. That precisely is the issue, and it is a major element of Christian teaching to which we shall return in subsequent chapters. God loves us into loving and frees us into freedom. We are neither the source nor the control of the power that can do this for ourselves or for anyone else. But what God's Word of grace does in its coming is activate and work through our own particular powers for love and freedom in all their given uniqueness.

The affirmations that have just been traced in this section on interpretation of Christian teaching regarding the Word of God condense into the following essentials.

Christian faith professes that God has spoken and continues to speak, revealing who God is. The words and acts that convey this revelation are embodied in what happens concerning Jesus Christ as this is testified to in the scriptures of the Bible and attested to in the ongoing ministry of the church. What happens concerning Jesus is believed to be the taking place of God's own acts of creation, judgment, and salvation. Insofar as these acts are humanly known to faith, they are known through the same environmental media of language, action, and perception involved in any other human knowing. But these media in themselves have no power to make the revelation of God occur through them. God's Spirit alone confirms this revelation and grants it free receptivity in the human heart. Nor is what happens concerning Jesus restricted to the ministry of the church, or to Christianity, or to Christians. Throughout the time and space of all creation, and all traditions, cultures, and peoples in their interactions with the whole realm of nature, events witnessing to the self-communicating Word made flesh in Jesus Christ are professed to occur and reflect this glory of God.

Proposed Disbeliefs

Drawing from this interpretation of the six topics suggested by Paul's statement in 2 Corinthians 4:5, the disbeliefs of Christian faith that have been proposed for recognition with respect to the doctrine of the Word of God may now be summarized as they have been stated.

Christian faith as affirmed in the doctrine of the Word of God refuses to believe:

1. all spirits or teachings that either deny God's otherness, or that interpret God's otherness as noncommunicative.
2. all teachings that tend to equate the Word of God with some object, including the Bible, and thus turn God into a thing.
3. any claim that God from the beginning has withheld from the church truth that is essential to saving faith.

4. any claim that God's Word can be confined and is not now free to speak wherever and as God chooses.
5. that God has no new things to say through the continuing proclamation of the canonical scripture as God's living voice.
6. that God's Word occurs for earthly human knowing without the mediation of ordinary historical means necessary for communication.
7. that any ordinary historical means necessary for communication can cause God's Word to occur for earthly human knowing.
8. that there can be an essential contradiction in faith between what is congruent with scripture as God's Word and what is consonant with experience as God's Word.
9. that the Word of God in scripture violates the internal witness of God's Word in the heart.
10. that the internal witness of God's Word in the heart denies the Word of God in scripture.
11. all positions that appeal to the past and to the particular narrated memory of scripture in such a way as to rob the present and the future of the scripture's promissory hope for God's making "all things new" (Rev. 21:5).
12. all positions that appeal to the scripture's promissory hope for the new in a way that severs it from the scripture's particular narrated memory.
13. any claim suggesting that God, when truly known apart from scripture, is of a different identity from that of God revealed through scripture.
14. that there is any Word of God that does not bear witness to the way, the truth, and the life revealed in Jesus Christ.
15. that witness to Jesus Christ is restricted to explicit use of the words "Jesus Christ," or to the speech, scriptures, and traditions of Christianity.
16. that faithful response to the Word of God is a result of human agency.
17. that faithful response to the Word of God as God's gift occurs apart from, or in violation of, human agency.

If these proposed disbeliefs are accepted as meeting the tests for doctrinal faithfulness, they provide grounds for reply to the four initial objections presented at the beginning of this chapter.

The refusals to believe that there can be an essential contradiction in faith between what is congruent with scripture and what is consonant with experience, that faithful response to the Word of God is the result of human agency, and that faithful response to the Word of God as God's gift occurs apart from, or in violation of, human agency, speak directly to the first of these objections, that Christian teaching concerning the Word of God seems to demean human responsibility by imposing an external authority over human beings. Any teaching regarding the Word of God that so demeans human responsibility is to be recognized as false. The authority of God's Word is the authoring of human life in ways that never violate the integrity of human creatureliness. Responsibility before God is the enabled ability to respond to reality freely, and in this sense rightly, that comes from God's Word. When it is truly the event of God's Word, the external and the internal witness confirm one another and do not conflict. The objection against all views that deny this ability-to-respond in love and freedom, either by misrepresenting God's agency or ours, is sustained.

The second initial objection, that it would seem that Christian teaching concerning the Word of God in effect attempts to turn God into a tangible object or a phenomenal entity, is specifically addressed in the refusal to believe all teachings that tend to equate the Word of God with some object, including the Bible, and thus turn God into a thing. Any attempt to reify the revelation of God's Word as a tangible object or a phenomenal entity is hereby rejected. The freedom of God's Word to occur for human knowing through creaturely means is not subject to creaturely means. This point is made in the refusal to believe any claim that God's Word can be confined and is not now free to speak wherever and as God chooses, and in the refusal to believe that any ordinary historical means necessary for communication can cause God's Word to occur for earthly human knowing.

The third objection, that Christian teaching concerning the Word of God seems to make God exclusive to Christianity and to deny that God can be known elsewhere, is also addressed in faith's refusal to believe that God is not free to speak wherever and as God chooses, and most particularly in the refusals to believe either that there is any Word of God that does not bear witness to the way, the truth, and the life revealed in Jesus Christ, or that this witness to Jesus Christ is restricted to explicit use of the words "Jesus Christ," or to the speech, scriptures, and traditions of Christianity. The exclusivity having to do with the issue of masculine imagery in speaking of God, which is raised in this third objection, will be a subject to which we return in the next chapter dealing with the being of God. Other aspects of inclusivity and exclusivity in Christian doctrine will be subjects for subsequent chapters, but the disbeliefs recognized here concerning the Word of God mark the course to be followed.

Finally, the fourth objection to any Christian teaching concerning the Word of God which presupposes that God is known apart from ordinary media required for human communication is shown to be sustained by faith's disbelieving that God's Word occurs for earthly human knowing without the mediation of ordinary historical means necessary for communication. This reply is coupled with the refusal to believe that any ordinary historical means necessary for communication can of themselves cause God's Word to occur for earthly human knowing. The conclusion of most Christian doctrine on this point can be stated simply. God's Word employs ordinary means. But ordinary means cannot employ God's Word.

Chapter 7

THE BEING OF GOD

Introduction

How in Christian faith is God to be described? To pose this question is to prompt the rejoinder, "Well, maybe God is not to be described. Maybe one of the realities of God is indescribability." And in one respect this is precisely what most Christian teaching from earliest times has said. That is, the fullness of God has consistently been held to be indescribable in the sense that God's reality is not circumscribable. The God known in faith is affirmed as not one of a kind whose being can be predefined by a generic label, even so general a label as "reality" or "being." *Deus non est in genere* is the commonly held theological axiom.[1] As the Deuteronomic author puts it, besides the Lord God "there is no other" (Deut. 4:35). At the very outset of any discussion of the way that God is God, Christian doctrine therefore registers its disbelief of all claims that presume to circumscribe, or to encapsulate by generic labeling, the One that is addressed and expressed in faith by the use of the word "God."

But the commonly held doctrines of the church also teach that God's being is indeed describable in the sense that the way that God is God can be characterized. We cannot fathom the mystery of God, but we are given in faith to know its character. As we noted in the previous chapter on the Word of God, Christian faith refuses to believe that God remains unidentified. God's unfathomable and uncomprehended depths are not without disclosure of identity. On this premise dogmatic theology addresses the doctrinal loci associated with the being of God.

The life of faith itself eventuates in what may be called an identifying characterization of God. Christian faithfulness does not exist apart from news, from the gospel, concerning what it is that God has said and done and is now saying and doing. Thus to live in relation to such news is already to engage in characterizing God — or, to put it more exactly, to engage in becoming instantiations of the ways that God's character identifies or attests itself. These ways are both individually personal and communal. None of us perceives life and lives out our calling in exactly the same time and space and circumstances of anyone else. Yet these ways that call us into being who we are as persons (although custom made, as it were, to each individual's irreplaceable uniqueness) are never private to us alone, but relate our individuality to that of others in the continual shaping of an ever-open community.

When in dogmatics we ask how God is faithfully to be described, we must recognize from the start both the limits of this question and the necessity. A refusal to believe that God's being is describable in the sense of circumscribable, and a refusal to believe that God's being is indescribable in the sense of unidentifiable or uncharacterizable, are the two disbeliefs that point out the navigational course by which a dogmatics of church teaching is to steer.

The recognition of the limits finds expression within biblical traditions where there is not only a reticence but a stern caution against using the divine name. Thus we read, "You shall not make wrongful use of the name of the Lord your God, for the Lord will not acquit anyone who misuses his name" (Exod. 20:7). Similarly, as we have previously noted from the New Testament, "Not everyone who says to me, 'Lord, Lord,' will enter the kingdom of heaven" (Matt. 7:21). The proscription of vain God-naming is part of the biblical call to faith.

If speaking of God's reality in Christian faith is necessitated by the attempt to tell what happens with Jesus of Nazareth, dogmatics cannot simply adopt what may be acceptable as descriptions of deity in other contexts.[2] If, following the New Testament focus, theology is approached from christology, then, as Dietrich Bonhoeffer has put it, a faithful confession begins with silence, yet a silence that paradoxically enough refuses to be silenced because it evokes gospeling: "The proclamation of Christ is the church speaking from a proper silence."[3]

Early in the second century we find words similar to Bonhoeffer's in Ignatius of Antioch's letter to the Ephesians: "It is better to be silent and be real, than to talk and to be unreal.... Whoever has the word of Jesus for a true possession can also hear his silence."[4] That is why the true proclamation of Easter can only be made by those who, in concert with Rachel's voice, have first been silenced by Good Friday.

But along with these limits arises the necessity of speaking in some description of the way God is. For the silence of Good Friday is only truly heard in the victory shout of Easter. The figure of Rachel is remembered not only because of her refusal to be consoled but because her refusal, according to Jeremiah, is heard by God who promises hope for her future and, in the Matthean depiction, embodies that promised hope within the sound of her voice at Bethlehem, in proximity of Ramah and of Rachel's tomb. The Cross would cast no shadow were it not for the light of Resurrection morn.[5] If Easter cannot be known apart from Good Friday, so Good Friday cannot be known apart from Easter. What limits faith's speaking of God is precisely what necessitates faith's speaking of God. The word of Jesus and his silence go together.

Whatever talk of God may proceed from other contexts, we are here concerned to trace the characterization of God's being that arises from the context we have just considered in the preceding chapter on the Word of God. In the native context of Christian faith the question of the being of God is "*Whose* life was given forth in Jesus, and *who* raised that life from the dead?" In the particular narration and promise of the Gospel message the "Who" in each instance is identified and characterized as "God."[6] Steering this course, we encounter the further disbelief: Christian faith disbelieves the purported identification of any "being" as the being of God that is not both *the-being-given-forth* of life in Jesus of Nazareth and *the-being-that-raises-up* this life from the dead. Ontic description, that is, description of the way God is understood to be God in Christian faith, proceeds from these markers.

In the history of church theology the traditional elements having to do with the being of God have been configured in many different ways. Certain matters are greatly expanded in some theologies and nearly ignored in others, depending upon the emphases and concerns of the community to which the theology is primarily responsive. Yet in most treatments of this doctrinal area two topics are usually dealt with in the consideration of the way in which God is God. One is the topic that in the older theologies is most often designated as the divine attributes; the other is the trinity or triunity of God.

The essentials of what the Christian doctrine of the being of God is about can be stated in a sentence: *God's being is a being-One-with-Another-in-a-unity-of-Spirit that is the dominion of love.* Most of the issues dealt with in dogmatics under this doctrinal rubric can be shown to refer to points condensed within this statement.

Initial Objections

If we ask whether it is indeed the case that a description of God's being is necessitated by Christian faith, and whether, if so, such a description properly takes the form of affirmations regarding God's attributes and triunity, initial objections along the following lines may be anticipated.

1. *It would seem that the ontic descriptions of God found in much dogmatic tradition conflict with the biblical testimonies they purport to affirm.*

Tertullian's question applies particularly at this point: "What has Athens to do with Jerusalem" when it comes to characterizing the One whom Christian faith worships as God? Conceptually, the answer must be, if based upon the history of doctrine, quite a bit. The metaphysical writings of the Greco-Roman environment of early Christianity provide the conceptual terminology for discussions of God's being and as such predetermine how questions are posed as well as addressed within this discussion. But should they today? Once Christianity officially became a "licit" religion under Constantine in the fourth century, the ensuing hellenization of dogma and canon law transformed the gospel into what it had not previously been, a metaphysical philosophy and a legal system. Not only does much of this "Platonism for the masses,"[7] to use Nietzsche's famous phrase, lack concrete meaning and fail to persuade many Christians of its coherence today, it ignores the social consequences endemic to its primary assumptions and thus perpetuates rejections that do not arise out of faith.

Such rejections include most notably all depictions of God's vulnerability. Once defined metaphysically as Necessary Being whose essence is self-contained permanence, at once forever independent and forever unaffected by that which is other, this Being ceases to be credible as One who makes and keeps promises and of whom a story of what happens with Israel and with Jesus may be told. The consequences for self-understanding if human beings are to see themselves as made according to the "likeness" (Gen. 1:26) of this God are disastrous. The human ideal becomes that of the self-contained, uninvolved, dispassionate, and singular individual. The free life is presumed to be one long declaration of independence. High value is placed upon self-sufficiency; low marks go to any admission of need. To be commendably strong is not really to need anyone else; to be in need, on the other hand, is to risk disgrace and failure. Something is intolerably wrong with such an interpretation. Is it more congruent with scripture and more consonant with experience to conceive of God's freedom as ultimate independence rather than as ultimate interdependence? Or to portray the love revealed in Jesus Christ as, at least in essence despite appearances to the contrary, devoid of all passion and suffering? Or to think of God's oneness as a relationless singularity of changeless invulnerability?

The mind boggles at the contradiction between this so-called Necessary Being of classical metaphysics and the scriptural depiction of the ways of God. One need not stress unduly the differences between Greek and Hebrew thought patterns to recognize why such hellenization imposed upon the gospel accounts of Jesus has been described as "the tyranny of dogma."[8] If ultimate being is by definition necessarily immutable, impassible, and timeless, then the God of Christian faith surely cannot be said to *be*.

2. *It would seem that faith can only confess the impact of God, not the being of God as such.*

This category of initial objections can cite a variety of traditions in historical theology to argue its case. If God is known only by way of creaturely means and media, must not this knowing be said to be based upon the effects of God somehow implanted within creation?

Thomas Aquinas, for his part, attributes to the natural powers of human reasoning apart from revelation the ability to demonstrate the existence of God, not by intuitive self-evidence, but from evident effects.[9] Melanchthon's more personal argument that "to know Christ is to know his benefits" was expanded in early Reformation thinking to include all faithful knowing of God.[10] Characteristic of Luther's teaching is the strong insistence that a theoretical god who makes no practical difference is not the God of biblical faith but a scholastic idol. So it is with Calvin as well, whose initial premise is that the knowing of God is inseparable from the knowing of ourselves. For Schleiermacher the so-called attributes of God are to be understood not as ontic referents within God but as descriptions of the relation of human self-consciousness to God.[11] Later existentialists elaborate similar themes and interpret them to mean that ontology can only be explicated anthropologically.

The point is that any characterization of God that arises out of biblical faith must be a description that is, to use the traditional dogmatic shorthand, *pro me* and not *per se*, or as it is more commonly stated, not *a se*. This means that faith only knows God as being for us and disposed toward us; it cannot presume to speculate about God's being in and of itself. Thus doctrines that attempt to describe the *aseity* of God, God's inner being apart from its relation to our own, lack both congruence with scripture and consonance with experience.

It appears that the only faithful characterization of the way God is must be in moral terms and not metaphysical terms. God's character is known in faith as God's moral will and not as God's ontic actuality.

3. *It would seem that the doctrine of the Trinity attempts to deify the language of "Father," "Son," and "Holy Spirit" as irreplaceable masculine terms for God's being.*

To argue that any terminology for God has as such a revealed status is to mistake the linguistic means of revelation for God's Word that occurs through them. It is to confuse the cultural context in which a text originated with the cultural context in which God's Word may speak through that same text today. An idolatrous verbal fetishism is the result. To construe trinitarian appellations for God as privileged discourse exempt from the finite limitations of all other images and symbols used in Christian worship for God is to engage in a fundamentalism of terminology, a reification of God's being through the incantation of an irreplaceable formulaic expression.

It is ironic that those who insist upon the unsubstitutable status of the traditional threefold designation for God's being must do so without the explicit support of scripture itself or of tradition claiming apostolicity up until the fourth century. What is now often insisted upon as essential to Christian faith and to the catholicity of its teaching, the rule of naming God exclusively as "Father, Son, and Holy Spirit," One in Three and Three in One, is something that apparently was unknown to the apostolic writers of the New Testament and to the earliest Christian communities. Traditions of spirituality within Christian history that have employed female imagery for God, even when in conjunction with the Trinity, have for the most part come to be dismissed as marginal and insignificant.[12]

This sort of dismissal represents a disregard for the criterion of consequence. The results of officially characterizing God's being exclusively in the male terms of "Father" and "Son," and of referring to the Holy Spirit as well solely by the use of masculine pronouns, must today be taken into account. Any refusal to do so can only be exposed as a rejection that does not have its basis in Christian faith. It is a nontheological rejection arising from some other source.

A significant and rapidly growing scholarly literature is now available on this subject that cannot responsibly be dismissed without a hearing.[13] There is the question of scriptural interpretation and of both the contents of the writings and the ways in which they are appropriated by church worship and teaching.[14] There is the historical question of Christian origins and of the influences that shaped the conciliar decisions of the first five centuries, and the undeniable antifemale bias that is endemic to much of the history of doctrine. There are the current questions of social criticism having to do with the analysis of cultural assumptions and practices regarding gender roles. All of these contemporary areas of research speak to issues involved in the theological testing of the spirits.

It will no longer do to say, as the church always has, that God's being is without sexual differentiation, and still continue to say, as the church for the most part does, that the triunity of this God can only be ascribed as "Father," "Son," and "Holy Spirit," who is such all by and within "Himself." (If certain words as vocables for God are themselves thought to be "revealed" and cannot ever be altered, why not still insist upon "Holy Ghost" in English because it represents an older usage than

"Holy Spirit"?) The incoherence of such an intolerable position would appear to be obvious.

Interpretation

With these initial objections before us, a tracing of the content of Christian teaching with respect to the being of God directs our attention to the subjects of the divine attributes, the Trinity, and the appropriate language in Christian faith for addressing and expressing God.

1. The Divine Attributes

What characteristics are to be attributed to God, and how is such attribution made?

Historically, Christianity has incorporated ontic descriptions of deity from what it took to be the best of classical Greek and Roman philosophy, and throughout its history it has been forced to reconsider these appropriations. Some of the borrowed descriptions have proved consistent with the identifying depictions of God in scripture, and others have not.

To contend, for example, that only God is the source of the way God is, and that God's being is not *effected* from some other source, is a definitional principle of classical metaphysics generally accepted by Christianity as an entailment of its own message. But to conclude from this that God's being as self-sustained is not *affected* from elsewhere, with the consequence that God is impassive to human suffering and cannot feel the groaning of creation, is irreconcilable with biblical testimony. "It won't preach." According to the depictions of this testimony the biblical God may appropriately be said to have need, not in order to be, as if such need were dictated by some more ultimate constraint, but because this is the way God has chosen to be. Words of the prophet Hosea convey the point:

> When Israel was a child, I loved him,
> and out of Egypt I called my son.
>
> The more I called them,
> the more they went from me;...
> How can I give you up, Ephraim?
> How can I hand you over, O Israel?...
> My heart recoils within me,
> my compassion grows warm and tender.
> ...For I am God and no mortal,

the Holy One in your midst,
and I will not come in wrath.

Hos. 11: 1–2, 8–9

As we noted with regard to Luther's discussion of the *theologia crucis* in chapter 2, speculative descriptions of God as the most glorious reality conceivable are radically reordered from the scandalous standpoint of a crucified Messiah. We encounter here the following disbeliefs: Christian faith refuses to believe that God's way of being is the effect of something else; Christian faith refuses to believe that God's way of being is unaffected by anything else. Within these parameters dogmatic testing proceeds.

But if one seeks descriptions of God that are congruent with the import of the characterizations found in scripture the question of how language that applies to creatures may also be said to apply to God remains.[15] Whatever we say of God, whether our forms of speech are metaphysical or figural, our expression consists of anthropomorphisms. To speak of God at all is to employ language that we also use in speaking of subjects other than God. Differences between the uses in each instance must be acknowledged, but to claim that such differences were total would be to deny that God could ever be either addressed or expressed. Thus, while references both to God and to creatures may be made in the same words, it is generally held that between these two frames of reference there exists neither a parity of meaning (univocity) nor a complete disparity (equivocity). Rather, theistic signification is said to be proportionate, in some sense, to its subject (analogy).[16]

Why this should even be a problem may not be obvious at first glance. Can we not say that God is like certain things we already know and unlike certain things we already know, and simply leave it at that? Some may imagine God as like a father, or like a mother, or not even like a parent at all, but like a mighty warrior, or a still small voice, a thunderstorm, or the lilies of the field. The possible similes and images would appear to be as unlimited as the whole range of human experience. Then again, can we not proceed next to make the necessary qualifications of these anthropomorphic and creaturely likenesses by simply adding that God is also unlike creatures who inhabit restricted locations in space and time and cannot be everywhere and always at once, who are destructive of good and subject to death, and whose word is not always trustworthy? Certainly descriptions of God are given in just this manner. But in testing these, dogmatic questions lurk, about which there remains considerable debate in Christian theology.

One question is how much in fact we actually do "already know" of the likenesses and unlikenesses of the predicates attributable to God. Another question is what to make of the fact that Christian confession not only says "God is *like* or *unlike* such and such," employing the language of simile or metaphor; it also says "God *is* such and such," employing the language of a proper name.

Not surprisingly, if we take into account the initial objections of this chapter, differences arise in interpreting what the so-called analogical sense involves.[17] If the meaning of one use of a term is taken to be proportionate to that of another use of the same term, the two meanings are not considered to be equivalent but comparable in that they are alike in certain respects and not alike in others. But in speaking of God's being, where are appropriate comparisons to be found? Much attention is given to this question in the history of doctrine.

Chapter 40 of the prophecy of Isaiah introduces the reader to several dimensions of this question. To recall the words of the prophet, "To whom then will you liken God," or with what likeness make comparison with the Holy One (Isa. 40:18, 25)? Clearly the incomparability of God is here emphasized. What the scholastics later meant by stating that God is not part of a genus or class is here prefigured in the form of Hebrew prophecy.

Yet in the same passage from Isaiah 40 comparisons are in fact made. On the one hand, there are descriptions given of the Holy One in which this incomparable One is said to be like creatures we know. These descriptions speak of God as "feeding his flock like a shepherd," as "gathering the lambs in his arms, and carrying them in his bosom," as "bringing princes to nought, and making the rulers of the earth as nothing," and as "giving power to the faint, and strengthening the powerless." We at least have some comparable sense of what these descriptive accounts are telling us because we say these things of creatures. We can visualize a meaning.

On the other hand, the Holy One is also described in Isaiah 40 as "measuring the waters, the heavens, and the dust of the earth," as "weighing the mountains in scales and the hills in a balance," as "sitting above the circle of the earth," as being "everlasting," the "Creator of the ends of the earth," as being One who "does not faint or grow weary," and whose "understanding is unsearchable." Again the words are common to our vocabularies, but attempts at visualizing their meanings in this instance require us to imagine God in certain respects not as like creatures we know but as unlike creatures we know. None of these descriptions is applicable to creatures. Our sense of what they mean comes by contrasting them with the limited way we exist as finite beings.

Translated into the traditional dogmatic terminology, the divine attribute of "feeding his flock like a shepherd," of "gathering the lambs in his arms, and carrying them in his bosom," and of "giving power to the faint, and strengthening the powerless," becomes *compassion;* "bringing princes to nought, and making the rulers of the earth as nothing," and "measuring and weighing" all creation becomes *justice* in the sense of *righteousness;* the attribute of "sitting above the circle of the earth" becomes *omnipresence;* the attribute of being "everlasting" becomes *eternity* and *immutability;* the attribute of being One who as "Creator of the ends of the earth" does not "faint or grow weary" becomes *omnipotence;* and the attribute of being One whose "understanding is unsearchable" becomes *omniscience.* These characterizations are all attributed to the "Holy One," that is, to God's being as *holiness* and as *unity*, and finally as *glory* that shall be universally revealed (Isa. 40:5). Thus translated into descriptive categories we have a traditional list of divine attributes: compassion, justice as righteousness, omnipresence, eternity, immutability, omnipotence, omniscience, unity, holiness, and glory. Additional descriptions elaborate these.

While the same words are common to us from using them in comparison and contrast with reference to creatures, when Isaiah uses them within the frame of reference in which they testify of God, we know that their definitive meaning — what Thomas Aquinas calls their "primary" (*prius*) signification — derives not from a general context of usage but from the particular context in which reference is being made to God. The incomparable God of biblical faith thus enables creaturely meanings to become proportionally comparable in faithfully characterizing the way God is. Language for God is appropriate insofar as God appropriates it as faithful witness. Such is the commonly held view regarding the role of analogy, in its most basic theological sense, in speaking of the divine attributes.

The dogmatic problem of accounting for the meaningfulness of Christian discourse in characterizing the being of God can thus be summed up in three points. (1) God is affirmed as not part of a genus or class. Therefore, no description of God can be understood as a generic label. (2) But all language, and thus the only language we have to speak of God, is generic in that words as such have commonly understood meanings. (3) Hence, there is no truth to any predicate we attribute to God unless God enables what we say in creaturely terms to become proportional to the way God is in God's own terms.

In traditions of dogmatic theology this enabling of proportional or analogical reference has been explained in several different ways. One explanation of how our human language may be said to be applicable to God appeals to our created nature as its frame of reference. Since human beings are created "after God's likeness," it is reasoned that this enables us to compare and contrast God's being who God is with our being who we are. Thus Thomas Aquinas speaks of the "analogy of being" (*analogia entis*).[18] Another explanation appeals not to our created nature as its frame of reference, but to God's grace of justifying our fallen nature in the act of reconciling us. Since human beings are justified by faith and made a "new creation" (2 Cor. 5:17) through the grace of Christ's saving work, it is reasoned that only God in similar fashion can justify human expressions of God and enable them to become what in themselves they have no natural power of becoming, namely, analogues of the grace of Jesus Christ. Prophecy as the gift of grace, Paul writes, leads to speaking "in proportion [*analogion*] to faith" (Rom. 12:6). Thus, Karl Barth writes of the "analogy of faith" (*analogia fidei*) or the "analogy of grace" (*analogia gratiae*).[19] Still a third explanation interprets faithful God-talk primarily within a frame of reference, neither of original nature nor of justifying grace, but of coming glory. Chief regard in this instance is given not so much to creation or to reconciliation but to eschatology, to the yet to be realized universal glory (*doxa*) of God that, according to the scriptures, is God's promised destiny for all creation and reconciliation. Since the coming glorification of God in "a new heaven and a new earth" (Rev. 21:1) is praised in the community of faith, it is reasoned that all descriptions of God's being are to be understood as analogous to the ascriptions of this glory in worship. They are anticipatory, or proleptic. Thus Wolfhart Pannenberg, among others, characterizes analogical statements as issuing forth in open-ended doxological statements that praise God's coming glory yet to be. "The correspondence of our words to God himself has not already been decided, but is yet to be decided. . . . We utter them in the hope of a fulfillment which by far overcomes the distance fixed in the analogy."[20]

In biblical contexts the enabling of human words and actions to bear faithful witness to the "I AM" who is God is acknowledged to be the necessary condition for all true prophecy. "God said to Moses, 'I AM WHO I AM. . . . Thus you shall say to the Israelites, "I AM has sent me to you'" (Exod. 3:14). Implicit in this account of the "I AM" commissioning Moses to speak is the promise, "I WILL BE WHO I WILL BE."[21] All that follows is seen to be premised upon and commissioned by this sending.

Disagreements arise over the extent to which the common meanings of terms retain their ordinary significance from a creaturely frame of reference when they are used to refer to God. To illustrate, Christian doctrine affirms with Johannine traditions that "God is Spirit" (John 4:24), and that "God is love" (1 John 4:8), but like these Johannine traditions it does not reverse these statements of faith and profess that all spirits are God or even that love is God.[22] To do so would be to engage in generic labeling, to assume that who God is conforms to some class of things that we already know how to categorize correctly as "spirit" and as "love." It would be, as Thomas Aquinas put it, to fail to recognize that the definitive meaning of words such as "spirit" and "love," when used to describe who God is, comes primarily from God to the creature and not the other way 'round.

This is why it is argued that the meanings of the same predicates when referring to God and when referring to ourselves are never identical or univocal. But to conclude from this that these meanings are totally different, or totally equivocal, and that there is no sense in which words such as "spirit" or "love" mean something similar when attributed to God and when attributed to human beings would be to deny the faith that God becomes identified to us through creaturely means and can be meaningfully confessed in human speech. The meaning of such speech as analogical is proximate and proportional to the way in which God is God as differentiated from the way in which creatures are creatures.

Karl Barth was critical of Thomas Aquinas for what he saw to be a tilt toward univocity in Thomas's treatment of analogical predication in allowing the predicates too much likeness between their attribution to creatures and their attribution to God. At least this was the later influence of Thomas, as Barth initially viewed it in 1932, evident in those Roman Catholic and liberal Protestant tendencies that, as Barth charged, reason not "in proportion to faith" from God's eventfully enacted identity in Christ to our own, but in proportion to some predefined anthropological self-understanding that is then projected onto God. As such the *analogia entis* evades christology and by so doing — Barth minced no words — becomes "the invention of Antichrist."[23]

Barth notwithstanding, Thomas to the contrary emphatically denies any generic connection between God's being and that of creatures: "They do not even share a common genus."[24] Yet he does hold that causes are known only from their effects. Even with words used primarily of God and only derivatively of creatures, ostensibly words such as "spirit" and "love," for example, we at least know their meaning first as it applies to creatures.[25] Such is the nature of language acquisition.

In his determination to reverse what he saw to be the mistaken application of this position to theological reasoning, and to refute all grounding of Christian theology in a general ontology or anthropology, Barth's own view of the analogy of faith (*analogia fidei*), which he saw as a corrective to the alleged Thomistic analogy of being (*analogia entis*), may for its part be faulted in turn for tilting too heavily toward equivocity. If predicate nominatives such as "spirit" and "love" lose all their regular meaning when used in sentences with God as the subject, and are in this one frame of reference defined solely by their subject through a miraculous and instantaneous bestowal of new meaning, as Barth's early view suggests, the question of which predicates are appropriate in characterizing God's being would seem to become a matter of indifference.[26] Apparently any words whatsoever may be used since the subject will totally redefine them. Yet in his own extensive account of the divine attributes or "perfections" in the *Church Dogmatics* II/1 Barth in practice clearly does not take such a capricious result to be the case.[27]

Theological differences in interpreting the significance of analogy should not cause us to overlook fundamental agreements. Upon examination it turns out that whether one bases one's account of analogy primarily upon creation, justification by grace, or eschatology, any claim to what we "already know" about the applicability of predicates for God is premised upon what we are assuming God's proper name as the "I AM" to be. This is equally true for the positions of Thomas, Barth, and Pannenberg, which obviously are not theirs alone, but which as distinguishable perspectives have a history of variations. Another way of putting the same point is to say that within the frame of reference of faithful attribution to God all common nouns are to be treated as proper nouns; all predicates become true only insofar as their meaning conforms to their subject. We shall see the pertinence of this point and the disbeliefs it illuminates when we return to the specific questions posed by the third initial objection of this chapter having to do with the traditionally ascribed trinitarian threefold name of God.

Common to most Christian teaching are two inseparable disbeliefs regarding the interpretation of the divine attributes. Each of the descriptive categories we have just noted in drawing upon the prophecy of Isaiah 40, along with any additional synonymous nouns that may be used, are to be defined in church doctrines according to two basic faith claims.

One is that to think of God's being as the life being-given-forth in Jesus of Nazareth is to disbelieve any characterization of this being that is other than one of *love*. God is not almighty except as love. According to Christian proclamation God enacts and thereby defines love in what happens with Jesus. God is thus confessed not as being *like* love in certain respects and *unlike* love in other respects; God *is* love. All human likenesses and unlikenesses to genuine love derive their comparability from here.

The other faith claim is that to think of God's being as the being-that-raises-up this life in Jesus from the dead is to disbelieve any characterization of this being that is other than one of *dominion*. God is not compassionate except as Lord. According to Christian proclamation the power that raises the life in Jesus from the dead is the power that has dominion over all things, and over all that opposes love, including death itself. God is thus confessed not as being *like* lordship in certain respects and *unlike* lordship in other respects; God *is* Lord. All human likenesses and unlikenesses to genuine authority derive their comparability from here. Disciples are instructed by Jesus' teaching not to "lord it" as the Gentiles do (Matt. 20:25).

With each category of divine attributes, whether that of God's compassion, justice as righteousness, omnipresence, eternity, immutability, omnipotence, omniscience, unity, holiness, or glory, the dogmatic task is to show how God's love is to be understood as God's dominion and how God's dominion is to be understood as God's love. This duality of focus upon love and dominion is what is at stake in standard dogmatic references to the moral and the metaphysical attributes, or to the communicable and the incommunicable attributes, or to God's immanence and transcendence, relatedness and absoluteness, love and freedom, yet it states this duality less problematically today than do some of these labels.

The point is that what the love of God means cannot be understood apart from the dominion that is God's way of being. Equally, what the dominion of God means (God's exercise of lordship or sovereignty) cannot be understood apart from the love that is God's way of being. This is but another way of saying that the Cross, and all the passion leading up to it, cannot be understood apart from the Resurrection and the victory it proclaims. Cross and Resurrection, the love of God in all its humility and suffering of being-given-forth, and the dominion of God in all its victory and glory as being-that-raises-up what is given forth over all opposition, even unto death and the depths of hell itself, cannot be separated in the signifying of the gospel. The one has no actuality apart from the other.

Yet theological speculation has sometimes tended, in effect at least, to separate them. The so-called metaphysical attributes affirming God's almightiness, what the early creeds literally referred to as the "dominion over all [*pantokrator*]," becomes translated as *omnipotentem* and interpreted apart from its native creedal context to mean an all-powerful almightiness not defined by the character of God's love. While at the same time the so-called moral attributes affirming God's gracious compassion and justice, the ways of God's mercy and holiness, may become interpreted merely as abstract ideals or values, good intentions on God's part, but possibly ineffectual and incapable of exercising dominion over all opposition in reality. With regard to the first of the initial objections raised concerning the apparent conflict of much ontic description of God with the biblical testimonies they purport to affirm, we can now respond that *God may be said to be invulnerable only in the sense that God alone does not cease to be vulnerable.* "Love bears all things" (1 Cor. 13:7).

In the history of the church's attempt to describe the reality of God, despite the different terms from scripture and from philosophy that are employed, the basic conviction expressed is that the ways of God's dominion and the ways of God's loving are ultimately one and the same, distinguishable only for human meditation upon the mystery of God's being. To know what love means in reference to God is to know how God exercises dominion. To know what dominion or sovereignty means in reference to God is to know how God loves. The ways of God are beyond all human comprehending, but to Christian faith both this love and this dominion are enacted as the naming of who "I AM" is in the events culminating in Holy Week.

The truth of the faith affirmed in the doctrine of the divine attributes may indeed harbor falsehood if the entailed disbeliefs of this faith are not recognized. When all of the affirmations have been distilled to their essence two of these disbeliefs emerge as most basic. Christian faith refuses to believe that love, as defined with reference to God, is subject to final defeat by any opposition. Christian faith refuses to believe in any form of domination that is not the dominion of this love.

2. The Triunity of God

The distinctively Christian explication of deity as loving dominion is to be found in the doctrine of the Trinity. Unitarianism stands as a continuing reminder that this explication has not always proved convincing.

Very few Christians indeed have a mind for the metaphysical abstractions that are the spinoff of scholastic speculation regarding God's being as Three in One. If tested by the appeal to consequences alone, much historical evidence would count heavily against the doctrine. What other teaching of the church has so served not only to befuddle the faithful, but to burn dissenters at the stake? "Whoever wishes to be saved," so the still most definitive creedal account of God's triunity written in the fifth century concludes, "must think thus of the Trinity."[28] The sixteenth century Reformers were no less definite. Bullinger, for example, commends Christian emperors for being "right to appoint capital punishment for those who should spread new teaching on this dogma and teach different things with insult to God."[29]

Granted the indubitable history of confusion and persecution attendant upon the doctrine, why does it persist as the major Christian attempt to describe the being of God? Either one must dismiss its continuance as an exercise in ecclesiastical sadism or search for the source of its durability elsewhere. If true to faith as apostolic tradition, the doctrine of God's triunity nevertheless through misuse harbors the lie of the betrayal of God's loving dominion when it becomes Judas tradition. In this instance the recognition of the relevant faithful disbeliefs becomes crucial.

The explicit persistence of the doctrine of the Trinity in Christian teaching since the fourth century arises from the continuing importance of the question that this doctrine seeks to address; namely, Who is rightly to be called "the Lord God" in light of what happens with Jesus of Nazareth? How can one faithfully say, "Hear, O Israel: The Lord our God is one Lord" (Deut. 6:4), and also faithfully address Jesus Christ, in the words of the disciple Thomas following the Resurrection, as "My Lord and my God!" (John 20:28)? Expressed in terms of disbeliefs, what characterizations of "God" are proscribed if, as the author of Colossians puts it, "In him [Jesus Christ] all the fullness of God was pleased to dwell" (Col. 1:19); and, "The Father and I are one," to cite words attributed to Jesus in the Gospel of John (John 10:30)? One view that was emphatically proscribed as avowed by Marcion and his followers in the second century is indicated in the refusal of Christian faith from the beginning to believe that the God who is confessed as dwelling in Christ and being one with Jesus is a different God from the God of Israel.

When the church at what is regarded as its first general or ecumenical council at Nicaea in 325 C.E. affirmed that what happened in, to, and through Jesus was not less than ultimate, not less than God, but was "of the same reality with the Father" (*homoousion to patri*), it did from an ontic point of view a very curious thing. The foundation was thereby laid for recognizing that somehow the oneness of God, what the ancients called Necessary Being as by definition the way reality most ultimately is, is a oneness in the sense of being one-with-another. As the Johannine prologue had earlier expressed it, the Word that became flesh and dwelt among us was from the beginning "with God and . . . was God" (John 1:1). Just over a half century later a second general council (Constantinople, 381) made explicit acknowledgment of the church's faith that the Holy Spirit as well is the "Lord" "who with the Father and the Son together is worshiped and glorified."[30] By these conciliar declarations two further disbeliefs are registered, the refusal of Christian faith to believe that what occurs with Jesus, including the presence of the Spirit, is less than God, and therefore the refusal to believe that God's being as "I WHO AM" is not innately relational.

Calling the one God's way of being Lord by the three terms "Father, Son, and Holy Spirit" emerges in the first instance because the gospel message contains a threefold referentiality. If the story of what happens with Jesus could be told without a threefold reference to God there would be no church doctrine of the Trinity. A manner of speaking that proves to be unavoidable in expressing Christian faith becomes more or less formalized as a rule of thought by which the church in turn recalls what its witness to the gospel, even without always realizing it, is in fact confessing. The formal rule or summation is that, as recounted in the community that lives its life in reference to the gospel, God is Lord by being One-with-Another-in-a-unity-of-Spirit.

Analogies to this triunity of God as a way of thinking have been drawn primarily according to the three ways of interpreting analogues of God that we have noted in discussing the divine attributes, that is, with respect to alleged vestiges in human nature as created in God's image, with respect to God's announced saving work of justification by grace, and with respect to ascriptions of praise regarding God's eschatological *doxa* or coming glory that inform Christian worship.

In regard to human nature as created, Augustine, most notably, points to "certain trinities, each of their appropriate kind" in human beings, most particularly in the purest acts of the mind where he finds "traces of that highest Trinity which we seek when we seek God."[31] There is, Augustine suggests, a triadic structure detectable both in our being aware of ourselves, which involves not only our knowing that we are but also our loving that we are, and also in our being created with a mind that can only function through a threefold exercise of remembering, understanding, and willing. But, Augustine cautions, such vestigial similarities, while apt indicators of the triune God in whose image we have been created, are only to be viewed as creaturely approximations.

With respect to God's saving work of justification, the description of God's triunity is drawn not from analogies of the mind or psyche but from the way in which God is said in the gospel to accomplish the dominion of love within creation in the sending of Christ as Savior and in the giving of the Spirit. Through such accomplishment, or *economy*, to use the traditional term, we see in these missions of sending and bestowing an inseparably threefold character of how God is God. A dominion or sovereignty that is inseparably threefold in its administration is not thereby divided or threatened with a loss of unity. So argued Tertullian, himself a lawyer, who in the second century was the first to apply the term *trinitas* to God's rule and to use the expression *one substance* and *three persons* in refuting charges of polytheism.[32] No impetus to trinitarian doctrine is stronger than the conviction of Christian faith that in the coming of Christ and in the gift of the Spirit salvation *as only God grants it* occurs. In the triunity of this economy of salvation the triunity of the way that God is self-related is said to be revealed.

With respect to the anticipation of God's coming glory, the approach to trinitarian doctrine is primarily through an analysis of the language of such anticipation, that is, of doxology. This way of accounting for trinitarian doctrine through doxological ascriptions is at once both ancient and contemporary. It attempts to adhere to the *Lex orandi est lex credendi* principle that "the rule of prayer is the rule of belief" and thus appeals for its support to the criterion of consistency with worship. Doxological ascription, nevertheless, is not to be thought of simply as a language of human response. It is in the first instance taken to be revelatory language congruent with scriptural testimony in that the glory of God is believed to be named by God and only then ascribed by the worshiper in faithful praise. "Ascribe to the Lord the glory of his name; worship the Lord in holy splendor" (Ps. 29:2).

Basil of Caesarea, from the region of ancient Cappadocia in Asia Minor, exemplifies this approach. He and his brother Gregory of Nyssa, and their friend Gregory of Nazianzus, also Cappadocians, were the most influential in the development of the trinitarian doctrine that emerges with the decisions of Constantinople in 381. Basil's treatise on the Holy Spirit, *De Spiritu Sancto*, is directed against those who were unwilling to ascribe the full glory of God to the Holy Spirit, as well as to the Son — the fourth-century followers of Arius, or Arian subordinationists by dogmatic designation. It begins as follows:

> Lately when praying with the people, and using the full doxology to God the Father in both forms, at one time "with the Son together with the Holy Ghost," and at another "through the Son in the Holy Ghost," I was attacked by some of those present on the ground that I was introducing novel and at the same time mutually contradictory terms.[33]

"Worshipping as we do God of God," writes Basil, "we both confess the distinctions of the Persons, and at the same time abide by the Monarchy.... The sovereignty and authority over us is one, and so the doxology ascribed by us is not plural but one."[34] From the writings of the Cappadocians is derived the classical formulation of God's triunity as *one ousia* and *three hypostases*. Whether one uses this Greek terminology of the Cappadocians, or the Latin terminology of Tertullian's *one substance* and *three persons*, the affirmation of faith being made is that God's one sovereignty or dominion is an equally inseparable but distinguishable threefold dominion of love.

These abstracted formulas asserting that God's being is one reality in three actualizations are said to encode as derived summations the innate structure of Christian worship as it confesses the One to whom glory is to be ascribed as the Lord God. The *Gloria Patri* is equally and inseparably, though distinguishably, a *Gloria Filio* and a *Gloria Spiritui Sancto*.

Traditionally the church has most often associated the manifestation of the triunity of God with the liturgy of baptism. In the account of Jesus' baptism in the synoptic Gospels we find a threefold reference. As Mark has it,

> In those days Jesus came from Nazareth of Galilee and was baptized by John in the Jordan. And just as he was coming up out of the water, he saw the heavens torn apart and the Spirit [Matthew puts it, "the Spirit of God" (3:16), and Luke, "the Holy Spirit" (3:22)] descending like a dove on him. And a voice came from heaven, "You are my Son, the Beloved; with you I am well pleased." (Mark 1:9–11)[35]

In Matthew 28:19 the so-called Great Commission is given to the disciples by the resurrected Christ: "All authority in heaven and on earth has been given to me. Go therefore and make disciples of all nations, baptizing them in the name of the Father and of the Son and of the Holy Spirit." The commission to baptize in the threefold name has been very influential in the history of reflection upon the doctrine of the Trinity. Fourth-century figures such as Athanasius and Basil of Caesarea emphasize it.[36] John Calvin develops a similar line of reasoning to arrive at what he takes to be the import of scripture for faith. In book 1, chapter 13 of the *Institutes* Calvin calls attention to words of the Epistle to the Ephesians:

> There is one body and one Spirit, just as you were called to the one hope of your calling, one Lord, one faith, one baptism, one God and Father of all, who is above all and through all and in all. (Eph. 4:4–6)

Here, says Calvin, we have the connecting of baptism, faith, and God. Since we believe that there is only one baptism, then we believe that there is only one faith, and one faith means that there is only one God. Thus baptism witnesses to the oneness of God. Yet in order to understand the baptism that is of God we must hear the injunction of our Lord, "Go and teach all nations, baptizing them in the name of the Father, and of the Son, and of the Holy Spirit." "What else is this," Calvin concludes, "than to testify clearly that Father, Son, and Spirit are one God?"[37]

While the import of these and other scriptural passages are taken to infer the doctrine of God's triunity, the explicit articulation of the doctrine is not found prior to the Cappadocians of the fourth century. God's one reality (*ousia*) is affirmed as indivisible, but as realized in three actual ways (*hypostases* or *persons*). Immediately, Basil warns, in hearing this talk of One in Three and Three in One we must not be deceived by an "ignorant arithmetic."[38] With regard to God's being, there are no quantities to be counted; nor are there gradations or series. The threefold enumeration involves no addition, subtraction, multiplication, or division, no circumscribed limitations. God's being is not partitioned so that in part, as it were, one-third of God operates through the Father, and another one-third through the Son, and still another one-third through the Holy Spirit. Rather the three hypostases, persons, or actual ways of being each share fully in the others, although in the distinctive manner that is proper to each.

This sharing was denoted by the Cappadocians as *perichōrēsis*, a fascinating concept derived from the same verb that gives us the term *choreography*. The fullness of God's being, it is suggested, is to be thought of as dancing equally throughout the three inseparably distinctive ways that the one God is God.[39] What such faith disbelieves is that God's being as Father, Son, and Holy Spirit is tripartite or that there are three Gods. What is also disbelieved is that God's being is a metamorphic series in which God first is only the Father, and then no longer the Father but only the Son, and then no longer the Son but only the Spirit, each in turn but not altogether, a persistent misrepresentation of God's threefoldness historically labeled after its alleged third-century advocate, Sabellius, as Sabellian modalism.

In response to questions and disputes raised by the gospel's threefold depiction of God's saving economy and the threefold ascription of praise to God in Christian worship the summary description of God's ontic triunity is drawn. The spare but carefully honed words of the fifth-century Pseudo-Athanasian Creed express it as follows:

> The Father is made of none; neither created, nor begotten. The Son is of the Father alone: not made, nor created: but begotten. The Holy Spirit is of the Father and of the Son:[40] neither made, nor created, nor begotten: but proceeding. So there is one Father, not three Fathers: one Son, not three Sons: one Holy Spirit, not three Holy Spirits. And in this Trinity there is none before, or after another: none is greater, or less than another. But the whole three Persons are coeternal, and coequal. So that in all things, as aforesaid: the Unity in Trinity, and the Trinity in Unity, is to be worshiped.

While the history of dogmatics contains repeated endeavors to spell out the coherence (some would say incoherence) of what is asserted in this brief trinitarian affirmation, the fundamental disbelief enjoined by the faith here expressed remains. Proscribed as false witness to the gospel is any attempt to characterize God as being God other than in one properly named threefold relationality.

3. God's Proper Name

The Trinity is not professed to be simply any triad or threefold relation. We come back to the issue of the proper name of God's triune being and to the appropriate language in Christian faith for the God of the gospel to whom glory is to be ascribed.

In the biblical context the name of God is understood to be communicated by God. It is in this sense that God's name is revealed as a proper and not a generic name or an appellation chosen by human preference. According to ancient tradition in Genesis the names of creatures are chosen by human selection: "whatever the man called every living creature, that was its name" (Gen. 2:19). Not so with the name of God. So sacred is this name in Hebraic tradition that it is not spoken. Another word, "Lord" (*Adonai*), is substituted in its place wherever the original

YHWH appears in the Hebrew texts. We read in Exodus of God speaking to Moses when Moses asks to know God's name: "Thus you shall say to the Israelites, 'The LORD, the God of your ancestors, the God of Abraham, the God of Isaac, and the God of Jacob, has sent me to you': This is my name for ever, and this my title for all generations" (Exod. 3:15).

Two observations regarding this text from Exodus 3 have a bearing upon our subject. The first is that the word "LORD" is not the word "YHWH" but is used to signify the unspoken tetragrammaton. The second is that this naming of God is revealed, as it was explained in the discussion of revelation in chapter 6, in the form of story and of promise. That is to say, the identification of this LORD is narrated in the accounts of Abraham, Isaac, and Jacob, and by extension all the other men and women in Hebrew scriptures involved in the story of God's covenant people. Furthermore, this story is continually recalled as the bearer of God's promise. If God's promise in the story is not heard, who God is is not revealed. Moses, for example, is instructed to tell the elders of Israel that God says, "I have given heed to you and to what has been done to you in Egypt. I declare that I will bring you up out of the misery of Egypt" (Exod. 3:16).

The emphasis upon story and promise in connection with the identifying name of God figures prominently in twentieth-century theology. "The name of God," writes Jürgen Moltmann, "is a name of promise" the revelatory knowledge of which is "always bound up with the recounting and recalling of history and with prophetic expectation."[41] If we apply these insights to the question of the proper naming of God's triunity we are brought back again to the fact that the stories that comprise the message of the gospel involve a threefold reference to God.

This threefold referentiality, while not uniform in the New Testament writings, is used consistently in saying some things about each of the referents, Father, Son, and Holy Spirit, that are not said about the other two. We may take it as a working principle that no language for God is faithful to the gospel message which violates the gospel's storyline with its pattern of threefold reference. Nor is such language faithful if it betrays the promise this pattern of threefold reference serves to convey.

The One crucified is confessed by the centurion and the others keeping watch at the Cross in the words, "Truly this man was God's Son!" (Matt. 27:54). Nowhere in the New Testament is the crucified One referred to as the Father or as the Holy Spirit. The One who is said to give the only-begotten Son, the One from whom the Spirit is said to descend upon Jesus, and the One to whom the crucified Jesus calls out in the passion of the Cross, is referred to as the Father, not as the Son, and not as the Holy Spirit. The One who is recounted as descending upon Jesus, and as coming upon the disciples on the day of Pentecost, is referred to as the Holy Spirit, not as the Father, and not as the Son.

Yet the inseparability of these three distinguishable referents in the gospel story is as pronounced as are the distinctions in the way these terms are used. We have already noted this inseparability with regard to the account of Jesus' baptism (Mark 1:9–11). But other statements make the point as well. In the concluding discourse of Jesus in the Gospel of John we read, "When the Advocate [or Helper] comes, whom I will send to you from the Father, the Spirit of truth who comes [or proceeds] from the Father, he will testify on my behalf" (John 15:26). In Luke's account of Peter's sermon on the day of Pentecost these words tell of the "Jesus God raised up": "Being therefore exalted at the right hand of God, and having received from the Father the promise of the Holy Spirit, he has poured out this that you both see and hear" (Acts 2:33). A threefold reference in Paul's writings may reflect an early form of liturgical benediction: "The grace of the Lord Jesus Christ, the love of God, and the communion of the Holy Spirit be with all of you" (2 Cor. 13:13). To the Romans Paul writes that the indwelling Spirit is "the Spirit of him who raised Jesus from the dead" (Rom. 8:11).

The problem of the appropriate language in Christian faith for God may now be stated more precisely. It is how to reject the idolatry of deifying the generic meanings of the male images (nouns and pronouns) with their sexist distortions while at the same time not violating the gospel's storyline with its threefold reference expressed by verbs, prepositions, and gerunds. This storyline, which forms the structure of the church's liturgy, conveys the contextual relation of the three triune referents by identifying Who sends Whom into the world, Who is begotten by Whom, Who is conceived by Whom, Who descends from Whom upon Whom, Who is raised from the dead by Whom, ascends to Whom, is now present among us in Whom, and shall come from Whom. Hearers and tellers of the gospel story will recognize which "Who" in each of these instances refers to "the Father," which to Jesus Christ "the Son," and which to the "Holy Spirit." Gerunds, such as "the giving," "the sending," "the being begotten," "the surrendering up," "the dying," "the descending," "the ascending," and "the proceeding" contextualize the identifiable relation of the three persons referred to in the gospel's promissory narration as the one Lord. *In Christian faith the proper name of God is the continuing and unfinished story of the gospel's threefold referentiality with its all inclusive promise of the vindicated dominion of love.* Faithful disbelief is thereby enjoined against any description of God's being, whether metaphysical or figural, whether conventional or revisionary, that violates the contextualized relationality of the threefold referents in the gospel's story and promise. Current debates within the church over the faithfulness of its language for God in worship and doctrine fail in testing the spirits if they do not recognize and account for their positions with regard to this disbelief.

Proposed Disbeliefs

Through attempting to trace the contours of commonly held church teaching regarding the attributes and triunity of God we have in this chapter proposed that affirmations of Christian faith enjoin and entail the following disbeliefs:

1. that God's being is describable in the sense of circumscribable.
2. that God's being is indescribable in the sense of unidentifiable or uncharacterizable.
3. that the being of God is not both the being-given-forth of life in Jesus of Nazareth and the being-that-raises-up this life from the dead.
4. that God's being is the effect of something else.
5. that God's being is unaffected by anything else.
6. that love, as defined with reference to God, is subject to final defeat by any opposition.
7. that any form of domination is of God that is not the dominion of this love.
8. that the God who is confessed as being in Christ and being one with Jesus is a different God from the God of Israel.
9. that what occurs with Jesus is less than God.
10. that God's being is not innately relational.
11. that God's being as Father, Son, and Holy Spirit is tripartite or that there are three Gods.
12. that God's being is a metamorphic series in which God is first one and then another of the triune persons singly in turn but not altogether.
13. that God is God other than in one properly named threefold relationality.
14. that any description of God's being, whether metaphysical or figural, whether conventional or revisionary, is faithful if it violates the contextual relationality of the threefold referents in the gospel's story and promise.

As in the case of any dogmatic claims, these proposed disbeliefs must themselves be tested according to the ten criteria of accountability that have been set forth. Insofar as they are recognized as faithful, a definite course for further understanding and inquiry is marked.

To respond to the argument made at the beginning in the first initial objection, that the ontic descriptions of God found in much dogmatic tradition seem to conflict with the biblical testimonies they purport to affirm, these disbeliefs rule out any idea of God as One whose life can be characterized as introverted detachment. The oneness of God is not to be thought of as a quantitative numerical unit but as a relational unity. Ultimate Reality is not known to faith as a single isolated Ego, self-enclosed, without relationship, but as One whose unity is realized only with Another in a reciprocity of Spirit. The Other with whom God is One in Spirit is the rejected, crucified Other. This means that, contrary to some classical concepts of Necessary Being, God does suffer. But the trinitarian understanding does not deify suffering for its own sake or foster masochism. The rejected, crucified Other is also the resurrected and vindicated Other. As portrayed in the gospel, God not only knows what it is to give one's life in suffering. God knows what it is to suffer the pain of having a loved one suffer. In the reciprocal Spirit, proceeding from and uniting these distinguishable but inseparable sufferings, and relating the Giver of the Only Begotten and the Only Begotten, Christian faith confesses to know in life and death an incorporation into the one dominion of love in Christ which overcomes all opposition.[42]

To recall the case raised in the second objection, that faith can only confess the impact of God, not the being of God as such, there has been no disagreement registered here with the claim that faith only knows God by God's being for us and disposed toward us. But from this it does not follow that the gospel account of the ways God relates to us does not tell also of how the three referents to whom Christian worship ascribes praise as God distinctively relate to each other. We shall have reason to look further at this question of God's triune self-relatedness in chapter 9 on the Holy Spirit. What is communicated through the gospel *pro me* or *pro nobis*, in relation to us, is expressly the threefold referential relationality of God that as storied promise is clearly also *per se* or *a se*, that is, also innately a self-relationality. In this sense at least of keeping on the track of the gospel message, one must grant Karl Rahner's point, which is appropriated by others as well, that "the Trinity in the history and economy of salvation" "is the immanent Trinity," for the reason that confessing how God relates to us in union with the Word and the Spirit necessarily involves confessing God's own threefold self-relation.[43] Any dichotomy between the economy of God's ways with their impact upon us and the ontic reality of God's aseity is hereby rejected. Moral characterization of God's doings involve some ontic characterization of the doer as well. Nevertheless, such description, as the second initial objection rightly emphasizes, can only be drawn from the impact God makes upon us in faith. The being-that-raises-up life in Christ is only known insofar as it is the being-given-forth to us of life in Christ.

To recall the third objection, that the doctrine of the Trinity attempts to deify the language of "Father," "Son," and "Holy Spirit" as irreplaceable male terms for God's being, we have now recognized that generic meanings of "father" and "son" and of masculine pronouns are, according to these disbeliefs, to be repudiated along with all other generic meanings when they are either explicitly or implicitly attributed to God. This third objection rightly calls for an acknowledgment of the destructive consequences of such false witness today in both the church and society.

In chapter 6 we observed that Christian affirmations of faith with regard to the Word of God entail the refusal to believe that the Word of God is equatable with some phenomenal object, or that God's self-communication can be reified in the words of any text. For example, in treating the Lord's Prayer John Calvin writes, "We would not have it understood that we are so bound by this form of prayer that we are not allowed to change it in either word or syllable. . . . Though the words may be utterly different, yet the sense ought not to vary."[44] In this chapter the disbelief of any form of domination that is not the dominion of love, and the disbelief of any description of God's being that violates the contextual relationality of the threefold referents in the gospel's story and promise, combine to provide a framework for assessing what Calvin calls "the sense [that] ought not to vary" of "words that may be utterly different" in ascribing praise to God's triunity.

Churches that maintain the traditional language of Father, Son, and Holy Spirit as closest to the sense of the gospel's referential relationality have the responsibility of discrediting generic meanings of these terms with their sexist consequences and of contextually supplementing these terms to convey the analogy of femaleness and maternity of the Lord who says through the prophet Isaiah, "As a mother comforts her child, so I will comfort you" (Isa. 66:13).[45] Churches that determine it crucial to faithfulness to revise the traditional language of Father, Son, and Holy Spirit and use different words because of consequences of the traditional ascriptions that are perceived to betray the sense of the gospel have the responsibility to find nominative terms that conform to the verbs, prepositions, and gerunds by which the threefold references to God in the gospel are contextually interrelated.[46]

When Julian of Norwich, approximately six centuries ago, wrote of the "motherhood" in God she expressed it precisely by dwelling upon the interrelation of the three Persons:

> I understand three ways of contemplating motherhood in God. The first is the foundation of our nature's creation; the second is his taking of our nature, where the motherhood of grace begins; the third is the motherhood at work. And in that, by the same grace, everything is penetrated, in length and in breadth, in height and in depth without end; and it is all one love.[47]

Revised formulations such as "in the name of God who is the Source of our life in Christ Jesus by the Holy Spirit,"[48] or "in the name of God who through the Word and in the Spirit creates, redeems, and sanctifies,"[49] come near to summarizing the gospel's interrelated threefold referentiality. On the other hand, "in the name of the Unoriginate, and of the Begotten, and of the Procession," though technically accurate, is, as Athanasius held, too abstracted from the gospel story for the service of worship, and the more currently favored substitution, "in the name of the Creator, and of the Redeemer, and of the Sanctifier (or Sustainer)" fails to convey how the three gospel referents themselves are related to one another in the recounting of God's work of creating, redeeming, and sanctifying (or sustaining).

Today the continuing efforts in the churches to test the spirits in seeking the most faithful expression and confession of the being of God prompt a renewed consideration by both linguistic traditionalists and revisionists of what Christian faith refuses to believe.

Chapter 8

JESUS CHRIST

Introduction

In the previous chapter we observed that Christian doctrine speaks of the being of God with reference to what happens *with* Jesus of Nazareth. In the language of the Gospel of John, the Word that in the beginning was "with God and was God" is confessed to have become enfleshed in Jesus (John 1:1). How God's being is faithfully proclaimed as One *with* the Word made flesh in a unity of Spirit is the foremost issue of dispute leading up through Nicaea in 325 to Constantinople in 381 with the resulting affirmation of God's triunity. Overlapping this subject is another traditionally labeled in dogmatic texts as "the person of Jesus Christ." Turning now to this locus, we are led to consider that, in short, Christian doctrine speaks of who the Word made flesh is in terms of what happens *in*, and *to*, and *as the future of* Jesus of Nazareth. These matters of the existence of Jesus Christ in relation to the triunity of God's being come to the fore in those disputes of antiquity leading through the third of the commonly recognized general councils, Ephesus in 431, to the explicit affirmation at Chalcedon in 451 of the doctrine of Christ's so-called two natures.

To the question, "Who is God if Jesus Christ is the Word become flesh?," the result of Nicaea and Constantinople provided the church ecumenical with an answer, "the Trinity." To the overlapping question, "Who then is Jesus Christ if God is triune?," the result of Ephesus and Chalcedon provided an answer, "the Incarnation of the Word as truly God and truly human." This understanding of Christ's person cannot be separated from what is usually dealt with under an additional dogmatic rubric as "the work of Jesus Christ," but most of the discussion of that subject will be reserved for chapter 11, which deals with salvation.

If the doctrinal contours of the two previous chapters have been accurately traced, the picture as mapped is already clear in showing that the primary datum on which all praise of God is focused in the beginning of Christianity is the significance of Jesus of Nazareth. This has to do with the answer of faith given to the formative question that Jesus addresses to his disciples in Mark 8:29, "But who do you say that I am?" On the answer to this question everything else depends, including the answer to the further question, "What do you think of the Christ?" (Matt. 22:42). "He himself is before all things," so the Letter to the Colossians puts it, "and in him all things hold together [*synestēken*, 'have their coherence']" (Col. 1:17).

Despite the many different and sometimes conflicting ways in which the significance of Jesus has been interpreted, there are in church teaching two inescapable factors that are always in some manner to be taken into consideration. One is the *historical factor*. The name "Jesus of Nazareth" is held to refer not to a fictional character but to an actual human being who lived and died at a specific time and geographical location recalled in creedal formulation by the phrase "under Pontius Pilate." Whatever the literary composition and figures of speech in the gospel portrayals, the significance of Jesus is thus always in one instance to be understood as a historical significance. Even so, the extent we are to think of "history" with respect to the person of Jesus as the Christ is one of the disputed questions in christology. The other factor is the *soteriological* or *saving* factor. According to the gospel testimony, Jesus of Nazareth becomes significant to faith as a matter of life and death importance, in an ultimately saving way. The story of what happens concerning him is seen to enable all followers to tell their own life story as a story of hope. In the commonly held teaching of the ecumenical church there is no Christ (*Messiah*, from the Hebrew title, "God's Anointed One") other than this Jesus (a name that means "God saves"). Conversely, Jesus of Nazareth has no significance for faith other than as the ultimately saving Christ.

Thus, when in Christian confession the name "Jesus" is joined with the title "Christ," the reference is to a life span that includes, but also reaches beyond, the first-century individual who once existed *sub Pontio Pilato*. The term "Jesus Christ" encompasses the ultimate destiny of the first-century Jesus' life and death which transcends, by coming both before and after, the time and locality designated as "under Pontius Pilate." When the church confesses that Jesus is the Christ it is confessing the universal reach as well as the historical particularity of the life, death, *and destiny* of Jesus of Nazareth.[1] Christology may be said to be the study of the present-day significance of the church's confession of the life span of a particular Jesus as the ultimate and universal Christ.[2]

That the ultimacy of Jesus is inseparable in the church's faith from his earthly life and death can be seen in the fact that the New Testament writings never speak of the earthly existence of Jesus except in this light. They relate a pattern of events in which what comes to be affirmed in Christian teaching as the Incarnation, the Resurrection, and the Parousia is articulated along with the sayings and doings of the first-century ministry of Jesus. Rubrics such as the Incarnation, the Resurrection, and the Parousia designate, to be most concise, what is said to happen *in* Jesus, *to* Jesus, and *as the future of* Jesus. More exactly, the term "Incarnation" denotes what is affirmed as occurring *in* Jesus' life and death. "For in him the whole fullness of deity dwells bodily" is one expression of this faith (Col. 2:9). Or, as we have noted, "The Word [who in the beginning was with God and was God] became flesh and lived among us" (John 1:14). "Resurrection" denotes what happens *to* Jesus' life and death. "This Jesus God raised up" (Acts 2:32). "Parousia" denotes what *will happen* concerning Jesus. " 'Surely, I am coming soon.' Amen. Come, Lord Jesus!" (Rev. 22:20). These happenings which are presented in the New Testament as essential dimensions of the full life span of Jesus Christ are what is meant here by the use of the term "destiny" along with earthly "life" and "death."

The ultimacy that Christian doctrine attaches to the person of Jesus Christ is based upon the New Testament conviction that the origin and future of all creation is bound up with this life, death, and destiny. What happens exclusively in a specific and particular pattern of events is held to be decisive for what finally happens inclusively to all creation and to all of us as creatures. No human story shall be concluded without reference to this story. Such a conviction may have arisen among some of those who came into contact with Jesus during his earthly ministry, but the Resurrection is the primary reference point from which the apostolic testimony announces this conviction. The entire New Testament is written from a post-Resurrection perspective. Faith knows no life and death of Jesus abstracted from his destiny.

The story of the gospel, as observed in chapter 6, like the story of God's Word throughout the Bible, contains references to events in this world's history as well as references to events that do not fall within the limits of such history. We see this especially in the accounts of Jesus comprising the New Testament christological pattern of events. The movement from Christ's preexistence as the Word in the beginning to the Parousia at the end is narrated as a movement from outside our ordinary boundaries of time and space as historians would define them, into them, and outside them again. This produces problems for christology in understanding how best to interpret the coherence of the reality of Jesus Christ today in terms that are faithful to this complete pattern.

Different tenses and frames of reference are obviously involved in saying that Jesus was with God before Abraham in the beginning, was the only-begotten eternal Word become flesh who came down from heaven, was of David's lineage, was conceived by the Holy Spirit of the Virgin Mary, was born of a woman under the law, was a Jewish rabbi from Nazareth who went about proclaiming God's Kingdom of release to captives, was crucified under Pilate outside the gates of Jerusalem, was dead and buried, descended into hell, was raised and is risen, ascended into heaven, is present in the Spirit, and is seated at the right hand of the Father from whom he will come to judge and make all things new. There are space-time juxtapositions both dissonant and contrapuntal within these various elements of testimony which cannot be dismissed as simply the discordant notes of an outdated cosmology. Yet disagreements arise over how best to understand today the historical and soteriological significance of the past, present, and future of Jesus Christ in heaven and on earth according to these gospeled juxtapositions.

What is generally taken to be indisputable is that, according to the New Testament pattern of events, the life span designated as "Jesus Christ," whether interpreted primarily "from above" or "from below" in its space-time juxtapositions, has to do with a *coming* into the world and with an *overcoming* of the world. Jesus Christ is presented as coming under the conditions of earth, in Luther's words, as "an earthworm in the feedbox of a donkey,"[3] and undergoing death on the Cross. "He came to what was his own" (John 1:11). Jesus Christ is also presented as the One exalted who overcomes the full sway of death that permeates the conditions of this world. "In the world you face persecution. But take courage; I have conquered the world!" (John 16:33). Christology is about this coming and overcoming.

Initial Objections

At the barest minimum Christians by definition must be said to be people who acknowledge the primary importance of Jesus Christ. We are not, therefore, attempting to prove that Jesus has importance for Christian faith or to refute objections that would simply deny any primary importance. Rather, the initial objections that must be considered here are those that have to do with the ways in which this importance is to be understood today in faith. If we sift the major complaints on this subject that have been raised historically and are still being raised we may condense the import of most of them into four categories of objections.

1. *It would seem that if the existence of Jesus Christ is truly historical it cannot be ultimately and universally saving.*

If the role of Christ as Savior is tied too closely to the historical figure of Jesus of Nazareth any saving benefit would appear to be restricted in two respects. Salvation becomes limited either to those who live in the closest historical connection to Jesus or to those who can most identify with the earthly particularities of Jesus.

Historical proximity need not mean that one must have been a first-century contemporary of Jesus. Clearly no church teaching early or late has taught such a view. But if the saving power of Christ is held to be mediated historically (in any manner in which historians would apply that term) then some chronological connection linking benefit to source, or effect to cause, must be affirmed. Those cultures and peoples for whom a chronological continuity with this particular past of first-century Palestine cannot be established historically then become off-limits to whatever has to do with Jesus. This is the net result of doctrines equating apostolic continuity with historical connection — such as an uninterrupted succession of bishops — as well as of doctrines equating, to use Schleiermacher's phrase, "the redeeming influence of Jesus of Nazareth" with historical influence stemming from the actions of the earthly Jesus.

Further, if the historical existence of Jesus is held to be definitive for the image of the Christ to whom, in Paul's words, our natures are "predestined to be conformed" (Rom. 8:29), large segments of humanity would appear to be excluded at the outset.[4] What would a natural resemblance to this Jesus entail? Is maleness to be preferred as more Christ-like than femaleness, celibacy as more Christ-like than sexual fidelity, the Semitic culture of first-century Palestine as more Christ-like than that of any other time or place? There have been teachings answering Yes to each of these questions. Yet it may be argued that within the New Testament itself such concerns are clearly out of context with respect to what the gospel message stresses as important. They do not reflect a faithful regard for Jesus Christ but a reading of him that in Paul's terms is *kata sarka*, a way of thinking that is "according to the flesh," or better in this instance, "according to an alienated perspective." "From now on we regard no one *kata sarka;* even though we once knew Christ *kata sarka*, we know him no longer in that way" (2 Cor. 5:16).

Viewed strictly as a question of historical research and scholarship it is difficult to see how the claim could be supported that the influence of Jesus has always been a benefit. At best historical judgments about matters of ultimate significance remain ambiguous. Who is to deny the persecution, anti-Semitism, colonial missionary imperialism, and varieties of inhumane discrimination that the history of Christianity claiming continuity with Jesus of Nazareth includes? Certainly no reputable historian could make such denials.

On the other hand, if the influence of Jesus Christ is truly saving, as Christian faith affirms, then we cannot relate to it as we relate to inferences arrived at by historical research. If one takes a position like that represented by Søren Kierkegaard, the historical reality of Jesus Christ must be said to be paradoxical in that "the historical fact that God has existed in human form" is essential to faith only as the point of departure or moment for an eternal contemporaneity with Christ that is not dependent upon historical sources or details, nor can it be documented by them. "We see at once," writes Kierkegaard, "that the historical in the more concrete sense is a matter of indifference . . . ; if only the Moment remains, as point of departure for the eternal, the Paradox will be there."[5]

In Christian faith the ultimate soteriological significance of Jesus Christ takes priority over all other interest and importance, and this significance is not reducible to any particular reconstruction of past history. What is ultimately saving is not "the historical in the more concrete sense," as Kierkegaard puts it, but rather, in Paul's words, "the freedom for which Christ has set us free" (Gal. 5:1).

2. *It would seem that the dogmatic interpretation given to Jesus Christ in the classical christological formulations in effect denies that the existence of Jesus Christ is really historical, and, in this respect, fully human.*

Christian orthodoxy in the statement of Chalcedon explicitly affirmed as a matter of faith what, it may strike us today, should have been unquestionable from the start, namely that Jesus Christ is truly human. "The same reality [*homoousion*] as we are with respect to being human [*kata tēn anthrōpotēta*]" is the way Chalcedon expressed it. Yet this explicit affirmation came over a century later than Nicaea's primary confession that Jesus Christ is "the same reality [*homoousion*] as the Father," and the godliness of Jesus retains a priority over the humanity of Jesus in classical christological interpretation. Before declaring the true humanity of Jesus, Chalcedon's statement reaffirms with Nicaea that Jesus is "the same reality [*homoousion*] as the Father," now adding, "with respect to being godly [*kata tēn theotēta*]." The two respects, however, of being human and of being godly are not treated with equal emphasis. The humanity remains secondary to the divinity.

A case can be made to support this claim by pointing to the conceptual terminology of the Greek-speaking theologians who were most influential against their opponents in shaping the elaboration of this christology. In the coming of Jesus the divine Word or *Logos* takes on human flesh. The human flesh of Jesus does not, it is said, take on or assume the divine Word. The divinity, as preexistent *Logos*, is thus given ontic priority over the humanity in these accounts of the person of Jesus Christ. The *hypostasis* (as the Eastern theologians spoke of an "actualization" of reality) of the divine nature of Jesus Christ is held to serve as the bearer of the human nature as well. The human nature as such, unlike the divine, has no *hypostasis* or, in English, "actuality" of its own. Christ's human existence is thus said to be *anhypostatic* (without a *hypostasis*), or better, *enhypostatic* (having its *hypostasis* or actuality in that of the divine nature).[6]

Translated in terms of its logical consequences, it would seem that what is being said with the conceptuality of *hypostasis* is that it is the godly nature of Jesus that actualizes and reveals Jesus' humanity; the humanity of Jesus does not provide the revelatory actualization of deity. Whether or not this result was the intention of the Chalcedonian defenders, the point is that the concentration upon the divinity of Jesus Christ, as the eternal Word [*Logos*] or Second Person [*Hypostasis*] of the Trinity who in the fullness of time becomes incarnate, leads to a disregard of any historical existence of the person of Jesus such as our own. Words of Albert Schweitzer written at the beginning of the twentieth century sum up the objection of many: "That the historic Jesus is something different from the Jesus Christ of the doctrine of the Two Natures seems to us now self-evident."[7]

3. *It would seem that the actual identity of Jesus Christ cannot be determined, and thus this so-called person lacks any reality other than that which we fashion.*

The reference to Albert Schweitzer leads to the consideration of this third category of objections. It is Schweitzer's book, *The Quest of the Historical Jesus*, first published in German in 1906, that provides the best-known study of post-Enlightenment attempts to trim back ancient myth and metaphysics from the figure of Jesus in the pursuit of the person as he actually existed in first-century Palestine. The aim of these so-called liberal lives of Jesus was to provide an alternative to the classical dogmatic formulations of Christian orthodoxy by reconstructing the earthly life of Jesus as responsible historians would reconstruct any other. Yet after completing his sympathetic examination of these attempts, Schweitzer states his conclusion: "It is not given to history to disengage that which is abiding and eternal in the being of Jesus from the historical forms in which it worked itself out, and to introduce it into our world as a living influence. It has toiled in vain at this undertaking."[8]

Unlike the second objection, this third one disputes the claim that the historical factor — as historians define it — is significant for faith in Jesus Christ. More than the first objection, it questions whether the historical significance of Jesus can even be determined. As in the case with Kierkegaard, Schweitzer concludes that what can be known of Jesus through historical investigation is a matter of indifference to Christian faith. "It is not Jesus as historically known . . . who is significant for our time and can help it." It is "not the historical Jesus . . . that . . . overcomes the world."[9] The limitation of historical investigation is that it has no means for arriving at what the early theologians call the *Logos*, what Kierkegaard calls the eternal Moment, and what Schweitzer calls the spirit of Jesus. "Jesus as a concrete historical personality remains a stranger to our time, but His spirit, which lies hidden in His words, is known in simplicity, and its influence is direct."[10]

We encountered in chapter 2 Troeltsch's claim that the Christian religion is not bound to the historical personality of Jesus and Barth's claim that the historian as such cannot arrive at what the Bible refers to as revelation and thus "do justice to Christianity." If the historical existence of Jesus is indeed as inaccessible and irrelevant to faith as these otherwise differing viewpoints insist, it appears that the person of Jesus Christ can be portrayed simply to suit the prevailing self-interests of every community or interpreter. The saving factor becomes no more subject to identification than the historical factor. Rather than humanity being conformed to the image and likeness of God incarnate in Jesus Christ, the truly human One, it would seem rather that Christ is made to conform to our image. The term "Jesus Christ" is defined according to the vagaries of human fantasy in conformity with whatever the current self-understanding of the human interpreters happens to be.

4. *It would seem that the definite articles should be replaced by indefinite ones in referring to the person of Jesus Christ, that Jesus is to be confessed today not as "the" Christ but as "a" Christ.*

The case for this fourth objection is usually made on three grounds: that of tradition, of consequence, and of coherence. By *tradition* what is meant in this instance is the diversity of thought within Christian origins prior to the christological decisions of Nicaea and Chalcedon that set the guidelines of orthodoxy. The appeal to *consequence* inquires into the fruits that result from christological exclusivity. The appeal to *coherence* questions the sense it makes to speak of the one and only Christ in view of the many ways in which this Christ has been represented in various times and cultures throughout Christian history.

It would be difficult to mount a convincing argument that confession of Jesus as "a" Christ rather than as "the" Christ represents tradition that might legitimately be considered apostolic. Following the Johannine use of the term *monogenes* ["only begotten"],[11] the words of both the Apostles' Creed and the Nicene Creed affirm faith in Jesus Christ as the Father's "only Son." Chalcedon in turn speaks of "one and the same Christ, Son, Lord, Only-begotten." Yet pre-Nicene and pre-Chalcedonian christologies were far more fluid than the later catholic orthodoxy.[12] A full fledged ecumenical doctrine of "only-begottenness," in distinction for example from either a Gnostic series of "emanations" or from an Arian subordinationist christology of "first-born creature," awaited the Nicene decisions of the fourth century. The early concept of the *Logos* pervading all reality, a concept with antecedents in pre-Christian thought that was emphasized in the second century by Justin Martyr, may be proposed as offering alternative possibilities to thinking of Jesus as the one and only Christ. Justin himself acknowledged the presence of the *Logos* among certain pagan philosophers of antiquity and among the Hebrew prophets, a position that generally came to be accepted as orthodox.[13]

A modern view that draws upon such reasoning is expressed in the following words by John Hick:

> If, selecting from our Christian language, we call God-acting-towards-mankind the Logos, then we must say that *all* salvation, within all religions, is the work of the Logos and that under their various images and symbols men in different cultures and faiths may encounter the Logos and find salvation. But what we cannot say is that all who are saved are saved by Jesus of Nazareth. The life of Jesus was one point at which the Logos . . . has acted; and it is the only point that savingly concerns the Christian; but we are not called upon nor are we entitled to make the negative assertion that the Logos has not acted and is not acting anywhere else in human life.[14]

The consequences of an exclusivistic christology are of concern not only with respect to the specific issues of salvation and of other religions to which Hick draws attention.[15] An understanding of the necessary ingredients for a contemporary Christian ethic is at stake. Even if the basic outlines of the historical existence of Jesus of Nazareth are agreed to, they do not in themselves provide a sufficient basis for contemporary Christians to make responsible ethical judgments, and it is hypocritical to pretend that they do. The "imitation of Christ" is a deceptive notion if it assumes that the vocation of the Christian is to be a copy of the first-century Jesus. The differences between cultural environments as the social contexts of moral responsibility cannot be ignored. All attempts at such imitation outside of the original environment are inevitably selective. No datum from the past as such embodies the ongoing life of the present and the future. Historical circumstances are never simply duplicated. By appealing to a first-century Jesus as the sole embodiment or incarnation of God's Word, the one and only Messiah or Christ, the church in its history has resisted new insight and opposed new movements of the Spirit that were subversive of popular prejudice and entrenched cultural wrongs.

In addition to both the diversity of tradition within Christian origins, and also the consequences of an exclusivistic christology in church attitudes and teachings regarding salvation, other religions, and the approach to contemporary ethical issues generally, this fourth objection also cites the test of coherence. Even if it is insisted that Jesus of Nazareth must be affirmed as "the one and only" Christ, the only-begotten Son of God incarnate, the representations of Christ in the church have plainly not been "one and only." The biblical testimonies that portray the Messiah or Christ in both the prophetic expectation of the Old Testament and the apostolic remembrance of the New are themselves a composite of literary materials reflective of both the Hebraic and the Hellenistic environments of the ancient world. There is obviously no single uniform portrayal of Jesus Christ identical in all details. Similarly, the subsequent history of Christianity shows how changing cultural influences have continually shaped the interpretations that have been given to the figure of Christ. What then does it mean to speak of Christ as "the one and only"? It is incoherent to maintain that the church in affirming the one incarnate "only-begotten Son" has in practice ever professed anything other than a series of Christs, each image or representation bearing more or less the traits of a family resemblance.

The rejection of the definite article in speaking of Jesus as the Christ or Messiah, and of his person as the sole incarnation of God, would, so Maurice Wiles has argued, not violate Christian faith. "It would still be possible to see Jesus not only as one who embodies a full response of man to God but also as one who expresses and embodies the way of God towards men. . . . The most likely change would be towards a less exclusive insistence on Jesus as *the* way for all peoples and all cultures."[16]

Interpretation

If we examine the faith affirmations of the teachings held in common by most Christian churches regarding the person of Jesus Christ, what disbeliefs do they enjoin and entail? How do these four categories of initial objections look when viewed with the question in mind, What does Christian faith itself *refuse* to believe about Jesus Christ?

In the account given in Acts 5:42 it is written of the apostles that "every day in the temple and at home they did not cease to teach and proclaim Jesus as the Christ [*ton christon Jesoun*]." This verse provides a good starting point from which to proceed because it offers a typical instance of how the three terms "Jesus," "the Christ," and "teaching and proclaiming [*euangelizomenoi*, 'gospeling']" are associated in the church's christological doctrines. Ecumenically considered, Christian faith entails disbelieving any confession of this particular Jesus other than as the universal Christ and any confession of a Christ other than this Jesus. Further, and this cannot be overlooked, it refuses to believe that Jesus as the Christ is significant to faith, either historically or soteriologically, apart from the ongoing apostolic testimony of teaching and proclaiming that in New Testament language is called "gospeling." These refusals may be said to represent three of the Christian faith's most elemental christological disbeliefs. They immediately raise additional questions that lead to the recognition of further disbeliefs and to the further clarification, with respect to objections, of what such refusals do not mean.

Most simply put, what is denoted by referring to the "person" of Jesus Christ is the life span. This life span includes both the earthly existence of Jesus of Nazareth and the ultimate destiny, meaning what comes of this existence, as well. What comes of this existence is proclaimed in the gospel testimonies as "eternal life." "What has come into being in him was life," so the words of the Johannine prologue express it, "and the life was the light of all people" (John 1:4). "The free gift of God," writes the Apostle Paul, "is eternal life in Christ Jesus our Lord" (Rom. 6:23). The life of Jesus Christ as gospeled, therefore, is confessed to be both that of the human Jesus of first-century Palestine and that of God's own eternal life in union with it.

The actual (*hypostatic*) union within this life span of what is of the same reality as God with what is of the same reality as humanity becomes affirmed, in the language of the four adverbs used at Chalcedon, as concurring "unconfusedly [*asygchytōs*], unalterably [*atreptōs*], undividedly [*adiairetōs*], inseparably [*achōristōs*]."[17] While such adverbial reiteration may strike today's reader as mere redundancy, these Chalcedonian adverbs are precisely directed against specific christological positions that were perceived either as mistaking the unity of Christ's two natures by separating them (Nestorianism), or as mistaking the two natures of Christ's unity by fusing them (Eutychianism). The important dogmatic question is what such adverbial reiteration amounts to. I suggest that it amounts to the disbelief of any claim that the reality faithfully confessed as "Jesus Christ" is an amorphous life that has no particular spatio-temporal identity, or is a historically restricted life circumscribed by its particularity in space and time. The life of Jesus Christ is thus affirmed to be both human life and eternal life; but neither the one without the other. And the span of this life is thus affirmed to be both chronologically and geographically locatable "under Pontius Pilate" and also universal in its scope "in heaven and on earth and under the earth" (Phil. 2:10): "And remember, I am with you always" (Matt. 28:20), the same identity, not as a static past or present with no new future, but as the one person or life span "yesterday and today and forever" (Heb. 13:8) that has yet "many things to say" (John 16:12).

Confessed in this manner of speaking about the eternal and the not-yet, the past and the present, heaven and earth and the Kingdom to come, not all dimensions of the reality of Jesus Christ are thus subject to signification in the same time and space frame. Different frames of reference, both with respect to tense and setting, appear in the gospel testimonies. To recall the discussion in chapter 6 of revelatory language as narration and promise, the life span in question is both a life story and a life promised; again, it is not one without the other. There is a story of Jesus Christ, but the destiny of Jesus Christ as narrated in this story spans life that is promised but has not yet taken place. "Beloved, we are God's children now; what we will be has not yet been revealed. What we do know is this: when he is revealed, we will be like him, for we will see him as he is" (1 John 3:2). The dimensions of Jesus Christ that do not yet appear are historically and soteriologically significant to faith as the life promised that is inseparable from the life story in the union of the past, present, and future reality that Christian faith affirms as the one "Jesus Christ."

The union of this narrative particularity and promissory universality in the person of Jesus Christ has continued to pose hard questions for theological interpretation in the history of the church. Numerous accounts reflecting varied modes of thought are given of this so-called paradox of the two natures, this alleged concomitance of frames of reference that are at once in their scope so bafflingly exclusive and so all-inclusive in tense and setting. Yet before looking more specifically at what Christian doctrine basically confesses regarding the Incarnation, and regarding what is gospeled as happening not only *in* Jesus, but *to* Jesus (the Resurrection), and *as the future of* Jesus (the Parousia) as well, we can already recognize the primary buoy marker in Christian faith for the determination of its christological disbeliefs. Proscribed is any spirit or claim that denies the exclusively all-inclusive union within the one life span of Jesus Christ of life that is truly human with its particularity and life that is universally and eternally God's own. Now we must explore further where this marker of particular universality, or exclusive inclusivity, leads.

1. The Incarnation

It is in the testimony of Good Friday, and not only of Christmas (and certainly not of romanticized nature), that Christian faith in the Incarnation takes its bearings. The witness of Rachel's refusal, as Luther saw, points to the connecting link between the Nativity and the Cross. Not only is the Incarnation a coming of God's Word to birth in the flesh of Jesus Christ. It is, in language used by Paul, a coming into the flesh of slavery unto death, "even death on a cross" (Phil. 2:8). Paul stresses to its full extremity the depths of this coming in his statement to the

Corinthians — still as shocking if one thinks about it as it must have sounded in the first century — that Christ who "knew no sin" was even "made to be sin" (2 Cor. 5:21). So scandalous is the way of Christ's enfleshment that Joseph, to whom Mary is betrothed, is depicted in the Matthean nativity account as resolving to divorce himself from the risk of shame that attends it. Precisely because he is just, we are told, Joseph resolves to divorce Mary quietly to avoid the shame of the new life which the Lord God is conceiving to bring into this world (Matt. 1:18–25). Christ comes, so the gospel proclaims it, where even the just cannot conceive that it is proper for God to be.

"Conceived by the Holy Spirit, born of the Virgin Mary" is the way that the Apostles' Creed expresses it. "Who, for us humans and for our salvation, came down from heaven, and was incarnate by the Holy Spirit of the Virgin Mary, and was made human" is the expanded statement of the Nicene Creed. Trivialization amounting to prurient interest attaches itself to this affirmation if it is abstracted from its gospel context, and if thought is not given to discerning the disbeliefs that the faith being affirmed entails. Such an abstraction from the gospel context amounts to what Paul calls *kata sarka* ["according to the flesh"] thinking; that is, interpretation that is irreconcilable with the reality of Jesus Christ (2 Cor. 5:16–19). Discernment of faithful disbelief, as we noted in chapter 3, requires what the Johannine author calls *en sarki* ["in the flesh"] thinking. In Pauline language a similar meaning, in its theological implications, is expressed as *kata stauron* ["according to the Cross"] thinking.[18] The difficulty and task of dogmatic testing is to interpret the significance of the creedal affirmations in a manner that is, to use this shorthand, *en sarki* (or *kata stauron*), but not *kata sarka*. Equally proscribed by the gospel context are any confessions of Jesus Christ that are not *en sarki* and any confessions that are *kata sarka*. This distinction becomes crucial for dogmatics when we consider the significance of the Incarnation.

As mentioned, the New Testament accounts of Jesus are all written from a post-Resurrection perspective. It is only in view of what happens *to* Jesus' life and death that the New Testament speaks of what happens *in* the conception of Jesus' life and death, including his preexistence and birth. His overcoming, that is to say, discloses where he comes from. Christological categories arise because ordinary anthropological categories prove inadequate to convey Jesus' destiny, but they in turn give false witness to this destiny if they serve to deny his anthropological reality as truly human.

Christians disagree over how "literally" to interpret the Virgin Birth. Is "conceived by the Holy Spirit, born of the Virgin Mary" the same kind of statement as "suffered under Pontius Pilate, was crucified, dead, and buried"? Or is its significance more like the clause "ascended into heaven, sits on the right hand of God the Father Almighty"? Plainly the time and space frame of reference differs somewhat in each of these three clauses. Here is an instance in which the disbeliefs of a Christian confession may be clearer to state than the belief. I will propose for consideration seven of them.

First, Christian faith refuses to believe that the life of Jesus Christ is not fully human. This faith is confessed by refusing to believe any claim that would make his birth (as well as his death) not fully human. The heresy of docetism, of denying full humanity to the reality of Jesus Christ, ranks as arguably the oldest and most persistent christological heresy in the church.

Second, Christian faith refuses to believe that the life of Jesus Christ is ultimately subject to any other life. The conviction underlying the affirmation "conceived by the Holy Spirit," when taken in the context of the gospel, expresses the faith that every spirit is subject to the one Spirit that is the source of Christ's being. The Power that puts the future into the hands of this crucified human being is no human power. From his prophesied advent, annunciation, birth, and presentation in the Temple to his betrayal, crucifixion, and burial in a tomb the life span of Jesus Christ is graphically portrayed in scripture as being delivered over into human hands. With the Resurrection the proclamation is that all things are now subject to his hands, and the birth as well as the passion and death of Jesus are now seen in this light. Here is said to be the one birth and death of a human subject to which all other human births and deaths are subject.

Third, Christian faith refuses to believe that the workings of the Holy Spirit in bringing forth life are subject to documentation by historical methods, or any other. In a biblical perspective the term *Spirit* as applied to God resists all human attempts to define the Deity as an objectifiable or certifiable reality. We shall return to this point in chapter 9. The Spirit is said to move where it will, and like the wind one may hear the sound of it but can never observe where it comes from or where it goes: "So it is with everyone who is born of the Spirit" (John 3:8). This should be enough to clue us in that the working of the Holy Spirit in the conception of Jesus Christ defies all obstetrical definition. The ways of the Spirit cannot be dissected in terms of any of the mechanisms of this world, viewed either as nature or as history. The notion of a god mating sexually with a human being, or, as the more pious musings within Christianity have expressed it, impregnating her through the ear, is *kata sarka* thinking alien to the import of the gospel witness. It leads to such prurient trivialization as some of the scholastic speculations over whether Mary's virginity remained physically intact *post partem*, during and after as well as before the birth of Jesus from her womb.

Fourth, confession of the faith that Jesus Christ "was conceived by the Holy Spirit" entails the refusal to believe that male prowess, sexual or otherwise, is the source and cause of salvation. The importance of this disbelief has not been lost on some who have suffered the personal and social consequences of an undeniably inhumane male dominance. Sojourner Truth's address to the Akron Woman's Rights Convention in 1851 offers a prime example. To a male clergyman who announced that women cannot have equal rights with men because Christ was not a woman, former slave Sojourner Truth, described by one eyewitness as rising "with outstretched arms and eye of fire," responded, "Where did your Christ come from? Where did your Christ come from? From God and a woman. Man had nothing to do with him."[19] Interestingly, by contrast, in another cultural context, that of late medieval Christendom, Martin Luther found it crucial, in combating what he saw to be an idolatrous works righteousness implicit in the church's manipulation of the cult of Marian devotion, to call for recognition of the disbelief that Mary's virtue is the source and cause of salvation. "For not her humility but God's *regard* is to be praised."[20] This regard, of which the Magnificat in Luke 1:48 speaks, Luther associates with God's gracious promise to redeem Israel. "This same promise," he writes, "the Mother of God here lauds and exalts above all else, ascribing this work of the Incarnation of God solely to the undeserved promise of divine grace, made to Abraham."[21]

Fifth, the life that is "conceived by the Holy Spirit" is also confessed in the words of the Apostles' Creed to be "born of the Virgin Mary." By this affirmation Christian faith in the first instance disavows belief that the coming of Jesus to Mary is merely one in appearance and not in bodily birth. *Born* is the term receiving the initial emphasis. In the writings of Paul, which provide some of the earliest testimony of the gospel that we have in the New Testament, there is no mention of the virginity of Mary (indeed only in the nativity accounts of Matthew and of Luke is Mary, with reference to Isaiah 7:14, explicitly described as "a virgin, *hē parthenos*"). Yet the childbirth is twice stressed by Paul in stating that, "when the fullness of time had come, God sent his Son, born of a woman, born under the law" (Gal. 4:4). "Born of the virgin Mary" is but the beginning of a series of antidocetic affirmations in the Apostles' Creed entailing the disbelief of a phantom Christ, one in human semblance only, removed, as the Gnostics and Marcionites taught with their false understanding of spirit, from the materiality of physical existence. A fleshless Jesus would not be born of an actual woman's body, would not suffer under an actual ruler in history, be crucified at an actual time and place, die at an actual hour, and be buried in an actual tomb. The antidocetic character of these creedal affirmations culminates in the summary confession that Jesus Christ descended into the full extremity of death, into hell itself.

The naming of "Mary," although not a historically documentable figure in the same sense as Pontius Pilate, serves even further to underscore the professed historical facticity of this birth. Entailed here as well is the disbelief that Jesus Christ, while said to be "born," is only born figuratively speaking, as some mythical or metaphysical idea engendered by the fantasies of the religious imagination. The birth of Jesus from Mary's womb is not of the recurrent order of, say, the birth of Springtime from the womb of Mother Nature, or, for that matter, the birth of an infant New Year as the progeny of Father Time. It is not the same as a birth of consciousness within the heart. There is a nonmetaphorical factuality to the "birth" which is made "incarnate by the Holy Spirit of the Virgin Mary."

A sixth disbelief is enjoined when the title of "the Virgin" is used for Mary in the apostolic church to confess that her motherhood is the "bearer of God" (*Theotokos*). What once again is disbelieved by the affirmation of this title is that a human capacity originates the life span of Jesus Christ that is born of Mary. Physiological speculation beyond the canonical context intrudes upon the eschatological, or ultimate, mystery here, and thus must be rejected as thinking that is *kata sarka*. Insofar as this speculation results from the assumption that sex as such is evil, and virginity is a nobler state, or that procreation is the carrier of sin as a genetic taint, it is to be recognized as falsehood, as we shall consider in chapter 10, according to the Christian doctrine of creation. But if conservative "literalists" generally are tempted in the direction of physiological *kata sarka* falsehood, liberal rejections of the Virgin birth for their part sometimes tend toward falsely spiritualized docetic denials of the *en sarki* reality. In this respect both positions fail to recognize the disbeliefs entailed by the affirmations.

The key term of coherence for an incarnational understanding of the affirmation "born of the Virgin Mary" when considered in the context of the gospel testimonies, as Luther saw, is promise. In these testimonies it is not a question of determining the limits of what is, either naturally or supernaturally, genetically possible *kata sarka*. Rather, the emphasis is upon God's promise as that which originates life *en sarki* that is not subject to the flesh. This is where the importance is placed in biblical prophecy. Mary's song blesses the Lord God for the power now actualized in showing merciful remembrance of what has been promised "to Abraham and to his descendants for ever" (Luke 1:54–55). Recalled by her Magnificat is the birth of Isaac to Sarah and Abraham that issues from a promise of pregnancy when all thought of physiological possibility is, so the accounts in Genesis make explicit, quite laughable (Gen. 18:9–15, 21:1–7). Hence both naturalistic and supernaturalistic methods of explanation, when applied to the accounts of the Virgin Birth either to refute or to defend possibilities of human parthenogenesis, prove to be incommensurate with the gospel message itself.

As a seventh disbelief, therefore, we may observe that faith in Jesus Christ as "born of the Virgin Mary" is not a belief about genetic possibilities. It is a refusal to believe that human existence is the actualization of its own possibility or potential in the present rather than the actualization or "coming to pass" of the future that God promises to the present. The difference, as the biblical prophets saw, between a promise to the present and a possibility of the present is that a promise carries a commitment for a future into the present. This has implications for a theological understanding of what constitutes "history." There is, biblically speaking, no history of the past except from the perspective of a future that is committed to the present.[22] This point brings us to the heart of the gospel's proclamation of the incarnate Christ's destiny as the Resurrection.

2. The Resurrection

The transition between the death and the resurrection of Jesus Christ in the affirmations of the Apostles' Creed occurs in the clause "he descended into hell." Although the date of the addition of this clause is later than some others in the Creed, it serves to point up the essential message of both the coming and the overcoming that the gospel attributes to Jesus Christ. Here the frame of reference obviously shifts from the earth of space and time which locates the crucifixion under Pilate, but it does not become otherworldly in the sense of having no relation to this earth. On the one hand the extremity of the suffering and death of the Crucified One is emphasized. The descent *ad inferna* affirms that the reality of Jesus Christ extends in scope to the uttermost depths of human misery and alienation. By this affirmation Christian faith refuses to believe that there is any earthly suffering or betrayal of the good that is off-limits to Jesus' suffering and betrayal by sinners. There is no dimension of death and loss that his reality does not encompass.

> Never a burden that He doth not carry,
> Never a sorrow that He doth not share.[23]

On the other hand the exaltation of the Resurrected One is emphasized, for the descent into hell also affirms that all creation, past as well as present and future, is invaded by the life of God in Jesus Christ. By this affirmation Christian faith refuses to believe that Jesus Christ's relating to others is confined by earthly time and space or any other circumstance. Wherever human destinies reach, there the destiny of Jesus meets them. In some doctrinal traditions the humiliation of the descent as the final act of the Crucifixion is stressed. In other doctrinal traditions the exaltation of the descent as the first act of the Resurrection is stressed. But both elements are involved in the faith here expressed. Thus the gospel is seen as "proclaimed even to the dead" (1 Pet. 4:6): "For Christ also suffered for sins once for all, the righteous for the unrighteous, in order to bring you to God. He was put to death in the flesh, but made alive in the spirit, in which also he went and made a proclamation to the spirits in prison, who in former times did not obey" (1 Pet. 3:18–20).

The resurrected life "in the spirit" is not affirmed as a disembodied life; in this respect the Incarnation is not abrogated by the Resurrection. It is only, as we have noted, in light of the Resurrection that the gospel speaks of Jesus' preexistence, birth, and death. Despite the variety of ways in which the different writers of the New Testament portray the Risen Christ there is a primacy of witness to the Resurrection. Thus Paul, whose testimony contains no nativity accounts, writes to the Corinthians, "If Christ has not been raised, then our proclamation has been in vain and your faith has been in vain" (1 Cor. 15:14). What is confessed is that in the person of Jesus Christ all that opposes creation is defeated, including the final enemy of death itself. The humiliated Servant is in reality the exalted Lord. The One who was delivered over into the hands of sinners is now revealed to faith as the One who holds all sinners in his hands. The writer of 1 Peter speaks of "the resurrection of Jesus Christ, who has gone into heaven and is at the right hand of God, with angels, authorities, and powers made subject to him" (1 Pet. 3:21–22).

Dogmatics continually is faced with the problem and task of discerning how the Resurrection is faithfully to be interpreted in a way that is *en sarki* but not *kata sarka*. As one might expect, theological accounts of the bodily Resurrection of Jesus, as well as the bodily Incarnation, do not always agree, but there can be no denial of the fact that Christian doctrine teaches a "bodily" Resurrection.[24]

"But someone will ask, 'How are the dead raised? With what kind of body [*sōmati*] do they come?' " (1 Cor. 15:35). By questioning "the kind of body" in which the dead are raised these words of Paul to the Corinthians contain acknowledgment of the continuity of the Incarnation in the Resurrection. It is interesting in this passage that while Paul addresses such a questioner as "Fool!" he then proceeds to give serious attention to an answer (1 Cor. 15:36–53). Three attempts are traditionally given in dogmatics to explicating the "how" of the Resurrection. Being raised from the dead is said to be analogous to a seed that must die, or germinate, before it can grow: "But God gives it a body as he has chosen, and to each kind of seed its own body" (1 Cor. 15:38). The analogy is also made to the change between sleeping and being awakened from sleep: "But in fact Christ has been raised from the dead, the first fruits of those who have fallen asleep" (1 Cor. 15:20). More central to the gospel testimonies than either of these similes, however, is the proclamation of Jesus' Resurrection as the ultimate future that is coming. This is what the expression "first fruits [*aparchē*]" emphasizes. What happens in the Resurrection of Jesus Christ is the embodiment of that future which is promised to creation. It is in this sense the embodiment of a future that is both universal and eschatological. Paul refers to such embodiment as the "spiritual body [*sōma pneumatikon*]" given in the resurrection of the dead and distinguishes it from the "physical body [*sōma psychikon*]" of existence prior to death. This "spiritual body" cannot be known *kata sarka* as a possibility of the "physical." Flesh and blood according to the terms of the "physical body" can neither inherit nor reveal it. But resurrected life in the Spirit is not for this reason to be thought of as incorporeal. In this respect, the Resurrection does not render void the Incarnation; it too is destiny that is *en sarki*, in the sense of embodied, but not according to the conditions that pertain prior to the final overcoming of death and all opposition to creation.

To test for witness to the Resurrection that is faithful confession *en sarki* and thus not *kata sarka* requires in this instance as well that attention be given to the disbeliefs involved. Discussion of some of these disbeliefs will more properly arise when we come to the topic of "the work of Christ" as it pertains to the doctrinal subjects of salvation and humanity. Here the area of doctrine before us concerns "the person of Christ" seen in terms of what Christian faith refuses to believe in its affirmation of the Resurrection as the destiny of Jesus.

The canonical context of the expression "third day" with reference to Jesus' rising from the dead recalls words of the prophecy of Hosea: "Come, let us return to the Lord; for it is he who has torn, and he will heal us; he has struck down, and he will bind us up. After two days he will revive us; and on the third day he will raise us up, that we may live before him" (Hos. 6:1–2). Paul passes on the oral tradition delivered to him that Christ "was raised on the third day in accordance with the [Hebrew] scriptures" (1 Cor. 15:4). According to Luke's account in Acts of Peter's testimony, "They put him to death by hanging him on a tree; but God raised him on the third day and allowed him to appear" (Acts 10:39–40). Likewise in the Gospel of Luke we read of the risen Jesus saying to the disciples, "Thus it is written, that the Christ is to suffer and to rise from the dead on the third day" (Luke 24:46). Emphasis upon "the third day" both incorporates the prophetic claim that it is *God's* action to raise the stricken on the third day, and it equally serves to maintain the particularity of the raising of the crucified, dead, and buried Jesus. The life of Christ as resurrected, while not subject to the conditions of the "physical body," is nevertheless affirmed as neither a timeless nor amorphous generality.

From this we may recognize two entailed disbeliefs. Christian faith refuses to believe that the Resurrection involves a loss of particular identity. Christian faith refuses to believe that the Resurrection is subject to the conditions of physical nature. Neither as a recurrent rite of spring nor as the resuscitation of a corpse is the *en sarki* reality of the risen Christ faithfully confessed. Theories that speak of the immortality of the soul, and by so doing posit either a deathless element in human existence that has a capacity of its own nature to evade death, or an objective immortality with loss of subjective identity, are thus shown to be contrary to Christian faith.[25]

Interpreters disagree as to the significance of references to the empty tomb.[26] Strictly speaking there are no such references to the tomb's emptiness in the New Testament, although it can be argued that some are definitely implied. The Four Gospels provide our only sources here, for they alone tell of the women's visit to the sepulchre at daybreak following the sabbath.[27] What is explicit in these passages is that the resurrected body of the Christ is said not to be in the tomb in which his crucified body had been buried. The burial cloths do not contain the bodily reality of Jesus. "When they went in, they did not find the body" (Luke 24:3). We may assume that Luke here means that the women did not find a body of any sort. Yet a *kata sarka* trivialization of this gospel testimony results from speculation in terms of contemporary physics about what constitutes a resurrected body. This preoccupation has sometimes led to arguing that the reality of the Resurrection is in principle either confirmable or falsifiable by the absence or presence of Jesus' physical remains. Can one speak without self-contradiction of a fully human body and yet say that in death it leaves no physical remains? From a standpoint of contemporary physics what would be said to qualify as physical remains? Are tests for possible fingerprints from an earthly lifetime and chemical analyses of the wood of the cross (not to mention such once reputed relics as the imprint left by a corpse on the Shroud of Turin) to be classified as the traces and residue of an earthly body? Are all of these physical data to be thought of as comprising elements of the corpse of Jesus that is resuscitated in the Resurrection? If not, does this suggest that there is merely a quantitative difference between fingerprints or chemical residues as bodily remains and skeletal remains? We can see how this sort of speculation if pursued to its logical conclusions quickly results theologically in a *reductio ad absurdum*. Surely, according to the import of the gospel witness, the Risen Christ is not to be found through any such approaches of carbon dating or the verification of phenomena by the physical sciences. Since no relics are known to exist, the arguments are purely hypothetical anyhow. But they also represent a credulity contrary to the entailed disbeliefs of the gospel. Flesh and blood as the *sōma psychikon*, to use Paul's terms, neither inherits nor reveals the resurrected *sōma pneumatikon*. The recognition of the Christian refusal to believe that the Resurrection is subject to the conditions of physical nature rules out all interpretations based upon the idea of a resuscitation of a corpse.

But some interpreters who do not argue for the resuscitation of the corpse of Jesus nevertheless contend that the bodily resurrection of Jesus is denied if any elements of the physical body of Jesus are assumed to have remained. In their view the mere assumption that in theory there might have been physical remains amounts to a denial not only of the gospel writers' intent but of the *en sarki* or somatic identity of the risen Christ. Jesus becomes risen only as a datum of consciousness in the existence of his followers. These critics who reject both conservative fundamentalism and liberal existentialism propose a view that is not of a corpse's resuscitation to its former physicality, which they agree represents *kata sarka* thinking, but rather of its transformation without remainder of its former physicality, which they hold to be an understanding that is properly *en sarki:*

> Make no mistake: if He rose at all
> it was as His body;
> if the cells' dissolution did not reverse, the molecules reknit, the
> amino acids rekindle,
> the Church will fall.[28]

In this understanding, however, the physical body, while not itself resuscitated but instead miraculously transformed into a spiritual body, still cannot be said to have left any remains that might have "corrupted in the tomb."[29] The difficulty with the theological coherence of this transformational logic is that it assumes that the fact of the existence of physical remains would indeed have the power to falsify the Resurrection. But this position, it is plain, disregards the refusal of faith to believe that the destiny of Jesus as risen is subject to the conditions of physical nature, either, we may now add, as a source of possible falsification as well as of confirmation.

Yet the reality of the Resurrection is not confessed *en sarki* unless the actual conditions of physical nature are themselves understood to be subject to the destiny of Jesus:

> The stone is rolled back, not papier-mache,
> not a stone in a story,
> but the vast rock of materiality that in the slow
> grinding of time will eclipse for each of us
> the wide light of day.[30]

"He ascended into heaven, and sits at the right hand of God the Father Almighty [or simply, 'the Father']" is the way the two ecumenical creeds express this. In the earliest traditions the Resurrection and the Ascension are considered part of the one event of Christ's exaltation. Only Luke with his concern for the sequence of events places the Ascension forty days after the Resurrection: "As they were watching, he was lifted up, and a cloud took him out of their sight" (Acts 1:9). Here is a typical instance of what Rudolf Bultmann defines as a "mythical" expression of faith. A spatial description is used to indicate transcendence.[31] But not all Ascension language in the New Testament is spatial, and none of it obviously assumes the same conditions that science would define today as space. To "go up" in this instance refers primarily to status and not to spatial location. In the biblical context reference to a cloud often serves to denote God.[32] "Far above all rule and authority and power and dominion, and above every name that is named, not only in this age but also in the age to come" is the way the writer of Ephesians describes God's raising of Jesus Christ (Eph. 1:21). In this instance it is not a meteorological phenomenon or a defiance of the pull of gravity that marks the Ascension but a defiance of the sway of death. Yet death's sway is not viewed as otherworldly in the sense of unearthly, nor is its defiance. Neither this age nor that which is to come is depicted as a state of affairs devoid of the presence of governing powers. Jesus is not said to rise in relation to thin air. The exaltation is not a levitation. The *en sarki* reality of the Resurrection is the vindication of the will and way of Jesus Christ precisely in relation to all existing power structures, and not in disregard of them.

The understanding of corporeality or "spiritual body" as a governance of vindication, a bringing of all "rule and authority and power and dominion and name" into subjection, is emphasized in the creedal affirmation of the Risen Christ's session at the right hand of God the Father. Recapitulated here against all false spiritualizations is the primary category provided by Hebrew messianic prophesy for interpreting the significance of the Incarnation: "Authority [government] rests upon his shoulders" (Isa. 9:6). The confirmation of this *en sarki* reality of Jesus Christ is proclaimed in the message of the Resurrection: "The kingdom of the world has become the kingdom of our Lord and of his Christ, and he will reign forever and ever" (Rev. 11:15). Influential among New Testament writers in this connection are the words of Psalm 110:1, usually thought in their origin to apply to a royal coronation, "The Lord says to my lord, 'Sit at my right hand, until I make your enemies your footstool.'" To sit at the "right hand" of a ruler is to share in the power and sovereignty of this ruler. Christian faith, by affirming that the risen and ascended Christ sits at the right hand of "the maker of heaven and earth" commits itself to the disbelief of any confession of the transcendent destiny of Jesus Christ that does not have to do with actual governance in all its forms of this-earthly, as well as heavenly, power relations and jurisdictional authority.

To be sure, this governance of Christ's vindication is indeed said to be "not from this world" (John 18:36), but only in respect to its derivation and, so to speak, base of operations. Its exercise is scripturally depicted precisely in relation to what is happening on the same earth in which Herod and Pilate issue commands. Thus Christ's ruling and overruling cannot rightly be thought of as otherworldly in its field of operations. In a biblical perspective heaven is held to have much more reality in connection with earth than is suggested in the ways we generally hear the word *heaven* spoken today. The "vast rock of materiality," as the words of Updike's verse put it, is not evaded by an ascent into heaven. Such an ascent sets the actual parameters for social realism according to the gospel. To sit at the right hand of "the maker of heaven and earth" is not to be absent now from the affairs of this earth on sabbatical leave, as it were, in some never-never land beyond the sunset. Instead, it is to be present in the sense that imminence may be said to be a form of presence that brings both incarnate immanence and resurrected transcendence to bear materially upon current affairs. "At hand" is a term used in the New Testament to express this imminence. In the Gospels of Matthew and Mark it figures prominently in introducing the accounts of Jesus' preaching and teaching: "Repent, for the kingdom of heaven is at hand" (Matt. 4:17); "The time is fulfilled, and the kingdom of God is at hand; repent, and believe in the gospel" (Mark 1:15). Paul, referring to the risen Christ, uses the same term in writing to the Philippians, "The Lord is at hand [*engys*]" (Phil. 4:5). The presence of that coming future which is proclaimed as "at hand" is conveyed in Christian faith by denoting Jesus Christ's destiny as the Parousia.

3. The Parousia

The ascended Lord who is at God's right hand is confessed in faith now to be "at hand" — but not in hand. "From thence he shall come to judge the living and the dead" is how the Apostles' Creed expresses this. For Christian faith the "person" or life span of Jesus Christ includes the coming to pass of a future destiny as well.

We shall focus particularly upon this doctrinal subject when we discuss issues involved in Christian eschatology, or "last things," in chapter 14. Then we will turn to the question of the soteriological significance of the coming of Jesus Christ as a "judgment" of the living and the dead and inquire into the faithful disbeliefs of that part of the Christian credo that speaks of "the life of the world to come." To conclude this chapter on the person of Jesus Christ it remains for us to ask in what respects the life span of Jesus Christ, as we have traced it, exhibits the reality of "history."[33]

If a governance through the Cross is to be understood as now constituting the resurrected body of Christ this is not an embodiment of the same age that deals death to Jesus, but of the promised age to come. As such it is only realized by faith as a "coming," which is most simply what the Greek word *parousia* means. The happening suggested is that of a yet to be completed arrival upon the scene that already is changing the scene. Having no place among powers that presently can command death but not life, it eventuates by making a new place. A coming or *parousia* that has no place in prior circumstances but that eventuates as a new place of different circumstances is what in New Testament language is also called an *apocalypse*. We must say more about apocalyptic motifs later. Here we will only observe that the term *apocalypse* is characteristically used in scripture to designate both the constituting and the disclosing to faith of a new and still generally secret future state of affairs, revealing the real world now to be not what seems to be publicly in place but what currently is coming to take place. I deliberately say "what is *coming* to take place" rather than "what is *going* to take place" because the scriptural emphasis is usually upon a more immediate sense of the future's presently impending reality.

The author of 2 Thessalonians, for example, writes of "when the Lord Jesus is apocalypsed from heaven" (2 Thess. 1:7). The Resurrection of Jesus Christ that is confessed as having already happened is also confessed as not yet an established vindication universally evident throughout creation. Its reality still goes unrecognized by all powers at enmity with it which presume to rule the present age on other terms as yet unmindful of their footstool status. The public overcoming of all opposition to the life crucified in Jesus Christ is thus not evident *kata sarka*, or according to what Paul refers to apocalyptically as "the present form of this world [that] is passing away" (1 Cor. 7:31).

Understood in this apocalyptic manner, what aspects of the life span of Jesus are to be labeled "history"? This question, about which so much has been written in modern christology in examining what is meant by such terms as *historical fact, historical consciousness* or *perspective*, and *historical process*, cannot be addressed without giving due regard to two primary christological disbeliefs.

In the first instance, Christian faith refuses to believe that the life of Jesus Christ does not involve a fully human earthly existence in the particularities of time and place and environment designated as "under Pontius Pilate." This means that any confession of Jesus Christ as One whose human ancestry is not from the Jews and of the lineage of Israel's David is proscribed.

Christian faith equally refuses to believe that this life of Jesus Christ exists other than in union with the destiny of God's eternal life happening in it, to it, and as its future. This means that Jesus' earthly existence, just as in the case of every one of us, has its actuality only as its particular individual destiny comes to pass. But it also means that, unlike the case of every one of us, the life that is subject to death in Jesus Christ becomes actual through every power of death universally becoming subject to it. For this, the gospel testifies, is Christ's destiny. This concomitance of crucified and risen life coming to pass in the events of the Cross is what is proclaimed by the gospel and attested in the ongoing community of faith as the unique actuality of Jesus Christ. Christian faith refuses to believe that the life of Jesus *as the Christ* actually exists other than as this concomitance.

I have intentionally reiterated the words *actuality* and *actually* in the last two sentences in order to call attention to three different ways of thinking about "what actually is" that figure in modern christological disputes over what may be said to constitute "history" as far as the life, death, and destiny of Jesus Christ is concerned. One of these ways has already been mentioned. It is the influence of the classical Greek theologians' employment of the word *hypostasis* in the fourth and fifth centuries.[34] Another way follows from the definition of history as *wie es eigentlich gewesen ist* ["what actually happened"] made famous by the German philosopher and historian Leopold von Ranke in the nineteenth century.[35] The third is the apocalyptic perspective of the gospel testimony to Jesus Christ's life as incarnate, risen, and coming. Each of these ways represents a purported reading of reality as it actually is and is intended by its adherents as a reality description.

While the Greek word *hypostasis* carries a range of meanings in antiquity, it may be said most characteristically to represent a manner of speaking about that which is believed to be actual, the way something really is, that of which one can be confident. The introduction of the Letter to the Hebrews, for example, refers to God's Son as bearing the glory and imprint of God's *hypostasis* (Heb. 1:3) The Cappadocians for their part paved the way for ecumenical Christianity in the fourth century to think of God's triune being as one reality [*mia ousia*] realized in three actualizations [*treis hypostaseis*]. Following upon this usage, Cyril of Alexandria and his supporters in the fifth century influenced the Council of Chalcedon to think of the concurrence of what is human and what is divine in the incarnation of the Word, said to be the Second Hypostasis (or in Latin, the Second Person), as a "hypostatic union." Such a union is thus confessed to be the actuality of the person of Jesus Christ. In affirming the hypostatic union of the two natures of Jesus Christ Christian faith logically commits itself to disbelieving that either nature may be said to be actual apart from the other. This is what the four Chalcedonian adverbs, "unconfusedly, unalterably, undividedly, and inseparably," serve to make emphatic. Admittedly, debate over this disbelief continues, as has been acknowledged in the second initial objection of this chapter, and we will come back to it.

When the term *history* is defined in Leopold von Ranke's often quoted expression as *wie es eigentlich gewesen ist*, "what actually happened," certain stipulations are imposed upon the definition of what may be called an "actual happening." What actually happens is now defined as that which comes to pass on the earthly scene and occupies a documentable place within the space and time continuum of this earth. Some historians today would further refine von Ranke's definition by adding "and is recountable in a story." Acknowledging that all attempts to recount "what actually happened" presuppose the interests and selectivity of the interpreter, this commonly held modern viewpoint nevertheless aims to tell of human events that permit of publicly accessible evidence to document their reputed occurrence within the nexus of space and time.[36] Actuality, as defined in this instance, thus becomes synonymous with historical factuality or facticity. Stories that are not factual in von Ranke's sense of the term may be "true to life" in profound respects, as in the case of religious myths or great works of fiction, but they are not classifiable as history because they do not meet the rules used for defining "what actually happened."

By refusing to believe that the life span of Jesus Christ is not fully human, or did not involve an actual childbirth from Mary or death under Pilate, Christian teaching does affirm that the reality of Jesus Christ includes some historical factuality of first-century existence. In most cases this facticity is what is usually meant by references to "the historical Jesus." By this definition, it is plain to see, all that comprises the destiny of Jesus Christ does not qualify as "history" because it does not qualify as documented fact confined to the nexus of space and time.

In affirming the Parousia of Jesus Christ, Christian faith acknowledges yet another reading, an apocalyptic reading, of "what actually happens" that differs in significant respects from both the hypostatic and the historically factual reality descriptions. In this third perspective what comes to pass as the reality of Jesus Christ includes not only what is already in place, as it were, either as a fixed "union of two natures," or as a publicly documentable "historical fact." The reputedly hypostatic and historically factual dimensions of Jesus Christ's life span are here taken up in a dynamic frame of reference that discerns a current relating of all things to the vindication of the life crucified in Jesus. What is acknowledged to be the real world in this manner of describing reality is the coming to pass, or the actualization, of the future that is promised to the present.

An apocalyptic reading of the Two Natures casts the hypostatic union as concomitant events. *Hypostasis* is not *stasis* in the sense of static fixity. The description of "faith" given in Hebrews 11:1 shows this apocalyptic connotation: "Now faith is the *hypostasis* [actualization] of things hoped, the proving true of things not yet evident."[37] An apocalyptic reading of historical factuality, for its part, sees the significance of past "facts" always determined by their future. The actuality of the future is admittedly never known under the same documented conditions as the actuality of the past, but there is no historical perspective except from the horizon of a future to which past events are seen to be related.

For this reason some christological interpreters argue that the life span of Jesus Christ may be said to exhibit "history" in yet another sense from that of von Ranke's factuality. The Resurrection and Parousia as the destiny of Jesus Christ are confessed in faith to be the universal future to which all that actually happens is ultimately related. If this is so, the apocalyptic destiny of Jesus Christ may be said to provide the ultimate horizon for historical consciousness, or historical perspective. Worldviews that rule out this promised destiny of Jesus Christ as off-limits to reality are themselves thus called into question and challenged for seeking in effect to foreclose consideration of the universal horizon required for the full story of "what actually happens."[38]

Still a further respect in which the life span of Jesus Christ may be said to exhibit "history" arises from the disbelief of any confession of the resurrected destiny of Jesus Christ that does not have to do with actual government in its social and political forms of power relations and jurisdiction. History is not only a matter of facticity, and not only a matter of consciousness or theoretical perspective; we also speak of the course of human events and of a historical process as well. The idea of Christ's coming and overcoming as a description of the course or process of history most readily calls to mind the names of Hegel and Marx. The roots of the understanding of history as a dialectical movement and social process are biblical and christological insofar as "what actually happens" is seen as a movement for the vindication of what is just, a rectification that is both incarnate and apocalyptic. Historical reality is defined in this instance not only as a question of facticity or theoretical perspective, but also as a time of testing, a freedom struggle. The course of human events is viewed as a trial process in the practical working out of which contested rights of domain are being adjudicated.[39]

To sum up this section, it is plain that in interpreting the significance of Jesus Christ the entailed disbeliefs of the faith affirmations concerning the Incarnation, the Resurrection, and the Parousia serve to inform one another. There is no faithful confession of Jesus Christ risen apart from Jesus Christ incarnate, and no faithful confession of Jesus Christ incarnate apart from Jesus Christ imminent. Similarly, christological coherence requires that the hypostatic, the historically factual, and the apocalyptic ways of thinking about "what actually happens" in the particular universality, or the exclusive inclusivity, that is the life span of Jesus Christ be understood as integral, each to the other. This is the point to be underscored. With Jesus Christ there is no hypostatic union apart from apocalyptic vindication, and no apocalyptic vindication that does not involve factual history.

Proposed Disbeliefs

Keeping in mind, as always we must, the interpretative context in which the foregoing christological disbeliefs have been proposed for recognition, we may now list them in the order stated.

The following have been pointed out as positions and claims that are refused credit and credence by the commonly held affirmations of Christian faith:

1. any confession of Jesus of Nazareth other than as the universal Christ and any confession of a Christ other than this particular Jesus.
2. that Jesus as the Christ is significant to faith, either historically or soteriologically, apart from the ongoing apostolic testimony of teaching and proclaiming that in New Testament language is called "gospeling."
3. that the reality faithfully confessed as "Jesus Christ" is an amorphous life that has no particular spatio-temporal identity, or is a historically restricted life circumscribed by its particularity in space and time.
4. any spirit or claim that denies the exclusively all-inclusive union within the one life span of Jesus Christ of life that is truly human with its particularity and life that is universally and eternally God's own.
5. any confessions of Jesus Christ that are not *en sarki* and any confessions that are *kata sarka*.
6. that the life of Jesus Christ is not fully human.
7. that the life of Jesus Christ is ultimately subject to any other life.
8. that the workings of the Holy Spirit in bringing forth life are subject to documentation.
9. that male prowess, sexual or otherwise, is the source and cause of salvation.
10. that the coming of Jesus to Mary is merely one in appearance and not in bodily birth.

11. that Jesus Christ is only born figuratively speaking, as some mythical or metaphysical idea engendered by the fantasies of religious imagination.
12. that a human capacity originates the life span of Jesus Christ that is born of Mary.
13. that human existence is the actualization of its own possibility or potential in the present rather than the actualization or "coming to pass" of the future that God promises to the present.
14. that there is any suffering or betrayal of the good that is off-limits to Jesus Christ's suffering and betrayal by sinners, or any dimension of death and loss that Jesus Christ's reality does not encompass.
15. that Jesus Christ's relating to others is limited by time and space or any other circumstance.
16. that the Resurrection involves a loss of particular identity.
17. that the Resurrection is subject to the conditions of physical nature.
18. any confession of the transcendent destiny of Jesus Christ that does not have to do with actual governance in all its forms of this-earthly, as well as heavenly, power relations and jurisdictional authority.
19. that the life of Jesus Christ does not involve a fully human earthly existence in the particularities of time and space and environment designated as "under Pontius Pilate."
20. that this life of Jesus Christ exists other than in union with the destiny of God's eternal life happening in it, to it, and as its future.
21. that either of the two natures of Jesus Christ may be said to be actual apart from the other.
22. any confession of Jesus Christ risen apart from Jesus Christ incarnate, or of Jesus Christ incarnate apart from Jesus Christ imminent.
23. that with Jesus Christ there is hypostatic union apart from apocalyptic vindication, or apocalyptic vindication that does not involve factual history.

If the coherence of the church's christological doctrines is sought in line with these disbeliefs, the first of the initial objections is shown to be correct in recognizing the *kata sarka* issue. Christian faith does not worship the historical figure of Jesus of Nazareth abstracted from his destiny, or trust that salvation comes from any creaturely capacity. The life of Jesus Christ as incarnate, risen, and coming is not therefore like the lingering effect of other past events upon the present, nor can these dimensions of this life be documented by physical phenomena. The influence of Jesus Christ is not the influence of the dead. Conformity to Jesus Christ is not conformity to a first-century environment. Most important, the life span of Jesus Christ is not to be equated with the history of Christianity or with cultural Christendom. The vindication of this life span is not the "absoluteness," as it has sometimes been referred to, of the Christian religion. All such ideas the first objection rightly protests as intolerable.

Yet the influential Kierkegaardian view appealed to in this objection is shown to be less adequate, in light of these disbeliefs, when tested for an *en sarki* witness. By its indifference to factual history it fails to take sufficient account of Christ's life span in its connection with governing powers in their social and political aspect. What is assumed to matter for faith is not world history in its sociopolitical aspect but the self of the contemporary disciple in its existential historicity. A failure occurs in not distinguishing adequately between significance that is "according to the flesh" apart from faith and significance that is "enfleshed" in the Word made flesh.

A similar problem appears in a number of attempts in the nineteenth and twentieth centuries to speak of the biblical accounts of God's saving acts, especially as these are seen to culminate in Christ's destiny, as depicting a history of their own, a "sacred history" or a "salvation history," not to be defined according to the parameters of "world history." Much christological discussion of the past century, in line with the title of Martin Kähler's text cited above, employs a distinction in terminology between "history" as historical factuality (in German, *Historie* or *Weltgeschichte*) and history as God's saving acts (in German, *Heilsgeschichte*). Increasingly today, however, more exegetical and theological interpreters are critical of what they see to be the docetic tendencies implicit in speaking of "God's history" or "salvation history" as distinguishable from all other history.[40] The task of faithful disbelief in seeking christological coherence calls for an *en sarki* interpretation that equally rejects any *kata sarka* alternative.

With regard to the second category of initial objections, issues having to do with the apparent conflict between the formulations of classical christological dogma and the historical significance of Jesus Christ, the disbeliefs we have noted illuminate the heart of the dispute. What is shown to be at stake in pitting the so-called Jesus of history against the Christ of dogma is a conflict in christological interpretation between the historically factual and the hypostatic ways of reading "what actually happens" that reflects a mutual disregard of an apocalyptic reading.

Neither ontic nor factual references to the life of Jesus Christ have significance for Christian faith apart from their apocalyptic context in the gospel. Argument over whether christological coherence is to be approached *von oben* or *von unten*, "from above" or "from below," is based upon a false alternative that fails to take into account the gospel's witness to the actuality of Jesus Christ as a future vindication now taking place in relation to presently governing powers. The person of Jesus Christ is not known to faith either as a fleshless Word in heaven or as Word-less flesh on earth.

This second initial objection rightly points to what may be viewed as the docetic qualification of a Cyrilian, or Alexandrian, christology in attributing, as it were, more actuality to the divinity, since it, being the *Logos*, is said to be hypostatic, than to the humanity that in the Incarnation is said to be brought into union with this hypostasis. Yet attempts to reconstruct the factual biography of the earthly Jesus against "the tyranny of dogma," as Schweitzer puts it,[41] mistakenly presuppose that the humanity in the life span of Jesus Christ is reducible to the dimension of earthly existence subject to death — that is, to historical factuality. Tested by the disbeliefs proposed, claims of ontic priority or inequality in the hypostatic union of the Two Natures become docetic as a purported reality description to the degree that this union is not understood apocalyptically as a vindication of the life to which death is subject, in actual relation to all life that is in fact subject to death. In short, the divinity of Jesus Christ *is* the vindication of true humanity.

The proposed disbeliefs bear upon the third initial objection as well with its expression of skepticism regarding the identifiable reality of Jesus Christ. In the context of ongoing gospel witness, or "gospeling," the truly human actuality of Jesus as the Christ is not identified as such in severance from its vindication. Attempts therefore to search for this actuality within the strictures of historical factuality inevitably miss their intended subject. The record of this mistake Schweitzer's study documents. But here the final disbelief on our list becomes instructive. Who Jesus Christ really is, in actuality or as *hypostasis*, is only identified when *apocalypsed*, and only apocalypsed in relation to the course of factual *history*. In the context of the ongoing testimony of the gospel in which Jesus as the Christ becomes significant to faith these three ways of recognizing reality, the hypostatic, the apocalyptic, and the historically factual, mutually inform one another. The life story of Jesus Christ identifies the life promised always in connection with what is going on at present, the external and internal freedom struggle of creation in its "travail," to recall Paul's phrase, "until now" (Rom. 8:22–23).

As the incarnate "*hypostasis* of God" (Heb. 1:3) "*apocalypsed* from heaven" (2 Thess. 1:7) Jesus Christ is identified as God's revealed Word is identified, through ordinary historical means necessary for communication, as we considered in chapter 6, but not by the power of these means or methods in and of themselves.[42] The third initial objection rightly acknowledges the second half of this statement but fails to give adequate cognizance to the first, that is, to the necessity in responsibility to the gospel for historical-critical thinking in seeking a faithful christological coherence today. Historical-critical study of the gospels, writes Ernst Käsemann, can detect "decisive pivotal points" of continuity linking the content of Jesus' own teaching and that of the early church's proclamation of his saving significance. These points "are not capable of being used as components in a reconstructed biography of Jesus; but they do give to the '*that* of the coming of Jesus' certain unmistakable traits of his individuality" without which preaching would "only be docetic in nature."[43] Here again we see an *en sarki* emphasis being reasserted, but in a way that also attempts to avoid the *kata sarka* misconceptions of the older nineteenth-century quest for the historical Jesus.

From the standpoint of the proposed disbeliefs some of these misconceptions do appear in the case presented in the fourth initial objection. Most glaring is that the particular universality of what the gospel proclaims as happening *in, to*, and *as the future of* Jesus is disregarded as essential to the actual life span of Jesus Christ. Jesus is referred to only as a provincially particular first-century figure or Christian symbol lacking universality. Universality, as John Hick's quote suggests, is attributed to a more comprehensive *Logos* portrayed as having no one identifiable actuality in particular. The "tyranny of dogma" in this instance is seen as the sanction given by the doctrine of the Incarnation as a hypostatic union of the Two Natures to an imperialistic Christianity. Against any such exclusivism of religion or culture this objection rightly protests. Yet, if the proposed disbeliefs are to be recognized as faithful, to deny the Incarnation is to deny the Resurrection and the Parousia as well, and thereby to misrepresent the true historical significance of Jesus Christ by abstracting it from the hypostatic and apocalyptic frames of reference that inform it.

What is confessed to be "only begotten" is falsely assumed in this fourth objection to imply a single religion, culture, or first-century life to which all others are bound to conform. But this again is to confuse the province of Jesus Christ with the province of Christianity or of world religions. Christian faith refuses to believe that what is "only begotten," however religiously or nonreligiously labeled, is other than the dominion of love in the actual vindication of true humanity. How this exclusive inclusivity identified in the gospel as the life of Jesus Christ is attested in all life is addressed in faith affirmations of the church concerning the Holy Spirit.

Chapter 9

THE HOLY SPIRIT

Introduction

The word "spirit" (Hebrew, *ruach;* Greek, *pneuma*) in ordinary English usage comes laden with a variety of connotations. Common to everyday speech are such expressions as "getting the spirit," or "getting into the spirit." We speak of team spirit, school spirit, national spirit, the spirit of the electorate, or more broadly, the human spirit. An influential reader in feminist religious thought published in the late seventies bears the title *Womanspirit Rising.*[1] Familiar as well is the German expression, the *Zeitgeist*, or the "spirit of the times," and the French *esprit de corps*, or "spirit of group honor." Tourist bureaus advertise with such slogans as "The spirit of Massachusetts is the spirit of America," or, a bit less assertively, "Discover the Spirit in North Dakota, then keep it a secret." Even programs of church denominations, to take the United Methodists as one example, are sometimes promoted with a byline such as "Catch the Spirit." The ambiguity of this last phrase for a church pronouncement is most curious. Does one "catch" the *Holy* Spirit? If so, is this more like catching a ball, or a cold, or a plane? Often in secular usage the word "spirit" seems to mean no more than a "mood."

Contrary to this, in the call of 1 John 4:1 not to believe every spirit the word "spirit," as was observed in chapter 1, may initially be said to designate a *claimant* for attention and allegiance, most especially one who claims to speak for God. The idea is that not every voice claiming to speak for God (the biblical definition of a "prophet") does so and deserves to be heeded. Faith in God, therefore, involves a distinguishing between true and false prophets, or true and false spirits as claimants. Within this context of usage it is consistent both to say that "God is spirit" (John 4:24), the sovereign claimer of all life in the dominion of love, and also that not every "spirit" that claims to be of God is from God (1 John 4:1–3).

In addition to the meaning of "spirit" as *claimant*, the testimony that "God is spirit," in its context in the Fourth Gospel, also suggests *presence*. With reference to God the term "spirit" denotes *presence that is both ultimate and unrestricted*. It is in this sense that we speak of *the* Spirit. To the Samaritan woman at the well who said to Jesus that her ancestors worshiped on that mountain but that Jesus' people worshiped in Jerusalem, implying a localization of divine presence, the reply of Jesus given in the gospel account is that true worship will be neither on that mountain nor in Jerusalem, but "in spirit and truth" (John 4:20–24).

Such testimony to God's spirit as ultimate and unrestricted presence is consistent with a broad range of scripture. The Psalmist writes:

> Where can I go from your spirit?
> Or where can I flee from your presence?
> If I ascend to heaven, you are there;
> if I make my bed in Sheol, you are there.
> Ps. 139:7–8

The "you" addressed in these words of Psalm 139 is depicted as the One who is omnipresent in dwelling place, both in the heights and in the depths. Yet this omnipresent indwelling of God's spirit is not simply equated by the Psalmist with either the heights or the depths that it is proclaimed to inhabit. God's spirit is thus affirmed to be everywhere but not to be everything. The ultimate indwelling that is God's presence distinguishes itself from that which it dwells in. Distilled to the most basic point, Christian doctrines of faith in the Holy Spirit may be seen as attempts to explicate the twofold conviction that in what happens with Jesus Christ, God presents God as everywhere but not as everything.

In dogmatic terminology the doctrinal rubric in which attention is paid to such ultimate indwelling presence is labeled pneumatology. We observed in chapter 6 that this subject is closely linked with that of the Word of God. If the Word is rightly described as God-communicating, the Spirit in turn may be said to be God-communicated, that is, the achieved communication. What is communicated of God *through* the Word is thus professed to be communicated *in* the Spirit.[2] The Word of God may be signified, but this Word only becomes significant for faith, as Paul expresses it, by "that very Spirit bearing witness with our spirit" that we are its "heirs," that this Word is meant for us (Rom. 8:16). Without the internal witness of the Spirit the outer witness of the Word meets with no receptivity. This testimony of Paul, like that of the Psalmist, distinguishes the Presence that is God from our presence where its indwelling is confessed to bear witness.

The most commonly held affirmations of the church on this subject are to be found in the words of the Apostles' Creed and the Nicene Creed. The Apostles' Creed in its second article affirms the life of Jesus Christ as "conceived by the Holy Spirit" and in its third article associates belief in the Holy Spirit with the full scope of the life of faith in referring to "the holy, catholic church, the communion of saints, the forgiveness of sins, the resurrection of the body, and the life everlasting." The Holy Spirit is thus affirmed in connection with holy life. This is more readily apparent in the original Latin and Greek versions of the creed, in the sequence, "*Spiritum Sanctum* [in Greek, *Pneuma to Hagion*], *sanctam ecclesiam* [*hagian ekklēsian*], *sanctorum communionem* [*hagian koinōnian*]": "the Holy Spirit, the holy church, the communion of the holy," together in "everlasting life, *vitam eternam* [*zōēn aiōnion*]." The Nicene Creed, for its part, describes Jesus Christ as "incarnate by the Holy Spirit of the Virgin Mary" and professes faith in the Holy Spirit as "the Lord and Giver of life, who proceeds from the Father (and the Son), who together with the Father and the Son is worshipped and glorified, who spoke by the prophets."

In both instances we can see that the long-standing creedal emphasis is upon the Holy Spirit, not as a mere mood, but as *God giving life*.

We may, therefore, trace most plainly the contours of this doctrinal locus and attempt to recognize the faithful disbeliefs entailed by looking at this subject of *God giving life* under three headings: the Holy Spirit as Gift, the Holy Spirit as Giver, and the Gifts of the Holy Spirit.

Initial Objections

The main objections that arise with respect to teachings concerning the Holy Spirit tend to fall for the most part into three categories. Each of the three represents a different reaction to the church's trinitarian understanding of God's being. The first complaint is that the logic of trinitarian doctrine in effect restricts God's spirit, as *God giving life*, to the boundaries of Christianity, thus denying God's omnipresent indwelling. The second is that even within the acceptance of trinitarian doctrinal traditions the role of the Third Person, in distinction from that of the First and the Second, remains subordinate and undeveloped. The third is that proposed pneumatologies that disregard or reject the triune relations are not faithful to the identification of the Holy that occurs in the threefold referentiality of the gospel testimonies. Reasons offered in support of these three different judgments may be condensed as follows.

1. *It would seem that a trinitarian interpretation of the Holy Spirit in effect denies the omnipresence of God.*

Most simply stated, if the Spirit of God is said to be operative only in relation to the One whom Jesus called "Father" and to the life span of Jesus as the Christ, it is difficult to see how Christians can confess that God is present outside of the symbolic world of Christianity. Whatever is valid in another religion or history becomes, to Christian eyes, merely a partial and yet to be realized tendency toward Christianity. The arrogance of such a perspective cannot be reconciled with the gospel message of God's universal dominion of love as the basis of the injunction to love one's neighbor. One reason why this is so is that the attitude amounts to the saluting only of your own kind that is warned against in the words of Jesus on the mount, as recorded in Matthew 5:47.

Indigenous testimonies to the Spirit are to be found among nearly all peoples from the earliest records of antiquity. Such indigenous witness to God's presence has often been disregarded without testing as false in principle by a colonialist missionary mentality that confused faith in God with conformity to its own exported culture. In an age of increasing global communication across multicultural lines new attention is required to eliminate chauvinistic aspects of church teaching concerning the Holy Spirit.

Insofar as trinitarian doctrine results in the attempted sacralization of only one sequence of history, that of biblical messianism as it culminates in what happens with Jesus, an idolatrous equation is made between this history and the sacred presence of God's Spirit. Such an interpretation cannot consistently allow for the Spirit to be present elsewhere in all times and places.

2. *It would seem that the distinctiveness of the Holy Spirit remains suppressed and undeveloped even within trinitarian doctrine.*

The charge of a deficient or underdeveloped pneumatology is often made against the more characteristic trinitarian theological traditions of the West, both Roman Catholic and Protestant, in contrast to the churches of Eastern Orthodoxy, to Pentecostalist communities, and to those proponents of liberal religion who see in the universal presence of the Spirit the most inclusive basis for a humane unity and dialogue among all peoples and religions. This objection contains the following elements.

Historically, it is a fact that with respect to the formation of trinitarian doctrine the equality of status of the Son with the Father was affirmed before the equality of status of the Holy Spirit with either the Father or the Son. Early Christian testimony has been characterized as being more binitarian than trinitarian.[3] The confession of the Son as *homoousion* with the Father was made explicit at Nicaea in 325, but the confession of the Holy Spirit as "with the Father and the Son worshipped and glorified" awaited the decisions of Constantinople in 381. Admittedly, this delay was due in part to the circumstance that the deity of the Holy Spirit was not as vigorously challenged until the Nicene definition of the status of the Son had been promulgated. But even following Constantinople in 381, the term *homoousios* for the equality of the eternal status of the Third Person was not used in the Creed.[4]

It is particularly in the West, however, that the logic of Augustinian thought, so the accusation is made, undercuts, even if without intending to do so and explicitly arguing otherwise, the full actuality of the Holy Spirit as a third distinctively coequal *hypostasis* or *person* of God's being. The reason for this is that the term "Holy Spirit" is said by Augustine to denote the bond of mutual love between the Father and the Son, "that which both are in common."[5] Even if unintended, the result of so interpreting the Holy Spirit as the mutuality of love between the Father and the Son is to reduce pneumatology to christology and to reduce the trinity to a binity of the Father/Son relation. Thus only in the West did the phrase "and the Son" [*Filioque*, or *et Filio*] gradually come by the late sixth century to be added to the original affirmation of the Nicene-Constantinopolitan confession two hundred years earlier that "the Holy Spirit . . . proceeds from the Father." The result of so subordinating divine presence to the Father/Son relation is that the unrestricted indwelling of God's Spirit in all of creation as equally a way of God's triune being with its own proper actuality, or *hypostasis*, tends to become a less regarded theme. An answer to the "So what?" question is that one practical consequence of such disregard appears in the failure of much Christian teaching to deal adequately with the mounting problems of the environment and with the newer ecological awareness of the late twentieth century. The role of the Spirit in creation is neglected with almost total emphasis placed upon the role of the Spirit in personal salvation. Correspondingly, the natural world is exploited as if devoid of God's presence and subject only to human disposal.

Another approach to arguing this same objection calls attention to the apprehension and disapproval with which ecclesiastical authorities historically have tended to view pentecostal and charismatic movements. The charge of "enthusiasm" against individuals or groups that are perceived to be disloyal and separatist for allegedly claiming to be spirit-filled arises early within Christianity.[6] Paul apparently viewed some of the Corinthians as such divisive pneumatics: "Already you have all you want! Already you have become rich! Quite apart from us you have become kings!" (1 Cor. 4:8). Tertullian became associated with the Montanists of late second-century Phrygia who professed to experience the promised apocalyptic outpouring of the Spirit. Sociologically interpreted, institutional consolidation and concentration of power within the church have been said to lead to a "routinization" of the spirit.[7] In reaction to this fixity an emphasis upon the Holy Spirit has often characterized countercultural Christian groups outside the mainstream of the established church governance. One thinks of the Anabaptists who were fiercely opposed as subversive fanatics by Luther and Calvin, of John Wesley and his followers condemned as "enthusiasts" in eighteenth-century England for preaching "heart religion" in "a catholic spirit," and of the Quakers refusing to deny the "inner light." Manifestations of the Holy Spirit become suspect when they occur outside of official ecclesiastical jurisdictions.

Further support for this second objection comes from the contention that a more thoroughly trinitarian designation of the full coequality of the Holy Spirit serves to mitigate a restrictive and exclusionary christocentrism in Christianity.[8] Especially where conflicts arise today over the patriarchal and masculine terminology used in speaking of God as "Father" and "Son," the term "Spirit" would seem to provide a less controversial alternative. According to the logic of trinitarian doctrine, the Spirit is not restricted to the incarnation of the "only-begotten" Word.

3. *It would seem that nontriune depictions of the Spirit violate the gospel's threefold identifying referentiality concerning God.*

The doctrine of the Trinity, so its proponents who represent this third objection argue, serves to ward off all interpretations of God's omnipresence as pantheism. This is what the critics of a trinitarian pneumatology fail to recognize. In the threefold referentiality of the gospel accounts, God is presented as identifying *with* the world in such a way that the world cannot be identified *as* God. The concern behind this third objection is that revisionist pneumatological proposals that seek to heighten the emphasis upon the Spirit by rejecting or disregarding the triune relations will end up precisely by confusing God's indwelling with that which God dwells in. The result, even if unintended, is that God's presence everywhere is mistaken for God's purported presence as allowably anything and everything. Because of severance from its scriptural context, the term "Holy" thus ceases to describe the Spirit that is of God as designated in the gospel. As a practical consequence the theological critique of evil and social injustice is undercut.

A variant on the confusion of omnipresence with pantheism is the reduction of pneumatology to anthropology. The distinction the Apostle draws between God and ourselves in writing of the "Spirit bearing witness with our spirit" (Rom. 8:16) is lost. "The divine being" becomes, in the words of Ludwig Feuerbach, "nothing else than the human being . . . freed from individual limits [and] objectified."[9] The equation of God's Spirit with any form of creaturely spirit, whether it be that of an individual, a gender, or a community such as a race, class, culture, or nation, it is contended, represents a betrayal of the "Holy" according to the import of the gospel message.

Interpretation

In approaching the doctrine of the Holy Spirit we do well, having taken account of these three categories of initial objections, to start out by reflecting upon the point that it is *life* that God is being confessed to give. It is easy to forget this if we dwell only upon the abstractions of pneumatological theories and conceptions. There is one subject in theology (not only beginning students confronted for the first time by the awesome history of Christian doctrine need to be reminded) in which each of us is the world's greatest authority. That is the subject of how the life God gives us looks in faith from where we are in our particular time and place. We each occupy a unique spatio-temporal position. Not one of us ever stands exactly where another stands. And although the life of faith is always a communal way, a shared way,[10] none of us even among our closest peers within the same immediate culture represents merely a carbon copy of someone else's joys, sufferings, and insights. To recognize that the Christian faith is a lived way, a movement, a pilgrimage, is to recognize that we do not find ourselves today where we were ten years ago. We may expect that ten years from now we will see some things differently from how we see them at present. But if theology is not an abstract system of theorems that one can learn as a fixed calculus and thus have mastered, but rather is a continual accounting of a faith community's current reason-for-being en route, then how each individual member of the community attests to this life in his or her particular circumstances is important. No vantage point is to be repressed or disregarded as being of no account.

Ralph Waldo Emerson's "Divinity School Address" at Harvard in 1838 contains the following paragraph:

> I once heard a preacher who sorely tempted me to say I would go to church no more.... A snow-storm was falling around us. The snow-storm was real, the preacher merely spectral, and the eye felt the sad contrast in looking at him, and then out of the window behind him into the beautiful meteor of the snow. He had lived in vain. He had no one word intimating that he had laughed or wept, was married or in love, had been commended, or cheated, or chagrined. If he had ever lived and acted, we were none the wiser for it. The capital secret of his profession, namely, to convert life into truth, he had not learned. Not one fact in all his experience had he yet imported into his doctrine. This man had ploughed and

> planted and talked and bought and sold; he had read books; he had eaten and drunken; his head aches, his heart throbs; he smiles and suffers; yet was there not a surmise, a hint, in all the discourse, that he had ever lived at all.[11]

One need not subscribe to all of Emerson's theological opinions to appreciate this description of the preacher. The point is that the way and the truth of Jesus Christ is witnessed in Christian faith as life (John 14:6). And it is life both as given and as the Giver that is designated in Christianity by the term "Holy Spirit."

1. The Holy Spirit as Gift

The Pentecost referred to in Acts 2 as the promised empowerment of the apostolic mission "to the ends of the earth" (Acts 1:8), recalls the words of the Hebrew prophet Joel: "God declares, . . . I will pour out my Spirit upon all flesh" (Acts 2:17; Joel 2:28–29). The image of "pouring out" is one of unreserved giving "without measure" (John 3:34). The message of Paul to the Romans is that "God's love has been poured into our hearts through the Holy Spirit that has been given to us" (Rom. 5:5). This emphasis upon God's spirit as "poured out" by God is consistent with the Johannine epistle's testimony earlier considered in chapter 3 that it is God's spirit as "given" by God (1 John 4:13) which calls all other spirits into question. Elsewhere Luke recounts the teaching of Jesus that the heavenly Father will "give" the Holy Spirit to those who ask (Luke 11:13). The pentecostal gift is most especially associated with the promise of baptism:

> Peter said to them, "Repent, and be baptized every one of you in the name of Jesus Christ so that your sins may be forgiven; and you will receive the gift of the Holy Spirit. For the promise is for you, for your children, and for all who are far away, everyone whom the Lord our God calls to him." (Acts 2:38–39)

What faithful disbeliefs does such testimony today entail? We may, I think, recognize two refusals here as most basic. The first is that faith in the Holy Spirit refuses to believe all proposed objectifications of God. The second is that faith in the Holy Spirit refuses to believe all proposed subjectifications of God. Let us consider why this is so.

First, in the canonical context of scriptural usage the word "spirit" clearly serves to prevent us from objectifying God. Translators vary in deciding when or not to capitalize the original Hebrew and Greek, but insofar as the term "spirit" is seen to be applicable to God it resists a fixed phenomenal delineation. The human intellect can formulate metaphysical theories that speak of absolute spirit or — following Kant perhaps more than Hegel — formulate ethical theories of the human spirit that postulate an absolute, and still not know, according to biblical perspectives, the life of God's spirit. Nor is God's spirit subject to ritual performance. In the writings of the Bible the Spirit of God is viewed as properly to be invoked, but never conjured or contrived. This gift cannot be harnessed or domesticated. No one has a grasp on it or a mastery of it. There is a freedom and spontaneity indicated by the word "Spirit" in biblical references to God that escapes all human controls.

The image that spirit-language both in the Old Testament and the New Testament brings before us is that of "breath" or of "wind." In the opening lines of Genesis we read of the "*ruach* ['spirit' or 'wind'] from God" upon the face of the waters in creation (Gen. 1:1–2).[12] In one creation account the Lord God is portrayed as "breathing" into human nostrils the breath of life (Gen. 2:7). What is depicted is the human being [*adam*] animated by God's own animation. Such breathing of God's spirit into human creation contradicts any claim that "God" is One who is solely an external object to us. Rather, as the story in John's Gospel reports Jesus saying to Nicodemus: "The wind [*pneuma*] blows where it chooses, and you hear the sound of it, but you do not know where it comes from or where it goes. So it is with everyone who is born of the Spirit [*pneumatos*]" (John 3:8). Thus in both the Old and New Testament scriptures, despite a variety of references to "spirit," the term functions consistently to prevent the objectification of our understanding of God.

An important significance of this faithful disbelief occurs with the realization that objectification in human reasoning is a means of control. It is a means of gaining power. In some cases, such as in the natural sciences and technology, this may be publicly demonstrable power. In others, such as in the social and behavioral sciences [the so-called *Geisteswissenschaften*, or "sciences of the human spirit"], the power may take more subtle forms. Theological education for ministry ceases to be faithful as a "steward of the mysteries of God" and becomes dehumanizing as a false "peddler of God's word" whenever it leads to thinking of faith communities and individuals within them as objects, such as cases, clients, or social classes, to be dealt with or controlled by professional "training," whether purportedly theoretical or practical. The quaint and less clinical term for pastoral ministry in the church, the "care of souls," if it is understood biblically to mean embodied souls or ensouled bodies, is closer to the reality of human life, both individually and communally, as the gift of God's spirit.

With respect to the second faithful disbelief, the New Testament identification of the Holy Spirit as the Spirit of Jesus Christ equally serves to prevent us from subjectifying God, that is, from deifying our subjectivity.

To be sure, it is said that "the Spirit blows where it chooses." It is not battened down to historical particularity in the same way that is Jesus Christ. Not all predicates applicable to the Holy Spirit can be applied as well to the Son. A distinction, for example, is clear in the gospel message between the Christ as literally "the anointed one" and the Holy Spirit as "the anointing Spirit." The two referents, Word (or Son of God) and Holy Spirit, are not synonymous. Yet, in the testimonies of the gospel the Holy Spirit is said to declare the things that are of Jesus Christ and to have no other content of its own. The Spirit is represented as the linking up of the life span of Jesus Christ, the incarnate Word, with our own life span. Nothing is seen to be holy or of God, in the apostolic writings, that is not of Jesus Christ. Thus to worship in faith is not to follow after every spirit, after every wind that blows, but after the *Holy* Spirit, namely, the Spirit that conforms to the will and way of the Holy One, Jesus Christ.

As we trace our way here we must keep the three initial objections that have previously been noted in mind. The New Testament does not provide us with only one uniform interpretation in this instance, but the relation of the Spirit to the event of Jesus is maintained throughout. When the Gospel of Matthew relates the Nativity, for example, it is said of Mary that "she was found to be with child from the Holy Spirit" (Matt. 1:18). In the Gospel of Luke the angel's promise to Mary is "The Holy Spirit will come upon you, and the power of the Most High will overshadow you; therefore the child to be born will be holy" (Luke 1:35). Following the birth narratives, at the baptism by John that marks the beginning of Jesus' public ministry, the Spirit is said in the three Synoptic Gospels to descend upon him as a dove (Matt. 3:16, Mark 1:10, Luke 3:22). Jesus' ministry itself of exorcising the forces of bondage and setting at liberty those who are oppressed is further depicted as carried out in the power of the Spirit (Matt. 12:28, Luke 4:16–21). Similarly, in reference to his death, Paul writes that this same Jesus has been designated "Son of God with power according to the spirit of holiness [*kata pneuma hagiōsynēs*] by resurrection from the dead" (Rom. 1:4). In the Gospel of John the Holy Spirit is called the Paraclete, or "Encourager," whose promised sending, Jesus tells the disciples, is to occur after Jesus has gone to his death and has returned to the Father. The Spirit is thus described as "the guide into all truth," the "declarer of the things that are to come," even the "many things" Jesus has yet to say which the disciples cannot presently bear. Even so, such things will all glorify Christ because the Holy Spirit, as John relates Jesus' farewell discourse, "will take what is mine and declare it to you" (John 16:12–15). Still again, this time in the Gospel of Mark, the "blasphemy against the Holy Spirit" seems to be identified with blasphemy against Jesus' spirit — "for they had said, 'He has an unclean spirit' " (Mark 3:29–30).

Hence, despite the variety of ways in which the point is made, the New Testament message clearly is that the Holy Spirit is the Spirit of the life, death, and destiny of Jesus Christ.

To avoid misunderstanding such a conclusion, it is crucial to recall once again the christological discussion of chapter 8. The term "Jesus Christ" in the context of the New Testament accounts denotes the full life span, including what happens *in, to*, and *as the future of* Jesus of Nazareth, and is not limited merely to the factuality of Jesus' first-century historical existence.[13] This means that the Spirit of Jesus Christ referred to in these testimonies as the Holy Spirit is not reducible to the mood, or consciousness, or personality of a first-century historical figure.[14]

Faith in the Holy Spirit as a refusal to deify human subjectivity is the basis for the critical assessment of the many sources of ecstasy, as it were, currently blowing in the wind. The argument that one should not be overly concerned with whether a spirit is holy but should simply "go with the flow" and "do what comes naturally" is challenged in biblical faith. The reason why it is challenged is that, as the gospel witnesses view this matter, human existence evidences self-destructiveness toward the good of its own created naturalness. In so doing, it loses the capacity freely to be itself. Thus God's Spirit is required, not simply spirituality per se, but the Spirit that will bring wholeness — which is what "holiness" suggests — into human life. Only then is what humans do truly natural, that is, true to the good of their created nature. By the indwelling of the Holy Spirit, and not by any alleged self-actualizing of our own spirits, we relate to others in ways that result in freedom and communion. We shall consider this tenet of faith further when we come to the doctrines of salvation and humanity. Here the point to be underlined is that faith in the Holy Spirit as gift leads to the disbelief of all attempts both to objectify God and to deify human subjectivity.

2. The Holy Spirit as Giver

In the case of the Holy Spirit the gift of God is confessed in Christian faith to be none other than God giving. The name denotes an agent, a "life giver," and not simply an attribute, a disposition, or a quality. The Holy Spirit comes to be praised, along with the Father and the Son, as distinctively God in person, the one Lord. Augustine, whose thinking is formative in shaping the traditional interpretation of the Holy Spirit as gift and love, writes in the early part of the fifth century that the Holy Spirit is "given as a gift of God in such a way" as also to be the giver.[15] Elaborating upon this theme of "the Gift of God giving [*Donum Dei dantis*],"[16] Thomas Aquinas in the second half of the thirteenth century argues that to speak of the Holy Spirit as the Love relating the First and

Second Persons is not to speak merely of a relationality as such, but of a characteristic act of relating on God's part. As Thomas puts it, the *nexus* is also an *actus*.[17]

In the language of the Nicene Creed, not only the Father and the Son, but also and with them the Holy Spirit as well, is to be "worshipped and glorified as the Lord." "The Holy Spirit" is thus acknowledged in the discourse of Christian faith along with the terms "the Father" and "the Son" to be the subject of active verbs that are distinctively appropriate to the agency of God. "When they bring you to trial and hand you over, do not worry beforehand about what you are to say; but say whatever is given you at that time, for it is not you who speak, but the Holy Spirit" (Mark 13:11). In addition to "speaking," the Holy Spirit is also characteristically said to "teach" (1 Cor. 2:13), to "descend" (Luke 3:22), to "come upon" (Acts 19:6), to "proceed" (John 15:26), and, as has been mentioned, to "indwell" (Rom. 8:11). This list of active verbs could be extended. Christian faith therefore refuses to believe that the Holy Spirit is a mere quality or attribute derivative of anything creaturely, either of the world of nature and history more objectively considered, or of the conscious and unconscious subjectivity of the human psyche.

In trinitarian doctrine the Holy Spirit as Giver denotes for Christian faith the way that God, according to the import of the biblical writings, is said to live, both in self-relation and in relation to creation. As presented by the threefold referentiality of the gospel testimonies, God lives as life-giving Spirit, not incommunicado in self-retained and unforthcoming isolation, but as a proceeding forth that is the realization of relation which is fully loving in its will for the good of the other and, as such, fully free.

An ancient image sometimes appealed to in attempting to think of such proceeding forth is that of an inexhaustible fountain that is at once a self-propelling source and spray. In scholastic terms, the source of deity is traditionally characterized as the First Person, the *hypostasis* or actuality of God as ungenerated generating, the *fons et origo*. Most often in scripture the word "God" is used in speaking of the First Person. The spray streaming forth is characterized as the Second Person, the *hypostasis* or actuality of God distinguished now not as an unconfigured font and origin, but as a manifest configuration, the *only-begotten* Word. The fountain's surge or propulsion, so to speak, its pouring forth, is characterized as the Third Person, the *hypostasis* or actuality of God that is distinguished in this third instance neither as the unfathomable font and origin, nor as the only-begotten configured manifestation, the Word, but as the *vivifying procession* of the Holy Spirit. From God as source both the spray of the fountain's manifestation and the surge that propels it come forth as God's own being and not as creatures other than God. But the Word and the Spirit come forth from the Father in distinguishable ways. There is an eternal begetting forth of the Word and an eternal breathing forth (a *spiratio* for the metaphysically stout-hearted!) of the Holy Spirit. The God of the gospel is praised as eternally self-related in this inseparably threefold way of the unbegotten Source, the only-begotten Word, and the surging Spirit that proceeds.

This image of an everflowing fountain may serve to stimulate thinking about God in dynamic rather than static terms, but like all creaturely images of God's being it is only partially apt to the import of the gospel message. The dimensions of a fountain are not personal relations. The configuration of a fountain's spray is not that of a life story faithful to its promise. One may, therefore, prefer to think of God's coming forth as performative utterance or speech which, according to creaturely analogy, requires both self-committing word and breath. Or again, the analogy is sometimes drawn between the Word as God's self-knowing and the Spirit as God's self-willing. The attempt in each of these anthropomorphisms is to call to mind the biblical portrayal of God as active forthcoming, both in the configured Word made flesh in Jesus Christ and in the unbounded life-giving power of the Holy Spirit.

All imaginings of this sort, the fourth-century interpreters emphasized, must be guided by the import of the threefold referentiality of the gospel message that is enacted in the sacramental liturgy of Christian worship. A key example of such threefold referentiality with regard to the Spirit can be seen in Paul's announcement of the good news to the Romans that if the Spirit of the One who raised Jesus from the dead dwells in them, the One who raised Christ from the dead will give life to their mortal bodies also through this same Spirit which dwells in them (Rom. 8:11). Here we find reference made to the One who raised Jesus, to the Risen Christ, and to the indwelling Spirit of resurrection life. Whatever the Holy Spirit has not said in speaking the scriptures, wrote Cyril of Jerusalem about the year 350, "we dare not say" about the Holy Spirit.[18]

Cyril's own teaching merits comment here. In his sixteenth and seventeenth addresses of catechetical instruction to candidates for baptism we find a fourth-century account of proposed faithful disbeliefs entailed in Christian affirmations regarding the Holy Spirit. Alasdair Heron provides the following helpful summary of these refusals.

> Warnings are . . . given against Marcion's separation of the Spirit in the Old Testament from the Spirit in the New (XVI.34); against tritheism and Sabellianism (XVI.4); against thinking that the Spirit is a mere power or energy without its own enhypostatic reality and agency (XVII.5) for it "lives and subsists and speaks and works" (XVII.2); against the claims of heretics from Simon Magus through Montanus to Mani, the founder of Manicheeism, to possess the

> Paraclete (XVI.6–10); and against imagining that the Spirit takes *violent* possession of humans as evil spirits do (XVI.15–16). The point is also made, by no means unnecessarily, that not every reference to *pneuma* in Scripture is to the Holy Spirit (XVI.13).[19]

Cyril of Jerusalem was not faced in the fourth century by the dispute over the *Filioque* phrase that came to be included in the Western versions of the Nicene-Constantinopolitan confession two centuries later. We must now try to see what is at stake for faith in this dispute that continues to divide the church East and West.

Debates over the *Filioque* are really debates over the First Person of the Trinity. It is remarkable the extent to which the First Person, "the Father," has become the most problematic of the three trinitarian hypostases for contemporary theology. If manifest only through the Word and known only in the power of the Spirit, how is God's distinctiveness as First Person thus to be confessed? We shall look at this question again when we come to the doctrine of creation. At issue here is how most faithfully to affirm the *source* of the Spirit's distinctive forthcoming in God. In standard trinitarian doctrine, as we have observed with the metaphor of the fountain, the source of all deity is traditionally attributed to the First Person who as *fons et origo* is also designated as the ungenerated generator, God as at once unbegotten and begetter. The source of God's forthcoming is affirmed as one. To suggest otherwise, the East argues, is to threaten the very basis of biblical monotheism, or what the ancients called the divine *monarchia*. But is this ultimate oneness of source better expressed as that of only "the Father," or as that of "the Father and the Son" in relation? And furthermore, judged by the tests of consequence and of cruciality, what real difference, if any, does the answer given make for the life of faith today?

The first, we will call it the Eastern, view tends to think of the three Persons from the standpoint of origin and emphasizes that God the Father is unoriginate, or unbegotten. The second, or Western, view tends to think of the three Persons from the standpoint of their relation and emphasizes that God the Father is begetter. Neither position denies the other characterization, but differences result, depending upon which emphasis, that of the Unbegotten or that of the Begetter, is treated as primary.

Consider first the idea that the source of God's forthcoming is to be attributed only to God as Unbegotten. If we think of the three triune Persons with respect to their origins, the Father alone is said to denote God as without origin, or unoriginate. Nowhere in biblical testimony is God the Father referred to as engendered. The eternal Son, in distinction, is confessed as God's only-begotten [*to monogenēs*] (John 3:16), and the Holy Spirit is confessed as proceeding [*ekporeuomen* or *ekporeuomenon*] from the Father (John 15:26). Both the Son and the Holy Spirit are thus scripturally proclaimed to be originate, but not to be created.[20] They are engendered of the Father who is not such without them, and they are engendered in distinguishable ways, the Son by the Father's begetting, and the Holy Spirit by proceeding forth as the Father's breathing, or "spirating." The figural language of scripture is thus transposed into the ontic concepts of trinitarian theory. As a Latinism the technical term *spiration* loses some of its awkwardness if we try to think of it as a shortened form of such terms as *respiration* (having to do with breath), *aspiration* (having to do with intention), and *inspiration* (having to do with an enlivening indwelling). Such forthcoming, or *spiration*, as a "proceeding from the Father" characterizes God's being, or the way God is, as a communion of Spirit. God's breathing forth the breath of life is biblically depicted as God's own aspiring to inspire. This "spiration" is distinguished in the gospel accounts, although never separated, from the forthcoming that is the begetting of the Word who in the fullness of time becomes flesh and dwells among us. The eternal source engendering both the Word and the Spirit is to be attributed only to God as unoriginate, that is, to the First Person, or the Father.

Consider next the idea that the source of the Spirit's forthcoming is to be attributed to the Father and the Son in relation. If the way God is, as denoted by the term "First Person of the Trinity," is to be characterized not only as "unbegotten" but also as "the begetter of the Son," the confession that the Holy Spirit "proceeds from the Father" can only mean that the Holy Spirit proceeds from One-with-Another, or from the Father as related to the Son. The term "Begetter" entails a relation to a "Begotten" that the term "Unbegotten" or "Unoriginate" does not.[21] Historically the phrase "and the Son" is indeed a western addition to the Creed of 381, an addition generally ratified only in the West at the Council of Toledo in 589. Logically, so its proponents from Augustine through Thomas to Barth have argued, the phrase is not an addition of content but rather an explication of the original Nicene content of the word "Father." There is in Christian worship, Nicaea declares against the Arians, no Father to be praised without the Son who is *homoousion to patri*. A residual Arianism in the West in the sixth century was held to be reason enough to make this explication necessary. Without the redundancy of the *Filioque*, it is argued, the *Homoousios* tends to be evaded. The confession that the Holy Spirit "proceeds from the Father *and the Son*" is thus advocated as a necessary reaffirmation against Arianism, and similar tendencies, of the original Nicene refusal to believe that the God of the Gospel is Father without being Son.

If we examine the *Filioque* controversy with respect to the test of apostolic tradition, the judgment follows that the phrase is undeniably later than the original creed, and some ecumenists would advocate dropping it as an obstacle to the unity of the church for this reason. Yet apostolicity in tradition is not equatable merely with historically precedent wording. Further testing is needed.

If we examine with respect to the test of congruence with scripture, four texts may be taken as representative of issues in the debate.[22] Most often cited is the statement from the discourse of Jesus to the disciples found in John 15:26: "When the Paraclete comes, whom I will send to you from the Father, the Spirit of truth who comes [*ekporeuetai*, "proceeds"] from the Father, he will testify on my behalf." Here Jesus' words portray his role in the "sending" of the Spirit but distinguish this mission from the "procession" of the Spirit that is said to be "from the Father." Similarly, the antifilioquist position of the East affirms the Son's *sending* of the Spirit in the economy of God's relation to the world, but it distinguishes this economy, or "energy" as it is called, of *sending* or *mission* from the *procession* of the Spirit as a self-relation within God.

The role of Jesus in sending the Spirit is reiterated in a resurrection appearance to the disciples, also recorded in John: "Jesus said to them again, 'Peace be with you. As the Father has sent me, so I send you.' When he had said this, he breathed on them and said to them, 'Receive the Holy Spirit' " (John 20:21–22). Still a third text exemplifies the inseparability of the Father and Jesus that the Johannine author recounts with respect to the Spirit: "All that the Father has is mine. For this reason I said that he [the Spirit] will take what is mine and declare it to you" (John 16:15). In yet a fourth instance, this time a text from Revelation, a depicted procession symbolic of the Spirit may arguably be interpreted as actually suggesting the sense of "from the Father and the Son": "Then the angel showed me the river of the water of life, bright as crystal, flowing [*ekporeuomenon*, "proceeding"] from the throne of God and of the Lamb" (Rev. 22:1). From these and similar scriptures contextually interpreted the import of the canonical witness for faith in the Holy Spirit continues to be sought, with much agreement, but with as yet somewhat different conclusions, by East and West.

We come to the "So what?" question when we turn to the test of consequence and ask what difference the *Filioque* issue makes today. The gist of the claims and counterclaims that it provokes includes the following.

The major argument against the *Filioque*, other than its being a later alteration by only part of the church catholic of an ecumenically acknowledged creed, is that only one principle of origination is consistent with the biblical depiction of God. If the Spirit is said to proceed from the Father "and the Son" two sources of God's forthcoming appear to be posited, and the distinctive actuality attributed to the First Person as *fons et origo* in trinitarian doctrine is violated. The procession of the Spirit *ex Patre* may be understood to mean "from the Father through the Son," as indeed John of Damascus in the eighth century and others before him taught, but "Only the Father is cause [*aitios*]."[23] Put less abstractly, attribution of the Spirit's cause to the Son, it is contended, in effect leads to the reduction of pneumatology to ecclesiology, with the church as the "body of Christ" assuming the role of dispenser of the Spirit.

On the other side, the argument for the retention of the explicative significance of the *Filioque*, even if not the actual wording, stresses the inseparable relation of the Father and the Son. To recall the words of Thomas Aquinas cited earlier, with respect to the relation of Begetter and Only-Begotten this *nexus* or relationship in God is also God's *actus* or way of acting. Stated less technically, the Holy Spirit is God relating as Begetter and Begotten, not one-sidedly, as it were, hierarchically from the top down, but in a mutuality in which neither the Father nor the Son is God without the distinct bearing of the other. If doctrines with all their creaturely limitations are to be read and critically assessed as proposed reality descriptions, it matters for daily life to say that Ultimate Reality is the act of the relating of One with Another in the Spirit of perfect love and freedom. It matters, that is, to those who profess that being human means being made in the image of God.[24] It may further be argued that the sense at least of the *Filioque* should not be lost in that it provides for an understanding of the Holy Spirit in a more sociohistoric and political perspective, one, that is, having to do with governance, as the writings of both the Old and New Testaments variously attest. Proceeding from the Father and the Son suggests a proceeding of the Spirit that is both eternal and yet involved in the fullness of time as the Word becomes flesh. Current events become more important as the arena of the Spirit's liberating movement. Such an engaged and event-oriented perspective, it is alleged, contrasts with a more quiescently mystical and metaphysical view of the Spirit as proceeding only from the primordial source of the great unfathomable Unbegotten. Different pieties, philosophies of history, and approaches to ethics and politics are arguably the long-term result.

Rejoinders to these claims include the response from the Eastern perspective that the inseparable relationality the filioquists seek is amply provided for already in the unaltered Creed with the affirmation "who together with the Father and the Son is worshipped and glorified." Further, the concern for history and social involvement as the arena of the Spirit's vindicating movement is also provided for and more properly articulated as the divine economy of the *sending* or *mission* of the Spirit and not its *procession*, that is, as God's relation to the world and not as God's self-relation.

The filioquists in turn respond to the charge of threatening the *monarchia* of God as source of the Spirit's proceeding forth by granting that the only-begotten Son is not cause as is the begetting Father. Yet, simply to follow the narrative configuration of the gospel accounts leads the church to conceive of a giving of the Spirit, not only from the side of the Father to the Son, but also, even if not in the same sense, from the side of the Son back to the Father. In the dialogical depictions of the passion of the Cross the Crucified One who is confessed by the centurion with the words, "Truly this man was God's Son!" (Mark 15:39, Matt. 27:54), is said to *give* the spirit, crying, as the Lucan account puts it, with a loud voice, "Father, into your hands I commend my spirit" (Luke 23:46), or as the Johannine account adds, "Then he bowed his head and gave up his spirit" (John 19:30). It is in this reciprocity of giving from both sides in their distinctive ways, so the gospel's narrative configuration governing trinitarian theory suggests, that the Spirit of God actually proceeds and is forthcoming for faith. In such recounting of the Cross, God is presented, and thus may be said to be Presence, not hierarchically, as it were, from the top down, but in this very reciprocity of "the Father and the Son." The First Person rightly is a designation of the ungenerated and unengendered reality of God. But there is consistent with the gospel message no Unbegotten source, no reality of *archē*, except as the Begetter, and no Father except in conjunction with the Son. The breathing or "spiration" of the Spirit may thus be said to be a *conspiring*, not in a sinister but in the truest etymological sense of the word. The *nexus* of the Father and the Son is indivisibly one as God's own *actus*.

If we analyze the *Filioque* dispute with attention to the disbeliefs entailed, we find that the agreement between the two sides, beginning with the two basic disbeliefs of all objectification and subjectification that we first noted regarding the Spirit, is considerable. Both positions refuse to believe that ultimate reality is not life-giving. Both positions refuse to believe that this life-giving originates from any source that is not primal or is other than God, or that this life-giving is less actually and distinctively the one God's own way of being God than is the way referred to scripturally as the Father and the way referred to as the Son. Both positions refuse to believe that this life-giving flows forth, or proceeds, from an origination in God that is ever unrelated to the eternal Word confessed in faith as God's Son. Within the parameters of such shared disbeliefs as these, as they are broken down ever more specifically on location in their ramifications, present-day ecumenical consideration of the *Filioque* issue may take its bearings and find the traffic signals to chart beyond any current impasse its further course. Together the question continually to be pressed in such dogmatic testing is "What does faith now call us to *refuse* to believe?"

From the disputed question of the *Filioque* as an ontic consideration of God's forthcoming or procession in self-relation, we now turn to God's giving of life as the Holy Spirit in relation to us and to the world. One finds throughout the scriptural canon testimonies depicting the role of the Spirit in creation, in salvation, and in the envisioned coming consummation. In these so-called economic (as distinguished from the ontic) respects the mission of the Holy Spirit is seen as commissioning the purpose of all existence. The Holy Spirit as the Giver of life is thus portrayed as the Giver of created life, the Giver of rectified life, the Giver of glorified life, and the Giver of commissioned life. These rubrics anticipate the subsequent chapters dealing with creation, salvation, humanity, the church, and the life to come.

Testimony to the Spirit as the Giver of created life comes primarily from the Hebrew scriptures. In Genesis, as we have noted, God's spirit is said to blow over the face of the waters at the dawn of creation and to breathe life into the human creature (Gen. 1:1–2, 2:7). This view is reflected in the book of Job where Elihu says to Job, "The spirit of God has made me, and the breath of the Almighty gives me life" (Job 33:4). In the New Testament the emphasis falls upon the new creation, or the rectified life, but not as a denial of the Old Testament testimony to God as Creator Spirit. The new life, as the author of the Colossian letter expresses it, is renewed "according to the image of its creator" (Col. 3:10). The groaning of the whole creation in all its futility and present suffering, writes Paul to the Romans, is actually the birthpangs of a glorious freedom because the creation, despite all appearances to the contrary, is shown in the resurrection of Jesus to be not subject to itself but to God's Spirit (Rom. 8:19–23). Christian faith refuses to believe that the Giver of rectified life is other than the Giver of created life. This is the faithful disbelief registered in the second century against Marcion's teaching that the God of salvation is not the God of creation.

As the Giver of rectified life the Holy Spirit is confessed as sanctifier, or Giver of holiness and wholeness. The creeds, as we have seen, associate the Holy Spirit with a forgiven people in a holy universal community. The Spirit makes life right. Life that has gone wrong is referred to by Paul as being of the flesh and by this manner is contrasted with life that is of the Spirit. Romans 8 is especially instructive here. "But you are not in the flesh, you are in the Spirit, if in fact the Spirit of God dwells in you" (Rom. 8:9). There is definitely in Paul's accounting a corpus of death. "But if Christ is in you, though the body is dead because of sin, the Spirit is life because of righteousness" (Rom. 8:10). Yet, and somewhat unexpectedly, the flesh/spirit and body/spirit discourse in Paul proves not to conform to a docetic or Gnostic disembodied spiritualism. Although the sinful body is dead, God's indwelling Spirit of the resurrection over sin and death is said to "give life to your mortal bodies" (Rom. 8:11). The awaited deliverance is "the redemption of our bodies [*tou sōmatos hēmōn*]" (Rom. 8:23). There is a corpus of life confessed by Christian faith in such incarnate and somatic creedal terms as "holy catholic church," "communion of saints," and "resurrection of the body."

The eschatological emphasis upon the Spirit as the Giver of glorified life, or the life to come, is prominent in both the Old and New Testaments. The prophecy of Joel 2:28–29 with its telling of what shall "come to pass" is repeated, as was mentioned, in Acts 2:16–21 as part of Luke's account of the outpouring of the Spirit on the day of Pentecost. A key characterization of the Spirit in this connection, one that we find three times in the Epistles, is expressed with the word *arrabōn*, a fascinating fiscal term conveying the sense of a down payment and a promissory note as proof of future payment. The *arrabōn* is an unconcluded proving true of God's promised future. It is precisely this word for a commitment currently proving true that is used to describe the gift of God's life-giving as Spirit.

In his second letter to the Corinthians Paul writes, referring to Christ,

> For in him every one of God's promises is a "Yes." For this reason it is through him that we say the "Amen," to the glory of God. But it is God who establishes us with you in Christ and has anointed us, by putting his seal on us and giving us his Spirit in our hearts as a first installment [*arrabōn*]. (2 Cor. 1:20–22)

The Holy Spirit is here depicted as the presence of the coming God with us. Both the sense of presence and the sense of coming are accented. They enable us to recognize two more major disbeliefs inherent in Christian faith in the Holy Spirit. As presence, the coming vindication and glory of Jesus Christ is not pie in the sky bye and bye but is now given in the Spirit as a living foretaste and shown to be proving itself true. As a coming glory that is still coming due, this presence of the Spirit allows for no sacralized stasis of the present order, no closing of accounts as the deification of any status quo.

Again, in the same letter to the Corinthians Paul writes a second time regarding the glorified life to come that "we have a building from God, a house not made with hands, eternal in the heavens." He then concludes that the One "who has prepared us for this very thing is God, who has given us the Spirit as a guarantee [*arrabōn*]" (2 Cor. 5:1, 5). In a third epistolary passage the author of the Ephesians letter, whether Paul or another, writes similarly that, "In him [Christ] you also . . . were marked with the seal of the promised Holy Spirit that is the guaranty [*arrabōn*] of our inheritance until the redeeming [*apolytrōsin*, "redemption"] of the saving to the praise of his glory" (Eph. 1:13–14).[25]

Faith in the Holy Spirit as the present *arrabōn* of coming vindication and glory includes the refusal to believe that the present life God gives has no future yet to be realized, and allows for nothing new, and the refusal to believe that the future life God promises to give is not currently being witnessed, and is not now in every present situation proving to be true.

That in giving life as creation, rectification, and glorification the Holy Spirit commissions life with a purpose is a consistent theme of the scriptures. To live trusting in one's creation, justification, and promised fulfillment by God's Spirit is to live as participants in what is proclaimed as God's own ministry and mission. As expressed by the prophecy of Isaiah that is recalled by Jesus in his home synagogue at Nazareth, the anointing by the Spirit brings good news to the poor, proclaims release to the captives, recovery of sight to the blind, and tells the Lord's own time of favor (Isa. 61:1–2; Luke 4:18–19). The Holy Spirit as gift, and the Holy Spirit as the Lord and Giver, commissions gifts that are described as the "fruit" of the Holy Spirit.

3. The Gifts of the Holy Spirit

In contrast to all that represents opposition to God's dominion Paul writes to the Galatians that "the fruit of the Spirit" is such things as "love, joy, peace, patience, kindness, generosity, faithfulness, gentleness, and self-control" (Gal. 5:22). In his second letter to the Corinthians Paul addresses himself in Chapter 12 specifically to this subject of spiritual gifts. Not everyone receives the same gifts of the Spirit, or in equal measure. To some is given one gift especially, to others, another. Yet although there are varieties of gifts, they are of the same Spirit, the main point being that "to each is given the manifestation of the Spirit for the common good" (1 Cor. 12:7).

In the messianic prophecy of Isaiah the spirit of the Lord is said to rest upon the "shoot that shall come out from the stump of Jesse." Early Christian writers reading this Hebrew text in the Greek translation known as the Septuagint made much of the "seven-fold" gifts they saw indicated in the Prophet's proclamation of "the spirit of wisdom and understanding, the spirit of counsel and might, the spirit of knowledge [and piety] and the fear of the Lord" (Isa. 11:1–2).[26] In the New Testament the variety of the Spirit's manifestations is understood to embrace nothing that is not an ingredient of faith, hope, and love. These three "theological virtues," as Thomas Aquinas designates them, are set forth in Paul's own discussion in 1 Corinthians 13 of the three things that "abide" (1 Cor. 13:13). Also to the Thessalonians Paul writes of his thankfulness to God in remembering their "work of faith and labor of love and steadfastness of hope in our Lord Jesus Christ" (1 Thess. 1:3).

This wording of the statement to the Thessalonians in which Paul speaks of their work, labor, and steadfastness as being of faith, love, and hope is instructive as a concise reminder of two governing convictions that inform much of the later interpretation in the history of Christian doctrine. First, as gifts of the Spirit, faith, love, and hope are viewed by Paul as not of our own doing. Second, these gifts are such that they result in our own doing. They empower the ministry and mission of human acts. We will take up this second point again when we come to the topic of grace in the chapter on salvation. Here the significance of the first point for pneumatology and the disbeliefs entailed invites attention.

To confess that faith, love, and hope as gifts of the Spirit are not of our own doing involves a refusal to believe that they are either universal human attributes or particular human achievements. Rejected is the presumption that we can produce faith, or love, or hope either within ourselves or within anyone else. This is profoundly important for Christian ministry and mission. Looked at anthropologically the gospel testimonies concur that not all have faith, walk in love, and continue in hope. Looked at theologically, however, God is said to be faithful to all, to love all, and to be the hope of all. Words from 2 Thessalonians express this dual emphasis: "For not all have faith. But the Lord is faithful" (2 Thess. 3:2–3).

While the language of "possessing" the Spirit is sometimes used, the meaning more exactly in keeping with the import of the canonical witness is rather "being possessed by" the Spirit. This is consistent with the understanding of the gifts of the Spirit in the first instance as God's own indwelling that is not subject to our control. Yet the meaning as we shall discuss later is never that the recipient is rendered passive. Quite the opposite, to be inhabited by the Holy Spirit is, according to the gospel message, to become activated in freedom. It is precisely to come to life in one's own integrity. This is the point of Cyril of Jerusalem's fourth-century catechetical instruction cited earlier "against imagining that the Spirit takes *violent* possession of humans as evil spirits do." The Holy Spirit does not rape. Christian faith refuses to believe that any violation of human freedom and integrity is possession by the Holy Spirit. Herein lies the theological basis for the critique of all totalitarian religion and compulsive ritual practice. Life in the Spirit is freedom to act with a purpose and a mission that serves the common good. In such freedom of human agency faith indeed works, love labors, and hope remains steadfast.

Luke's account in Acts 2 of the day of Pentecost portrays those who are possessed by the sudden outpouring of the Holy Spirit as given the ability "to speak in other languages [*lalein heterais glōssais*]" (Acts 2:4). We should not leave the topic of the gifts of the Spirit without reflecting upon the pneumatological significance of this gift of *glōssolalia*.

"Speaking in tongues," as the term is most often used for the mark of the baptism of the Spirit, has historically been a disputed subject in the church. In sorting out the issues today three points should not be overlooked.[27] The first is that the manifestation of ecstatic expression of some sort in reference to the Spirit is clearly part of the church's history. Biblically one finds acknowledgments of such possession in the Old Testament, where in the instance of Saul, for example, the "spirit of God" is said to cause "prophetic frenzy" (1 Sam. 19:23), and, most prominently, in the New Testament passages of Acts 2 and 1 Corinthians 14.

A second point would have to be that ecstatic utterance as such is by no means a phenomenon peculiar to biblical faith. Thus this form of ecstasy, as indeed all others, has to be tested to discern which spirit is holy, the One "who spoke by the prophets" as the Creed puts it, the Spirit of Jesus Christ. The temptation is always to worship the ecstatic expression as such, to mistake a form of spirituality for God's Spirit. It is an ancient and still widespread practice to attempt to induce religious sensations by the use of drugs. It is also the case that forms of psychotic illness exhibit characteristics similar to some expressions of religious ecstasy. At the anointing of Saul, Samuel says to him, "Then the spirit of the Lord will possess you, and you will be in a prophetic frenzy" (1 Sam. 10:6). This will occur, Samuel tells Saul, when "you will meet a band of prophets coming down from the shrine with harp, tambourine, flute, and lyre playing in front of them; and they will be in a prophetic frenzy" (1 Sam. 10:5). Yet later when falling into a frenzy before Samuel, Saul, so the story has it, "stripped off his clothes . . . and lay naked all that day and all that night." And the text adds tellingly, "Therefore it is said, 'Is Saul also among the prophets?' " (1 Sam. 19:24).

The third and most important observation is to be found in Paul's advice to the Corinthians. It amounts to this: the test of speaking in the Holy Spirit is how much this speech communicates God's life-giving to other people. "How," Paul asks the Corinthians who are speaking in tongues, "can anyone in the position of an outsider say the 'Amen' to your thanksgiving, since the outsider does not know what you are saying?" (1 Cor. 14:16). This for Paul is the primary concern, and it allows no Christian community to go unchallenged whether it claims to be pentecostal and charismatic or not — what about the others, the outsiders? Is the spirit in question one of self-preoccupation or one of communication with those who are different? Thus Paul sums up his comments on this matter by saying, "I thank God that I speak in tongues more than all of you; nevertheless, in church I would rather speak five words with my mind, in order to instruct others also, than ten thousand words in a tongue" (1 Cor. 14:18–19).

The challenge Paul poses is totally missed if the issue is cast today merely in psychological terms as a preference for intellect over emotion, or in sociological terms as a classist preference for the more prescribed worship of the culturally established churches over the more spontaneous practices of the often (but not always) poorer so-called sects.

Foremost in the life commissioned by the Holy Spirit, as Paul sees it, is the concern to communicate God's life-giving with the outsider.

This third observation would seem to be borne out by Luke's narrative of Pentecost in Acts 2 as well. In it we read that the influence of the Spirit upon the company of the apostles enabled them to communicate with all people present. Devout persons from every nation under heaven heard in their own language the apostles' message. From every land visitors to Jerusalem reported, "In our own languages we hear them speaking about God's deeds of power" (Acts 2:11). It is striking that here the *glōssolalia* of the Spirit is depicted not as "unknown tongues," but exactly as the opposite, "known tongues" that make communication possible.

Proposed Disbeliefs

If we look back over the foregoing interpretation as it has attempted to trace the way through doctrinal issues associated with faith in the Holy Spirit, we will find the following disbeliefs proposed for recognition. In summary, I will now list them as they were stated and in the order set forth.

Christian affirmations of faith in the Holy Spirit entail the refusal to believe:

1. all proposed objectifications of God.
2. all proposed subjectifications of God, or attempts to deify human subjectivity.
3. that the Holy Spirit is a mere quality or attribute derivative of anything creaturely.
4. that ultimate reality is not life-giving.
5. that this life-giving originates from any source that is not primal, or is other than God.
6. that this life-giving is less actually and distinctively the one God's own way of being God than is the way referred to scripturally as the Father and the way referred to as the Son.
7. that this life-giving flows forth, or proceeds, from an origination in God that is ever unrelated to the eternal Word confessed in faith as God's Son.
8. that the Giver of rectified life is other than the Giver of created life.

9. that the coming vindication and glory of Jesus Christ is pie in the sky bye and bye and is not now given in the Spirit as a living foretaste and shown to be proving itself true.
10. that, as a coming glory that is still coming due, the presence of the Spirit allows for any sacralized stasis of the present order, any closing of accounts as the deification of the status quo.
11. that the present life God gives has no future yet to be realized, and allows for nothing new.
12. that the future life God promises to give is not currently being witnessed, and is not now in every present situation proving to be true.
13. that faith, love, and hope as gifts of the Spirit are either universal human attributes or particular human achievements.
14. that we can produce faith, or love, or hope either within ourselves or within anyone else.
15. that any violation of human freedom and integrity is possession by the Holy Spirit.

These disbeliefs provide parameters for evaluating the three initial objections stated in this chapter.

The first objection, that a trinitarian interpretation of the Holy Spirit in effect seems to deny the omnipresence of God, raises the issue of the role of the Spirit in life outside the symbolic world of Christianity. This question will face us again in connection with the doctrines of salvation and the church. Looked at specifically as a problem for pneumatology, we can now say that any restriction of God's life-giving presence to one sequence of world history is opposed by Christian faith as an attempted objectification of God. The source of God's Spirit is neither historic Christianity nor the subjectivity of Christians. The fact that God calls forth life outside of historic Christianity and that all created life is indeed the gift of God's Spirit is the pneumatological conviction that this first objection rightly seeks to underscore. Life's diversity is to be respected precisely in seeing creation's differences as a variety of manifestation for the common good. When cultural imperialism and chauvinism govern a Christian community's teaching, the result is either the idolatrous objectifying of God's life-giving as a circumscribed part of world history, or the attempted deifying of the subjectivity of that community's own adherents. The first objection rightly calls attention to and repudiates such doctrinal corruptions.

Nevertheless, by refusing to divorce the source of all life-giving from its rectitude, Christian faith is led to a trinitarian interpretation of the

Holy Spirit. Not everything in life is to be attributed to the working of the Spirit. The Spirit that is everywhere is not everything. For a faith that refuses to believe that the Spirit of creation and the Spirit of rectification are not one and the same, the variety of gifts for the common good cannot be said to include in their cultural diversity that which is not right for creation and does not serve the common good. That is, God's life-giving does not include anything that is inimical to life, to its rectitude and wholeness. The inevitable question for all life becomes, how is such rectitude and wholeness identified? By refusing to believe that the Giver of rectified life is other than the Giver of created life, Christian faith commits itself to the eternal relation of the source of all life with the destiny of the Word of life crucified, risen, and coming. This is the point of the conviction that there is no life-giving in God that is ever unrelated to the eternal Word confessed in faith as God's Son. A trinitarian interpretation, therefore, when pursued in recognition of what Christian faith refuses to believe with respect to the Holy Spirit, shows itself to be antithetical to the very corruptions that the first objection rightly exposes.

Further, it is in keeping with the concerns expressed in the first objection that faith as defined contextually by the New Testament *pistis* not be confused with adherence to Christianity as a religion. Yet neither can such faith be confused with a general characteristic of human nature, with the putative anthropological fact that every human being may be said to rely on or believe something. Faith as the Spirit's life-giving is in the first instance God's doing. It is God's relating to human beings in such a way as to relate human beings to each other in ministering to the common good. How, and when, and where God's omnipresent Spirit achieves this relatedness is not subject to human control. The Spirit's working for freedom is revealed only by the free working of the Spirit. The gospel message is that not all presently live by faith, but equally the message is that there is never a time or place without the Spirit's witness to God's faithfulness.

The second initial objection, that the distinctiveness of the Holy Spirit remains suppressed and underdeveloped even within trinitarian doctrine, finds a generally increased acceptance in late twentieth-century theology. The historical evidence cited to this effect in the second objection deserves careful consideration. The understanding of Christian faith from the perspective of the Third Article calls for the church's further attention. Here the proposed disbeliefs serve to point the way toward a more authentically triune way of thinking. Especially pertinent is the refusal to believe that the life-giving of the Spirit is less actually and distinctively the one God's own way of being God than is the way referred to scripturally as the Father and the way referred to as the Son. The relevant problem of the masculine language of such scriptural reference to "Father" and "Son," as well as the use of male pronouns for the Spirit, has been addressed in earlier chapters. We need in this connection to recall the disbelief, recognized in chapter 6, of any claim that the Word of God is reified in the words of a text, and the repudiation of the generic meanings of all terms attributed to God enjoined by the faithful disbeliefs having to do with the being of God that were discussed in chapter 7.[28]

As far as the matter of ecclesiastical authority raised by the second objection is concerned, we have earlier confronted a similar issue also in the chapter on the Word of God. Here we may appeal in addition to the disbeliefs associated with the gifts of the Spirit. As with respect to faith in the Word of God, so with respect to faith in the Holy Spirit, there is no authority recognized that does not author faith, love, and hope. In this regard charismatic movements require testing as much as any other.

Finally, the third objection, that nontriune depictions of the Spirit violate the gospel's threefold identifying referentiality concerning God, is shown to be sustained if the proposed disbeliefs have been accurately recognized. Yet insofar as these pneumatological proposals witness to the life of peoples and communities that have been suppressed or previously disregarded as God's gift by the more official circles of orthodoxy they call for a faithful hearing that resists a prejudiced dismissal without testing. Conservative defenders of so-called tradition who tend to value correct formulations and abstractions over life itself in all the untidy richness of its cultural diversity will find no cause for self-congratulation in Christian faith concerning the Holy Spirit. Yet neither will tendencies toward pantheism and the equation of the Holy Spirit with creaturely spirit of any kind. Christian faith in the Holy Spirit refuses to credit or give credence to any sacralized stasis of the present order. At the same time it refuses to credit or give credence to any violation of human freedom and integrity purporting to be possession by God's Spirit.

These disbeliefs obviously do not put an end to all of faith's questioning. Debates continue. Yet the call to faithful disbelief remains. In providing faith room to maneuver these refusals chart a course ahead to the next doctrinal area. The locus to which we now turn is usually said to be the first of the triune God's works, that which Christian faith confesses to be *creation*.

Chapter 10

CREATION

Introduction

Creation is sometimes referred to as if it were a self-evident fact. But we need not listen long to what is said about it to recognize that this is not the case. That we inevitably experience ourselves as part of a world, or that there is something rather than nothing, as philosophers have put it, may indeed be a self-evident presupposition of all human activity and awareness. But the presupposition that something exists says nothing about whether or not it has been created. Existence is not identical in meaning with creation, nor, when we think about it, is origination. Not all talk about the origin of the universe, or cosmic emergence, is talk about the creation of the universe, although often such language is loosely used as if the terms were interchangeable.

Contingency as well is another matter. In the world as we know it contingency is generally acknowledged to be empirically demonstrable. At least within our space-time system, parts of nature can be shown to depend upon other parts of nature for their continuance. Without the requisite conditions of a favorable environment certain things do not occur, and when the necessary support system no longer is present they cease to exist as before. But is the whole space-time system itself demonstrably contingent as a totality upon that which is other than itself? Here from the time of antiquity philosophers of nature have disagreed. Some attribute the origin and continuance of the universe to its own inherent resources, while others attribute this origin and continuance to a more ultimate necessity distinguishable from the universe itself. Cosmologically the latter view may be harder to conceptualize, but neither position can rightly claim to have proven to be persuasively self-evident.

The first requirement in studying the doctrine of creation is thus to clarify the focus of the inquiry. All investigation, as Thomas Aquinas reminds us, may in some respect be said to be about the world; what distinguishes one sort of inquiry from another is the frame of reference in which the world is viewed.[1] Every investigation looks at its subject in a certain light. For Christian theology that light is the frame of reference provided by the creation talk found in a particular context of usage, namely the Bible as scripture attested in the communal life of the church.

Creation doctrine in the church is an article of faith in the triune God as Creator. The same need not be said about the creation teachings developed within other frames of reference. Comparative mythology, natural science, and metaphysics, for example, each pursue their particular focus of inquiry into nature's origins without necessarily presupposing such faith. Nevertheless, as we observed in chapter 4, the test for a faithful coherence applied to church doctrine opposes any tendency on the part of Christian theology to disregard the insights other disciplines afford. How the claims to knowledge about creation made in the context of Christian faith agree or differ with the current state of knowledge claims made in other contemporary disciplines requires a dogmatic accounting.

Ernest Nagel defines what philosophical atheism for its part judges to be untenable about theism with reference to creation doctrine:

> And by theism I shall mean the view which holds, as one writer has expressed it, "that the heavens and the earth and all that they contain owe their existence and continuance in existence to the wisdom and will of a supreme, self-consistent, omnipotent, omniscient, righteous, and benevolent being, who is distinct from, and independent of, what he has created."[2]

Dogmatic testing, however, questions every theory of theism as well as of atheism. It asks first what the words in Nagel's statement are held to mean and how such language is rightly to be understood.

Within a biblical and ecclesial context of usage, "creation" may most simply be defined as *all that comes from God but is other than God.* Such usage rules out as creatures the Word and the Spirit, on the one hand, and evil, on the other. While the Word and the Spirit are indeed acknowledged as coming from God, who is their ultimate and unengendered source, they are explicitly praised as not being creatures who are other than God but as God's own coeternal forthcoming. And evil, while not God, is also seen in faith as not coming from God in the sense that would make it God's creation.

Christian doctrine has to do with this faith in God as the Creator who brings into being that which is other than God. In the historic creeds the creation is referred to comprehensively as "heaven and earth," including "all things visible and invisible." Since it is believed to come from God as its Maker, whatever is created is confessed to be good, never evil. Since it is believed to be other than God, whatever is created is confessed not to be deity, and thus never a subject of worship.

Initial Objections

If we ask where church traffic tends to become stalled today in the area of creation doctrine, four alleged roadblocks may be pointed out. Some of these objections are longstanding, while others have only begun more recently to be noticed. They register complaints against (1) the devaluation of nature, (2) fatalism, (3) hierarchy, and (4) anthropocentrism.

1. *It would seem that church doctrine regarding creation devalues nature.*

The case to support this contention includes the following elements. The New Testament itself contains comparatively few references to creation. By far the primary emphasis is upon the saving work of God in the events having to do with Jesus. Creation is relegated to a minor theme subordinate to that of human sin and the message of salvation. Nature is viewed as having become flawed and fallen, indeed downgraded as the term "degradation" makes explicit, and as requiring re-creation and rebirth. One of the most influential New Testament passages in this connection illustrates the point. In the first chapter of Romans, cited by most all major figures in the later history of Christian creation doctrine, Paul's subject is the gospel as the power of God for salvation. Attention is directed to the wickedness of those who are said to "suppress [*katechontōn*] the truth" (Rom. 1:18). Creation is alluded to only to explain how this suppression of the truth occurs.

> Ever since the creation of the world his [God's] eternal power and deity, invisible though they are, have been understood and seen through the things he has made. So they are without excuse; for . . . they exchanged the truth about God for a lie and worshiped and served the creature rather than the Creator, who is blessed forever! Amen. (Rom. 1:20, 25)

The conclusion usually drawn from Paul's words, and the one that has been most prominent since Augustine in the history of doctrine, is that the truth about God remains suppressed in nature because of a willful human tendency to counterfeit what is there. *Ergo frustra nobis* is the way John Calvin expresses the point: "It is therefore in vain that so many burning lamps shine for us in the workmanship of the universe to show forth the glory of its Author."[3]

The result of such teaching is the depreciation of the natural world that is the common global habitat of all earth's creatures.[4] An alienation from nature is evidenced both on a personal level, in self-destructiveness that is distrustful of sensuous feeling, and on a social level, in the kind of human behavior that threatens and despoils the earth's environment. To regard God is to disregard, or to show remorse for, the physical existence that all creatures have in common. The conviction that nature somehow is fallen and a source of our turning away from God, while antedating Christian teaching, is yet perpetuated by it and must be charged with fostering such alienation.[5]

2. *It would seem that Christian creation doctrine is fatalistic.*

While the term itself has consistently been rejected by Christian interpreters, "fatalism" in this instance may nevertheless be taken to stand for that note of universal inevitability that critics charge against creation doctrine. There are several facets to this sense of the cosmos as somehow conclusively predetermined. "The heavens and the earth . . . and all their multitude" are indeed said to be "finished" in the opening account of Genesis (Gen. 2:1). On the seventh day, it is reiterated, God "finished the work . . . and rested" (Gen. 2:2). "Long ago you laid the foundation of the earth," prays the Psalmist, "and the heavens are the work of your hands" (Ps. 102:25). Yet even "before the foundation of the world [*pro katabolēs kosmou*]," in the words of the Epistle to the Ephesians, God "chose" those "destined" according to "a plan for the fullness of time, to gather up all things in him [Christ], things in heaven and things on earth" (Eph. 1:4–5, 10]. When such passages are interpreted to support a perspective of universal inevitability the results are far-reaching.

To think of the world as fated from before the beginning of time leads to the idea of fixed orders of creation. The physical world of nature becomes a closed, prearranged system, to be understood not from an empirical investigation into its own processes, but from the deductions of an imposed supernaturalism. In such a system there can be no room for anything new. The names of Galileo and Darwin remain as two of the best-known recipients of the church's fierce opposition to free scientific exploration in those instances when the reported findings are held to conflict with officially sanctioned opinion. But if the world is depicted as merely a foregone conclusion, it follows that its Creator, as Alfred North Whitehead has warned, is one for whom all is primordial abstraction and nothing is of actual consequence.[6] Surely such a view of the ultimate inconsequence of existence is not commensurate with the God of biblical faith.

Especially is this fatalism apparent in doctrinal claims that in the continuance of creation all things are governed by God's providential will. John Calvin's words on this point are not as atypical as they are sometimes represented: "We make God the ruler and governor of all things, who . . . from the farthest limit of eternity decreed what he was going to do, and now by his might carries out what he has decreed."[7] To such teaching the objection is that human apathy and social irresponsibility in the face of injustice are the intolerable moral outcome.

3. *It would seem that a hierarchical portrayal of creaturely existence is antithetical to the faith that all creation is good.*

The issue is not that there is order in creation, but the type of order and how this is to be understood. There is no question but that the most formative traditions of church teaching picture the created order both as good and as hierarchical. "God saw everything that he had made," the account in Genesis 1 has it, "and indeed, it was very good" (Gen. 1:31). Yet while everything created is confessed to be "very good" in God's eyes, some created things come to be looked upon as not so good in human eyes. These are things that are said to rank at the lower end of the ladder of being. The top of the ladder extends into the heavens themselves with its celestial hierarchy of angels.[8] In descending order that which is intellectual is seen as closer to being spiritual and ranks above that which is bodily and material, just as heaven ranks above the earth. The influence here of Plato and Aristotle is apparent.

Such ranking brings with it a particular power dynamics. The higher is meant to rule over the lower while the lower is fashioned to meet the needs of the higher. The capacity to impregnate is ranked above the capacity to become pregnant. What is considered lower on the scale of created being is taken to have value insofar as it is thought to serve the good of what is higher, thereby contributing to its glory. To be sure, the order of preference exercised in human desires often does not conform to the order of nature. Contemplative reason, so Augustine explains, sees the natural order very differently from those whose judgments are more faulty because they are dictated by "the necessity of the needy, or the desire of the voluptuous."[9] Yet the scale remains; contemplative reason ranks higher than that which is associated with bodily sense.

The consequences of hierarchical creation doctrine are not merely theoretical. Patterns of subservience attributed to the natural order of creation come to be reproduced in social structures of authority and behavior with utilitarian values determined by those who happen to be in the top positions of dominance. To quote Rosemary Radford Ruether, "The chain of being, God-spirits-male-female-nonhuman nature-matter, is at the same time the chain of command."[10] An ecological awareness of the reciprocities of nature is blocked. "So human beings are free to use creatures lower in the hierarchy as suits human interests with only instrumental concern for their well-being," writes Julian Hartt. "It remains to be seen whether the massive destructiveness of that conviction will become clear and urgent enough in the perceptions of Christian peoples to change the pattern and course of Western civilization before the planet is rendered uninhabitable for other forms of life as well as for humankind."[11]

4. *It would seem that Christian creation doctrine promotes a false anthropocentrism.*

The protest against a hierarchical portrayal of the order of creation overlaps with a fourth objection that questions the kind of role attributed to the human creature in the total scheme of things. Customarily what has been highlighted in Christian doctrine is the fact that in the creation account of Genesis 1–2:3 the blessing to humankind [*adam*], in this first instance understood as "male and female," is given along with the charge to "fill the earth and subdue it" and to exercise "dominion... over every living thing that moves upon the earth" (Gen. 1:28). In the account that follows after Genesis 2:3 the creation of *adam* comes before that of any other living thing, and when the Lord God plants a garden in Eden it is given for *adam* "to till it and keep it" and to "eat freely" as commanded (Gen. 2:15–17), a command to which both man and woman are later held accountable. Every living creature that moves is said to be formed to meet the need for a "helper" and "partner" of *adam* (Gen. 2:18). The last and only fit helper is then introduced as woman, who in this second instance is differentiated as formed from the rib of *adam* in order that "they become one flesh" (Gen. 2:24). According to the more customary reading, the central focus throughout these testimonies from Genesis is upon the dominance of the human creature, with a definite bias toward the priority of this creature as male.

Criticism of anthropocentrism as a theological falsehood is generally made on the grounds that were, in chapter 4, labeled coherence, comprehensiveness, and consequence. Because of the challenges raised initially from these standpoints the case for congruence with scripture comes to be rethought.

With respect to coherence, the argument is that the idea of the universe as somehow centered in the dominance of the human species is as incoherent scientifically as is the notion that the cosmos is geocentric or that the earth is flat. The premise of this charge is not that natural science should determine the church's faith in God as Creator. Rather, insofar as the doctrinal claims that confess this faith are anthropocentric they are said neither to be required for the internal consistency of the faith itself, nor to relate externally to the present state of knowledge claims in the sciences other than in a contradictory way. James Gustafson alleges this dual incoherence. First he faults "most modern theologians" for still not coming to grips "with the significance of what many developments in modern science have made clear: the minuscule place of human life in the order of nature."[12] Later he argues, "But even the Genesis account can be interpreted to indicate that the Creator viewed the whole creation as good, not merely as good for our species."[13] Anthropocentrism is held to fail the test of coherence both with regard to natural science and with regard to biblical faith.

The appeal to comprehensiveness combines with the appeal to coherence whenever it is argued that not all the relevant data have been taken into consideration in doctrines that place humanity at the center of creation. Further data that are deemed relevant may come not only from the natural sciences, and today's ecological concerns, but also from new construals of the scriptural testimonies and ecclesial traditions themselves. In addition to the accounts of creation in Genesis 1–2, appeal may be made to a broader range of scriptures in both the Old and New Testaments to show its bearing upon Christian faith in regard to creation.[14]

With respect to the test of consequence, the argument against anthropocentrism is similar to that made against hierarchy. In effect, the good of creation in God's sight comes to be understood primarily as a utilitarian "good for something" in human eyes. This is not to suppose that no inequities exist in nature apart from human interference. The empirical evidence of a predatory law of the jungle has to be acknowledged along with whatever favorable evidence there is for the more harmonious ecological balance of a pristine rainforest, or of the planet's totality as a mutually sustaining cybernetic system. But the prophetic vision sees the goal of all that God has made not in the survival of the fittest predators, but in "the wolf [that] shall live with the lamb, and the leopard [that] shall lie down with the kid" (Isa. 11:6). It is this vision of creation that informs biblical faith. The theme of exercising dominion and subduing other creatures militates against the recognition of the necessary environmental balances and reciprocities connecting all living things. The other than human creation, both animate and inanimate, is valued in terms of its potential development for human profit, with the least profitable viewed as the most expendable.

Increasingly the falsity of the anthropocentric perspective is recognized in the priority given to the male, or androcentrism, which is held to be this perspective's patriarchal corollary and its persisting cultural consequence.[15] Phallic androcentric motifs are seen to be reflected in ideas of creation by fiat, as an executive order issued from on high, and in the interpretation of the *ruach* [wind-spirit] sweeping over the face of the waters in Genesis 1:2 as thunder and lightning, vertical from above. Obscured by androcentric outlooks are such nonphallic scriptural images of creation as being born of, or birthed by, the Spirit (John 3:5–6) with the *ruach* of Genesis 1:2 understood as hovering over the face of the waters, more in the sense of a nesting and hatching prior to the existence of the formed world.[16]

Interpretation

By refusing to worship either Father Time or Mother Nature Christian faith may be said to represent a vast iconoclasm, a clearing away of some of the most readily available images of who God is as Creator. The same is true as well with regard to the less than mighty, gender unspecified, and yet to develop emergence of an Infant New Year. That this iconoclastic denial of ultimacy to the kind of giving and taking exemplified by Father Time, Mother Nature, and Infant New Year also applies in the case of totalitarian patriarchy is a question raised by the initial objections.

The language of an "Almighty Father, Maker of heaven and earth" would seem to offer a quintessential refuge for both a totalitarian and a patriarchal image of the Creator incommensurate with the import of the gospel. This language provides the most longstanding and familiar means of expression by which Christians articulate their creedal affirmation of faith in God. Commonly associated with baptism are the words of the Apostles' Creed: "I believe in God the Father Almighty, Maker of heaven and earth." Commonly associated with the eucharistic meal of holy communion are similar words of the Nicene Creed: "We believe in one God, the Father Almighty, Maker of heaven and earth, and of all things visible and invisible." Comparable usage is found in noncreedal Christian communities. To assess creation doctrine in its scriptural and ecclesial contexts requires an inquiry into the disbeliefs that faith in God the Creator enjoins and entails. What does faith in "God the Father Almighty, Maker of heaven and earth" *refuse* to believe?

1. "Let There Be": From Exodus to Genesis

Our focus upon the biblical and ecclesial context of creation discourse directs attention to the prominence of a recurrent antiphony in the first chapter of Genesis. The words, "Let there be," are followed by the statement, "And it was so." By this antiphonal repetition a primary characterization of who is and who is not to be acknowledged as Creator is indicated. None is Creator except the One whose calling forth of being is equivalent with the fact of being. In keeping with this antiphonal testimony, such equivalence is rightly attributable to no agency other than that of God. As antiphonally identified in Genesis 1, the Creator may be said to be Creator whether or not the creature so wills, but the creature is creature only if the Creator so wills. We are introduced to a basic volitional demarcation between the characterization of the Creator and the creature. Creaturely existence is that which is subject to a decision prior to its own. It has first been decided for and willed into being. Stated as a disbelief, such conviction refuses to believe that any command makes something so except the command of God. Hence in the Hebrew scriptures only the Lord God is the subject of the verb *bara*, "to create."

Within such a frame of reference the dogmatic task is to explicate what may be called the antiphonal import of Genesis 1 in its larger canonical context, both scriptural and ecclesial, by testing for what it does and does not mean for faith to confess today that God is the agent, or *subject of*, this antiphony and that creatures, by contrast, are *subject to* this antiphony. The familiar creedal juxtaposition of the terms "Father, Almighty, Maker" provides an outline of rubrics for this testing.

First, the term "Father." To the extent that paternal references for God tend to be understood as patriarchal in an androcentric manner that betrays the gospel, they cannot be said to convey the apostolic tradition of faith in "God the Father." Citing the cultural consequences of such an androcentric tendency some Christians today reject the older creedal language.[17] In addition to the question of *tendency* there is also the question of *intention*. What account is to be given of the faith intention expressed by the creedal use of the word "Father" in the context of Christian worship? A recognition of the faithful disbeliefs enjoined and entailed is essential to providing an answer.

To affirm faith in "the Father Almighty" as "Maker of heaven and earth" is to refuse to believe that the power that brings creation into being is of a Source other than the power of Jesus' resurrection. This linkage for Christian faith is the heart of the matter; what is intended by identifying the Creator as "Father" is reference to the One whom Jesus trusted as "Father" and who proved trustworthy by raising Jesus from the dead. The Jesus of the Gospels does not place trust in generic fatherhood. Nor does patriarchy, totalitarian or any other kind, raise this Jesus from the dead. To say "the One who proves trustworthy with Jesus" is to say what is intended by the use of the word "Father" within the creedal context of faith. Christian conviction affirms the Creator of heaven and earth to be "God, the One who proves trustworthy with Jesus, Almighty."

A clear example of the linkage made in early Christian testimony between the Creator of all things and the resurrection of Jesus may be seen in Acts 17. According to the account given of Paul's address to the Athenians, it is in the context of his "telling the good news about Jesus and the resurrection" (Acts 17:18) that Paul is led to proclaim that "the God who made the world and everything in it, . . . who is Lord of heaven and earth" is not the object of mortal manipulation or imaging (Acts 17:24). Assurance of who this One is who "made all nations to inhabit the whole earth" is said to be given to all "by raising [Jesus] from the dead" (Acts 17:26, 31).

Following this train of thought, if Christian faith is given its assurance of who the Creator is by the resurrection of Jesus, the threefold referentiality unavoidable in "telling the good news about Jesus and the resurrection" must be recognized as part of the intent of any faithful usage of the creedal term "Father." The gospel news of God's act of creating the world cannot be told except by referring to the Source of all things in connection with the Spirit's proving true of the power of Jesus Christ's resurrection. Within this particular linguistic framework the Creator is identified to Christian faith as triune.

Opera Trinitatis ad extra sunt indivisa is the way this recognition has traditionally been stated: "the external works of the Trinity are indivisible."[18] What this means is that unlike God's relations *ad intra*, God's self-relatedness, where designations such as *fons et origo* or Unbegotten Begetter are attributable solely to the First Person, and Only-Begotten is attributable solely to the Second Person, and *spirated* or Breathed-Forth Procession is attributable solely to the Third Person, God's relations to that which is not God as they are enacted in creation, salvation, and the fulfillment of all things are to be attributed to the working of all three Persons conjointly in their undivided unity. As the one God and sole Subject of the antiphony *"Let there be"/"And it was so,"* the Second and the Third Persons, or ways of God's being God, must be said to share fully in the work of creation along with the First.

But the sharing is in a manner that is distinctive of each. The three referents, while inseparable, are recognized within this framework of usage as not interchangeable. We do not tell of the Son of God or the Holy Spirit as the "Maker of heaven and earth" in the same sense that we tell this of the Father as the eternal Source of all forthcoming. Similarly, we do not tell of the Father or the Holy Spirit as the Savior in the same sense that we tell this of the Son, or tell either that the Father or the Son is poured out as the Sanctifier in the fulfillment of all things as we tell this of the Holy Spirit. The observation that the threefold referentiality involved in "telling the good news about Jesus and the resurrection" is both inseparable and yet not interchangeable explains why the term "Father," which involves reference to the Son and to the Spirit, is appropriated in speaking of the Creator in a way that the terms "Son" and "Spirit" are not. It is appropriate to speak of "the One who proves trustworthy with Jesus" as creating *through* the Son and *in* the Spirit. Creation is fully the work of all three Persons but according to the way that is distinctive to each. In the words of the Second Helvetic Confession, "This good and almighty God created all things, both visible and invisible, by his coeternal Word, and preserves them by his coeternal Spirit, as David testified when he said, 'By the word of the Lord the heavens were made, and all their host by the breath of his mouth' (Ps. 33:6)."[19]

If in Christian confession of faith in God as Creator the semiotic intent of the use of the term "Father" is "the One whom Jesus trusted and who raised Jesus from the dead" — in short, "the One who proves trustworthy with Jesus" — the agency operative in creation is affirmed not only to be self-relational but also personal. The Power of creation is thus referred to in biblical faith as a personal Subject, not as an impersonal object, a causal mechanism, or a principle of creativity. While our living, moving, and being have dimensions that are properly to be understood as physical, chemical, biological, psychological, and sociological, in the Athenian address as recounted in Acts Paul ultimately attributes such creaturely existence to a personal Source in *whom*, not in which, we are (Acts 17:28). As the Power that overcomes the crucifixion of Jesus, the Subject of *"Let there be"* / *"And it was so"* is not confinable within the explanatory categories of these other frames of reference. This means as well that when engaging in personal address for the Creator as the Power that overcomes the crucifixion of Jesus what is intended cannot be confined simply to ideas of personality and gender, whether masculine or feminine pronouns are used. The domain of the Resurrection is not restricted to frames of reference having to do with gender, the psyche, or the soul.

This brings us next to consider the creedal term "Almighty" (in the Greek, *pantokrator;* in the Latin, *omnipotens*).

Pantokrator is made up of two Greek words, *kratos*, which means "dominion," and *panta*, which means "all." Christian faith is confessed in the God who has dominion over all. This is affirmed originally against Manichean, Marcionite, and Gnostic forms of dualism. Disbelief is registered against any notion of more than one God. Faith refuses to believe that evil has equal status with the good, or that the opposition to the call "Let there be" can keep the good creation from being so.

To say that God as Creator is "Almighty" in this context is not to say that God has unlimited power, but rather power subject only to self-limitation. Just as the biblical testimonies to God's omnipresence do not exclude others from the presence of God, so the confession of God's omnipotence does not carry the semiotic intent of claiming that all power is excluded from creation that is other than God. In creating, God gives space and time to the creature. To be made in God's image is to be given creaturely "dominion" under God (Gen. 1:27–28).

With the faithful refusal to believe that the power of creation is of a different Source from the power that raised Jesus comes a radical redefinition of what is meant by "almighty" in the confessional context of usage. Luther emphasized this redefinition by pointing to a "theology of the cross" in contrast to a "theology of glory." If "Christ crucified" is "the power of God," as Paul writes to the Corinthians, then faith in Christ is led to confess that what Paul calls "the source of your life in Christ Jesus" "chose what is weak in the world to shame the strong" (1 Cor. 1:23–24, 27, 30). "The God of the Bible," to recall Dietrich Bonhoeffer's words from prison, "conquers power and space in the world by his weakness."[20] To the faith that recognizes the power which overcomes the world in what happens with Jesus the omnipotence of the Creator of heaven and earth means that nothing can ultimately defeat the crucified and risen Christ.

The doctrinal claim that God creates *ex nihilo* and that only God is Creator in this sense also is linked to faith that the Almighty's power is the power of resurrection. We find this expressed in the influential first-century Jewish writing of 2 Maccabees, a text often cited as the earliest explicit instance of the idea of *creatio ex nihilo* in Hebraic tradition. The writing narrates events of martyrdom set in the years 180–161 B.C.E. As sentence is pronounced on the last of seven brothers condemned to torture and death in a single day by King Antiochus for refusing to disobey the Lord's command, the faithful mother whispers to her sole remaining son:

> I beg you, my child, to look at the heaven and the earth and see everything that is in them, and recognize that God did not make them out of things that existed [or, made them out of things that did not exist]. And in the same way the human race came into being. Do not fear this butcher, but prove worthy of your brothers. Accept death, so that in God's mercy I may get you back again along with your brothers. (2 Macc. 7:28–29)

The theme is reiterated in the narrative that the seven brothers died cherishing "the hope God gives of being raised," a hope of "resurrection to life" (2 Macc. 7:14). The faith that the Ruler of the universe creates out of things that do not exist derives here not from cosmological speculation but from "the hope God gives of being raised."

The same may be said in the case of the two New Testament passages that are usually cited as suggesting some idea of *creatio ex nihilo*. In one of them, Hebrews 11:3, the claim, "By faith we understand that the worlds [*tous aiōnas*] were prepared by the word of God, so that what is seen was made from things that are not visible," follows a description just preceding in 11:1 of faith as "the actualization [*hypostasis*] of things hoped for, the proving true [*elegchos*] of things not seen."[21] Even more explicit in linking the Creator's almightiness to resurrection hope are Paul's words in Romans 4:17 that God "gives life to the dead and calls into existence the things that do not exist."

The third term is "Maker." It occurs along with "Father, Almighty" in the original wording of the fourth-century affirmations of Nicaea and Constantinople that come to comprise the Nicene Creed and is at least implicit in the origins of the Apostles' Creed. The best-known instance of these origins is the so-called Old Roman Symbol, a second-century baptismal formulary used in Rome from which the Apostles' Creed is thought to have developed. "Maker" seems only to have been added explicitly to this symbol somewhat later. Yet reference to the Father Almighty as the One "who made the heaven, and the earth, and the seas, and all that is in them" already is presented as traditional teaching by Irenaeus sometime around the year 200,[22] and additional commentary evidence further suggests that the meaning of "Maker" was most certainly understood in catechesis from the beginning to be implied in the confession of God as "Father, Almighty." Rufinus of Aquileia, our earliest extant source for the Old Roman Symbol, writing at the start of the fifth century, comments, "Almighty is applied to Him [God the Father] on account of the dominion He has over the universe."[23] What is more striking is that Rufinus goes on to explain that the designation of "Almighty" in the original Old Roman Symbol, where the term "Maker" is lacking, carries the meaning of Creator precisely because the Almighty is first confessed to be the "Father" of the Son through whom all things are said, in the words of the Epistle to the Colossians, to be "created."[24] "For in him all things in heaven and on earth were created, things visible and invisible, whether thrones or dominions or rulers or powers — all things have been created through him and for him" (Col. 1:16). Rufinus in this instance provides us with a good example of the attempt to set forth the semiotic intent of the juxtaposition of the words "Father, Almighty, Maker" in early Christian confession.

By linking the creation of "heaven" above with that of "earth" beneath, biblical and creedal language testifies in spatial imagery to a scope of God's dominion in conjunction with earth that is not presently visible as a phenomenon within the space-time continuum of earthly existence. It is noteworthy that scriptural references to descending and ascending with respect to heaven do not lend themselves to any characterization of this sphere that suggests a bypass or evasion of the reality of earth. In fact, just the opposite is the case. Prominent in the Gospel of Matthew, for example, is the message of John the Baptist (Matt. 3:2) and of Jesus (Matt. 4:17) that what is now "at hand" here on earth is precisely the "*basileia* of heaven"; that is, God's own unimpeded "kingdom" or "dominion" moving onto the scene. The disbelief implicit in this creedal language of "heaven and earth" should not be missed. Faith refuses to believe that the scope of creation is either limited to, or permits evasion of, those things that presently appear.

We have observed that by confessing "heaven and earth" to be God's creation biblical faith acknowledges that the world is not to be viewed as deity, nor is it to be viewed as evil. The cosmos itself, both seen and unseen in all its heights and depths, is the good gift of God. "Whatever *is* is good," writes Augustine, asserting not a disregard of evil, but emphasizing that whatever has being is good as that which has been decided for by God and called into being.[25] Evil, from this perspective, becomes defined as that to which God never says, "Let it be." We shall return to this point about evil in a moment.

More concretely, the doctrine of creation registers faithful refusal of all attempts to portray the natural world, the physical body, and sex as intrinsically bad and shameful. Equally refused are all attempts to sacralize the status quo, to deify such nature, and to confuse the creature with the Creator. We should notice what these disbeliefs amount to. In short, pantheism is shown to be the antithesis of Christian creation faith precisely because of its disregard for the existence and good of that which is *not* God. This undervaluing of the integrity of creation by pantheism is a fact often overlooked. From the standpoint of Christian faith in God as Creator, any effort to deify another human being at once dehumanizes that other by violating the creaturely integrity of the very one whom we are commanding to serve us as our god. No creature, human or other than human, can understand us completely, show mercy toward us unceasingly, and be with us through all our life and death. No creature is the source of the power of Christ's resurrection. An idol becomes such because of false pretensions, not for being what it really is. To know God as "Maker of heaven and earth" is to know the freedom that comes from letting others than God be who they are, the good company whom God has chosen not to be without. These consequences of Christian creation doctrine come to view in light of faith's disbeliefs.

The affirmation of God as "Maker" also involves the biblical idea of covenant. The testimony concerning creation on the part of Israel and the early church tells of their having been called into being as a people, as a community. Geophysics is not the primal frame of reference for this cosmogony, God's commitment is. In the Hebrew scriptures the Lord God is confessed as having created Israel by making a commitment. That is what "chosen people" means. Israel is depicted as having been decided for, or "elected," by God, not for special exemptions, but for a special mission, to be the bearer of God's blessing to all the nations of the earth. In this call, this election, Israel is created. From the historical reality of having been called into existence by an exodus from bondage in Egypt and identified as a people ultimately decided for and committed to, Israel confesses the faith articulated in the Genesis 1–3 accounts that this same Lord God is indeed the creator of the ends of the whole earth. "Israel looked back in faith from her own election to the creation of the world" (von Rad).[26] For this reason most interpreters today stress the point that the divine commitment to exodus deliverance is the premise of biblical faith regarding the genesis of all things.

The logical priority of the Resurrection in Christian confession of God as the Creator "who gives life to the dead and calls into existence the things that do not exist" (Rom. 4:17) finds its Old Testament counterpart in the logical priority of the Exodus in Israel's confession of the genesis of all things. This explains why the definition of creation, within a biblical frame of reference, is never simply equatable with origination or emergence. Creation is precisely that origination and emergence which enacts an ultimate self-commitment. As that which has first been decided for and committed to, creation involves the promise on the part of God to be with all that is called into being. The causality of giving life to the dead and calling into existence the things that do not exist is thus not presented scripturally as a putative scientific cosmology. The priority for faithful witness to creation is not some explanation of the origin of species but the ultimacy of the commitment made to species. What is at stake in affirming God as "Maker of heaven and earth" is the question of historical faithfulness in the making and keeping of covenant. Covenant is the promise of God to work for the good of creation in all that creation confronts in its existence. This particular character of biblical witness has often led theologians to speak of covenantal fidelity with creation as a contractual relation on the part of God, distinguishable from God's ontic self-relatedness, in two senses of the verb "to contract." First, as biblically depicted, the Subject of the antiphony *"Let there be"/"And it was so"* makes a commitment, God "contracts" to be with existence in time and space; second, in so doing God draws back, as it were, from being all that is, God "contracts" to make room for the other than God to be.[27]

2. "It Is Not Good": Knowing Evil

Within the canonical framework of creation discourse there is a "not good" to be heard in testimony regarding the creation of the good. Immediately following the call of *"Let there be"* references appear in the Genesis narratives to what shall "not" be. Not to be grasped by the creature for eating is fruit from "the tree of the knowledge of good and evil" (Gen. 2:17), a figural depiction of that which belongs solely to God's domain. Coupled with this declaration of Creator/creature boundaries is the pronouncement, "It is not good that *adam* should be alone" (Gen. 2:18). If creation properly denotes what God is portrayed as deciding for in saying *"Let there be,"* the "not good" must be said, within this frame of reference, to be other than creation. The "not good" is what God is portrayed as deciding against in saying *"Let there be."* Both the creation, as everything made and seen by God to be "very good," and also the "not good," enter the biblical picture and come on the scene with the call *"Let there be."* But only of the good creation, and never of the "not good," does the antiphon of Genesis 1 conclude, *"And it was so."* Herein for biblical faith lies the difference, and with it the problem of recognizing evil.

The theological import of these figurative accounts when taken as putative reality descriptions is that evil is real, but not as the Creator is real and not as creation is real. Evil "is," but only as that which "is not" to be so. It is presented as coming upon the scene of creation as a usurper of what is to be, "looking for someone to devour" (1 Pet. 5:8). Much analytic attention has been given in the history of philosophy and theology to the kind of reality and meaning that is denotable by such terms as "not good," "not being," and "no-thing."[28] Faith in God as the good Creator of a good creation thus leads to a consideration of what is "not good."

A problem arises at the very heart of Christian faith in God the Creator, the problem of powerful opposition to all that God has made. Along with the good creation of heaven and earth, of humankind, and all creatures great and small, there is an opposing force that seeks to annihilate the covenant life that God has called into being.

The church tells of this opposition in preaching the gospel message of what happens with Jesus of Nazareth. The narrated events of the Cross reveal the extent to which the will and way of Jesus are under attack in this world. If, as Christian faith confesses, the will and way of Jesus are to be recognized as the will and way of Emmanuel (Matt. 1:23), "God-with-us" incarnate, then the events of the Cross reveal the extent to which the very reality of God is under attack within the good creation God has made.

Christian faith also witnesses to the fact that this opposition is personally encountered as one follows the life that is given in Christ. The gospel conflict exposes a current conflict within our existence as well. We face in our own life stories a struggle against forces that are antithetical to the love and freedom in which, so the gospel message promises, God has created us to live. Creation is thus recognized to be under a constant onslaught of opposition manifest by the Cross of Christ itself and the annihilation and destructiveness which in various ways haunts each of us and the lives of those we love.

What comes to be labeled "the problem of evil" is actually twofold. It is in the first instance, and most crucially, the problem of *withstanding* this opposition, the issue of salvation, to which attention will be directed in the next chapter. But it is also, while secondarily and as part of the first, the problem of *understanding* this opposition from the vantage point of creation testimony as far as faith in God as "Father (the

One who proves trustworthy with Jesus) Almighty, Maker of heaven and earth" permits.

In the stipulations of the usage we have been attempting to follow, the word "evil" as the "not good" is properly applicable only to that which opposes God as God is and opposes creation as creation is called to be. By its refusal to believe that either the Creator or the creature as created is to be characterized as evil, Christian faith in fact registers two profound disbeliefs. Rejected is any claim that evil is something essential to the good. Rejected as well is any claim that there is evil that cannot become subservient to the good. The consequence is that all ultimate dualisms that seek to pair good and evil as necessary opposites in an equilibrium are disallowed. Any opposition that is essential to the health and wholeness of creation, whether viewed cosmologically or psychologically, is not opposition to the good, or evil. The delimitation of evil as opposition to Creator and creature thus is not to be confused with those contrasts that are depicted biblically as comprising God's good creation: that is, night as well as day, dark as well as light, shadow as well as sun, and even travail as well as joy.

At the level of a conceptual understanding, the recognition of the kind of reality that evil may be said to possess becomes a matter, within a biblical frame of reference, of recognizing rights of domain. God the Creator — as trustworthy, almighty, and maker — is depicted as good and as having dominion over all. Humanity in turn is said to be good, as created, and to be given dominion under God (Ps. 8:6). For its part, evil as the "not to be so" is configured as opposition to the good that asserts dominion over creation, but does so only under God. The dogmatic task becomes one of seeking a faithful accounting of how this "over and under" is to be understood. How may the opposition to Creator and creature that asserts dominion *over* the creation but *under* God be said in faith to be "known"?

Taken canonically, scriptural traditions require the interpreter to use the word "know" when referring to evil in four distinct senses: how God as Creator knows evil, how the creature knows evil in the Fall, how God as Savior knows evil, and how the creature knows evil in salvation.

First, God as Creator is said to have "knowledge of good and evil" (Gen. 2:17). The tempter in the garden of Eden is depicted as saying, "When you eat of it [the forbidden fruit of the tree which is in the middle of the garden] your eyes will be opened, and you will be like God, knowing good and evil" (Gen. 3:5). At the initial stage of creation God thus is reported already to "know" evil by defining the "not good" that is rejected by willing the existence of the good. The conception is one of God knowing what is not to be so by rejecting all that it is not good for the creature to be. God as Creator is thus first presented in the creation accounts as the Rejecting One with respect to evil.

Second, in the ensuing story of Eden the creature may next be said to "know" evil, not by rejecting it but by electing it. This point will be addressed when we come to the doctrine of salvation. In this chapter we need only observe that the evil the Creator rejects is disclosed in this second instance as that which is desired and accepted by the creature. The message of Eden is that the creature decides *for* what God has decided *against* in willing the creature's good to be. Such creaturely disorientation in willing and delusion in knowing is what is meant by "the Fall." We are thus introduced to a second meaning of "know" with respect to evil, as a falling for it. The "not good" boundary violation of the Creator/creature relation is apprehended in the creature's knowing as the exposure of "nakedness" and "hiding" that is the "not good" of being alone (Gen. 3:7–8).

Third, as the story of salvation develops in the Bible, God as Savior is said to "know" evil as the bearer of it, the Suffering Servant who becomes the Rejected One. This testimony provides yet a third meaning of "knowing evil." The One who cannot be said to know evil in the sense of desiring it, or falling for it, is now said to undergo its opposition in the events of the Cross. Paul writes of the crucified Messiah, "For our sake he [God] made him to be sin who knew no sin, so that in him we might become the righteousness of God" (2 Cor. 5:21).

Fourth, in the gospel proclamation of salvation the creature is described as knowing evil for what it is by knowing the victory of the Rejected One. The Resurrection testimony provides yet a further way of speaking of the knowing of evil. This is not the knowing of the first instance when God in creating is said to know the "not good" as the Rejecting One. It is not the knowing of the second instance when the creature in the Fall may be said to know evil as an act of defiantly choosing what is "not to be." It is not the knowing in the third instance when God as Savior may be said to know evil by bearing its opposition as the Rejected One in crucifixion. Rather, it is the knowing of evil for what it is by the cost of its being overcome. All that is "not good" and "not to be so," even as willed in self-opposition and self-destructiveness by the creature, is pictured as unable to prevail against the power of the Rejected One's resurrection from the dead.

Within the parameters of these four kinds of reference to the knowing of evil certain purported explanations for why "bad things happen to good people" are shown to be ruled out.[29] Faith stands with Rachel in refusing to be consoled by them. Disbelieved are all claims to the effect that (1) no really bad things happen, that evil has no bad reality but is only good disguised or misconceived—the denial of evil, (2) that evil, if it does happen, does not happen to the good, that is, that those who suffer bad things were not created good people — the denial of faith's affirmation of "Maker," (3) that God, even as the good Creator, does not exercise dominion over all — the denial of "Almighty," and (4) that God, even as the Creator who exercises dominion over all, does not do so in ways that prove trustworthy for the creature's good — the denial of the creedal intent of "Father."

To join Rachel in her refusal is finally to disbelieve every hypothetical attempt to understand evil in abstraction from its actual withstanding. The deeper issue for biblical faith when confronted by inexplicable opposition to creation's good is not, as many speculative theodicies have assumed, How in the face of such evil can we vindicate the ways of God?, but instead, How in the face of such evil does God vindicate us? With respect to this latter question of withstanding, to anticipate the theme of the next chapter, the testimony is that the Creator stands with us as Savior.

3. "The Lord Will Provide": Creation's Continuance

The creation that is not self-evident in its origins is certainly no more so in its continuance. That an ultimate decision for, and commitment to, the good of all things visible and invisible in heaven and earth remains currently in effect can only, if so, prove to be so by a provision greater than our own. By giving currency to ancient traditions of Rachel's refusal of comfort at the slaughter of the innocents the Matthean nativity account acknowledges forthrightly at the start that this is indeed a world in which those subjected to the likes of Herod's fury continue to be mourned as "no more" (Matt. 2:18). This testimony runs counter to all romanticized claims for divine providence that base their appeal upon evidences of physical advantage or prosperity to be found within nature and history.

In the face of opposition, and without denial of the earthly loss of those good gifts of creation that are indeed "no more," Christian faith in God as Creator rejects every spirit that proclaims that the conditions of covenant existence cease to remain in effect. This is the primary disbelief entailed in the doctrine of providence. The point is graphically conveyed by the Genesis account of Abraham and Isaac at the sacrifice on the mount in Moriah, an account from which the doctrine of providence derives its name. At this initial threat to the continuance of life in covenant exemplified by the offering up of the covenant-child Isaac, the sudden appearance of a ram in the thicket provides Abraham with a burnt offering for sacrifice instead of his son. "So Abraham called that place 'The Lord will provide'; as it is said to this day, 'On the mount of the Lord it shall be provided' " (Gen. 22:14).

Much has been written and questioned about this story of Abraham's testing by the command to sacrifice Isaac. What is plain is that provision of the ram in the instance of the offering up of Isaac is dramatically recounted as occurring precisely at the necessary moment, and not ahead of time, or before the place of offering is reached. The Lord is thus depicted as providing concretely in a timely rather than a timeless manner. Viewed from this perspective, the idea of providence, unlike the idea of creation *ex nihilo*, presupposes the prior existence of time and space.

If the word "creation" is appropriately used to denote the conditions of life in covenant first brought into being by God's *making* of the promise of deliverance from bondage, "I will take you as my people, and I will be your God" (Exod. 6:7), the word "providence" in turn may be said to denote God's *keeping* of this promise in all subsequent circumstances of creaturely existence. Just as faith in the making of God's commitments is not equatable to a theory of natural science, so faith in the keeping of those commitments is not equatable to a theory of historical progress. Such faith subverts all imperialistic claims to manifest destiny by refusing to believe that earthly privilege and the power to subjugate are the signs of divine endorsement. The only manifest destiny, from the standpoint of faith in providence, is the trustworthiness that God alone can manifest in keeping covenant with Rachel's refusal of consolation in the face of all within nature and history that currently seeks to oppose and destroy the creature's good.

God's providing for the continuance of the conditions of life in covenant has traditionally been referred to in the history of Christian doctrine as God's "maintaining" (*manutenentia*) or "conserving" (*conservatio*) of the creature's good.[30] What is disbelieved is that this providence is a maintenance or preservation of the status quo. Withstanding the threat to creaturely existence is not a *stasis*, a standing still either in time or place. Both Old Testament and New Testament narratives witness not to a static but to a dynamic providence occurring en route to a sabbath fulfillment. Provision of *manna* in the exact amounts needed for the day is said to be given so as to be gathered afresh "morning by morning" en route through a wilderness to a promised land (Exod. 16:21). The appeal of ten lepers to Jesus is said to be met with healing that is commanded to take place en route: "And as they went, they were made clean" (Luke 17:14). The maintaining of covenant relation is thus seen in the first instance to be something only God can do. Creation sets the stage for the free play of covenant love to unfold. But the drama of this unfolding is always new, never a series of old reruns. What is continuing to take place in every present situation is a fresh vindication of this love against whatever it is that may currently be working to destroy it.

Providence as a continuing but ever new vindication of the conditions of life in covenant is traditionally referred to doctrinally as God's "governing" (*gubernatio*) of creation. Rachel's refusal serves as faith's reminder that this vindication is not yet visibly established throughout the course of nature and history. Despite all attempts to rationalize it, mourning for the good that is "no more" still intensifies in this world beyond human powers of comprehension. Job's would-be comforters prove false. Evil would not be the problem that it is if the answers given to explain it truly satisfied. How God is presently ruling so as to work out creation's good in all circumstances is yet hidden from view, but that this vindication is now concretely occurring is faith's scandalous confession.

The complexity of this confession is illustrated by the words of the Heidelberg Catechism of 1563. To Question 27, "*What do you understand by the providence of God?*," the following response is given:

> The almighty and ever-present power of God whereby he still upholds, as it were by his own hand, heaven and earth together with all creatures, and rules in such a way that leaves and grass, rain and drought, fruitful and unfruitful years, food and drink, health and sickness, riches and poverty, and everything else, come to us not by chance but by his fatherly hand.

Any interpretation of this instruction to the effect that God ordains for injustice and misery to be met with human apathy and acquiescence clearly violates the import of the biblical message for faith. To identify the Creator's upholding and ruling of all things with any opposition to the creature's good amounts to perpetuating not the truth of the doctrine of providence but the lie that it harbors when its faithful disbeliefs are not recognized. What then is the disbelief here being confessed? The clue is to be found in the phrase "not by chance." At stake in the catechetical response is the active refusal of faith to believe that some circumstances are not subject to God's hand but rather fall beyond the bounds of God's providential working for good, thus mocking the prayer, "Thy will be done." To teach that God fails to see to the good in all things, John Calvin reminds his readers, quoting both Basil of Caesarea and Augustine more than a thousand years earlier, is in effect to attribute some ultimate dominion to fortune and fate, those ancient idols of chance, whose eyes, mythically characterized, are blind.[31]

Against such perceived idolatry the alternative vision of biblical faith sees the range of God's covenantal providence to be all encompassing, extending, in Karl Barth's memorable phrase, to every "wing-beat of the day-fly in far-flung epochs of geological time."[32] While biblical testimony concerning all things as coming from God's own hand leads to such seemingly contradictory statements as "Although he [the Lord] causes grief... he does not willingly afflict or grieve anyone" (Lam. 3:32–33), what has consistently been rejected by Christian teaching is the belief that any part of creation is ever outside of God's provision for its good.

This brings us to the third traditional category addressed in Christian doctrines of providence, that designated as *concursus*. The term may best be interpreted as the "conjoining" of divine and creaturely actions. In maintaining and conserving the creature's good we have noted that God is confessed to be vindicating this good in all things. Along with faith in both this upholding and ruling of creation now must be added the third affirmation that God does so by using creaturely means. Today as in the past the idea of providential *concursus* raises some of the most fascinating issues in Christian theology.

At the heart of this faith is the refusal to believe that God's ways of upholding and governing creation ever violate the freedom and integrity of the creature who is being upheld and governed. Perhaps no disbelief of Christian faith continues to be less recognized by critics of the doctrine of providence than this one. God's providing is always custom made to fit the creaturely recipient so that the creature's own freedom is never abrogated but activated. The point deserves underlining. This emphasis upon the conforming of God's grace to the created integrity of its recipient is one of the most consistent themes present throughout Christian doctrine. Disallowed by this faith is any claim that human beings are rendered mere puppets or robots, less than free agents, by their provision from God's hand. This faithful disbelief entailed in the affirmation of the divine *concursus* is already plain from what has been said about God's *conservatio* and *gubernatio* as the upholding and vindicating of each actual creature's good.

In this instance the sense of what faith refuses to accept has traditionally proven easier to explain than the sense of what faith asserts positively in confessing that all things come from God's hand. We have encountered this difficulty in the second of the initial objections raised regarding the appearance of fatalism.

The medieval scholastics, to be sure, gave much attention to the question of how God's providence for creation may be said to rule and overrule in such a way as not to deny the integrity of creaturely agency and of contingent circumstances. "The effect of divine Providence," so Thomas Aquinas argued with his usual deftness, "is for a thing to come about . . . in its own proper style, necessarily or contingently as the case may be."[33]

This effectual conjoining of God's care with creaturely means finds characteristic expression as well in the following declaration of faithful disbelief from the Second Helvetic Confession: "We disapprove of the rash statements of those who say that if all things are managed by the providence of God, then our efforts and endeavors are in vain . . . and we will not have to . . . do anything."[34]

Yet it is equally recognized that God's free conjoining with what we do in the upholding and vindicating of creation's good may also relate to our doings, not in concurrence in the sense of harmonious concert, but rather by going against their intent whenever and wherever these means are found to be set against themselves and against their own creaturely good. In the words of the Westminster Confession of 1647: "God, in his ordinary providence, maketh use of means, yet is free to work without, above, and against them, at his pleasure."[35] There is at this point disagreement in Christian theology over whether it is coherent with faith in the Incarnation to speak of God providing for creation, as the Westminster Confession puts it, "without" any creaturely means.

The faithful disbelief at stake can be more plainly stated. Christian faith refuses to believe that God is not free to relate to all creaturely means and contingencies in ways that conserve and vindicate creation's good. Once again, it is a narrative testimony from Genesis which most tellingly epitomizes the scope and character of God's providence, this time in the sense of *concursus* as a conjoining of divine and creaturely agency even where there is not a concurrence of intent. Recounted in the final chapter are these providentially paradigmatic words of Joseph's benediction to his brothers who once sold him into Egyptian bondage: "Even though you intended to do harm to me, God intended it for good, in order to preserve a numerous people, as he is doing today. So have no fear; I myself will provide for you and your little ones" (Gen. 50:20–21).

4. "See, I Am Making All Things New": Creation's Expectancy

When the identification of the Maker of heaven and earth is confessed from a standpoint of faith in the One who proves trustworthy with Jesus, the past and present dimensions of creation become configured with the imminent sense of a future that is coming to be. The finished origin and providential continuance of covenant existence are seen in the gospel message to involve an expectancy that still awaits realization. The Spirit's proving true of God's trustworthiness in connection with Jesus takes time and space, indeed all creaturely times and spaces.

Paul writes to the Romans that in "the sufferings of this present time . . . the creation waits with eager longing for the revealing [apocalypse] of the children of God" (Rom. 8:18–19). The metaphor Paul here chooses for creation, that of the contractions of the womb in travail just before childbirth, denies neither the current intensity of suffering nor the attendant hope of its longing: "We know that the whole creation has been groaning in labor pains until now; and not only the creation, but we ourselves, who have the first fruits [*arrabōn*] of the Spirit. . . . But if we hope for what we do not see, we wait for it with patience" (Rom. 8:22–23, 25).

The New Testament witness to a new creation draws upon the prophetic and apocalyptic testimonies of the Old Testament in announcing what takes place with Jesus Christ. Jeremiah speaks of a "new covenant with the house of Israel and the house of Judah" (Jer. 31:31). Isaiah tells of the Lord God saying, "For I am about to create new heavens and a new earth" (Isa. 65:17). In the prophecy of Ezekiel the promise is, "A new heart I will give you, and a new spirit I will put within you" (Ezek. 36:26, see also 11:19).

Against this background, the author of Hebrews portrays Christ as "the mediator of a new covenant" (Heb. 9:15) while the author of 2 Peter recalls the apocalyptic vision of the Lord's coming day: "But, in accordance with his promise, we wait for new heavens and a new earth, where righteousness is at home" (2 Pet. 3:13). That the new creation occurs in what happens with Jesus Christ is Paul's message to the Corinthians: "So if anyone is in Christ, there is a new creation: everything old has passed away; see, everything has become new!" (2 Cor. 5:17). Similarly Paul writes to the Galatians, "For neither circumcision nor uncircumcision is anything; but a new creation is everything!" (Gal. 6:15). The Ephesian letter speaks of "one new humanity" created in Christ (Eph. 2:15). The Colossian letter reminds its recipients that in their life with Christ in God they have clothed themselves with "the new self, which is being renewed in knowledge according to the image of its creator" (Col. 3:10). Finally, the Revelation of Jesus Christ to John contains the apocalyptic vision of "a new heaven and a new earth" (Rev. 21:1) with the words of the One seated on the throne saying, "See, I am making all things new" (Rev. 21:5).

There are significant differences among these texts. What is common to them all when they are read and heard in conjunction with the creation accounts in Genesis is a reference to something "new" with respect to creation. Talk of God's "finished" work of creation and of the provision for its continuance as *manutenentia* or *conservatio* may appear to be contradictory to apocalyptic motifs with their stress upon discontinuity with what has gone before. How the "new creation" is to be confessed in relation to the one Creator and Provider of all things from the beginning is a question that a biblical framework of usage poses for dogmatics. Here two disbeliefs mark the course to be followed. Christian faith enjoins disbelief of all claims that creation has no future that is new. Christian faith enjoins disbelief of all claims that the new comes from another source than that of the same triune Creator in the beginning. God's providence for creation, we have already noted, is not depicted biblically as a maintenance of the status quo. Rather it is an ever-new maintaining, conserving, and vindicating of the creature's "good."

The "new" for which the whole creation until now is said to be in expectancy is described by Paul as "the freedom of the glory of the children of God" (Rom. 8:21). In the words above from 2 Peter, this "new" is "where righteousness is at home" (2 Pet. 3:13). The witness of both accounts is consistent. Only where the right relationships dwell that constitute true freedom for God's children does creation come to its promised sabbath rest. We shall look further at what this "new creation" means for faith in our final chapter, "The Life to Come." What should not be overlooked at this point is that faith's expectancy regarding the God who is now "making all things new" refuses to believe that any ordering of relationships that opposes covenant fidelity in freedom, no matter how long established in a society or culturally entrenched, reflects the order of God's creation.

Proposed Disbeliefs

Looking back over the interpretation that has just been given of the main contours of Christian doctrine regarding creation, we may now review in summation the disbeliefs that have been pointed out and enumerate them in the order recognized. Christian faith, it has been proposed, refuses to believe:

1. that any command, except that of God, makes something so.
2. that the power which brings creation into being is of a Source other than the power of Jesus' resurrection.
3. any notion of more than one God.
4. that evil has equal status with the good.
5. that the opposition to the call "Let there be" can keep the good from being so.
6. that the scope of creation is either limited to, or permits evasion of, those things that presently appear.
7. all attempts to portray the natural world, the physical body, and sex as intrinsically bad and shameful.
8. all attempts to sacralize the status quo, to deify such nature, and to confuse the creature with the Creator.
9. that evil is something essential to the good.
10. that there is evil that cannot become subservient to the good.
11. that no really bad things happen, that evil has no bad reality but is only good disguised or misconceived.
12. that evil, if it does happen, does not happen to the good.

13. that God, even as the good Creator, does not exercise dominion over all.
14. that God, even as the Creator who exercises dominion over all, does not do so in ways that prove trustworthy for the creature's good.
15. every hypothetical attempt to understand evil in abstraction from its actual withstanding.
16. that the conditions of covenant existence cease to remain in effect.
17. that earthly privilege and the power to subjugate are the signs of divine endorsement.
18. that providence is a maintenance or preservation of the status quo.
19. that some circumstances are not subject to God's hand but rather fall beyond the bounds of God's providential working for good.
20. that any part of creation is ever outside of God's provision for its good.
21. that God's ways of upholding and governing creation ever violate the freedom and integrity of the creature who is being upheld and governed.
22. that human beings are rendered mere puppets or robots, less than free agents, by their provision from God's hand.
23. that God is not free to relate to all creaturely means and contingencies in ways that conserve and vindicate creation's good.
24. all claims that creation has no future that is new.
25. all claims that the new comes from another source than that of the same triune Creator in the beginning.
26. that any ordering of relationships that opposes covenant fidelity in freedom, no matter how long established in a society or culturally entrenched, reflects the order of God's creation.

The first initial objection, that church doctrine regarding creation devalues nature, raises certain issues that can better be dealt with when we come to consider the topics of sin and the Fall in the next chapter on salvation. Nevertheless, at this point we can say that, if the disbeliefs listed above are faithful ones, nothing that may be taught about nature after the introduction of sin can cancel the Christian conviction that all nature as created by God is good. This first objection rightly criticizes all elements of traditional church teaching that lead to a disparagement of the body and the natural world. What is original in biblical testimony regarding created nature is definitely not sin or fallenness but God's beholding of all creation as good.

The second objection, that Christian creation doctrine is fatalistic, is addressed especially by faith's refusal to believe that God's providential governance of creation violates the freedom and integrity of the creature. Controversial questions remain, but the disbeliefs implicit in faith with respect to creation provide a necessary corrective to certain ideas of universal inevitability. Disallowed by faith, on the one hand, is admittedly any claim that the conditions of covenant existence which God has called into being cease to remain in effect. God's constancy in proving trustworthy is confessed to be eternal and universal. But equally disallowed, on the other hand, is any claim that this ultimate constancy of covenant fidelity imposes a fixed order upon creation that allows no room for anything new, or further, that God is not free to relate to all creaturely means and contingencies in ways that conserve and vindicate the creature's good. What is constant is the vindication of true freedom in ever new states of affairs.

The third objection, that a hierarchical portrayal of creaturely existence is antithetical to the faith that all creation is good, is addressed most specifically by faith's refusal to believe that any ordering of relationships that opposes covenant fidelity in freedom, no matter how long established in a society or culturally entrenched, reflects the order of God's creation. If any appeal to hierarchy violates covenant fidelity in freedom, according to this disbelief, it betrays Christian faith in God as Creator. Failure to recognize this disbelief results in corruptions of creation doctrine with the destructive consequences set forth in the objection. We shall have more to consider on this subject when we come to chapter 12 on the doctrine of humanity.

A similar argument can be made with the overlapping fourth objection, that Christian creation doctrine promotes a false anthropocentrism with androcentric cultural consequences. If the "dominion" given the human creature is one of serving God's own *conservatio* of creation's good, a very different picture arises from that of the profiteer or exploiter, whose power to "subdue" in the sense of subjugate is seen as a sign of divine endorsement. Theologically considered, responsibility toward creation centers not in any human dominance over the environment, but in God's providential *concursus* in which human agency is conjoined with God's purpose of making a home for righteousness. How that righteousness is confessed, and our responsibility in it, is the subject of salvation which next invites our attention.

Chapter 11

SALVATION

Introduction

Announcements of salvation presume that there is something to be saved from and for. This presumption is dealt with in Christian soteriological doctrine. I use the word "presumption" here because where neither threat nor loss is obvious, talk of saving insinuates that all may not be as well as it appears. The fortune cookie that predicts "You will triumph over disaster" is hardly the cookie most of us would prefer for dessert following the satisfactions of an enjoyable meal. On the other hand, where threat or loss is all too obvious it may be hard to hear that there is anything left other than disaster for which to triumph over and be saved. "Who warned you to flee from the wrath to come?" John the Baptist is reported to have asked the crowds who came out to hear him at the Jordan (Matt. 3:7, Luke 3:7). Who indeed?

In addition to the work of creating, the God of biblical testimony is described, to borrow the words of the Psalmist, as "working salvation in the earth" (Ps. 74:12). A common address of praise in the Psalms is "O God of our salvation" (Ps. 65:5). Indeed throughout the scriptures generally the appeal to God as Savior may be said to be the implicit, if not the explicit, salutation of all prayer. According to the prophecy of Isaiah, recalled in the Gospel of Luke, the voice in the wilderness preparing the way of the Lord cries, "all flesh shall see the salvation of God" (Luke 3:6).

Such an announcement is made with reference not only to the evil of being wronged, but also to the evil of doing wrong. Deliverance is said to be both from the *affliction* of evil and from the *infliction* of evil. We have already in the previous chapter, where God's providence for creation was discussed, given consideration to evil as opposition to the good. There we observed that Christian faith affirms God's continuance of creation in every affliction by confessing that, despite all appearances to the contrary, the Lord provides in this life and beyond for the conservation (*conservatio*) and vindication (*gubernatio*) of creation's good. We must now look further at the faithful disbeliefs entailed in this professed vindication insofar as it has to do with the inflicters of evil.

Along with the teachings of creation and providence the church's ministry of the gospel also speaks of a reconciliation in what happens with Jesus Christ. "All this is from God," Paul writes to the Corinthians, "who reconciled us to himself through Christ, and has given us the ministry of reconciliation" (2 Cor. 5:18). Reconciling presupposes a breach, the occurrence of a prior enmity. More than a *conservatio* is required. From the opposition to well-being that afflicts the innocent, that inexplicable destructiveness for which Rachel and her children are not to blame, we turn to that opposition to the good of creation for which we, like Herod's fury, are at fault. This is the destructiveness we have inflicted upon others and upon ourselves.

The opposition to creaturely well-being for which human beings are culpable has customarily been labeled moral evil. This is to distinguish it from the opposition arising from so-called natural or physical evils, such as the devastation caused by storms and earthquakes, or by any forces of nature not accountable as human actions.[1] Moral evil, involving fault, introduces the topic of "sin."

But if the idea of reconciling presupposes that a breach of enmity has occurred between two parties, it also speaks of an overcoming of this breach, of a rectification. This overcoming of sin is attributed in Christian teaching to "grace." "By grace [*chariti*] you have been saved" (Eph. 2:5). Any attempt to recognize the disbeliefs entailed in Christian faith regarding salvation and the work of Jesus Christ as Savior requires a consideration of the two biblical terms "sin" and "grace." The range of issues now before us is given one of its most paradigmatic summations in Paul's statement, "For our sake he [God] made him [Christ] to be sin who knew no sin, so that in him [Christ] we might become the righteousness of God" (2 Cor. 5:21).

Once again the carryover of the significance of words such as "sin" and "grace" from their canonical context into everyday speech may be shown to be quite limited and inadequate at best. For example, the trivialization exhibited by the cultural use of such an expression as "living in sin," whether old-fashioned or new, suggests that such raciness (once quaintly defined as "living without benefit of clergy"!) surely is the last thing anyone needs to be saved from. More significantly, in the rhetoric of nations the only sin or evil that is generally acknowledged is that which is alleged of one's enemies.

Similarly, according to secular usage, we may still speak of someone as being "gracious," but "gracious" in this sense, or "graciousness," tends for the most part in our day to connote gentility, proper manners, and correct etiquette. Such characteristics are usually assumed to be the marks of "gracious living." And to be "graceful" has come to be understood as the opposite of being clumsy. Even if we translate "grace" rather straightforwardly from the original Greek *charis* and speak of "charity" and "charisma" these translations do not, as we commonly find the words used today, tell us what the "grace" of salvation is all about. "Charity" has come to have a demeaning sound, so that the only people who like to talk about it are the ones who conceive of themselves as offering it. The expression "to live on charity" is generally intended and taken as an insult. "Charisma," in like fashion, has suffered a reversal of meaning in ordinary discourse and is now usually held to designate a characteristic *belonging* to an individual, such as a radiant or magnetic personality, an inspiring presence, and the like. The same reversal can be seen in our adjective "gifted" whenever it is applied in order to credit an individual for being "accomplished."

To be distinguished from this usage is the commonly held testimony of the Christian church that all salvation is the accomplishment of God's grace in Jesus Christ. The Incarnation, Resurrection, and Parousia that mark the life span of this person have their purpose affirmed in the words of the Nicene Creed as taking place "for us humans and for our salvation." We are led now to focus our attention upon the recognition of the disbeliefs entailed in the confession of Christian faith that salvation as the reconciling work of the triune God is (1) by grace, (2) from sin, and (3) for righteousness.

Initial Objections

The dissatisfactions expressed throughout Christian history with respect to church teachings regarding salvation for the most part may be said to fall broadly under two general rubrics. One class of objections protests the role of soteriological doctrine in fostering human irresponsibility. We have earlier looked at a similar line of questioning in considering the doctrine of the Word of God. The other is primarily concerned with the issue of divine favoritism. The two themes are played out with multiple variations.

1. *It would seem that the confession of salvation by grace is a confession of human irresponsibility.*

There are five primary grounds most often cited in arguing this objection. The first has to do with the idea commonly referred to since Augustine as "original sin." While Christian teaching affirms that all God's creation is good, this is immediately qualified by adding "as created." Between the good as created and every form of human creaturehood as we know it there is said to have occurred the great divide of human fault and failure known as the Fall. The willful succumbing of Adam and Eve to the serpent's temptation to be "like God," as recounted in Genesis 3, is construed as involving the lapse of all subsequent humanity. "In Adam's fall, we sin-ned all" is the Puritan couplet used to catechize this conviction. Whether our current complicity in original sin is interpreted to mean our inheritance of a genetic taint from our primal forebears, as most of the older theologies from Augustine until the Enlightenment maintained, or whether it is thought of more as a parable of the human condition, "*As* in Adam's fall, we sin-ned all," the insistence upon a self-imposed degrading from which humanity is forever powerless to extirpate itself remains. The Genesis story of the Garden suggests that for the human creature as God's good creation prior to the Fall it is possible not to defy God's will, and thus not to sin. This is a state of innocence characterized in Augustine's famous shorthand as *posse non peccare*.[2] In distinction, so it is argued, once the initial defiance has occurred and forever thereafter there exists for the human creature no possibility, whatever the remaining options, except to sin, a state that can only be described in contrast as *non posse non peccare* ("not possible not to sin"). Such Augustinian teaching, as the opposing Pelagians insisted, appears to have the logical consequence both of making God immoral as One who, in commanding us to do the good, commands that which is impossible, and of making us unaccountable for our actions, since we cannot because of the Fall, it is claimed, voluntarily do other than to sin.

A second reason for this objection is the tendency of Christian soteriological doctrine to portray Jesus Christ as a "substitute" for the rest of humanity. Ideas of Christ "representing" us and "taking our place" appear to contribute to the sense that as human beings we are not responsible for our actions. It is Jesus Christ who assumes our humanity and "recapitulates" our life, as Irenaeus puts it, thereby granting us a "passive righteousness," in Luther's phrase, upon which all humankind is "absolutely dependent," to recall Schleiermacher, for its salvation.[3] The primary emphasis in teachings of this sort seems to be upon human replacement, passivity, and dependency.

A third difficulty arises with the idea that salvation is "predestined." This is similar to the charge of apparent fatalism in Christian teaching regarding creation and providence. Whether God's determination of who gets saved is said to be an eternal decision logically prior to the idea of humanity's "lapse" in the Fall, the so-called *supralapsarian* view, or is alleged to have been made in recognition of the Fall, the *infralapsarian* position, the conundrum remains that in either case it all takes place over our heads. Although he insisted upon it as biblical testimony,

John Calvin has at least been more candid than most in characterizing as "a horrible decree," and beyond all human validation, the doctrine that God secretly predestines before they ever exist some human beings to damnation while others are elected to salvation.[4]

A fourth line of questioning raises concerns about teachings that concentrate upon individual salvation from sin to the neglect of the more societal and even ecological interconnectedness of which all human life is part. The link between the individual and corporate dimensions of salvation, as depicted biblically, becomes ignored. The slavery of sin is addressed with no reference to the sin of slavery. Christ is proclaimed as the Savior of souls as if salvation did not involve the whole of creation, body and soul together. The individual sinner is pronounced justified by Christ's atoning sacrifice even though the wider environment remains unjust, bound up with unchallenged systemic evils of social and economic destructiveness.

Finally, if God's grace is professed to be extrinsic to all human actions, such primary scriptural injunctions as the call to love one's neighbor and to "do justice" (Mic. 6:8) are finally of no practical consequence. Movements for peace on earth, struggles to set the captives free, the adjudication of rights, and all sociopolitical efforts for the healing of nations and the global environment would appear to be rendered superfluous and even inimical to the message of an ahistorical salvation, not by works, but by grace alone. A soteriology in which God's Kingdom or Realm of grace is viewed as otherworldly to the sufferings and destructiveness of the present time becomes a main obstacle for sustained Christian commitment to liberation struggles. In the words of José Míguez Bonino's criticism of the prevailing influence of much European and North American theology, "Any extrinsic relation between Kingdom and history is insufficient to support a serious concrete engagement."[5]

2. *It would seem that Christian soteriological doctrine portrays God as favoring some human beings with love over others.*

John Calvin's frank use of the words *decretum horribile* to designate the doctrine that some individuals are predestined to eternal rejection prior to their existence illustrates the profound difficulty for faith in understanding biblical testimony of God as at once universally benevolent but not universally saving. The one eternally good God is said to elect some and to reject others. Paul's words to the Romans, citing the Hebrew scriptures, epitomize this testimony:

> As it is written, "I have loved Jacob, but I have hated Esau." What then are we to say? Is there injustice on God's part? By no means! For he says to Moses, "I will have mercy on whom I have mercy,

> and I will have compassion on whom I have compassion." (Rom. 9:13–15)

In the Acts of the Apostles Luke recounts Peter's preaching of a "universal restoration [*apokatastasis*] that God announced long ago through his holy prophets" (Acts 3:21). Yet the attempt to interpret this universal restoration as universal salvation has, more often than not, come to be repudiated in Christian orthodoxy since the time of Origen's censure at the Fifth Ecumenical Council (II Constantinople) in 553 for the alleged heresy of teaching such an *apokatastasis*. In opposition to universal salvation the Augustinian view has tended to prevail, asserting that since Adam's fall the human race has been divided into two distinct groups, the elect showing forth God's gracious mercy, and the rejected showing forth God's righteous judgment.[6] Thomas Aquinas agrees, holding that while God does indeed antecedently wish for all to be saved, God nevertheless allows for the consequent rejection of sin to inflict the just penalty of damnation. "Some people God rejects."[7]

It is true that the announcement of the glorious coming of the Son of Man in Matthew 25 pictures a judgment scene in which the goats will be separated on the left hand from the sheep on the right, with the former going "away into eternal punishment, but the righteous into eternal life" (Matt. 25:46). But it is also true that the idea of two groups, the one recipients of salvation and the other not, has historically played itself out in countless expressions of a "we-they" mentality that betrays the gospel by fostering social bigotry, the persecution of difference, and moral arrogance. The consequence of restrictive covenants for wronging perceived outsiders cannot be ignored today in any faithful testing of the spirits. A restricted covenant of grace in which God is alleged to save selected human beings by sheer favor without any deserving on their part, while all others not so favored are consigned to unending rejection, surely mocks any confession that God's righteousness is both just and abounding in steadfast love.

Interpretation

Christian confession affirms that in the Incarnation, Resurrection, and Parousia of Jesus Christ God accomplishes the reconciliation of creation. Sifted to the heart of the matter, all technical terminology aside, what trust in this reconciling work entails is the refusal to believe that any situation is hopeless — *any* situation. When all is said and done, and whatever else is involved, this faith amounts to disbelieving that either the affliction or the infliction of evil, as the opposition to the good of creation, finally prevails. What is proclaimed to happen *in, to*, and *as the future of* Jesus is praised by the church even in the face of direst tragedy and loss as nothing less than the happening of ultimate salvation. The movement of the descent, ascent, and coming that comprises the life span of Jesus as the Christ according to the gospel message is a movement that is reported to connect this life span with that of every creature anywhere and everywhere without exception.

The bold insistence upon this connection, with its attendant risk of sentimentalizing Rachel's voice in the gospel and thereby harboring lies, now leads us to question how the christological rubrics of Incarnation, Resurrection, and Parousia that we considered in chapter 8 are to be faithfully understood as actually encompassing our own lives, and the lives of all others, by being "for us humans and our salvation."

Friedrich Schleiermacher's repudiation of all christological formulations that are not explicative of this saving connection between Jesus' life span and our own reaffirms an influential emphasis of Melanchthon three centuries earlier that "to know Christ is to know his benefits."[8] It is useful to recall here the four faithful disbeliefs (previously mentioned in chapter 5) that Schleiermacher sets forth as the four "natural heresies" disavowed by Christian faith: (1) that human beings do not need salvation, (2) that humans are not salvageable, (3) that Jesus Christ is too like other humans to be uniquely able to save, and (4) that Jesus Christ is too unlike other humans to have access to them to save. How the saving access or connection between the life span of Jesus and our own life span is most faithfully to be drawn depends upon how the gospel witness to the Incarnation, the Resurrection, and the Parousia informs the present-day significance of the confessional claim that salvation is by grace, from sin, and for righteousness. Testing the spirits that publicly compete today with offers, both religious and secular, of personal, social, and economic salvation requires that dogmatics for its part ask what further disbeliefs are to be recognized by looking at the soteriological meaning of the Incarnation, the Resurrection, and the Parousia first with regard to grace, then with regard to sin, and finally with regard to righteousness.

1. Saved by Grace

Most simply stated, that God is "for us humans and our salvation" is in church usage precisely what the term "grace" means. God's grace is *God's being for us;* disavowed at the start by this conviction is any assumption that grace is something attributable to us or to any other creature. Grace, according to this ecclesial context of usage, is not God being us, the mere aura, as it were, of our own idealized humanity, but God being *for* us as neither we nor any other creature can be for ourselves. Disbelieved by such faith is every claim that human beings are the source of their own salvation or of anyone else's. The saving to which faith testifies is, in the words of an influential Ephesians text, "not your own doing (*ouk ex hymōn*)"; it is God's "gift" (Eph. 2:8). What is seen to be at stake is nothing less than humanity's misplaced confidence regarding the workings of the real world.

How in the ultimate nature of things life is disposed in our behalf, by what manner, through what means, and with what results are questions that arise in the church's attempts to account for the hope by which faith in the God of the gospel lives. But all the ramifications of this hope, according to the church's witness, hinge upon the one major premise that the current and final reality from which nothing past, present, or future can separate us is indeed not set against us but is unfailingly directed toward our well-being. In calling to mind without denial the suffering, futility, decay, and groaning present throughout creation, Paul asks in the Epistle to the Romans, "What then are we to say about these things? If God is for us, who is against us?" (Rom. 8:31). He concludes, "No, in all these things we are more than conquerors through him who loved us" (Rom. 8:37). Such is the scope of faith's testimony to saving grace.

Faith in God's being for us in the Incarnation more specifically refuses to believe that grace can be accounted for apart from recounting the story of the life span of Jesus with its crucifixion "under Pontius Pilate." Disbelieved in thus affirming that God's being for us is *en sarki* are all claims that saving grace is either timeless or amorphous, something in general rather than someone "only begotten" and crucified in particular. The cruciform Incarnation of God's loving the world takes definite time and space and involves bodies as well as souls in the full environment of their social interaction and suffering. Christian faith in salvation by grace, understood as incarnate grace, thus disbelieves that souls are saved by dismembering them from bodies in the environment of their specific social interaction. Salvation, if accomplished through Christ's incarnation unto crucifixion, is by definition neither individual nor societal disembodiment. "This is my body," so Christian worship recalls the saving words of Jesus, "which is given for you" (Luke 22:19; see also 1 Cor. 11:24).

Disbelieved also by faith in the Incarnation of God's being for us in the life span of Jesus is that grace is witnessed as some kind of reserve at the disposal of the church; rather, as we shall consider in chapter 13, the church is witnessed as a preserve at the disposal of grace. Further, what is proclaimed in the gospel message is that not only the church but God's entire creation to the depths of hell itself is at the disposal of this grace. When true to this proclamation of the Cross, faith dissents from believing that the grace of God is present only where its configuration as the life span of Jesus is recognized, or that the manner, means, and results of the incarnate grace enacted in this life span are enfolded only within the historical confines of institutional Christianity. "I have other sheep that do not belong to this fold," are the words of Jesus in John's Gospel (John 10:16). Grace is no more restricted to where it is recounted than is the Incarnation restricted to where it is recognized. "He was in the world, and the world came into being through him; yet the world did not know him" (John 1:10). Christian faith in God as Savior, thus precisely in its telling of grace as the enactment of the Word made flesh unto death on a cross, counters as false prophesy any belief that God's omnipresence is gracious only where its incarnation is truly recounted as being so. What is disbelieved is that faith is the precondition of saving grace. To the contrary, saving grace, if indeed God's being for us as narrated in the incarnate descent to the Cross, takes precedence as the precondition of faith.

Turning now to the Resurrection, faith in God's being for us, not only in the Incarnation unto the Cross but in the life span of the risen Jesus as it makes connection with our own, brings still additional disbeliefs with respect to saving grace. Here the connection involves us with promise as well as with story. "Because I live, you also will live" (John 14:19). An Easter faith equally refuses to believe either that salvation by grace is the bypass of worldly existence and its opposing powers of death, or that the limits of worldly existence with its opposing powers of death constitute the limits of grace. Specifically, the teaching that anyone who is not aware of "being saved" before death, or who at least is not intentional about it, is thereafter off-limits to the grace of salvation is disbelieved as a false spirit by faith that the scope and span of grace is the scope and span of Christ's resurrection. The "Jesus God raised up" (Acts 2:32) is proclaimed to be for those who were neither aware nor intentional about his vindication, "even to the dead," as the author of 1 Peter expresses it, "to the spirits in prison, who in former times did not obey," so that "they [who] had been judged . . . might live . . . as God does" (1 Pet. 3:19–20, 4:6).

By confessing salvation in the resurrection of Jesus, Christian faith disbelieves that grace is reducible to the teachings, the example, or some putative self-consciousness of the first-century Jesus. Not only what the first-century Jesus may have done and thought, but what was done to him provides the format of the gospel testimonies. Within this frame of reference, the saying that there is "no other name under heaven" (Acts 4:12) by which humanity is saved does not arise as a claim for the exclusive moral and intellectual superiority of a first-century figure's reported teaching and insight, and certainly not for the religion that bears his sign. It is rather a doxology of the Resurrection faith that there really is no universally inclusive "name that is above every name" to whom "every knee should bend, . . . and every tongue confess" except that which has the power even in death on a cross to embody and incorporate the glorious vindication of love and freedom against not just some but *every* crucifying opposition (Phil. 2:9–11).

Entailed in this praise is the refusal to credit or give credence to all claims that the betrayal and crucifying opposition of God's being disposed toward us in love and freedom — whatever amounts to our resistance to being loved and thus to being free — renders this disposition on the part of God null and void. In the perspective of Christian faith the crucifixion of grace does not eliminate its resurrection. Nor is the risen life span of Jesus ever recounted in the gospels as the result of any favorable dispositions toward it on the part of those for whom Christ died. The dawning of Easter morning is never portrayed as conditional upon anyone's acceptance of its being so. The glad song of the Resurrection is not some encore awaiting creation's prior applause. By proclaiming grace to be the power of the Resurrection the widespread impression, often perpetuated within Christianity and without, that salvation is somehow an effect of the human will, the result of a human choice, a decision, a leap of faith, an assent, or a consent is proscribed as the bearing of false witness. If the contention that our salvation depends upon our acceptance of it were in fact the case, our resistance to being loved and being free, our noncompliance, as it were, with life on its real terms, would be stronger and more eternal than God's loving and freeing us for life; the Crucifixion would indeed be able to prevent the Resurrection, and sin would have the power to hold grace bound as hostage. Easter as grace rejects this. By affirming that salvation is the taking place "for us humans" of the Resurrection, faith refuses to believe that saving grace is dependent upon, or a product of, our acceptance of its being for us.

But if this account is correct, does it then follow that human beings as recipients of salvation are indeed rendered irresponsible, as the first initial objection to this doctrine we have noted charges? The old controversies in the history of dogmatics over whether or not grace is ultimately resistible or irresistible have their point. Here we confront the question of the soteriological significance of the life span of Jesus, not only as the Incarnation and the Resurrection, but as the Parousia.

While Christian faith in the Incarnation and Resurrection refuses to believe that God's being for us as grace is the effect or product of our free choice, it also refuses to believe that grace is ever the abrogation of human freedom and not its initiation. To believe that God is disposed toward creation in love and freedom entails the refusal to believe that such disposing is ever the imposing of a will upon our existence that violates love and freedom. According to this faith, God loves us into loving and frees us into freedom. Our receptivity to the gift of grace is all the while part of the gift as it comes to us. No creature can dispose the will of another without imposing upon the other's integrity and freedom of self-determination. The disposing of eternal love and freedom on our specific behalf, in contrast, by definition involves no such creaturely imposition. To be motivated by love and freedom is, in the history of Christian teaching, precisely what it means to be freely self-determining.[9] This ability to respond in love and freedom, this response-ability, is confessed in the Christian life as itself the coming of grace. It is this coming of grace which is praised as the Parousia of the life span of Jesus.

The occurrence of the Incarnation and the Resurrection, as recounted in the gospel message, includes the occurrence of eyes being opened to recognize what is so. What is reported to take place in the particular time and space "under Pontius Pilate" is proclaimed to make connection with every human life by coming to all the different times and spaces where God has created human life to be. As enacted in the saving connection of the life span of Jesus with our own, grace as once-for-all "under Pontius Pilate" is not first confessed by all at once. The Incarnate and Resurrected Life in what happens with Jesus Christ does not first appear to human destinies simultaneously as if all human existence transpired simultaneously in first-century Jerusalem. Grace, as the connecting of the once-for-all life span of Jesus Christ with our own life span, is not an occurrence all at once because the lives of human beings are not all at once. In the past, present, and future tenses of the syntax of the New Testament pronouncements, Jesus Christ, so it is testified, has come and overcome, Jesus Christ is now coming and overcoming, and Jesus Christ shall yet come and overcome. "He was destined before the foundation of the world, but was revealed at the end of the ages for your sake" (1 Pet. 1:20). It is this once-for-all but not all-at-once coming of saving grace with its overcoming of all that opposes it that is affirmed as God's being for us in the Parousia.

Along with the story and promise of the Incarnation and the Resurrection, the Parousia of the life span of Jesus as grace is therefore said to come to us as a sacrament that incorporates our own lives, not as some timeless conglomerate of generic humanity in the abstract, but exactly as who we are, where we are, and when we are in all the individual variety and irreplaceable uniqueness of our particular existence. This faith in God's incorporating sacramental coming to us and for us as once-for-all but not all-at-once in the Incarnation, Resurrection, and Parousia refuses to believe that the connection of grace is not, so to speak, custom made to fit the actual circumstances of each and every recipient. That grace is always fitting to its recipient is one of the classical themes of Christian theology.[10] "Differentiated" toward every creature according to each one's "particular nature . . . in its particular place" is the way Karl Barth puts it, adding that "[God] is not like a schoolmaster who gives the same lesson to the whole class, or an officer who moves his whole squadron in the same direction, or a bureaucrat who once an outlook or principle is embedded in his own little head rules his whole department in accordance with it."[11]

Barth himself, true to his mentors in the Reformation before him, does not allow that the providential *concursus* of grace includes the conjoining of any human effort with that of God's as a contributing factor to salvation. With the other heirs of Luther and Calvin he rejects any doctrine of "working together" (*synergism*) that implies that salvation is not by grace alone. Yet the Apostle Paul does write of a synergism brought about as the result of grace, even if not its contributor: "Working together [with God], we urge you also not to accept the grace of God in vain" (2 Cor. 6:1); "But by the grace of God I am what I am, and his grace toward me has not been in vain. On the contrary, I worked harder than any of them — though it was not I, but the grace of God that is with (*syn*) me" (1 Cor. 15:10); "Work out your own salvation with fear and trembling; for it is God who is at work in you, enabling you both to will and to work for his good pleasure" (Phil. 2:12–13). Such proclamation that God's grace works through our working as cause and not effect, making our work to be never more truly our own than when it is God's working within us, has been called "the central paradox" of grace in the gospel message.[12] Disputes over how exactly human efforts may faithfully be said to play a role in the reconciliation of the world run throughout the history of Christian theology. Common to ecumenical church teaching, despite the longstanding confessional disagreements over the true significance of synergism, is the consistent refusal to believe either that there is no given ministry of reconciliation, or that any human role in the reconciliation of the world is something other than the effect of the coming upon the scene of God's reconciling grace. God's enacted prevenience in our behalf is confessed to be the given premise of all subsequent workings of grace.

Finally, to identify grace as the Parousia of the life span of Jesus is to recognize the eschatological inescapability of its coming. While the saving significance of what happens *in, to,* and *as the future of* Jesus is not, as depicted in the gospel accounts, first witnessed by all creation at once, the ultimate future of the Parousia is said to be a coming day of judgment for all creation all together without exception, the living and the dead. (We shall look further at this final judgment in chapter 14, on the life to come.) Just as the Incarnation is professed in Christian faith to involve not merely God's partial but full assumption of human existence unto death on a cross, and the Resurrection is professed to involve not merely God's partial but total subjection of the crucifying powers of evil that oppose creation's good, so the Parousia of Jesus Christ at the last day is professed to be not merely a partial future only for some but one that shall come to and encompass all. Faith that the ultimate future as the Parousia is indeed grace thus contains the refusal to believe that anyone or any part of creation whatsoever, at any time or at any place, is not met by the coming of this grace.

2. Saved from Sin

The Christian confession of what grace saves us from arises from what God's being for us in the Incarnation, Resurrection, and Parousia of the life span of Jesus is shown in faith to meet up with in making connection with human existence. As we have just done with the word "grace," we must now ask what the word "sin" means in light of each of these three christological rubrics.

In short, our existence is said to be shown in this connection to be in a state of opposition against being loved and being free. This disclosure of existence set against itself is the enigma Paul Tillich delineates phenomenologically with psychoanalytic insight in the mid-twentieth century as humanity's "estrangement" from its own essential being.[13] Various ways of interpreting sin as our being against whom God is for appear in the history of Christian theology. At issue in every generation for the dogmatic testing and rethinking of claims regarding sin is the present-day import for faith of the canonical witness of scripture that is currently being attested in the ongoing life of the church.

Few New Testament assertions regarding what grace saves us from pass muster as common sense. While it takes no great argument to admit that we all from time to time have made our share of mistakes, suffered our defeats, failed to live up to our full potential, even felt guilty for things neglected, and ashamed for things committed, the blunt announcement that we were dead, having in effect taken our own life, renders these admissions quite tame in comparison. Yet nothing less radical than this is what hearers of the gospel message are told. Whatever sense it all makes surely is most uncommon indeed.

Once again we may refer to the wording of Ephesians 2, which provides a brief for so much of the church's soteriological doctrine: "You were dead," "all of us . . . like everyone else" (Eph. 2:1, 3). The hyperbole here, whether construed as a metaphorical or to some degree literal vitiation of created being, plainly asserts more than our having been merely unaware, unconscious, or even in a coma, for we are further said to have been quite active in this state of death, and are described as while being in it having followed the course of this world under the deceptive sway of a spirit of defiance in the air. It is this deceptive state of affairs in defiance of life, amounting to self-inflicted death, that the author of Ephesians, and other New Testament writers in their distinctive ways, refer to as "sin." "You were dead through the trespasses and sins in which you once lived" (Eph. 2:1–2). Elsewhere Paul writes, "So death spread to all because all have sinned" (Rom. 5:12).

But how does faith today account for knowing this death in sin as more than mythical speculation? Here the attempt to recognize the disbeliefs entailed in such salvation testimony becomes pivotal. Clearly, within a canonical framework of New Testament discourse, sin, whatever is involved, may be said to be known for what it is only in reference to grace. Without grace there is no enmity against grace. Any claim that our being disposed toward death is revealed for what it is apart from God's being disposed toward our life is disbelieved by Christian faith. Everything follows from this disbelief. Sin, therefore, as spoken of in this frame of reference, is no more an anthropological characteristic than is grace. As grace is not a label for our own potentiality, so sin is not a label for some psychic state of guilt. Feeling guilty, to underline the point, does not equate in biblical depictions with being sinful any more than does not feeling guilty.

Only God's being for us shows the extent of our being against whom God is for. In a sentence, this may be said to be the gist of the gospel message concerning the disclosure of sin. The New Testament confession that "we were dead" in sin comes only, it should be noted, from those who confess to having been made alive in relation to what happens with Jesus. Faith in keeping with such testimony, far from identifying the awareness of sin with a masochistic preoccupation with guilt, refuses to believe that there is any true sense of sin that is not the sense of sin forgiven. According to this faithful disbelief, the only sin we actually know is the opposition that is overcome by God's being for us.

The christological rubrics of the Incarnation, Resurrection, and Parousia shape the church's recognition of how truly we are, so to speak, dead set against ourselves, against being loved and being free, and how costly is our reconciliation. Again this professed connection of the life span of Jesus with our own life span is made unmistakable in the hymnlike words of the Ephesians text that tell of what occurs "when we were dead":

> But God, who is rich in mercy, out of the great love with which he loved us even when we were dead through our trespasses, made us alive together with Christ — by grace you have been saved — and raised us up with him and seated us with him in the heavenly places in Christ Jesus, so that in the ages to come he might show the immeasurable riches of his grace in kindness toward us in Christ Jesus. (Eph. 2:4–7)

Whatever the mythical motifs this gospel message employs,[14] those who hear in it a description of reality, of the way things actually are in the real world, see their lives as taking place in connection with how the span of Jesus' life is portrayed as taking place. In this uncommon way of viewing the relationality of existence — as, even when dead through trespasses (Incarnation unto the Cross), being made alive, raised up, and seated in the heavenly places (Resurrection), and as being the showplace of God's kindness without measure in the ages to come (Parousia) — the word "evil" denotes whatever stands in opposition to life taking place in this way, and the word "sin" denotes our complicity in this evil. Because God is for us, all opposition to God and God's creation by definition becomes self-opposition. Our so-called trespasses and transgressions directed against God and other creatures are viewed as rooted in our unwillingness for our own life to take place. What grace does, according to the dynamics of this reality description, is overtake us with what our true place actually and amazingly is.

Located with respect to the Incarnation, our true place is disclosed as being where God's grace chooses to take flesh and come to life. Being human, from this faith perspective, is where incarnate grace takes place. "For it is clear that he [Jesus] did not come to help angels, but the descendants of Abraham" (Heb. 2:16). The human nature that God's eternal Word is said to "assume," in the *assumptio carnis* language of the Two Natures christological formulary, is not human existence as an abstraction currently uninvolved with our own. Such abstract detachment would not be grace. In Jesus Christ the human existence where the Word becomes flesh is acknowledged as once-for-all but not all-at-once, spanning the first-century environs of Jerusalem in its life story but also embodying in its life promised the existence of all whom God is for in every time and space.

This enfleshment is pictured as happening, as in the case of Joseph in the Matthean nativity account previously noted, where even the just do not conceive that it is proper for God to be, and where they thus resolve to divorce themselves from its reality (Matt. 2:18–21). Our own determined opposition to taking our place as those for whom Mary's child is born is given voice in faith's affirmative answer to the question of the spiritual, "Were you there when they crucified my Lord?" To be "there" at the Incarnation unto the Cross thus means two things: first, our place is where grace chooses to become enfleshed and dwell, and second, we are found to have placed ourselves at enmity in inimical denial of this place. To be found denying who we are and where we are is the searching judgment upon our sin that arrives with grace. If God's being for us occurs in Jesus Christ through this life lived for others unto death on a cross, then the existence of those whom God is for is shown to be located in what faced Jesus at the Cross.

To return to Paul's paradigmatic words, the One "made to be sin who knew no sin" (2 Cor. 5:21) is the One whose incarnate place is that particular nexus of events which reveals how our self-opposition to life is borne out bodily unto the death that it is, but not thereby embraced for what it is. Where that decisive nexus of events occurs the Cross as grace both there and now occurs. In this once-for-all but not all-at-once nexus of events Jesus is proclaimed as shouldering and freely bearing what he does not embrace, that is, "sin," by coming to the very place of utter aloneness and forsakenness where it is said in the Genesis story of creation that God pronounces it "not good" for the human creature to be (Gen. 2:18).

By affirming Jesus Christ to be "like we are in every respect, sin being the only exception," Chalcedon does not hold Jesus' life to be somehow less than fully human, but just the opposite, *not* less than fully human because not set against being human in any way. Exactly where God's favor toward us becomes incarnate in the space, time, and suffering of the life span of Jesus as it continues to make connection with our own life span is where, so faith confesses, we are shown by what culminates at the Cross to have determined ourselves not to be. When sin, therefore, is defined as that which is inimical to this Incarnation unto the Cross it has generally in Christian doctrine been called *superbia*, a term more aptly translated today as our "attempted usurpation" of a place not our own rather than as "pride."

From the depiction of Adam and Eve ducking behind the trees in the Garden (Gen. 3:8–9) to the report that "all the disciples deserted him and fled" (Matt. 26:56) the theme of human running away and hiding pervades the canonical story of God's approach to humankind. "All we like sheep have gone astray; we have all turned to our own way, and the Lord has laid on him the iniquity of us all" (Isa. 53:6). In taking the place of our own inimical denial of grace, Jesus Christ in the narrated and promised events leading to the Cross, does not thereby, as faith sees it, replace our own life story as expendable, but relates it in judgment both there and now irreplaceably with God's own.

Located with respect to the Resurrection, our place is shown in the gospel testimony to be, in the words of the Ephesians epistle, "made alive together with Christ," "raised up with him and seated in the heavenly places with Christ Jesus" (Eph. 2:5–6). If the Incarnation unto the Cross with its descent into hell reveals our true place in the crucifixion of grace's enfleshment there and now, the Resurrection reveals our true place at the vindication of this crucified grace there and now and, in this instance, also yet to come. Sin as our opposition to God's being for us in the Resurrection, in contrast to sin as our opposition to God's being for us in the Incarnation, is portrayed in the gospel's spatial imagery to reside not in the attempt of our conceit to usurp another place than our own by thinking too highly, and thus falsely, of where God is, but in the self-rejection of not thinking highly enough, and thus truly, of where we are. If the Cross reveals our betrayal unto death of the life of grace delivered to us in human terms, the Resurrection reveals our demeaning of the life of grace delivered from such death on God's terms.

Since in the reality depiction of the gospel message it is "Christ who is our life" (Col. 3:4) in each instance, this demeaning is just as truly a self-demeaning as is the betrayal a self-betrayal. Sin from the perspective of the Resurrection is not "pride," as an attempted usurpation of place, but the demeaning self-abasement of not looking up to ourselves where we really are to be found, that is, "raised with Christ." Such a recognition of sin as looking down on ourselves and other human beings and refusing to lift up our heads to behold our true life is given graphic articulation in the Epistle to the Colossians with its rhythmic cadence, "If with Christ you died" (Col. 2:20), "If then with Christ you have been raised" (Col. 3:1). We may pick out the reiterated images without distorting the larger context: "Do not let anyone disqualify you, insisting on self-abasement" (Col. 2:18); "Why do you submit to regulations" ostensibly "promoting rigor of devotion, self-abasement, and severity to the body"? (Col. 2:20, 23);[15] "Seek the things that are above, where Christ is.... Set your mind on things that are above... for you have died, and your life is hidden with Christ in God" (Col. 3:1–3). By contrast to *superbia*, self-demeaning abasement is the sin of looking down upon ourselves that is traditionally referred to in dogmatic theology as *acedia* (despair). This twofold enmity to grace, *superbia* and *acedia*, is confessed in Christian faith to be the opposition that comes to light in the twofold movement of grace as inseparably both crucified and risen.[16]

In short, while the Incarnation as grace is said to reveal sin as an attempt to look above or over the head of the God who descends to the Cross, an overlooking of "the sacred Head now wounded,"[17] or of what Luther called "God hidden in sufferings,"[18] the Resurrection as grace, in contrast, is said to reveal sin as a looking down upon ourselves and others, an undervaluation of the creaturely existence that is made new and raised with Jesus Christ. In each case the sinful life is seen to be one that is out of focus with reality.

Located still further with respect not only to the Incarnation and the Resurrection, but to the Parousia, our place is described in the gospel message to be where this reality that shows life to be out of focus comes to make a home. Human existence is thereby disclosed to be disputed territory in that the grace that comes home to us reveals the extent to which we are not at home with ourselves and others. In this sense the Parousia is portrayed as the coming of judgment.

The rejection of our true place there and now in the Incarnation and the Resurrection results in the sin of seeking to displace and misplace the good of all with whom our lives are interconnected here and now. Biblically comprehended, all sin against God and self is judged to involve sin against one's neighbor in an environmental context. More concretely, a nation's relationships with those who are referred to in Jesus' parable in Matthew 25:40 as "the least" secure of the human family are designated as the arena of trial for the rendering of the coming judgment. "Lord, when was it that we saw you hungry or thirsty or a stranger or naked or sick or in prison...?" (Matt. 25:44). "Truly I tell you, just as you did it to one of the least of these who are members of my family [*ton adelphon mou*], you did it to me" (Matt. 25:40). The willful displacement and misplacement of our neighbor's good that occurs in consequence of both our *superbia* and our *acedia* is the destructive wrongdoing and harming of others that since the Middle Ages has been labeled as the remaining five of the so-called seven deadly sins: greed as crippling the neighbor through acquisition (*avaritia*), envy as begrudging the neighbor's good (*invidia*), gluttony as overconsumption in neglect of others (*gula*), lust as violation of the integrity of another (*luxuria*), and fury as ill-will directed against another (*ira*).

Increasingly Christian theology has come to recognize the social as well as the individual dimensions of the traditional seven deadly sins, and contemporary awareness of sin is more likely to express itself today in terms such as racism, sexism, classism, and such other forms of the displacement and misplacement of creaturely good that involve the larger systems, institutions, and corporate structures of society. The cosmic judgment that accompanies the Parousia as grace reveals to faith the deceptive sway over the individual will of unjust social orders that put creaturely well-being in jeopardy. What in New Testament terms are spoken of as "the rulers, authorities, cosmic powers, and forces of evil in high places" that require faith to wrestle with more than "enemies of blood and flesh" (Eph. 6:12) are more generally referred to today as "systemic evils." Systemic evils are institutionalized structures of dehumanization. They are "the course of this world" insofar as its inhabitants are ensnared into a crowd mentality of complicity with the infliction of destruction and death (Eph. 2:2).

When what we are saved from is thus recognized christologically with reference to the Incarnation, the Resurrection, and the Parousia of the life span of Jesus Christ, any claim that salvation means exemption from suffering, trial, and death is disbelieved as a false spirit. We are not saved from the sound of Rachel's voice but from its unreconciled silencing. As the coming day of triumph is envisioned in the Book of Revelation, those who sing forth, "Salvation belongs to our God," are identified as "they who have come out of the great ordeal" (Rev. 7:10, 14). Christian faith, in not denying the ordeal of human existence, refuses to believe that there are any conditions inimical to the true taking place of life in love and freedom that are not overtaken by the apocalypse of rectifying grace. This saving apocalypse is referred to biblically as the coming of righteousness.

3. Saved for Righteousness

The images of placement continue in the gospel testimonies regarding righteousness. Just as in the case of what salvation is confessed to be *by* and *from*, so in the case of what salvation is confessed to be *for*, the depicted reality in each instance is located in relation to the life span of Jesus Christ. The One for our sake "made to be sin who knew no sin" becomes so, in Paul's description, in order that "in him we might become the righteousness of God" (2 Cor. 5:21). If God's being for us does in truth show the extent of our being against whom God is for, this extent is portrayed as not unbounded; it meets its boundaries in how grace is apocalypsed, or, as the sense of the verbal form of *apokalypsis* is here best translated, in how grace takes place.

To hear that the righteousness of God which we are said to become in Christ is "apocalypsed" is at the start to hear something jarringly different from the language of moral imperatives and religious obligations. The significance of the Greek word *apokalypsis* in this context is not adequately conveyed by the English word "revealed," since what is at stake is not only a making known, but a making way for, an initiating as well as a disclosing of a new state of affairs. The moralist's admonitions that everyone ought to do right rather than wrong and that everyone is obliged to observe right practices are set, as it were, almost beside the point by the Pauline claim that what righteousness is is actually grace taking place; the "righteousness of God is apocalypsed" (Rom. 1:17). Christian faith enters here into a realm of discourse alien to that which speaks of doing right and making something right as the upholding of a standard.

With particular regard to the Incarnation unto the Cross, what takes place in the apocalypse of righteousness is portrayed in the gospel accounts as the making of a space for the exercise of freedom. The taking place, so to say, makes a space that enables the working out of relationships of love and freedom. It is the "sphere of the lordship of Christ's body" into which we are incorporated, writes Ernst Käsemann in his exegetical commentary upon Paul's references to righteousness as a gift of grace: "For the apostle knows of no gift which does not also challenge us to responsibility, thereby showing itself as a power over us and creating a place of service for us."[19] Human works are thus not disregarded by the confession that salvation is solely by God's grace. Again the soteriological brief in Ephesians 2 is instructive in the attempt to trace later ecumenical church teaching; salvation is at once said to be "not the result of works" and also "for good works, which God prepared beforehand to be our way of life" (Eph. 2:9–10).

What is rectified in faith is, in one respect, our misplaced confidence regarding the workings of the real world, which is to say, the world of the one people God has made us to be that is "created in Christ Jesus" (Eph. 2:10). Where faith finds its life placed is within a life span where opposition to whom God is for is denied a place. Proscribed and disbelieved by the confession of this life "in Christ" is any spirit that claims that the full inclusiveness of love and freedom is not the full rejection of all that opposes love and freedom. Not everything encompassed by the span of love and freedom disclosed in what happens at the Cross is embraced. The entry of the sting of death is denied its occupancy in this new creation. Where righteousness is enacted in the Incarnation some things are not granted a place.

With particular regard to the Resurrection, what takes place in the apocalypse of righteousness is portrayed in the gospel accounts not only as the making room or space for the exercise of freedom, but as the taking time for it as well. Not only does the New Testament speak of our being "in Christ" by the incorporation of our human existence in the Incarnation unto the Cross, it also speaks of the Risen Christ being "in us" in the power of the Resurrection. While our life span is proclaimed to be fully included once-for-all in the life span of Jesus as the Christ, Christ's life span is proclaimed, in contrast, not fully to permeate our life span all at once. Thus the New Testament accounts speak of Christ being "in us" as a temporal relationship still being formed and nurtured to its full realization. There is a "not yet" as well as an "already" to the power and presence of the Risen Christ within and among us. The present time of faith, in this perspective, is one of prayer that Christ's life span, within which by grace we are now located, will more and more come to occupy our own.

The righteousness of right relatedness given by the Resurrection as grace involves a time of waiting that is not passivity but an ever-greater yielding to the new sphere that makes room and allows time for the exercise of freedom. This is a sphere to which, as the gospel writers see it, all those whom God is for have been delivered by Christ's victory. In this sphere of righteousness much remains to be undertaken, resisted, and suffered by sharing in the mission, resistance, and suffering that Christ's presence there and now at the scene of Rachel's refusal brings. Sin is acknowledged to remain, although no longer to reign.

Reorientation to the power dynamics of the life span of Jesus as it makes room and takes time for our own exercise of freedom is referred to in the gospel accounts as "repentance" (*metanoia*). This reorientation to what amounts in the gospel descriptions to a new energy field is seen as a life-long vocation in grace. The idea is not one of onward and upward developmental progress without struggle or regress, but a perseverance in yielding to the sway of God's righteousness. The imperative of the gospel message, while variously expressed by the different New Testament scriptures, comes down to this one command: *Live where you are because where you are in Christ is where there is time and space for the real exercise of love in freedom.* Because, as Paul puts it, under the grace that unites us once-for-all to the death and resurrection of Christ "sin will have no dominion," the call to life here and now is "do not let sin exercise dominion in your mortal bodies, . . . but present your members to God as instruments of righteousness" (Rom. 6:12–14). To live where we are "in Christ" is to remain in resistance against all destructive domination where we are in the world.

This struggle over dominion to which Paul refers, and who is to be domiciled where, is the issue of contested occupancy addressed in church teachings that speak of the atonement. Righteousness with regard to the resurrection of the Crucified One is seen to involve not only a moving in but also an eviction. We may best trace what unites and distinguishes the primary patterns of thought that are found in the most influential Christian atonement doctrines by noticing how rightful occupancy, on the one hand, and eviction, on the other, are described. To do this it is necessary to point out how this thinking in terms of placement is interwoven in Christian tradition with thinking in terms of payment.

Historically the church's attempts to give an "accounting for the hope" (1 Pet. 3:15) with regard to the transition of place from death in sin to life in righteousness have found expression in the language of transaction. In some cases the transaction recalled is that of a sacrificial lamb, in keeping with ancient Hebrew traditions of a sin offering. In other cases the transaction is more explicitly financial in connotation, the word "redemption" itself in origin a financial term, as is the payment of a ransom. Financiers still speak of "forgiving" a debt so that prior obligations are no longer held against one's account. Forgiving an imbalance of liabilities over assets in banking terms means calling it even. Such language of payment has been the vehicle of much dispute in soteriological doctrine over what the transaction is said to involve and how adequate the transactional concepts are for conveying the gospel faith that God's grace in what happens with Jesus accomplishes a transition of human existence from sin to righteousness.[20] We shall need to ask what faithful disbeliefs are here to be recognized.

"Righteousness" (Hebrew, *tsedaqah;* Greek, *dikaiosyne*) as the term is used in the context of the Old and New Testaments most basically entails being true to who one is, a being true that consists of being in the relationships that rightly constitute one's own being. In the giving of the Decalogue to Moses all God's commandments and law recall Israel's deliverance from captivity in the Exodus and are set within the context of God's promise of covenant relationship. Only God is acknowledged both to be righteous (*dikaios*) and to make righteousness (*dikaioō*), and this making righteous (*dikaiōsis*), this verifying and rectifying that is usually translated into English as "justifying" is confessed to involve a making up for or "atoning" for human sin. It is this making up for our sin as a prerequisite to making room for righteousness that Christian teachings address in combining ideas of placement and payment, or of transition and transaction, when speaking of the atonement. Since this making up for in order to make room for is said to include the overcoming of a breach, of that which formerly has been at odds, the term "atonement" also serves to connote the sense of righteousness as a rightful coming to be at one together, rather than at odds apart, a reconciliation that is therefore a true at-one-ment.

If we attempt to distill the logic of the main atonement concepts in terms of placement, and think of the transition from occupying a place of sin unto death to occupying a place of life resurrected for righteousness, we arrive at the following three characteristic depictions of the salvation that takes place in the victory of Jesus Christ.

First, in one of the early ways of describing the role of Christ as Savior the picture is presented of Christ as a ransom to the devil.[21] Our place in sin, according to the logic of this ransom motif, is identified as a place of abduction from our true home. This kidnapped state is portrayed as one to which we have become enticed with the result that we no longer recognize where our own life actually belongs. The abduction thus manifests itself in patterns of addiction that disorient us from the relationships of love and freedom to which God in creation has called us into being. As in all self-destructive addictions we lend a pseudo-legitimacy, as it were, to the very violence that removes us from where we were created to live. This violent displacement of existence by the power of sin and death, personified in the figure of the devil as our kidnapper, is said to be what Christ faced and endured at the Cross. By Christ entering the very place and condition of our own abduction the devil's demands on us are no longer subject to denial or cover up but shown finally for what they are, a pseudo-legitimacy that has no right to lay claim on us before the God who raises Jesus from the dead. In this sense the crucified and risen Christ is confessed as the ransom that does not evade but rather evicts the devil from a position of holding sway and thereby sets the captive sinner free.

Second, in the eleventh-century atonement doctrine of Anselm of Canterbury the role of Christ as Savior is presented not as meeting by ransom the pseudo-demands upon us of the devil — that is, the demands of sin and death featured by a being carried away from where we belong that our self-destructive addictions have vainly tended to legitimate — but rather as meeting instead the legitimate requirements of God's own righteousness. The logic of this second position is developed by Anselm in a soteriological tract entitled *Cur Deus Homo* (*Why God* [*Became*] *Human*).[22] Here Anselm argues that if true righteousness resides in relationships of love and freedom, then clearly we cannot live in love and freedom if we withhold ourselves from these relationships and refuse to give them their due. Such withholding of what is due on our part, as Anselm puts it, amounts to dishonoring God's own way of being righteous and just. According to this second perspective, sin is not so much addiction to the devil's captivation of us from our rightful place as it is a withholding on our part of the rightful place due God in the sphere of human relationships. By entering the sphere of human relationships Jesus Christ, as fully human, not only allows for love and freedom to occupy the entire space and time of one sinless life span, but, as fully divine in encompassing every human life span, allows for love and freedom to move into every space and time that has been withheld by every sinner.

Third, a theme often reiterated historically in Christian atonement doctrines is that the role of Christ as Savior is one of making a place within our affections. What is given primary emphasis in this third perspective is neither the illegitimate place of our captivation by the devil, nor the legitimate place we have withheld from the honor due God's justice, but the more existential and less juridical transition that occurs because of Christ's communion with us. In commenting upon the statement of Paul in Romans 3:21–26 that God put forth Christ as "a sacrifice of atonement" in order "to show his righteousness" to faith, Abelard (1079–1142), with whom this perspective is classically associated, writes that by such showing of supreme love we are united with Christ "in the closest possible way by indissoluble bonds of affection."[23] God makes room for righteousness not by moving us as unknowing pawns on a chessboard but by eliciting our faith and making us conscious through Christ's teaching and example that we are ultimately loved.

Taking now these same three atonement perspectives and looking again at them, not this time in terms of placement and transition, but in terms of payment and transaction, we may distill their logic as follows. In the first view of Christ as sacrificial ransom for us, the idea is not that the devil is rightly owed anything, a premise to which Gregory of Nazianzus in the fourth century strongly objected,[24] but that our addiction to the evil that captivates us takes its toll and exacts a cost and penalty that can neither be evaded nor ignored. In the second view of Christ as the One who meets for us the requirements of God's own righteousness, compensation is said to be made to cover that which we have withheld and is due God. The vital point here is that the righteousness, or right-relatedness, which is attributable only to the way God freely loves and not to us, is not devalued by our discrediting of it but is credited to our account. Forgiveness in this Anselmic interpretation does not abrogate the conditions of right relatedness that are intrinsic to the exercise of love and freedom. To the contrary, it reinstates them in the extension of Christ's life span to encompass our own by neither writing off our own indebtedness as if it did not exist nor foreclosing on the debt that we in our time and space actually owe. Due regard for what is right, for what it takes to love and to be free, remains to be satisfied. To say, in Anselm's words, that Christ makes "satisfaction" for the time and space we have withheld from God's purposes and cannot ourselves reclaim is not to portray God as a bloodthirsty despot who demands tribute but to say that there is no true reconciliation that is exempt from honoring the justice of our original obligation to love and freedom.[25] In the third view the idea of a financial transaction is not explicit, but the stress upon faith as the receptivity to righteousness brought about by Christ serves to counter any notion that the receipt of saving grace as credited to our account is a transaction that leaves us personally uninvolved.

Church history contains a number of attempts to spell out the dynamics of the atonement, but the Resurrection victory upon which all such analyses are premised informs the Christian view of righteousness as the overcoming by God's grace of all that overcame Jesus on the Cross. At the base of atonement doctrines with their recalling of blood and sacrifice is faith's professed conviction that the destructiveness of our lives can only be genuinely confronted in the presence and power of God because only in this light are we both utterly exposed without pretension and utterly healed without condition. The free gift of salvation as being for righteousness is not, in Bonhoeffer's words, "cheap grace."[26] Equally disallowed by this conviction is any teaching that in effect claims that righteousness does not come from beyond our capacity to save ourselves, that we are not involved in this rectification personally, and that this rectification as freely given does not come at the greatest cost.

Having now inquired into what is meant by "righteousness" as it is spoken of in Christian testimony with regard to the Incarnation and the Resurrection, we turn finally to ask how righteousness is to be understood with regard to the Parousia. At the end of chapter 10 we observed that the "new" reality for which all creation is said to be in expectancy is described as being one "where righteousness is at home" (2 Pet. 3:13). The author of 2 Peter in this instance shares a prevailing view of both the Old and New Testaments in affirming that the dwelling place of righteousness is associated with "the coming of the day of God" (2 Pet. 3:12).

This coming day is proclaimed biblically as one of judgment because where righteousness takes its occupancy, unrighteousness is evicted. The message is that in electing to have a world and love it into freedom God rejects all that stands in the way of this destiny. Thus there is eviction, rejection, exclusion, and even the hell of eternal damnation wherever the right relationships constituting love and freedom find a home. The question posed by the gospel is not whether righteousness as biblically delineated involves an eternal rejection; it does. The question is, what does God's work of salvation reject and what does it not reject? Here dogmatics confronts again the problem of the extent of salvation and the disputed idea of a "universal restoration [*apokatastasis*]" (Acts 3:21) raised by the second of the initial objections set forth at the beginning of this chapter. There is disagreement on the issue of universality in the history of Christian soteriological doctrine, and a clearer picture comes into view only if we attempt to recognize the disbeliefs that the church's commonly held affirmations of faith in God as Savior entail.

Origen's censure at the Fifth Ecumenical Council (II Constantinople) in 553 for advocating a doctrine of *apokatastasis* in which even the devil and all his angels would eventually be restored to an original state of sinlessness applies the anathema to any claim that salvation involves a loss of distinction between good and evil and results in an ultimately indistinguishable "identity" of nameless disembodied spirits without differentiation.[27] Several objections are ingredient in this conciliar censure, whatever its fairness in interpreting Origen's own intentions.[28] The primary point to be underscored here is the evident concern that has remained in church teaching to register disapproval against any view of universal salvation which appears to compromise the eternal rejection of evil. For his part Augustine, a century earlier, in discussing the eternal punishment of the lost raises a series of objections to Origen's positions, but central as well to his rebuttal of the *apokatastasis* argument is an insistence that the devil is not to be thought of as saved.[29] What is consistently disavowed is that God's rejection of all that opposes love and freedom is somehow less than eternal.

But equally disavowed in the logic of ecumenical church teaching historically is the view that the opposition to love and freedom is itself eternal. For that would be to say that evil itself with our complicity in it as sinners possesses the ultimacy of a second God and is not, as biblical faith testifies, ultimately subject to the one God of grace. Thus evil's eternal rejection by God can only be seen as a rejection that comes from the one God whose Parousia will not allow our complicity in this evil to defeat God's being for us and for the good of all creation. Even hell, if by this term is meant death in sin as our farthest remove from being at home to relationships of love and freedom, remains subject in biblical hope to God's righteousness as God's eternal coming to make a home for relationships of love and freedom with us. It is the hell of our homelessness, and never our true home itself, that is seen to be universally evicted, rejected, excluded, and eternally damned by the confession that "as all die in Adam, so all will be made alive in Christ" (1 Cor. 15:22). Only when grace as the source of righteousness is thought to be something other than God's being for us in the life span of Jesus, once-for-all but not all-at-once, does a lack of receptivity to grace become confused with a lack of grace itself. Faith as our receptivity to love and freedom in our time and place holds no priority over grace as God's being for us in making room and taking time for our love and freedom to take place; grace holds priority over faith.

Calvin with characteristic candor rightly observes in introducing the vexed topic of the predestination of some to salvation and others to damnation that "in actual fact, the covenant of life is not preached equally among all [humans], and among those to whom it is preached, it does not gain the same acceptance either constantly or in equal degree."[30] But from the obvious fact that not all come to a faithful receptivity to grace during their earthly life it does not follow, as the "horrible decree" asserts, that grace does not come unsurpassably to all in the Incarnation, Resurrection, and Parousia. If the gospel proclamation is faithfully heard as promising that in the Incarnation, Resurrection, and Parousia Jesus Christ lives and dies for all, is raised for all, and comes as the destiny of all, there is entailed in this hearing a refusal to believe that the extent of God's reconciling work of salvation in both its righteous judgment and mercy does not reach to all.

Proposed Disbeliefs

From the foregoing attempt to trace some of the main contours of Christian soteriological doctrine the following faithful disbeliefs have now been proposed for recognition. Listed in the order in which they have come into view and been stated, we have found entailed in Christian testimony these claims that a faith in keeping with this testimony does *not* believe:

1. that any situation is hopeless—*any* situation.
2. that either the affliction or the infliction of evil, as the opposition to the good of creation, finally prevails.
3. that human beings do not need salvation.
4. that humans are not salvageable.
5. that Jesus Christ is too like others to be uniquely able to save.
6. that Jesus Christ is too unlike other humans to have access to them to save.
7. that grace is something attributable to us or to any other creature.
8. that human beings are the source of their own salvation or of anyone else's.

9. that grace can be accounted for apart from recounting the story of the life span of Jesus with its crucifixion "under Pontius Pilate."
10. that saving grace is either timeless or amorphous, something in general rather than someone "only begotten" and crucified in particular.
11. that souls are saved by dismembering them from bodies in the environment of their specific social interaction.
12. that grace is witnessed as some kind of reserve at the disposal of the church.
13. that the grace of God is present only where its configuration as the life span of Jesus is recognized, or that the manner, means, and results of the incarnate grace enacted in this life span are enfolded only within the historical confines of institutional Christianity.
14. that God's omnipresence is gracious only where its incarnation is truly recounted as being so.
15. that faith is the precondition of saving grace.
16. that salvation by grace is the bypass of worldly existence and its opposing powers of death, or that the limits of worldly existence with its opposing powers of death constitute the limits of grace.
17. that anyone who is not aware of "being saved" before death, or who at least is not intentional about it, is thereafter off-limits to the grace of salvation.
18. that grace is reducible to the teachings, the example, or some putative self-consciousness of the first-century Jesus.
19. that the betrayal and crucifying opposition to God's being disposed toward us in love and freedom, whatever, that is, which amounts to our resistance to being loved and thus to being free, renders this disposition on the part of God null and void.
20. that salvation is somehow an effect of the human will, the result of a human choice, a decision, a leap of faith, an assent, or a consent.
21. that saving grace is dependent upon, or a product of, our acceptance of its being for us.
22. that either God's being for us as grace is the effect or product of our free choice or that grace is ever the abrogation of human freedom and not its initiation.
23. that God's disposing as grace is ever the imposing of a will upon our existence that violates love and freedom.

24. that the connection of grace is not, so to speak, custom made to fit the actual circumstances of each and every recipient.
25. that either there is no given ministry of reconciliation, or that any human role in the reconciliation of the world is something other than the effect of the coming upon the scene of God's reconciling grace.
26. that anyone or any part of creation whatsoever, at any time or at any place, is not met by the coming of this grace.
27. that our being disposed toward death is revealed for what it is apart from God's being disposed toward our life.
28. that there is any true sense of sin that is not the sense of sin forgiven.
29. that salvation means exemption from suffering, trial, and death.
30. that there are any conditions inimical to the true taking place of life in love and freedom that are not overtaken by the apocalypse of rectifying grace.
31. that the full inclusiveness of love and freedom is not the full rejection of all that opposes love and freedom.
32. that righteousness does not come from beyond our capacity to save ourselves.
33. that we are not involved in this rectification personally.
34. that this rectification as freely given does not come at the greatest cost.
35. that God's rejection of all that opposes love and freedom is somehow less than eternal.
36. that the opposition to love and freedom is itself eternal.
37. that the extent of God's reconciling work of salvation in both its righteous judgment and mercy does not reach to all.

If we ask how the first initial objection of this chapter, that the confession of salvation by grace seems to be a confession of human irresponsibility, accords with these proposed disbeliefs, we can see that there is no disagreement in the concern to target as a false witness any doctrine of grace that is disabling rather than enabling of the human ability to respond in relationships of love and freedom. The question is how such response-ability occurs. When asked who can be saved, Jesus is reported in Luke's Gospel as answering, "What is impossible for mortals is possible for God" (Luke 18:27).

Irresponsibility, as it is commonly understood, can mean either unaccountability in the sense of lacking self-determination, or unresponsiveness to what is needed for well-being. To be responsible, in contrast, is to be able to respond not merely with any reaction to stimuli whatsoever but in ways that are not imposed against our will and that are not destructive of well-being. Testimony to salvation by grace, from sin, and for righteousness, by refusing to believe that grace is something attributable to the creature, or that human beings are the source of their own or anyone else's salvation, provides an alternative reading of responsible freedom and self-determination to that presupposed by theories of autonomous self-sufficiency.

This first initial objection, as we have noted, is arguable on five grounds. One argument raises the issue of "original sin" as our alleged falling for that which makes relationships of love and freedom, as Augustine expresses it, impossible (*non posse*). The claim that only grace makes possible what love demands, which is the point Pelagius protested in Augustine's prayer, "Give what Thou commandest, and command what Thou wilt,"[31] has been subject to conflicting theological assessments historically depending upon how the term "grace" is being defined. If it is true that faith in keeping with the gospel disallows the belief that, rather than God's being for us in the life span of Jesus, grace is instead some kind of reserve at the disposal of the church, or a credit to be dispensed that leaves its recipients uninvolved, or an imposition upon the will that abrogates rather than initiates human freedom, the charge of no human response-ability in being loved into loving and freed into freedom is seen to be unfounded. For this faith the acknowledgment of true freedom is to be found in the words, "We love because he [God] first loved us" (1 John 4:19).

The same basic understanding that salvation is not *by* our good works but *for* our good works carries over in reply to the other four ways in which the charge of irresponsibility may be argued. Ideas of Christ as "substitute" do indeed prove false insofar as they suggest that in taking our place in sin Christ somehow makes our own lives replaceable rather than irreplaceably related in love and freedom with God's own. But this irreplaceable rather than replaceable relation may be said to be precisely the soteriological point of the "recapitulation" to which Irenaeus refers in writing of human existence as "summed up" in Christ, and of what Luther means by received or "passive" righteousness as that which alone activates us freely from the despairing passivity of a will in bondage, and of what Schleiermacher in his way speaks of as the "absolute dependency" that is fully realized, note, only in the *releasing* influence of Jesus of Nazareth. Similarly, with regard to the third argument, predestination to anything other than the good of the creature is denied by the refusal to believe that the extent of God's reconciling work of salvation in both its righteous judgment and mercy does not reach to all. As to the fourth argument, irresponsibility is granted to be the consequence of not recognizing faith's refusal to believe that souls are saved by dismembering them from bodies in the environment of their specific interaction. This faithful disbelief is applicable in evaluating the fifth argument as well. While not intrinsic to our works or to anything we do as self-derived, grace as incarnate, resurrected, and coming is never faithfully witnessed as a bypass of existence in this world or as extrinsic in the sense of extraneous to an engagement in the practice of good works.

The second initial objection, that Christian soteriological doctrine seems to portray God as favoring some human beings with love over others, rightly calls attention to the social consequences of teachings that foster a "we-they" mentality contrary to the gospel by claiming divine sanction for restrictive covenants of grace. To disbelieve that the crucifixion of grace prevents its resurrection and parousia anywhere in God's creation is to repudiate as faithless doctrine the "horrible decree" that God predestines some individuals to be forever excluded from grace in eternal opposition to love and freedom. But equally recognized as faithless in this context is any doctrine of "universal restoration" (*apokatastasis*) that treats God's rejection of all that opposes love and freedom as ultimately a matter of indifference and somehow less than eternal. What is eternally favored and destined for salvation, therefore, is the well-being of every creature; what is eternally disfavored and destined for rejection is all opposition, including self-opposition, to the creature's well-being.

Biblical depictions in some instances, as the second initial objection indicates, individualize and personalize these distinctions between God's favor and disfavor and speak not of "what" God rejects but of "whom" God rejects. That which is ungodly is described as those who are ungodly. Evil doing is referred to as evil doers. The coming of judgment is portrayed not abstractly as the defeat of wrong and the vindication of right, but figuratively as two people in the same bed from which "one will be taken and the other left" (Luke 17:34). The distinction between the saved and the unsaved is thus expressed as a distinction between two separate groups of individuals, those sinners to whose destiny God shows mercy, and those sinners to whose destiny God does not show mercy.

By contrast, on the other hand, there are also depictions equally characteristic of biblical testimony that do not allow for an equation of the evil God rejects with individuals (Ps. 99:8). There are said to be principalities and powers of death opposed to the will and way of Christ that are not reducible to "blood and flesh" (Eph. 6:12). In this way of speaking, the ultimately unsaved must be said to denote not certain individuals, for "as all die in Adam, so all will be made alive in Christ"

(1 Cor. 15:22), but rather all enmity, including self-enmity, that is directed against every creature's life taking place in love and freedom. The New Testament does not speak of anyone predestined to be outside the life span of Jesus Christ.[32] Only in this destruction of all enmity, Paul writes, will God be "all in all" (1 Cor. 15:28).

Disbelief that sin nullifies grace, or that there are any conditions inimical to the true taking place of love and freedom that are not overtaken by grace, casts the question of divine favoritism in a different light. Divine impartiality in accomplishing the well-being of all is revealed not as neutrality toward all but as divine partisanship toward setting all captives free. In this partisanship on the side of "scattering the proud" and "lifting up the lowly" (Luke 1:51–52) all captivity is eternally rejected, both in its affliction and infliction.

According to the Christian doctrines of creation and salvation it is never our human being, but our being dead set against our true humanity and that of others in relation to all God's creatures that God eternally does away with in accomplishing the work of reconciliation through what happens with Jesus Christ. From considering how the triune God is identified to faith as Creator and as Savior we next turn to inquire still further what it means to be human according to this frame of reference.

Chapter 12

HUMANITY

Introduction

In the early years of his teaching Karl Barth remarked to his class that not everything but a great deal about us can "be explained by the fact that we are continually hungry, sexually unsettled, and in need of sleep."[1] Barth said he was concerned that church theology not proceed to speak about human nature as if we had no metabolism. (Luther characteristically was even more explicit.) Dust we are, the Psalmist prompts us ever to recall (Ps. 103:14), but if our previous chapters tell the truth of the gospel, this is dust that is to be recognized as eternally valued.

When we ask how humankind is to be understood in Christian faith, we are not asking about something other than ourselves, but about our own proper identification and true destiny. This rubric in the older dogmatics was usually labeled the Doctrine of Man, or better, Theological Anthropology. The underlying question behind all the church's teachings regarding our human being is, "How are we most truly revealed as being who we really are?"

We know from a psychological standpoint that there is a profound sense in which who we are is only revealed in our relationships with others. When we enter into a relationship with someone we become who we could not be otherwise and learn things about ourselves that we did not know before. Not uncommonly we are surprised to realize how we tend to interact with others. In being children, and having children, in being loved, and loving another, in being rejected and misunderstood, as well as in being accepted and welcomed, we develop self-awareness and self-understanding, and the promise of our own life becomes a story.

Similarly, from a more sociological perspective we recognize that certain environments and circumstances serve to reveal things about ourselves. Something happens to our world that alters the landscape, a relocation or dislocation, and a side of ourselves is disclosed that may not have been apparent before. Facing a different scene brought out the best in us, it may later be said, or the worst in us.

It is the testimony of Christian faith that we are most fully revealed as who we actually are in relation to what happens concerning Jesus Christ. The author of the Epistle to the Colossians writes, "When Christ who is your life is revealed, then you also will be revealed with him in glory" (Col. 3:4). Our being human, so to say, involves having our human being brought to light in what takes place in connection with the life span of Jesus. Here in our surveillance of Christian doctrine we enter into the arena of those patterns of biblical speech that describe a human being as someone who is created in "the image of God" (Gen. 1:27), who is becoming conformed unto "the likeness [*eikona*] of Christ" (2 Cor. 3:18),[2] and whose body is "a temple of the Holy Spirit" (1 Cor. 6:19). Coming to terms with who we are is thus seen in Christian faith to be inseparable from coming to terms with who God is in Christ through the Holy Spirit.

The vocabulary in which these terms of self-identity find expression in the history of Christian anthropological teaching may be introduced most concisely by attending to the language of Paul in Romans 8:29–30:

> For those whom he [God] foreknew he also predestined to be conformed to the image [*eikonos*] of his Son, in order that he [the Son] might be the firstborn within a large family. And those whom he [God] predestined he also called; and those whom he called he also justified; and those whom he justified he also glorified.

Here we have the identifying terms of our human being stated as (1) foreknown and predestined, (2) called, (3) justified, and (4) glorified. How these terms are seen in faith to register our actual metabolism as those who in being human are "continually hungry, sexually unsettled, and in need of sleep" is the subject to which we now turn.

Initial Objections

Criticisms of the more commonly held church doctrines regarding humanity most often allege that some formal ordering of human existence is apparently being decreed to the exclusion of humanity's actual diversity. We may sum up the thrust of these criticisms by stating one overall objection and then spelling it out further in regard to the concepts of the *imago Dei* and the *similitudo Christi*.

1. *It would seem that Christian anthropological doctrine perpetuates a stereotypical view of human relationships which in effect denies the varieties of God's gifts.*

Looked at from the standpoint of creation, the Genesis accounts of Adam and Eve have been used historically to define the relationship that is affirmed in orthodox Christian teaching to be normative for humanity. Either a priority is attributed to the male, as the human creature first called into being from whose rib the woman is formed to be his helpmate (Gen. 2:18–23), or, even if male and female are said to be created equal and together (Gen. 1:27), the priority in their relationship is depicted as being for the purpose of procreation, of being fruitful and multiplying (Gen. 1:28). The only deviation from this norm to receive the church's blessing has been most notably in instances of monastic and priestly celibacy.

When tested by the criterion of consequence, the fruits of such teaching may be seen in the following sexual stereotypes. Sexuality becomes identified as a created good only insofar as it is equated with the act of procreation within the marriage bond. All human beings who do not marry and stay married, and who in marriage do not produce offspring, carry at least the implicit stigma of being in some sense either abnormal, unfaithful, or barren. Not only within the church, but within the larger civil society influenced by church teachings, those who do not fit the prescribed order have their humanity called into question and have often been viewed by the dominant culture as less than blessedly human.

Religious orders mandating celibacy have, for their part, generally denied that there is any created good of sexuality whatsoever for their members and have called for a sexless spirituality. All sexual relationships outside of monogamous heterosexual marriage have been condemned as incompatible with Christian teaching under the labels of fornication or adultery.

The possibility of homosexual fidelity is denied. This initial objection does not question that there is indeed evil, fornication, adultery, and all manner of sin present in relationships among human beings; it argues that such sin tends to be defined according to cultural stereotypes that are themselves not congruent with the import of the gospel message itself.

To illustrate, when looked at from the standpoint of salvation testimony, the procreative relationship as privileged in creation is clearly countered with the apocalyptic sense of the imminence of the new day of the Lord in which the announced purpose of human life is not defined according to one's status with regard to marriage or having children. Paul's advice to the Corinthians is that they either stay single, or if already married, live "as though not [*hōs mē*]" (1 Cor. 7:27–29). Yet this advice is not imposed by Paul as a general command: "I wish that all were as I myself am. But each has a particular gift from God, one having one kind and another a different kind" (1 Cor. 7:7). And, "Let each of you lead the life that the Lord has assigned, to which God called you. This is my rule in all the churches" (1 Cor. 7:17). This alternative perspective of differing gifts and life callings stands in marked tension with essentialist doctrines of humanity that tend to formalize certain orders of creation as normative of human relationships. 1 Timothy 2:11–15 provides an example:

> Let a woman learn in silence with full submission. I permit no woman to teach or to have authority over a man; she is to keep silent. For Adam was formed first, then Eve; and Adam was not deceived, but the woman was deceived and became a transgressor. Yet she will be saved through childbearing, provided they continue in faith and love and holiness, with modesty.

Stereotypical thinking extends as well to doctrines that formalize patterns of subservience to authority as obedience to command. Children are to obey their parents, slaves their masters, wives their husbands, and subjects their rulers. Yet scriptural citations containing such admonitions, it should be noted, when taken in their canonical context, are all conditioned by the firm underlying proviso that in no relationship is any human obedience to be given that involves disobedience to the will of God. All too often this radical proviso in scriptural testimony regarding obedience in human relationships has been ignored in maintaining systems of control.

2. *It would seem that interpretations of the* imago Dei *contribute to questionable anthropological dualisms of "higher" and "lower" natures that do violence to human integrity and mutuality.*

The claim that human beings are created in the image of God has been interpreted in several differing ways in the history of Christian doctrine. This second initial objection is arguable along three lines. One complaint targets the dominance attributed to human beings over all other earthly creatures. Another criticism points to the superiority ascribed to the intellect over the supposedly more physical or bodily aspects of human existence. Yet a third form of this objection focuses upon the denial of mutuality that is found in thinking that the *imago Dei* is reflected by a coexistence in which the man takes precedence over the woman who remains subsequent.

The original reference in the creation account of Genesis 1:26–27 provides the basis for the interpretation that what the imaging of God consists in is the dominion that God grants the human species to exercise over all the rest of nature. In the creation account of Genesis 2 humanity is portrayed as animated into life by God's own breath for the purpose of cultivating the garden God has planted as the human habitat. While the idea of cultivation is generally held to be more acceptable to ecological sensibilities than the idea of exercising dominion as a form of subduing the earth, in both Genesis 1 and Genesis 2 the imaging of God is said to consist in a humanity that is somehow over and above the rest of earth's creatures and not interdependent with all that God has made. We have previously confronted the charge of a false anthropocentrism in chapter 10 in our consideration of the doctrine of creation.

A second line of argument comes at this initial objection to a "higher" and "lower" dualism from a different angle. It challenges the bias toward equating God's image in this instance not with the exercise of dominion over "lower" creatures but with the intellect as ostensibly of a "higher" and more spiritual nature than the physical body. We can see how this equation of God's image with what is held to be incorporeal developed in the history of doctrine. Against the idolatry of constructing graven images, so prohibited in Hebraic traditions, the effort in the early church to interpret the *imago Dei* doctrinally becomes one of subordinating everything that appears to be anthropomorphic to the allegedly higher realms of animation associated not with the physical body but with the soul. This is a move also influenced by Neoplatonism. A dualism is posited between a human being's higher spiritual nature and lower physical nature. To say that human beings are made in God's image, so this teaching goes, is not to say that God has a physical shape and size like that of human bodies. Rather, the image of deity into which we are created resides not in our physique, but in our more intangible spirit, our soul. The soul as the locus of God's animation within us is thus portrayed as superior to the body; the body is portrayed as created to be subservient to the soul. As expressed by Augustine, what is most like God in human nature is "a soul endowed with reason and intelligence."[3] It is this rationality of the intelligent soul that most images the Creator and distinguishes humankind from all other "irrational creatures."[4]

Even if unintended, the consequence of this form of anthropological dualism is that a higher value is placed upon what is deemed to be rational and intellectual and a lower value upon what is deemed to be physical and sensual. To the extent that the image of God is identified with that which is judged to be rational but not corporeal a disparagement of the physical body occurs that conflicts both with the doctrine of the Incarnation as well as with the teaching that all nature as created is good. This disparagement of physicality as our lower nature results both in a nonincarnational understanding of spirituality and in an unwholesome estimation of what is involved in being human.

Theorists of the human psyche continue to debate whether or not there are in all of us discernible differences between what appropriately may be characterized as masculine and feminine modes of experience. Yet most typically that which is judged to be female and feminine has in the past been associated in influential theological anthropologies with what is held to be more sensual and less rational and thus, to the degree that a disembodied interpretation of the *imago Dei* prevails, less reflective of the divine image.

It is remarkable the extent to which this "higher" and "lower" thinking is carried over in yet a third way of interpreting the *imago Dei.* This way attempts to reclaim the testimony in the Genesis accounts that humankind is created as male and female in God's image (Gen. 1:27) to be together with one another, and not to be alone (Gen. 2:18). Such testimony gives rise to thinking of the *imago Dei* as a relationship with another rather than as an individual characteristic, whether it be rationality or whatever. We image God, in this third view, by being together in a relationship for good, which is how trinitarian perspectives affirm that God is God, rather than by any so-called higher spiritual nature that we each have by being alone as separate individuals. An analogy is drawn between being together as a human relation and God's being together triunely as One with Another in a unity of Spirit — but with this exception. While the trinitarian relations are confessed to be coequal, the relation of man and woman as created in the image of God is interpreted as not coequal.

Karl Barth's theology provides the most provocative representation of this position. On the one hand, it stresses repeatedly that the basic form of humanity is not man alone, or woman alone, but each in relation to the other, a relation of mutual respect and encounter in which each is equally necessary to the other and neither is of superior or inferior value to the other. But on the other hand, Barth holds that within this coexistence as created of male and female there is both a precedence and subsequence to be valued, a "superordination" given to the man and a "subordination" given to the woman.[5] Anthropological mutuality is thus denied on the basis of the priority given to man's higher status as creature over woman, an analogy more in keeping with that of the Creator as superior to the creation.

Appeal is made to the teaching in 1 Corinthians 11:7–9 which again shows the influence of the Genesis accounts. Here it is stated that man is "the image and reflection of God; but woman is the reflection of man. Indeed, man was not made from woman, but woman from man. Neither was man created for the sake of woman, but woman for the sake of man." As early as 1934 women of the church who had been encouraged by Barth's theology of cohumanity questioned why there could not be more explicit emphasis given to mutualism within the relationships of men and women. In reply Barth referred them to this text of 1 Corinthians 11: "The essential point, which cannot be too much stressed, is that Paul's concept of man's superiority [*Superiorität*] is merely a means to an end, merely to illustrate God's superiority over human beings. Read this passage carefully from this approach, and you will see that it excludes all idea of mutualism."[6] It also, even if "merely" as an illustration, identifies the man and not the woman with God.

3. *It would seem that becoming conformed unto the likeness of Christ, the* similitudo Christi *teaching, requires conformity to that which is male and Christian.*

In *The Gospel according to Thomas*, a text which may have its origins in the late first century, Jesus is reported to say with reference to Mary, "See, I shall lead her, so that I will make her male, that she too may become a living spirit, resembling you males. For every woman who makes herself male will enter the Kingdom of Heaven."[7] Admittedly, this text did not find eventual acceptance within the New Testament canon, nor is its teaching regarding women the doctrine of the church. But, granting this lack of later canonical acceptance, it would also appear that the doctrine of humanity's conformity to the likeness of Christ promotes a gender bias toward thinking of human perfection according to male, rather than female, similes. Not only is Eve said to be subsequent to Adam in creation, Christ is said to be the new Adam to whom all human beings are to be conformed in salvation. While no commonly held church teaching explicitly denies that women as well as men are equally loved by God in both their creation and salvation, the contention that men bear more of a resemblance to Christ than do women has been used historically to legislate that women, despite their own sense of calling, cannot really have been called by God to fulfill certain men-only ministries of the church.

Increasing contemporary awareness of issues of gender bias and sexism in doctrinal formulations makes the christological question, as posed by Rosemary Radford Ruether in the 1980s, inescapable for any dogmatics that seeks to be faithful to the test of consequence: "Can a male savior save women?"[8]

A second complaint raised against the *similitudo Christi* concept in church teachings regarding humanity is that here we have yet another factor that engenders an imperialistic attitude within Christianity. While even theological liberals in the nineteenth century apparently found nothing unusual in Schleiermacher's assertions that what was most human was most Christian, and that what was most Jewish was least Christian,[9] today any hint of implication that Jews are less human than Christians recalls the horrible fruits during the intervening years of Christianity's shocking complicity in anti-Semitism. The idea not only of Christianity as the absolute goal of all other religions, but of Christian self-consciousness as the absolute epitome of all that is truly human self-consciousness, would clearly seem to be the intolerable outcome of teaching that humanity is becoming conformed unto the likeness of Christ.

Interpretation

In attempting to set forth the coherence of church testimony regarding what it means to be human we start with recognition of the Christian refusal to believe that human identity is self-referential. That is to say, who we are as human beings is confessed in Christian faith by reference to how the life span of God's Word made flesh in what happens with Jesus Christ takes time and place with our own. According to the frame of reference articulated at Chalcedon this life span is of the same reality as God (*homoousion tō patri*) as far as deity is concerned and of the same reality as we are ourselves (*homoousion hēmin*) as far as being human is concerned. For such faith the reference to the story, the promise, and the sacrament of this life span, which we have just considered in the previous chapter, provides the primal orientation for human self-understanding. To be sure, we are identified within many frames of reference, from genealogical charts and census reports to our career records and medical files, but none of these tell us what is the primary news about ourselves in the gospel message, that we are ultimately loved, that our life belongs irreplaceably with God's own.

In contrast to all ideas of prepackaged identities and foreclosure, human existence within this orientation is portrayed as open to that which is new. Who we are is said to involve both that which is "now" and that which is "not yet": "Beloved, we are God's children now; what we will be has not yet been revealed. What we do know is this: when he [Jesus Christ] is revealed, we will be like him, for we will see him as he is" (1 John 3:2). Because this "not yet" is linked to Christ's destiny it is noteworthy here that the future is viewed with hope rather than anxiety: "And all who have this hope in him [Jesus Christ] purify themselves, just as he is pure" (1 John 3:3).

1. Foreknown and Predestined

The "now" and the "not yet" find expression in Paul's identification of who we are as foreknown and predestined to be conformed to the *eikōn* of God's Son. Precisely because this predestination is confessed to be in conformity with the destiny of Jesus Christ, faith disbelieves that God's foreknowledge of us is a foreclosure of our freedom; it is the destiny of Jesus Christ to set us free for the good that is "not yet." Biblical perspectives affirm that we belong to One who knows us before we know ourselves, to One who in electing to have a world and love it into freedom has chosen not to be without us. In believing that human life is instituted by God's decision, Christian faith disbelieves that who we are consists ultimately in our own decisions. God is for us even when we are not.

"Or do you not know . . . that you are not your own?" Paul writes to the Corinthians; "For you were bought with a price" (1 Cor. 6:19–20). This language of ultimate belonging is taken up in church teachings regarding humanity. John Calvin's words provide an often quoted instance: "We are not our own. . . . We are God's."[10]

Similar are the words of the Heidelberg Catechism of 1563:

> *Question*. 1. What is your only comfort, in life and in death?
>
> *Answer*. That I belong — body and soul, in life and in death — not to myself but to my faithful Savior, Jesus Christ.[11]

Humanity's calling, justification, and glorification are confessed to have their basis in our being foreknown and predestined by God to love and freedom through incorporation into the life span of Jesus Christ. In the Johannine testimony the words of Jesus to the disciples are that "You did not choose me but I chose you" (John 15:16). Prior to all our loving is said to be the One who "first loved us" (1 John 4:19). God's foreknowing and predestining is explicitly confessed in certain scriptures to occur before birth or even before life in the womb. The word of the Lord's call to Jeremiah may be taken as an example: "Before I formed you in the womb I knew you, and before you were born I consecrated you; I appointed you a prophet to the nations" (Jer. 1:5). Similar is the song of the chosen servant with whom Israel is identified in Isaiah: "The Lord called me before I was born, while I was in my mother's womb he named me" (Isa. 49:1). Likewise from the New Testament, Paul the Apostle declares himself to the Galatians to be someone who has been set apart by God for his eventual ministry "before I was born" (Gal. 1:15).

Disagreement occurs in church teachings today over the significance of such testimony with respect to the issue of fetal abortion. Does confession of God's foreknowing and predestining entail the position that abortion is never a faithful act under any circumstances? In the absence of a current consensus of belief both among church bodies and within them the following disbeliefs provide the parameters of a continuing dogmatic testing. While Christian faith in God's decision to institute human life, as just noted above, involves disbelieving that who we are consists ultimately in our own decisions, such faith, as we observed in the chapter on creation, equally disbelieves that God's ways of upholding and governing creation ever violate the freedom and integrity of the creature who is being upheld and governed, or that human beings are rendered mere puppets or robots, less than free agents, by their provision from God's hand. Thus to acknowledge that we are not our own but that we belong to God "body and soul in life and death" is to acknowledge that between God and every "body and soul" no violation of well-being is sanctioned. Disputed differences occur in church teachings over the questions of when, if at all, the fetus may be said to be a human body and soul in distinction from the human body and soul of the woman in whose womb it is carried,[12] and in cases where the well-being of the one conflicts with that of the other in the course of a pregnancy, which is to be accorded precedence, and by whose choice.[13]

2. Called

Already in considering the subject of creation we have noted that in biblical testimonies God is said to have called humanity into existence. "Let there be" are the words used in Genesis in depicting God's work of bringing creation into being. Such depiction portrays human life not only as foreknown and predestined but also as called for and called forth. This portrayal of being called provides the most comprehensive element in Christian self-understanding. Who we are called to be is pronounced as good, as made in the very image of God to live in covenant fidelity. This calling to image God in faithfulness to God's covenant is what is said to give human life its purpose, its real vocation. What is refused by adherence to this testimony is any claim that some human beings as God's creation are not called to covenant fidelity.

As the second initial objection of this chapter points out, the language of exercising dominion is associated in Genesis 1 with the call of humanity into creation in God's image. In the New Testament account of Colossians the human image of the invisible God is identified with Jesus Christ as the One "in whom," "through whom," and "for whom" all things are said to have been created (Col. 1:15–17). These two traditions of testimony are interwoven in Christian teaching regarding the *imago Dei.* To image God is understood to involve being in such relationship to the origin ("in whom"), the provision ("through whom"), and the end ("for whom") of all creation that God appears through us. To exercise dominion under God, according to God's call, is thus never to violate the integrity of any creature God has made but to be incorporated into the relation that Jesus Christ has with that creature — namely as the life span in whom, through whom, and for whom all things are called to be God's own.

In Genesis 3:5 the relationship established in creation is depicted as broken when the human creature seeks to be "like God" on terms other than God's own. This is seen to be the primal human temptation, the attempt to make God in our own image and thereby to violate the very relationship integral to being who we are, that is, human in God's image. The *imago Dei* as the integrity of the self in the relation God has called into being is expressed by Calvin as "visible in the light of the mind, in the uprightness of the heart, and in the soundness of all the parts."[14] Such integrity, writes Calvin, is not seen by referring to ourselves, as if our created light of the mind, uprightness of heart, and soundness of all our parts had remained inviolate from our creation; rather, this imaging of God that constitutes human integrity is seen by faith only as it is restored from self-violation in Christ, the Second Adam. In Christ we see the integrity of our creation.

The interweaving of the testimonies of Genesis 1–2 with New Testament testimonies regarding Jesus Christ as the image (*eikōn*) of God contributes further to the doctrine that the relation God has called into being in creating us in God's image is a relation not only with God but with God's creatures as well. Human integrity involves relationship for good at once with God and with those with whom God creates us not to be alone. Interpreted from the perspectives of Genesis 1–2 the image of God as a shared existence of being-one-with-another in helpfulness is presented as the relation of male and female. Interpreted from the christological perspectives of the New Testament accounts that speak of the image of God this shared existence of being-one-with-another in love and freedom is not limited to the relation of male and female. Jesus Christ's being for others as the image of God knows no such restriction to gender and sexual categories. For example, in Genesis 2:24 the account given of the creation of man and woman concludes with the words: "Therefore a man leaves his father and his mother and clings to his wife, and they become one flesh." In the New Testament these words of Genesis are interpreted by the writer of Ephesians as follows: "This is a great mystery, and I am applying it to Christ and the church [*ekklēsia*, 'those called forth']" (Eph. 5:31–32).

The initial objections of this chapter thus prompt us to recognize three further disbeliefs entailed by the faith that God calls humanity into being in God's image: Christian faith refuses to believe (1) that human integrity in God's image occurs without being-one-with-another in love and freedom, (2) that the "other" with whom we are created to be together for good is God without any creature, or any creature without God, and (3) that human creation in God's image restricts the good integrity of being together, as opposed to the not-good of being alone (Gen. 22:18), to gender and sexual categories.

Christian teaching not only speaks of humanity as called into being by God at creation, it also speaks of God giving human beings a calling, a vocation, which is their purpose in life. In everyday speech the word "vocation" is perhaps most often used to mean one's life's work. "Vocation" stands for what we think our occupation in life should rightly be. Secondary schools offer counseling in vocational guidance. Sometimes the word "vocation" is used for a particular skill. We speak of students receiving "vocational training" to develop these skills and conventionally proceed to contrast vocational schools and training with professional schools and training. Then again we hear the word used as if it stood exclusively for a religious professional such as a priest, a pastor, a member of a religious order, someone, that is, who has taken religious vows. The assumption develops from this latter manner of speaking that clergy are called, but that everyone else has to find a job.

A brief overview of how the term "vocation" has been used historically in Christianity enables us to recognize more plainly which usages are proscribed for disbelief as not congruent with the import of the scriptural witness for faith today.[15] The New Testament word for "call" is the Greek *klēsis*. In Latin this Greek word is translated as *vocatio*, from which we get our English term. In early Christianity the writings associated with the Apostle Paul were most influential in shaping the understanding of God's calling. What is significant to note is that in them *klēsis* consistently appears in the singular and denotes the "one calling" of all who belong to Christ. There is confessed to be one vocation that comes in many different circumstances. This is a vocation to be holy and thus whole, a call to all Christ's people to be saints (*hagioi*, "holy people"). The call to be whole is the one vocation to which all are summoned by the gospel. A major disbelief of Christian faith in God, often insufficiently recognized, here comes into view. *Christian faith refuses to believe that God calls anyone to reject the particular gifts that God gives uniquely to each human life to make it whole.*

Usage becomes more restricted in the latter part of the third century with the rise of monasticism. The example of St. Anthony provides an instance of this change in the definition of vocation. Having been inspired sometime around the year 285 by the gospel account of the Rich Young Man who comes to Jesus seeking eternal life,[16] Anthony followed the admonition to forsake all his own earthly possessions and withdrew to the wilderness of the Egyptian desert to live as a hermit. His aim was to become completely possessed by the contemplation of God free from all worldly distractions. The call of God is here interpreted as a call to renunciation such as that given to Abraham in Genesis 12:1, "Go from your country and your kindred and your father's house to the land that I will show you," and that given to the disciples by the words of Jesus as we find them in Luke's Gospel: "Whoever comes to me and does not hate father and mother, wife and children, brothers and sisters, yes, and even life itself, cannot be my disciple" (Luke 14:26). *Vocatio* thus comes to be applied only to monks. Only those individuals who renounce worldly occupations in order to keep God's presence perpetually in mind are now said to have a sacred calling.

While a hermit's vocation was associated more exclusively with contemplation rather than with an occupation of daily work, a further shift in Christian interpretation occurs with the rise of the German mystics in the latter part of the thirteenth century. What such people as Meister Eckhart and Johannes Tauler observed is that the sense of God's presence often came most powerfully to common laborers in their secular occupations. "For, truly, if you imagine that you are going to get more out of God by means of religious offices and devotions, in sweet retreats and solitary orisons, than you might by the fireplace or in the stable, then you might just as well think you could seize God and wrap a mantle around his head and stick him under the table!"[17] One could, therefore, remain in one's secular occupation and respond to God's calling. Even though the monastic ideal was still thought to represent a higher vocation, those who provide for the necessities of life could also be said to have a vocation. They are like Martha in the Lucan account who with her sister Mary extends hospitality to Jesus, though she receives for her part less commendation because she is "distracted by her many tasks" than does Mary who sits listening at the feet of Jesus (Luke 10:38–42).

Against this background Luther next developed his doctrine of the priesthood of all believers. Luther too appeals to Abraham, but what is seen to be essential is not that Abraham renounced home and family, but that he was pronounced justified by faith before God not because of good works but to enable good works wherever one was. The lowest level of useful work, if that is God's will for one to engage in, is on the same plane before God as that which may be considered the most spiritual. Luther cautioned the ruler Frederick the Wise against neglecting his calling to administer the affairs of state by devoting so much time to spirituality and religious devotions. Every Christian was called to pray for all, in this sense, to be a priest. The mistake in monasticism, Luther contended, was that it assumed that human beings could achieve blessedness through renunciation. Rather, God comes to us as we are, where we are, and calls us to be God's people then and there. God makes God's holy presence known to faith in all of life.

In sum, vocation and occupation are shown not to be synonymous terms when theologically considered. The one vocation of every unique human life is to be whole in the covenant fidelity of being one with another for good. Our occupations, on the other hand, are varied and numerous, none being higher or lower if it is where our call by God to wholeness is being realized. We live out our vocation through our occupations, but it is our vocation from God that defines who we are. This faith that our calling is not what we do but what God does refuses to believe that our vocation as human beings derives from our work or ceases when our ability to work ends. If the call to be human is from God, the loss of one's job cannot take away the loss of one's vocation. It follows that we are justified in occupying time and space, according to this understanding, by a sanction greater than our own or that of any other creature.

3. Justified

By what right do any of us exist as human beings? As we have attempted to follow it in the previous chapter, the gospel message attested by the church announces that the right to be human comes from God and not from any other source. This is the theme of justification which is given its classic orchestration in Paul's Epistle to the Romans. As Paul expresses it, God is righteous and proves to faith in Jesus that one's humanity is made right, or justified (Rom. 3:26). Through its interweaving of biblical testimonies Christian doctrine affirms that God not only identifies us in creation as called into being in God's image, God also identifies us in salvation as justified by a right to exist that we ourselves have disowned. In Paul's accounting, it is not as the godly whose ways are just that we are justified. Rather, it is as the ungodly who are set against our own good that we are identified in faith as justified in our right to be. Christian faith thus disavows the belief that the justification for our life is something to be earned. From Paul's day to the present the doctrine of the justification of the ungodly, rather than the godly, has offended the common sense of morality and flown in the face of all views of justice defined as what is deserved. Paul himself anticipates the perennial objection: "What then are we to say? Should we continue in sin in order that grace may abound? By no means! How can we who died to sin go on living in it?" (Rom. 6:1). Less recognized, perhaps, have been the following claims that are disbelieved by this faith, that the right to be human is derived from the state, from an acquisition of property or class advantage, from ethnic or genetic privilege, or from adherence to a particular religion or orthodoxy, including Christianity.

Since church doctrines of justification get their vocabulary from Paul we may now take up the thread from the previous chapter on salvation and reflect further on Paul's usage. In interpreting the difference Jesus Christ makes in human affairs, what traditionally comes to be labeled in dogmatics as the work of Christ, Paul writes, "But God proves his love for us in that while we still were sinners Christ died for us. Much more surely then, now that we have been justified by his blood, will we be saved through him from the wrath of God" (Rom. 5:8–9). Both the linkage and distinction here in Paul's teaching between the "now" and the "shall be" are clear. By this manner of speaking human life is pictured as involving a present of justification and God's further saving grace still to be realized. This further work of saving grace Paul denotes as "sanctification": "But now that you have been freed from sin and enslaved to God, the advantage you get is sanctification. The end is eternal life" (Rom. 6:22).

These two terms, "justification" and "sanctification," have received varying emphases in the history of church doctrine. Paul's own writings do not provide us with a theory in which every use of these words is consistent, and there is no single view in this matter which has assumed normative dogmatic status in Christian teaching. We can, nevertheless, summarize briefly the major tenets of faith that the terms "justification" and "sanctification" have historically served to emphasize.

The initial point to be recognized, as we first observed in the previous chapter, is that the English word "justify" is a translation of a Greek verbal form meaning "to make righteous." In the Greek used by Paul the noun meaning "righteousness" is *dikaiosyne*. The verb meaning "to make righteous" is *dikaioō*. And the noun which means "the act of making righteous" is *dikaiosis*. When the attempt is made to translate these Greek words into English it is apparent that there are no adequately corresponding cognates. English has the noun "righteousness" but no suitable verbal form. We cannot say in English "righteous-fy" to mean "to make righteous." Nor can we say "righteous-fication" to denote "the act of making righteous." Thus in English we find ourselves using the words "righteousness," "justify," and "justification" to translate the three etymological forms of the one Greek term, and in this manner of speaking the original contextual connection between the three meanings is obscured.[18]

The point is that in referring to justification Christian doctrine affirms Paul's testimony in Romans 3:26 that the God who *is* righteous *makes* human life righteous. God's "righteousness" is depicted biblically as God's faithfulness, that is, as God's keeping of God's Word and covenant. To be righteous in this sense is to be true to who one is in covenant relation. Christian faith confesses that what justifies our existence is finally not our own efforts or behavior, although these are judged in God's grace for the good as well as the bad that they are, and not the dominant powers of the present age, which may variously view us with favor or disfavor, and not even the way we look upon ourselves. Faith in justification is faith in the way God looks upon us, that is, as those whose own life cannot be separated from the life promised in Jesus Christ. This confidence is therefore not so much a faith in our knowledge of God, but rather, as Paul explains to the Galatians, a faith in how we are known by God (Gal. 4:9). God sees us as no one else does, as being within the relationships of ultimate love and freedom.

What is proclaimed to justify our right to be as God has created us is that God acts to claim us for love and freedom precisely where we have suffered from the rejection of love and freedom, and does so in such a way that we are brought home to the uniqueness of who we are as God's own. The news that God alone is righteous and makes us righteous announces that God makes us true to ourselves as God has called us to be. The "So what?" of this faith is the refusal to believe that the right of any one of us to occupy our unique time and space is something we ever have to justify. More concretely this means that when we are physically weaker, whether as children, as infirm, or as aged, we have no valid cause to feel that we are less worthy to "take up time" or to "be in the way" than when we are in the full strength of our active life. In God's eyes no life story is ever without promise. Our times are in the hands of a God whose will is ever to make a place that is right for us.

4. Glorified

If the word "justification" in Christian doctrine is rightly said to denote the faith that God now views us as living within the life span of Jesus Christ, "sanctification" may be said to denote the faith that God through the power of the Holy Spirit is enabling the life that is in Jesus Christ to move into our life span. "That we may evermore dwell in him and he in us" is the prayer for wholeness in communion at the Eucharist.[19] By such sanctification, in which, to follow the doctrinal terminology, human beings who are created in the image of God and are becoming conformed unto the likeness of Christ recognize their own bodies to be temples of the Holy Spirit, human life is confessed to be glorified.

Whatever the empirical evidence to the contrary, and without denying all that counts against us, Christian teaching holds that God glorifies the outcome of every human life. Once again, the teaching, if more than merely pious sentimentality, is most uncommon sense indeed. Human identity from this perspective is not static and never hopeless. The creation, writes Paul, "will be set free from its bondage to decay and will obtain the freedom of the glory of the children of God" (Rom. 8:21). This awaited freedom of glory Paul calls "the redemption of our bodies" (Rom. 8:23). Proscribed by this representation of faith is any claim that humans are glorified as disembodied spirits.

Augustine in the fifth century specifically addresses the question of what the human similitude with Christ in glory implies for women if such glory is confessed to include a redemption of the body. He condemns as false the teaching that, since all are to be conformed unto the image of Jesus Christ, this means that women in the final resurrection will be raised as men. Against a longstanding claim of his day that the female sex is to be considered a defect of creation, Augustine counters that "woman is a creature of God just as much as man is." "The [God] who created both sexes will restore both," that is, redeem and glorify both. In light of the glory of redemption, Augustine continues, women are not to be defined by male lust or exploitation, nor are women's bodies to be valued for their use in procreation. Instead, redemption will be "to a new beauty" (*sed decori novo*).[20] The claim that being conformed to the image or likeness of Christ is conformity to maleness is here pointed out for faith's disbelief.

If our glory comes in being made whole, sanctified, the present justification of the ungodly, of which Paul writes in Romans, is not the acceptance of ungodliness, a pretending that injustice makes no difference. This, so we have seen in the chapter on salvation, is the point that Christian teachings concerning the atonement seek to address. Every rejection of love and freedom, and hence of justice, exacts a cost from others and from ourselves. There is a price to be paid for every defiance of the relationships of love and freedom, an honoring of what true life in covenant is due. The suffering inflicted by our disowning of the good we are created to be is only turned into blessing, according to these atonement teachings, by being ultimately borne by a Power greater than our own which brings the afflictions encompassed by the life span of Jesus Christ to glory.

This talk of suffering in connection with glory harbors a lie of sadomasochistic proportions if the faithful disbeliefs it entails go unrecognized. "Those wounds yet visible above in beauty glorified," as a hymn to Christ's ascension expresses it,[21] when taken in faith as a reality description, are words acknowledging that the suffering inflicted in this world is not rendered invisible by the glorious outcome of what takes place at the Cross. The ascended Christ is identified as no other than the same Christ crucified whom God has raised up in victory over every opposing power of life and death, including our own. The ascended glory is not an ultimate coverup, as it were, of what the Cross uncovers about human betrayal and death dealing; the wounds are brought to a new light.

All this is but another way of saying that the glory of being human is witnessed in Christian faith not as a return to a state of innocence in an Eden where there is no awareness of having fallen and no need of healing. Rather, the glory of being human is that God's love for us in Christ proves stronger than whatever is against us in our life and death. Our very culpability itself turns out to attest to God's blessing. "*O felix culpa*" are the words of Thomas Aquinas, "*O blessed fault*, which merited such and so great a redeemer."[22] Paul, whose influential testimony in Romans 8 gives expression to this uncommon sense of what being glorified means, writes that "the sufferings of this present time are not worth comparing with the glory about to be revealed [*apocalypsed*] to us" (Rom. 8:18). Adherence to this testimony enjoins an equal refusal to believe that human life is ever glorified by rendering suffering invisible, or that there is any glory in suffering other than in its overcoming.

Faith that the glorification of humanity, together with every creature God has made, is revealed as the love that God has for God's own finds expression also in the Johannine scriptures.

As recounted in the Fourth Gospel, the prayer of Jesus that all may be one in him as he is one with the Father speaks of "the glory that you have given me I have given them . . . so that the world may know that you have . . . loved them even as you have loved me" (John 17:22–23). The understanding that being glorified means being ultimately loved is consistent with the import of other gospel testimonies regarding human destiny as well. What is confessed is that the one true glory of every life is that God's love for it does not fail.

5. Being Human Sexually

How being loved into human freedom by God is faithfully reflected in being human sexually remains one of the most contested questions facing the church in contemporary society.[23] To heed Barth's warning against theological pronouncements about humanity that ignore human metabolism, and to take account of the initial objections raised at the beginning of this chapter, we will need to ask more specifically about the metabolic implications of the foregoing interpretation. What claims does this interpretation of the Christian understanding of humanity disallow as faithful witness today regarding sexuality? What then is disbelieved about human sexuality in believing that human beings are created for covenant relation in the image of God, are destined for glory in conformity to the likeness of Christ, and are justified in being who God made them to be with bodies that are temples of the Holy Spirit?

As a focus for our testing of the spirits in this area of doctrine, wording from *The Book of Discipline* of the United Methodist Church provides a concise statement of a position that in its main conclusions at least is representative of most Christian denominations today across the ecumenical spectrum.[24] This position, in sum, affirms "fidelity in marriage and celibacy in singleness," with the added stipulation that, while "sexuality is a good gift of God," and "persons may be fully human only when that gift is acknowledged and affirmed by themselves, the Church, and society," and while "homosexual persons no less than heterosexual persons are individuals of sacred worth" who along with "all persons are entitled to have their human and civil rights ensured," nevertheless, "the practice of homosexuality" is "incompatible with Christian teaching."

In the United Methodist statement a governing principle for reaching this position is professed to be the test of consequence: "We reject all sexual expressions which damage or destroy the humanity God has given us as birthright, and we affirm only that sexual expression which enhances that same humanity, in the midst of diverse opinion as to what constitutes that enhancement." This governing principle for determining faithful affirmations with respect to sexual expressions calls to mind the Lucan account of the reply of Jesus to his critics who, by appealing to the law of their scriptures, opposed his feeding or healing anyone on the sabbath day of rest: "I ask you, is it lawful" (in keeping with the scriptures) "to do good or to do harm on the sabbath, to save life or to destroy it?" (Luke 6:9). Dogmatic testing requires that these commonly held claims of ecumenical Christianity put forth as "Christian teaching" be assessed today for their faithful coherence.

By believing that all human beings are created in the image of God we have noted that Christian faith affirms covenant relationship to be the basis of all human integrity. It is "not good" for the human being to be alone (Gen. 2:18). "Fidelity in marriage" is recognized to be an expression of the covenant fidelity that is, in the traditional rituals of Christian matrimony, said to be "instituted of God" in creation.[25] Such covenant fidelity of being made in the image of God who is confessed in the threefold referentiality of the gospel message as being-One-with-Another-in-the-Spirit-of-love-and-freedom is thus "the humanity God has given us as birthright," in the words of the United Methodist statement. This covenant fidelity, we have seen, is confessed to be both with God and with another creature, and not with either apart from the other. It is in this sense that traditional rituals of Christian matrimony also speak of "fidelity in marriage" not only as "instituted of God" in creation but also as signifying unto faith "the union that exists between Christ and his church." Covenant union, therefore, is professed to involve the significance to faith both of humanity's creation in the *imago Dei* and also humanity's conformity to the *similitudo Christi*. According to this testimony, all human beings are called by God to live in covenant fidelity.

While covenant fidelity is clearly presented in the creation account of Genesis 2:22–25 to involve the creation of man and woman to be together for good as "helper" and "partner" (Gen. 2:18, 20), the covenant union signifying what the Ephesians account calls "the great mystery" of "Christ and the church" (Eph. 5:31–32) does not allow for the restriction of this covenant fidelity and union to the marriage of man and woman alone. If Christian faith affirms with the testimony of the Apostle Paul that God has not called all human beings to marry, but that rather everyone is to be true to the gift God has given, then the creation and calling of man and woman to be human together cannot be restricted only to the sexual union of husband and wife. Admittedly, when the account in

Genesis 2:23–24 is abstracted from the larger canonical context of both the New and Old Testaments and the import of this canonical witness for faith today, this account does move from reference to the creation of man and woman to reference of "Therefore a man leaves his father and his mother and clings to his wife, and they become one flesh." To claim that this described transition in Genesis 2:23–24 from a relation to "woman" to a relation to "wife" is prescribed for all humanity would be in effect to claim that only married men and women who cling to each other as one flesh are human beings made in the image of God and that all unmarried people are not human beings. Such a teaching clearly violates the love that comes to embodied expression in the way that Jesus Christ is confessed in Christian faith to relate to the church.

How the scriptures that speak of marriage are to be reconciled with the love Christians confess to know in their own lives remains one of the most unsettled questions in the church today. For the last quarter century no part of the liturgy, especially in liberal Protestant communions, has been more deleted, transposed, patched up, and supplemented than the liturgy of matrimony. Only the sternest of traditionalists among the clergy have been able to resist revisions thrust upon them by apprehensive couples before the processional begins. Such vows as "I promise never to demand surrender or to surrender to demand" lead one occasionally to wonder if a covenant is being affirmed or a truce negotiated.

With the exception of the traditional passage from Ephesians 5, and the reference in John 2:1–2 to Jesus' presence at a wedding in Cana of Galilee, most scriptures read at Christian weddings do not explicitly mention marriage. And most of the scriptures that do mention marriage are considered too objectionable to be read at weddings. Passages used in the past to contend that wives are to be subservient to their husbands have become especially troubling.[26] Equally unmentioned is Paul's rather grudging concession that, in the blunt words of the King James translation, for those who cannot contain themselves "it is better to marry than to burn" (1 Cor. 7:9). The point is that "what the Bible says" regarding marital fidelity requires, as we noted in discussing the test of congruence with scripture in chapter 4, that consideration be given in this instance, as in all others, not to noncontextual prooftexting but to seeking out the import of the entire canonical witness for faith today. This congruence we have earlier seen to be explicitly affirmed in the words of the Second Helvetic Confession of 1566 as that interpretation of holy scripture that seeks to recognize not only the original form and locale in which a text appeared but also the meaning for faith today that is *cum regula fidei et caritatis congruit* ("congruent with the rule of faith and of love").[27] What constitutes "fidelity in marriage" for the Old Testament patriarchs, and for a Solomon who is reported to have numbered among his wives "seven hundred princesses and three hundred concubines" (1 Kings 11:3), is depicted quite differently in "what the Bible says" from the depiction with respect to the early Christians awaiting the imminent end time whom Paul admonishes when married to live together only as though not (1 Cor. 7:29).

Where the biblical depictions of marriage do reflect a remarkable consistency, it should be underlined, is in their portrayal of unfaithful sexual practice as idolatry — that is, as the covenant violation of the integrity of being created in the image of God and destined for conformity to the likeness of Christ.

Thus the marital infidelity of King Solomon is, somewhat shockingly by Victorian standards, not located in the polygamous excess of having one thousand wives, but in the fact that his wives turned away Solomon's heart so that he was no longer "true to the Lord his God" (1 Kings 11:4). Similarly, the "degrading passions" that Paul expounds in Romans 1:18–32 are said to be behaviors arising from having "exchanged the truth about God for a lie and [having] worshiped and served the creature rather than the Creator" (Rom. 1:25). On the other hand, whereas the description given in 1 and 2 Samuel of the covenant relation of David and Jonathan would most likely be considered by some as grounds for suspicion in disqualifying them "sexually" for either clerical ordination or military service in the United States, ancient Hebraic tradition honors without any indicated embarrassment the covenantal context of their love in fidelity to one another: "Thus Jonathan made a covenant with the house of David . . . Jonathan made David swear again by his love for him; for he loved him as he loved his own life" (1 Sam. 20:16–17); "(David) bowed three times, and they kissed each other, and wept with each other" (1 Sam. 20:41); and at the death of Jonathan, the grieving David laments, "Greatly beloved were you to me; your love to me was wonderful, passing the love of women" (2 Sam. 1:26). To be sure, both Jonathan and David are also depicted with wives and offspring. But the point is that, in this instance as well as in the account of Solomon's wives and of Paul's testimony in Romans 1 with respect to degraded passions, the issue of whether a behavior or practice constitutes sexual infidelity is presented as whether it constitutes a violation of the covenant fidelity instituted of God.

The understanding of marital fidelity as an expression of the fidelity that Christ shows toward those who know of their calling to be a covenant people, the *ekklēsia*, bears out further the consistent import of these scriptural testimonies. The traditional emphasis of the nuptial mass which, following Ephesians 5:32, proclaims that marriage signifies the mystery of the union that exists between Christ and the church, has been variously interpreted in the history of Christianity. Irreverent comment has sometimes been made of the insistence of the pious and passionate Moravian leader Nikolaus von Zinzendorff (1700–1760) who admonished his followers that at the very moment of sexual union in marriage the true Christian would be thinking only of the mystical union that exists between Christ and the church — a view, it has been remarked, hardly complimentary to one's spouse. In this connection George Hendry has quoted the words of Dietrich Bonhoeffer: "To long for the transcendent when you are in your wife's arms is, to put it mildly, a lack of taste, and it is certainly not what God expects of us."[28] But what the "mystical union that exists between Christ and the church," as the traditional marriage ritual expresses it, has to proclaim to those of the church who are not married has for the most part remained unconsidered. If the church includes the unmarried as well as the married, it follows that the covenant fidelity disclosed in this "mystical union that exists between Christ and the church" applies to the unmarried *in Christ* as well as to the married.

This application is precisely what we find in the one chapter in the New Testament that at first glance appears to be most opposed to marriage and indeed to all human relationships of intimate love: 1 Corinthians 7. It is most unlikely that one would ever hear this chapter read at a wedding. For here Paul gives his "opinion [*gnōmē*]," as he calls it, that it is better for all those in Corinth who do not already know the love of a husband or wife to remain unmarried, as he is. This sounds as if those who are not married will be better off alone, in Paul's opinion, than in sharing the love of another.

Surely here the apparent cacophony of "what the Bible says" seems almost to invite despair. No teaching would seem more to contradict the Genesis testimony that the Creator views it as "not good" for humans to be alone (Gen. 2:18), or more to betray the love that Christian worship confesses in its praise to know in Jesus Christ. Even those most sympathetic to Paul may conclude that in this instance he is at his worst in guiding us today to the mind of Christ.

Without attempting to make Paul say what he does not say, or to pretend that everything in the Pauline letters has equal validity for every situation in conveying to us the gospel, the following words that trace a train of thought in 1 Corinthians 7 at least invite our notice:

> Now concerning the unmarried [*parthenoi*], I have no command of the Lord, but I give my opinion . . . I think that, in view of the impending crisis, it is well for you to remain as you are. Are you bound to a wife? Do not seek to be free. Are you free from a wife? Do not seek a wife. But if you marry, you do not sin . . . I mean, brothers and sisters, the appointed time has grown short . . . I want you to be free from anxieties . . . I say this . . . not to put any restraint upon you. (1 Cor. 7:25–29, 32, 35)

And then these words from earlier in the chapter which may be taken to introduce the foregoing statements: "I wish that all were as I myself am. But each has a particular gift from God, one having one kind and another a different kind" (1 Cor. 7:7).

If in this testimony we hear only the "opinion" of Paul we may well conclude, and perhaps rightly so, that here he intends to speak only for the end of time, and not for all times, or for our time. But if we hear the preface to this opinion, another sounding for faith may be detected.

"Concerning the unmarried . . . no command of the Lord." In this preface the terms of human relationships are recast not as commands but as gifts. Whatever the pressures of Paul's time, or of our time, or of any time, there is no universal command to marry or not to marry. "But each has a particular gift from God, one having one kind and another a different kind" (1 Cor. 7:7). From the anxiety that one cannot fully give oneself to another in marriage for fear that the relation of fidelity in marriage will prevent the relation of fidelity in covenant with God, the import of this message delivers us. Equally, from the compulsion that we must get married, find the right person and by a certain age or our lives will never be fully human, we are delivered. We have earlier noted the Christian teaching that God never loves us in general terms. The grace of that love is always special to who we are and to our destiny, fitting always to its particular recipient.

If this hearing of the gospel is a faithful one, then what is being done at a celebration of Christian marriage blesses us all, married or unmarried, widowed, single, or divorced. Freed from the anxiety of both exclusion and compulsion, we are in this hearing brought to see signified in the couple's special love as gift that mystery of the special union between Christ and every one of us.

In addition to the affirmation of "fidelity in marriage" in the United Methodist statement there is the affirmation of "celibacy in singleness." While celibacy has long been honored in Eastern Orthodox and Roman Catholic traditions, its place in Protestant faith and teaching has tended to receive recent emphasis mostly in order to specify the only church-sanctioned way of being human with respect to sex other than the way of "fidelity in marriage." Yet the United Methodist statement recognizes that being celibate no longer can be thought of as being nonsexual.[29] The theological inadequacy of affirming "celibacy in singleness" as an alternative to "fidelity in marriage" becomes glaring in light of the faith that all human beings are called to fidelity, not simply those for whom marriage is an expression of covenant fidelity. Celibacy in fidelity, not in singleness, affirms the human calling of all to be one with another in the spirit of love and freedom. If the Holy Spirit's gift in the temple of one's body is for celibacy, then this is a faithful expression of covenant fidelity in that instance.

A recognition of celibacy, like marriage, as one special gift and not a universal command may be found in John Calvin's theological objection to the papist insistence that only celibates qualify for clerical ordination. With allusion to "You shall not tempt the Lord your God" (Deut. 6:16; Matt. 4:7), Calvin writes, "But this is to tempt God: to strive against the nature imparted by him, and to despise his present gifts as if they did not belong to us at all."[30] It is an act of unfaithfulness, of infidelity, in the view of Calvin here articulated, for anyone to despise God's present gifts of the nature imparted by God of one's sexuality as if these gifts did not belong to one at all.

What then, we must now ask, is the implication of such a faith position in testing the third claim of the United Methodist statement, that "the practice of homosexuality is incompatible with Christian teaching"? What constitutes such "practice" is left undefined, just as what constitutes the practice of heterosexuality is left undefined. Nowhere in "what the Bible says" as prooftexting is the full range of reciprocal affectional intimacy as it is considered today under the rubric of human "sexuality" spelled out in physiological detail. By the "practice" of any sexuality one may assume that orgasm and coitus may be included, but no coherent understanding of sexuality today would attempt to reduce its human expression simply to orgasm or to a coital act. Considerations of sexuality today are no more limited to coitus than is coitus limited to procreation. Most church teaching no longer holds that the only faithful form of sexual expression is one that results in "being fruitful and multiplying" (Gen. 1:28).

Yet it is equally the case that not all forms of faithful covenant relation involve a sexual relation in the explicit sense of feelings and behaviors that may be said to be inclined, at least, toward coital intimacy. The call of all human beings to covenant fidelity takes forms as varied as the gifts God grants and the diverse "circumstances" [*en panti and en pasin*, "always and in all things"], as Paul puts it, in which faith learns to find its contentment (Phil. 4:12): marriage, celibacy, family, neighborhood, community, friendship, partnership, companionship, each of which may involve a faithful way of being human relationally in the image of God, of being one with another in the spirit of love and freedom.

Blanket church objections to "the practice of homosexuality" as being contrary to "what the Bible says" are often either implicitly or explicitly determined by such selected texts as Leviticus 18:22, "You shall not lie with a male as with a woman; it is an abomination"; Leviticus 20:13, "If a man lies with a male as with a woman, both of them have committed an abomination; they shall be put to death"; Romans 1:26–27, "For this reason God gave them up to degrading passions. Their women exchanged natural intercourse for unnatural, and in the same way also the men, giving up natural intercourse with women, were consumed with passion for one another. Men committed shameless acts with men and received in their own persons the due penalty for their error"; 1 Corinthians 6:9–10, "Do you not know that wrongdoers will not inherit the kingdom of God? Do not be deceived! Fornicators, idolaters, adulterers, male prostitutes, sodomites, thieves, the greedy, drunkards, revilers, robbers — none of these will inherit the kingdom of God"; and, 1 Timothy 1:9–11, "This means understanding that the law is laid down not for the innocent but for the lawless and disobedient, for the godless and sinful, for the unholy and profane, for those who kill their father or mother, for murderers, fornicators, sodomites, slave traders, liars, perjurers, and whatever else is contrary to the sound teaching that conforms to the glorious gospel of the blessed God, which he entrusted to me."

In the case of each of these selected scriptural citations, and others similar to them, what is being condemned is clearly the violation of covenant fidelity and not its expression.[31] If we inquire into the import of "what the Bible says" for faith today by examining, as the Second Helvetic Confession of 1566 affirms, not only the original form and locale in which these texts originated, but also the meaning that is *cum regula fidei et caritatis congruit*, "congruent with the rule of faith and of love" in the full context of the canon, the subject being addressed in every instance is definitely not any expression of being-one-with-another in covenant that God calls into being and grants as the embodied gift of the Holy Spirit.

Without in the least denying such homosexual (as well as heterosexual and asexual) violation of creaturely good, the question facing the church today is whether "the practice of homosexuality" in any form or respect is to be acknowledged as an expression of the covenant fidelity that God calls into being in creation and as a gift to those whose bodies are indeed faithful temples of the Holy Spirit. The general ecumenical consensus of the church in the past has answered No. But it has done so with surprisingly little, if any, attempt to face up to the disbeliefs that Christian faith in this area entails.

Only those who give no theological heed to consequence as a legitimate test of doctrine can fail to take account of the fact that current church teaching is viewed by increasing numbers of Christians as setting up an intolerable contradiction between their creation as sexual beings and their calling to the Christian life. In what amounts to a Catch-22, their being human as God has made them and their being faithful as God calls them are presented as antithetical. Why is this so?

Two reasons are most often given. On the one hand, there are those who suffer from what appears to them to be the withholding of the gift of marriage, of intimate companionship, and family, all of which Christian teaching affirms. These include those who have never married because of health, handicap, or whatever reason. It also includes increasingly those who having once taken the vows of fidelity to another "until death us do part" now find that their marriage failed and died. It ceased to be for them God's good gift. Still there are others whose continuing marriage in form may appear outwardly fine, but inwardly they know that the real story is very different. On the other hand, there are others professing Christian faith for whom it is the case that the love they have been given, and for which they can do no other but thank God, is neither recognized nor acknowledged as such by the church. An illustration of this second situation is that of the love between same-sex partners. In their case the ancient test of Christian teaching as *lex orandi est lex credendi et agendi* ("the rule of prayer is the rule of belief and action") is not applied. There is for them no consistency between what the church is teaching about their sexuality and their prayers of thanksgiving for each other to God.

In this social context the United Methodist Church at its General Conference in 1984 was reported to have spent more time debating issues related to homosexuality than all other issues combined. By 2008, despite continuing objections and controversy, the official position had remained virtually unchanged. Subsequent conferences and judicatories of other denominations and church bodies have reflected a similar pattern. The fractured conscience of the church becomes plain in the logical incoherence of the following generally subscribed to conclusions:

1. Sexuality is a good gift of God, and persons may be fully human only when that gift is acknowledged by the individuals themselves, by the church, and by society.
2. Homosexual persons no less than heterosexual persons are individuals of sacred worth.
3. The practice of homosexuality is not to be condoned by the church; it is incompatible with Christian teaching.

Thus, among both groups within the churches, those who feel that a gift of love has been denied to them, as well as those whose thanksgiving for a gift of love is rejected and disallowed by others within the community, there is the intolerable fact today in ecumenical Christianity of unspoken pain about this subject and an unspeakable inner conflict.

For the churches to come to terms with their own incoherence over what faithful teaching should be, and thus to be in a position to speak responsibly from their faith to similar problems arising within the secular culture, it will be necessary to ask what disbeliefs on the subject of being human sexually are entailed by Christian faith affirmations. Do the present rejections in church pronouncements arise out of these affirmations of faith? Are the refusals ones that are enjoined and entailed by the faith confessions? Are they, finally, prompted by the spirit that confesses that Jesus Christ has come, as 1 John 4:1 expresses it, *en sarki*, "in the flesh" of the sufferings of this present time, or are they instead actually the evidence of some other spirit?

From our review of Christian doctrine thus far four faithful disbeliefs cannot be overlooked:

1. Christian faith does not believe that the way God makes us in creation, including our sexuality, ever presents us with a Catch-22. This disbelief is entailed in Christianity's confession that all that God creates is good.

2. Christian faith does not believe that the fulfillment of life in Christ can only occur in marriage. This disbelief is entailed in the Christian affirmation of salvation by grace regardless of marital status.

3. Christian faith does not believe that a life of lonely repression, and the absence of all reciprocal affection and its relatedness to others, is God's calling. This disbelief is entailed in the faith that human beings are made in the image of God, as people of God's covenant election, and that this God is triune, a God whose way of being is by being One with Another in a unity of Spirit.

4. Christian faith does not believe that who and what we are called to be in salvation conflicts with who and what we are called to be in our creation, that our justification and destined glorification are in conflict with our creation. This disbelief is entailed in the faith that "fallen" nature is never our creation but our being opposed to ourselves as God has created us.

In sum, doctrinally the issue boils down to whether a homosexual orientation is ever God's good creation, or always an evidence of the "fall" as a rejection of one's good creation, and whether it is ever the gift of God's Holy Spirit for human wholeness templed in the human body, or always an idolatrous defiance of God's embodied gift.

The disbeliefs that have been uncovered in this chapter in attempting to trace the Christian confession that human beings as foreknown and predestined, called, justified, and glorified, are made in God's image, to conform to the likeness of Christ, with bodies seen in faith to be temples of the Holy Spirit, lead to the following doctrinal proposal that currently is not the official position of any church. It seeks to contribute further theological reflection for the church's continuing attempts to arrive at the mind of Christ today on issues of human sexuality by drawing together the conclusions reached from a dogmatic testing for faithful disbeliefs:

The ultimate vocation is neither marriage nor celibacy but the covenant fidelity of being one with another in Christ. To this all are called by the gospel of grace.

To be one with another in Christ is to seek the freedom of the other through love and to love the other through freedom. This is to bear the *imago Dei* as the imaging of God's own triune relationality of being-One-with-Another-in-a-unity-of-Spirit and is God's wondrous gift whenever God grants it and thus makes it whole and holy.

How such covenant fidelity comes to spiritual and physical embodiment and expression will vary according to the "varieties of gifts" (1 Cor. 12:4) that "differ according to the grace given to us" (Rom. 12:6) and the "circumstances" (Phil. 4:12) in which Christ's Spirit claims us. For most this will indeed mean the marriage of man and woman, for others celibacy, and still for others further ways of being faithful, including covenants of same-sex fidelity. No gift of God's grace is to be held in dishonor.[32]

Such an understanding is opposed both to dehumanizing exploitation and to self-centered repression. It recognizes the biblical injunctions against fornication, adultery, sodomy,[33] and all uncleanness to refer to every violation of the call to the covenant fidelity of being one with another in Christ's embodied Spirit of love and freedom. To hear and follow this call is the stance of faith which looks to God for its fulfillment as a witness to God's own faithfulness in love and freedom to us all.

Proposed Disbeliefs

From the interpretation given in this chapter regarding Christian teaching concerning our humanity, the following disbeliefs of Christian faith as they have been proposed in context may now be summarized in review:

1. that human identity is self-referential.
2. that God's foreknowledge of us is a foreclosure of our freedom.
3. that who we are consists ultimately in our own decisions.
4. that any human beings as God's creation are not called to covenant fidelity.
5. that human integrity in God's image occurs without being-one-with-another in love and freedom.

6. that the "other" with whom we are created to be together for good is God without any creature, or any creature without God.
7. that human creation in God's image restricts the good integrity of being together, as opposed to the "not good" of being alone (Gen. 22:18), to gender and sexual categories.
8. that God calls anyone to reject the particular gifts that God gives uniquely to each human life to make it whole.
9. that our vocation as human beings derives from our work or ceases when our ability to work ends.
10. that the right to be human is derived from the state, from an acquisition of property or class advantage, from ethnic or genetic privilege, or from adherence to a particular religion or orthodoxy, including Christianity.
11. that the right of any one of us to occupy our unique time and space is something we ever have to justify.
12. that humans are glorified as disembodied spirits.
13. that being conformed to the image or likeness of Christ is conformity to maleness.
14. that human life is ever glorified by rendering suffering invisible, or that there is any glory in suffering other than in its overcoming.
15. that the way God makes us in creation, including our sexuality, ever presents us with a Catch-22.
16. that the fulfillment of life in Christ can only occur in the marriage of man and woman.
17. that a life of lonely repression, and the absence of all reciprocal affection and its relatedness to others, is God's calling.
18. that who and what we are called to be in salvation conflicts with who and what we are called to be in our creation, that our justification and destined glorification are in conflict with our creation.

To recall again the first of the initial objections raised at the beginning of this chapter, that it would seem that Christian anthropological doctrine perpetuates a stereotypical view of human relationships which in effect denies the varieties of God's gifts, we can see that a response is provided by the interpretation resulting in these disbeliefs. If these refusals are acknowledged to be faithful ones, it becomes plain that any stereotypical view of human relationships which in effect does indeed deny the varieties of God's gifts betrays the gospel message. The refusal to believe that human creation in God's image restricts the good integrity of being together to gender and sexual categories, or calls anyone to reject the particular gifts that God gives uniquely to each human life to make it whole, supports the objection that all such stereotyping represents faithless doctrine. To obey God in human relationships is always to disobey the commands imposed by any putative structure of authority whenever they violate the covenantal relations of love and freedom that God calls into being.

The second initial objection, that it would seem that interpretations of the *imago Dei* contribute to questionable anthropological dualisms of "higher" and "lower" natures that do violence to human integrity and mutuality, is also addressed by these disbeliefs. Insofar as such dualisms are taken to mean that human glory is to be located somehow in a "soul" or in an "intellect" that can be divorced from, or is of a greater value to God than what Paul calls "the redemption of our bodies" (Rom. 8:23), dissent is registered by disbelieving that humans are glorified as disembodied spirits.

Nor can the *imago Dei* doctrine be faithfully interpreted to suggest superior and inferior relationships between human beings in the covenant fidelity that is enacted by their creation in God's image. In this regard a further word is called for concerning the issues raised by Karl Barth's interpretation as cited in this second objection. Throughout the thirteen books comprising his *Church Dogmatics* Barth develops in a variety of doctrinal contexts the theme that "God is in relationship and so too is the man [the human being] created by Him."[34] God in God's own triunity, as indicated by the threefold referentiality of the gospel message, is depicted as not solitary but One who is in relationship in a self-communion of Spirit. Further, in the works of creating, reconciling, and redeeming, as they are recounted biblically, God is acknowledged by faith to be in relationship as a God who elects not to be without us, but rather is confessed to have become incarnate for us as the Word made flesh in the humanity of Jesus. It follows, in Barth's reading of these testimonies to how God is in triune self-relationship (*ad intra*) and in relationship to the world (*ad extra*), that any imaging of this God on a human level involves also our not being alone and solitary, but instead our existing together as one with another. This is not to be said, Barth repeatedly cautions, with any idea that our creaturely being is generically of a kind with God's own incomparable being. Rather, an analogy can be drawn between the testimony that God is in relationship and the testimony that humankind is created male and female in God's image, according to Genesis 1:27, to be in relationship, so to speak, as cohumanity.

Where the difficulty arises with this reading of humans in relationship in light of testimonies to God in relationship is that in the case of God the trinitarian relations are said to be coequal, but the relation of God as Creator to creature is not. If the analogy of relation in the concept of cohumanity is interpreted as an imaging of God's triune self-relations, then there is no basis for alleging any superiority of relation in our being one with another. But if the analogy of relation in the concept of cohumanity is interpreted as an imaging of the relationship that God has with the creation, then an inequality and superiority is involved. The creature's love for God and freedom toward God is never presented in biblical testimonies as coequal with God's love for the creature and freedom toward the creature.

Thus, in trying to give faithful account of the *imago Dei*, which of these two kinds of testimony to God in relationship should humans in their relationship be said to image? Barth's own way of addressing this problem is by attempting to minimize any perceived lack of correspondence between how God may be said to be in self-relation and how God is proclaimed in the gospel message to relate to us. He stresses a similarity in Christian doctrine between the sort of precedence attributed to the First Person of the Trinity as the *fons et origo* ("font and origin") of the Second and Third Persons, and the sort of precedence portrayed of God the Creator as the originator of the world, although he is clear in maintaining that this similarity is not an identity.[35] Yet the problem remains, as the quotation from Barth in the second initial objection shows, in that while in the first instance this precedence of origination in God's triunity must be said to involve, as Barth emphasizes, "mutual relations" with no "superiority and inferiority,"[36] in the second instance of the Creator's origination of the creature there is involved a superiority on the Creator's part and a lack of mutualism between the Creator and the created. This explains why, in reference to Paul's text in 1 Corinthians 11, Barth, in the quotation given that speaks out against mutualism, clearly refers to the precedence of the man over the woman as a precedence that images as an "illustration" the Creator's superiority over the creature.

It is fair to note that this rejection of "mutualism" between man and woman by Barth in 1934 stands in tension with his later elaboration in 1945 of precisely the theme of "mutuality" between man and woman. In discussing what he calls the only "structural differentiation" in humankind, that of male and female,[37] he writes that scriptural testimony to male "precedence" and female "subsequence" is never to be taken in faith as an assertion of "an inferior being,"[38] but that all truly human encounter, if based in love and freedom, involves the "mutuality" of looking each other in the eye, a mutual speaking to and listening to one another, a rendering of mutual assistance, and all these done with a "gladness" that seeks neither to be "tyrant or slave."[39]

Regardless of how one evaluates Barth's own interpretation of the similarity and dissimilarity between God's so-called, to use the shorthand of dogmatics, *ad intra* and *ad extra* ways of being in relationship, two of the faithful refusals here proposed lead to the rejection of any alleged higher and lower relations between human beings, or of any set ordering of who as a human being precedes whom in covenant relationships. The one is the refusal to believe that human identity is self-referential, that is, that it can be known apart from reference to Jesus Christ's way of being for others as the true human "image of God" (2 Cor. 4:4; Col. 1:15).[40] The other is the refusal to believe, precisely because Christ in relation to the church is taken to be the "image of God" into which we become incorporated as part of Christ's body, that this image can be restricted to gender and sexual categories.

In these two disbeliefs, as well as in the refusal to believe that being conformed to the image or likeness of Christ is conformity to maleness, and in the refusal to believe that the reality of Jesus Christ is limited to, or equatable with, Christianity (as earlier noted in the chapters on the Word of God and Jesus Christ), direct response has been made as well to the third and final initial objection, that becoming conformed unto the likeness of Christ, the *similitudo Christi* teaching, would seem to require conformity to that which is male and Christian. We may best conclude by looking at another aspect of the much discussed and controversial 1 Corinthians 11. Whatever the judgments made there regarding the relationship of man and woman, we have Paul's own concluding insistence that the context for all faithful judgment in these matters of our humanity is the communion meal of the bread and the cup of the Lord Jesus where, he writes, all brothers and sisters who eat and drink are to discern the true body (1 Cor. 11:29).

From the doctrine of humanity we are thus pointed ahead to consider next the faithful disbeliefs entailed in the doctrine of the church.

Chapter 13

THE CHURCH

Introduction

That the treasure of God's grace reaches us surrounded by garbage will not seem surprising to anyone who is personally familiar with life in the church. Church history provides ample evidence of this garbage. The Apostle Paul in his day did not hesitate to speak of the treasure as being "in earthen vessels (*en ostrakinois skeuesin*)" (2 Cor. 4:7). "In used pots and pans" may come closer to the point, for Paul finds association with such means of conveyance to be in some respects no more visibly impressive than "refuse," "offscouring," and "rubbish" (1 Cor. 4:13). (The New Revised Standard Version translation of "in clay jars," while technically accurate, sounds today far too earthenware chic!) Grace comes to us, so Martin Luther argues, hidden *sub contrario*, beneath its opposite.[1] From this perspective, any idealized view of the church as only treasure is as faulty a vision of reality as any cynical view that the church is only garbage. Mangers, by definition, are found where there is manure.

Our attention now turns to this ecclesial contrariety, to the doctrine of that community which confesses its life in grace to be somehow the body of the One born in a manger, and yet a body denied unto death by its own members. The *sub contrario* character of this confession marks the starting point of Christian testimonies regarding the church.

Objections to corruption in the church may be found in Christian history from the very beginning. Betrayal within the original company of the disciples is narrated in the gospel message as the traditioning, or handing over, of Jesus unto crucifixion by Judas Iscariot, and such betrayal has been seen to continue throughout succeeding generations. By the confession of their sins Christian congregations acknowledge that a Judas tradition accompanies the apostolic tradition of Christ's saving significance in their common life as the church. "But what storm at sea was ever so fierce and wild as this tempest of the Churches?" writes Basil of Caesarea in the fourth century: "If our enemy is not the first to strike us, we are wounded by the comrade at our side."[2]

In taking up the question of ecclesiology we are returning to a point considered in chapter 2, that dogmatics is an ecclesial as well as an academic discipline. Apart from the context of a community that professes to be called into existence by God's commissioning, the *ekklēsia* in the Greek of the New Testament as "those who are called out," there is no Christian theology as a testing of the spirits. According to biblical depictions, God's Word as "revelation" may be said to be a community-creating event. When God "speaks" to declare covenant fidelity with creation, a community of faith with both its affirmations and refusals comes into being.

It is a noteworthy phenomenon that this communal context of Christian theology is thus one that in certain respects is set against itself. Many within the academy as well as the church, and within the wider secular culture who are more or less detached from either, are quite ready to say a good word for love, or freedom, or justice, or peace. At least they do not object when others have a good word to say. The same is generally true also when it comes to saying a good word for Jesus. But speaking about the church as a continuing historical fact, either with a capital *C* or a lowercase *c*, is a different matter. Some Christians themselves confess to a much greater sense of alienation from the day-to-day existence of the church than do others, but none of us can long evade the radical contradiction with which inclusion in the church confronts us, namely that whatever glory of life-and-death significance is to be found there, it exists in tension with the most inglorious triviality and denial. In attempting to secure its prerogatives and defend its institutions the church finds itself running counter to the very commission that according to the gospel accounts, so to speak, got the show on the road in the first place. In attempting to take its gospel commission seriously the church again and again finds that the curtains are being lowered on its own self-seeking show. When no longer "stewards of God's mysteries" (1 Cor. 4:1), to recall the Pauline images noted earlier in chapter 3, all the best laid promotional strategies on the part of church agencies to advance their own institutional policies and programs are judged to exhibit the stifling futility of those who have in effect become faithless "peddlers of God's word" (2 Cor. 2:17).

Creedal affirmations of belief in "holy church" are thus no more to be equated with believing that all that is said and done in the name of the church is holy than are creedal affirmations of belief in the "Holy Spirit" to be equated with believing that every spirit that claims to speak for God is of God. Ecclesiological doctrines cover a large and often disputed territory by seeking to give an account of *where* the existence of the church is manifest to faith, *how* — or in what manner — it is manifest, and *what* its ministry and mission are manifest in faith to involve. It is possible to glimpse at least some of the main lines of demarcation in these three broad areas of ecclesiology by focusing our sights on the following headings: (1) Discerning the Body, (2) The Marks of the Church as Disbeliefs, and (3) Signs, Wonders, and Sacrament. But first there are initial objections to be considered.

Initial Objections

Along with the continuing protests against the church's undeniable failure historically to live up to its own faith professions regarding its calling, and to practice what it preaches, there are also complaints to be heard about these faith professions themselves. Objections of this second, more disputed type are given voice today in criticisms that address each of the three main areas of ecclesiology just noted: *where* the church claims to be present, *how* it is present, and *what* it professes its mission to be. Something of the gist of the plausibility of these three areas of criticism may be summarized as follows.

1. *It would seem that Christian ecclesiological doctrine acknowledges the earthly presence of the true* ekklēsia *of God only within church institutions of historical Christianity.*

When references to the *ekklēsia* in the New Testament writings are applied to the Christian church as it becomes institutionalized historically, the question arises as to whether such application is warranted as faithful testimony to the gospel message. This is so as much with regard to those reformers of later generations who appeal to the New Testament to criticize alleged abuses of church authority in their day as it is to those defenders of historical continuity whose appeal attempts to justify the church's current claims to jurisdiction. On either hand the implication appears to be that the only people "called out" as God's own since the time of Jesus are those who are members of Christian churches.

That the true church does not exist as spirit without body is affirmed in New Testament descriptions of the *ekklēsia* as "the body of Christ." The primary source of such description is Pauline tradition,[3] but other texts as well refer to "the temple of his body" (John 2:21), to the Passover loaf blessed by Jesus for the disciples as "This is my body" (Mark 14:22; Matt. 26:26; Luke 22:19), to "our sins" as borne in Christ's "body on the cross" (1 Pet. 2:24), and to our having "been sanctified through the offering of the body of Jesus Christ once for all" (Heb. 10:10).[4] The point is that, by characterizing the post-Constantinian institutional church of historical Christianity (whatever the differing forms it has eventually come to take in a divided Christendom) in the same manner as the New Testament *ekklēsia*, ecclesiological doctrine leads to the apparent conclusion that the institutional body of the modern church is the sole locus of the incarnate Christ prolonged on the earth.

It is significant to recall that as early as the beginning of the second century the great opponent of docetism with its denial of Jesus Christ's bodiliness, Ignatius of Antioch, linked the existence of the true church with the existence of a congregational overseer or bishop (*episkopos*). "Wherever the bishop appears let the congregation be present; just as wherever Jesus Christ is, there is the catholic church."[5] Thus the faith that "wherever Jesus Christ is, there the church is," the *ubi Christus, ibi ecclesia* claim in doctrinal shorthand, in effect becomes understood as "wherever the historical church is, there Jesus Christ is," *ubi ecclesia, ibi Christus*. As a consequence the body of Christ in the world, according to this way of thinking, tends to be equated with a historical succession of bishops. So writes Ignatius, "For as many as belong to God and Jesus Christ, — these are with the bishop."[6]

Objection arises because of what such thinking does to the gospel testimony that salvation occurs "in Christ." The confession of Jesus Christ as the Savior sent for the world God so loves (John 3:16) in practice seems hereby to be turned into a confession of the institutional church as the sole sphere and dispenser of salvation. "In Christ" means only "in the church." Insofar as the saving life, death, and destiny of Jesus as the Christ is alleged to span only the history of the institutional churches of Christianity, salvation within the body of Christ is interpreted to mean that "outside the church there is no salvation," *extra ecclesiam nulla salus*. Representatives of such an interpretation can be found in Christian history from the time of Ignatius onward.[7] Most influential in this regard have been the metaphors used by the third-century bishop Cyprian of Carthage in defending the unity of the church universal. By teaching that no one can have God as one's father who does not have the church as mother, and that human deliverance outside the church is no more likely than was human deliverance from the flood outside of Noah's ark, Cyprian bequeathed to later ecclesiological doctrine the metaphors of the church as "mother," upon whose nurture all are dependent for eternal life, and as "ark," within whose shelter alone are to be found the necessary means of rescue.[8]

To be accurate it must be granted that most ecclesiological teaching throughout the major branches of ecumenical Christianity shows a greater flexibility on this subject today and allows in varying degrees for the possibility of salvation also outside the institutional church to those who are of conscientious intent. Nevertheless, the acknowledgment of any outsiders as God's elect would still seem to be based upon their tending, whether knowingly or not, toward the life that is manifest within the baptized community of the church. They are, in Paul Tillich's words, the "latent church,"[9] or, in a term made famous by Karl Rahner, "anonymous Christians."[10]

Yet granting this allowance, all who are deemed to remain outsiders to the baptized community of the church in the intent of their lives (*in voto*), as well as in fact (*in re*), to employ a distinction from the decrees of the Roman Catholic Council of Trent in 1563,[11] would still appear even in this more flexible teaching to be excluded from being acknowledged among those who are "called out" as God's people. The result is supercessionist assumptions in Christian teaching that either explicitly or implicitly foster the view that Jews have now been superseded as God's chosen people by the church, the New Israel, and that indeed all religions of the world other than Christianity are to be viewed as outside the saving "body" of God's gracious choosing.

2. *It would seem that the most commonly held ecclesiologies recognize the true presence of the church more in the manner of right creeds than of right deeds.*

A second category of objections questions the emphasis placed upon correct formulations of belief in the church's attempts historically to identify its orthodoxy as well as its universality or catholicity. While the call to holiness of life is affirmed, all too often right doctrine seems to be given priority over just practices. The association of catholicity with episcopal oversight, as articulated by Ignatius of Antioch, is extended by Vincent of Lerins in the fifth century to include belief in that which is to be held "everywhere, always, and by all."[12] The true presence of the church is thus defined as those who assent to right belief as it is decreed by episcopal authority. The prayer of Jesus in Luke 22:32 for Peter that his "faith may not fail" comes to be appealed to in asserting the infallibility of this episcopal authority when it is properly promulgated through the pope as the successor of Peter.

The Protestant Reformers of the sixteenth century were accused of violating such catholicity by holding some papal teachings to be unfaithful. But they in turn may be said for the most part, with notable Anabaptist exceptions, to have argued for a catholicity that identified the true presence of the church not with the just practices of its members but with right preaching and the right administration of the sacraments.[13] According to the Augsburg Confession of 1530, as drafted by Philip Melanchthon, to take the earliest example, with regard to "the true unity of the Church, it is sufficient to agree concerning the doctrine of the Gospel and the administration of the Sacraments" even "though they be delivered by evil men."[14] Consistent with this ecclesiology was the characteristic Reformation insistence against the Medieval church's traffic of indulgences with its allocations of merit, upon justification in faith, not by works but by grace alone. Mainly the representatives of the so-called Radical Reformation, the Anabaptists, insisted upon "pure walk and practice," in addition, as an essential identification of the true presence of the church.[15]

Post-Enlightenment theologies influenced by Immanuel Kant did define the true presence of the church more in terms of moral practice than of metaphysical claims, ritual observances, or creedal formulations. "The true (visible) church," in Kant's words, "is that which exhibits the (moral) kingdom of God on earth so far as it can be brought to pass by men."[16] Also, liberation theologies in the second half of the twentieth century criticize a continuing preoccupation in theology with issues of God-talk rather than, as Frederick Herzog puts it, with a "justice church" intent upon "praxis seeking justice" as "God-walk."[17] Following the 1960s the term "orthopraxy" has come increasingly into use. Influential in this respect is the voice of Gustavo Gutiérrez:

> The intention... is not to deny the meaning of *orthodoxy*, understood as a proclamation of and reflection on statements considered to be true. Rather, the goal is to balance and even to reject the primacy and almost exclusiveness which doctrine has enjoyed in Christian life and above all to modify the emphasis, often obsessive, upon the attainment of an orthodoxy which is often nothing more than fidelity to an obsolete tradition or a debatable interpretation. In a more positive vein, the intention is to recognize the work and importance of concrete behavior, of deeds, of action, of praxis in the Christian life.[18]

Drawing upon the testimony of African American Christians from the annals of slavery and bringing it to bear upon the history of ecclesiological doctrine, James Cone has similarly called into question the "abstract theological maneuver [which] makes it possible for theologians to speak of the church as the 'body of Christ' without saying a word about its relation to broken human bodies in society."[19] Earlier, from the bitter social context of racial segregation, Martin Luther King, Jr., had asked regarding the massive church buildings so prominent across the restricted neighborhoods of the white American South, "Who worships here? Who is their God?"[20]

The objection to identifying the true presence of the church in terms of creedal God-talk rather than the practical deeds of God-walk finds support in such New Testament texts as the following: "Not everyone who says to me, 'Lord, Lord,' will enter the kingdom of heaven, but only the one who does the will of my Father in heaven" (Matt. 7:21);

"Whoever says, 'I abide in him (Jesus Christ),' ought to walk just as he walked" (1 John 2:6); "For just as the body without the spirit is dead, so faith without works is also dead" (James 2:26); "Truly I tell you, just as you did [or, did not] do it to one of the least of these..., you did it [or, did not do it] to me" (Matt. 25:40, or 45). Among the prophetic testimonies of the Old Testament scriptures none in this respect are quoted more often than those of Amos and Micah: "I hate, I despise your festivals, and I take no delight in your solemn assemblies.... But let justice roll down like waters, and righteousness like an everflowing stream" (Amos 5:21, 24); and, "What does the Lord require of you but to do justice, and to love kindness, and to walk humbly with your God?" (Mic. 6:8).

3. *It would seem that what the church professes its mission to be violates the created integrity of indigenous peoples.*

A third category of objections questions the extent to which the church's understanding of its commission to go into all the world contributes to the disregard of the prior good of that world as God's creation.

In the Greek of the New Testament the *apostoloi* are "those who are sent forth." What the church is sent forth to carry out in the world is thus spoken of in Christian teaching as the "apostolic" mission, or the "apostolate." With slight variation the synoptic Gospels of Matthew, Mark, and Luke recount that the disciples are first sent forth in apostleship during the earthly ministry of Jesus as "sheep in the midst of wolves"[21] with authority over "unclean spirits" and "demons" to cast them out.[22] Each of the three synoptic Gospels then attributes a more universal sending of the disciples to words of the Risen Christ: "Go therefore and make disciples of all nations" (Matt. 28:19); "Go into all the world and proclaim the good news to the whole creation" (Mark 16:15); "Repentance and forgiveness of sins is to be proclaimed in his [the Messiah's] name to all nations, beginning from Jerusalem" (Luke 24:47). In the opening lines of Acts the Risen Jesus is portrayed by Luke as telling the reassembled disciples, "You will be my witnesses in Jerusalem, in all Judea and Samaria, and to the ends of the earth" (Acts 1:8). Apostles are thus characterized as those who give "testimony to the resurrection of the Lord Jesus" (Acts 4:33). Paul, for his part, identifies himself to the churches of Galatia as "Paul an apostle — sent neither by human commission nor from human authorities, but through Jesus Christ and God the Father, who raised him from the dead" (Gal. 1:1). The urgency of announcing the resurrection of Jesus is highlighted by the haste depicted in the sending of Mary Magdalene and the other women as the first to witness to the disciples that the embodied life of Jesus is not dead in the tomb, but risen, and going on ahead of them.[23] By such gospel depictions Mary Magdalene becomes, as Elisabeth Schüssler Fiorenza has written, "the *apostola apostolorum*, the apostle of the apostles."[24]

Difficulties arise when New Testament references to apostles as those who are being sent forth as "sheep in the midst of wolves" with authority to "cast out unclean spirits and demons" are appropriated by the institutional church as defining its apostolate as a missionary expansion throughout the world. To the degree that such appropriation is made it would appear that the so-called mission fields into which the church's missionary activities are extended are assumed to be previously devoid of God's Holy Spirit. At best the indigenous religions and cultures of native peoples are to be viewed as shrines to "an unknown god," similar to the manner that Luke in Acts 17 narrates Paul's appraisal of the religiosity of the Athenians. At worst these other religions and cultures attest only to spirits that are "unclean" and "demonic." Professions of this sort plainly conflict with Christian faith affirmations regarding the unrestricted working of God's Spirit everywhere and the goodness of all life as created with God's providence eternally over all. Merely the abandonment in Christian discourse of such ancient labels of disrespect for outsiders as "pagans," "heathens," "infidels," or "the lost" does not make up for the lack of love of neighbor that recognizes no gift of God to be received from the difference of the neighbor.

Since its founding in 1976 the Ecumenical Association of Third World Theologians (EATWOT) has been at the forefront in repudiating any idea of the mission of the church as "a matter of spiritual conquest or religious colonization."[25] "In the colonial era Third World religions and cultures were marginalized and attacked. Jesus Christ of the colonial churches came as a religious Julius Caesar, not to dialogue, invite, enable, give life, and help grow, but to conquer, destroy, and supplant."[26] In contrast, these theologians from among the churches of Asia, Africa, Latin America, and North American minorities, with their common focus upon the overcoming of all forms of dehumanizing domination, call upon the churches "to share the gift of Jesus" in such a way as "to discover for themselves the wonder of God's grace in every history, culture, and people, and to celebrate that grace and give thanks."[27]

Interpretation

According to the terminology found in discussions of Christian ecclesiological doctrine, not every place that calls itself the church truly is the church, and not every place that truly is the church calls itself the church. Disputes have arisen historically over the marks of the "true" church in contrast to the "false" church and over the "visible" church in contrast to the "invisible" church. There is also said to be the earthly church "militant" and the heavenly church "triumphant." In addition, John Calvin writes that God at times preserves the church in this world precisely where its existence goes undetected, "*quasi in latebris* [as in hiding places]."[28] Discerning the whereabouts of God's *ekklēsia* as it is affirmed in Christian faith is thus one of the tasks of faithful disbelief.

1. Discerning the Body

The previous chapter ended with a reference to Paul's counsel to the Corinthians regarding "whoever . . . eats the bread or drinks the cup of the Lord" (1 Cor. 11:27): "For all who eat and drink without discerning the body, eat and drink judgment against themselves" (1 Cor. 11:29). "Now you are the body of Christ and individually members of it," Paul continues, with "varieties of gifts" "for the common good" that "God has appointed in the church" (1 Cor. 12:4, 7, 27–28). Reflection upon this testimony of Paul introduces us to some of the main issues of Christian ecclesiology.

Foremost among these issues is where the existence of the church is to be recognized when it is discerned from a practice of what Paul here calls eating the bread and drinking the cup of the Lord. It is to participants in the Lord's Supper that the question of discerning the body is addressed. What is plain from Paul's counsel to the Corinthians is a concern that those who share the Lord's bread and cup not misjudge, and thereby bring judgment upon, the very body that they are.

Viewed from this sharing of the bread and the cup, clearly one way of misjudging the whereabouts of the church today is to overlook the building so named on the corner and down the road where people gather around a common table. The first point to be recognized in ecclesiological doctrine is the most obvious: the church is a body of people. To find out where the church is located, one needs to check the Yellow Pages. When the Lord's Supper is taken as the context for discernment, theology cannot speak about the body of Christ without speaking about these bodies of people visibly gathered together. Theological description of the *ekklēsia* falsely spiritualizes the existence of these gatherings when it ignores what Schleiermacher called "church statistics," the description of the doctrine of a community "in conjunction with the other circumstances of that community."[29] The Christian church, with or without a capital C, does not exist apart from some particular human gathering embodied in the material circumstances of a specific location on the corner or down the road even when the mystical communion of that gathering is said to exceed its local boundaries and extend beyond death itself unto the very hosts of heaven. Schleiermacher's proposals for a "church statistics" in 1811 and 1830 may be seen as the forerunner of a sociology of the church and of the necessary place of such analysis in a dogmatic testing for the *en sarki* ("in the flesh") coherence of ecclesiological doctrine.

From the perspective of the bread and the cup, a second point of ecclesiological doctrine emerges: the church is a body of people giving thanks. What is common to the ecclesiological teachings of most Christian denominations is the affirmation that the church exists wherever a certain thanksgiving occurs. This thanksgiving, as nothing else, is what determines the true location of the church. Most simply defined, the church is those who thank God for loving all creation in Jesus Christ. This body of people, made up of the many bodies large and small gathered on the corners and down the roads, is the part of the world that in remembrance of Jesus continually thanks God for loving all the world.

The Psalmist, in characteristic Hebraic tradition, sings of the call to enter the gates of the Lord God with thanksgiving, to give thanks that the Lord of all the earth is good and steadfast in a love that endures forever in faithfulness to all generations (Ps. 100:4–5). New Testament accounts of Jesus giving the bread and cup to the disciples at the final Passover meal before the Crucifixion reiterate in five instances the words, "when he had given thanks."[30] The meal of the Lord's Supper, or Holy Communion, in Christian worship thus comes to be known in liturgical terminology by the Greek word for thanksgiving, *eucharistia*, as "the Eucharist." Similarly, the reminder to the Colossians of their call to be "in the one body" is immediately followed by the words, "And be thankful" (Col. 3:15). "And whatever you do, in word or deed, do everything . . . giving thanks" (Col. 3:17). Likewise, the writer of 1 Timothy interestingly identifies "those who believe and know the truth" as those who do not in the name of abstinence reject any of God's good creation "provided it is received with thanksgiving" (1 Tim. 4:4–5). In these characteristic testimonies, whatever is done in word or deed, and the truth that is believed and known, are both, either as deeds or creeds, seen to stem from and express a giving of thanks. Christian doctrine that is faithful to these perspectives concludes that what distinguishes the existence of the church is a certain thankfulness. Disbelieved as a false spirit by this ecclesiological understanding is any suggestion that what distinguishes church members from others is that they are more loved by God, or possess more goodness. Paul makes this point unmistakable in portraying what unlikely exemplars the body of people at Corinth are to whom he writes: "not many wise by human standards," "not many powerful," "not many of noble birth" (1 Cor. 1:26), with "jealousy and quarreling" among themselves (1 Cor. 3:3), and reports of "sexual immorality . . . of a kind that is not found even among pagans; for a man is living with his father's wife" (1 Cor. 5:1). All this a sociology of the church can document.

A third point of Christian ecclesiological doctrine neither sociological nor theological analysis can establish. It is Paul's claim that the church as a body of people giving thanks becomes manifest to faith in its thanksgiving, despite all its unlikeliness, as the body of Christ. The unlikely gatherings on the corner and down the road, so littered with the tedium of their denials and betrayals, are confessed in faith to become none other than the place where the love of God embodied in Jesus Christ is shown to encompass the whole world in all its depths and heights. Such discernment of the *en sarki* reality of the church as the body of Christ is not confessed to be a discernment that is *kata sarka*, or "according to the flesh" apart from faith. Other New Testament writings besides those of Paul provide a similar testimony in their distinctive terms. The Gospel of Matthew recounts the promise of Jesus to the disciples with the words, "Where two or three are gathered in my name, I am there among them" (Matt. 18:20). The Gospel of John recounts the prayer of Jesus for the disciples with the words, "The glory that you have given me I have given them, so that they may be one, as we are one, I in them and you in me, that they may become completely one, so that the world may know that you have sent me and have loved them even as you have loved me" (John 17:22–23). The author of the letter to the Ephesians writes that no one ever hates one's own body, but "nourishes and tenderly cares for it, just as Christ does for the church, because we are members of his body" (Eph. 5:29–30).

When the Lord's Supper is taken as the context for discerning the body that the church is, ecclesiological doctrines commonly affirm that the *eucharistia* or thanksgiving is a uniting of God and the church in holy communion. This poses the question of how God may be said to share in the act of thanksgiving with human beings. Scriptural usage does not speak explicitly of God giving thanks, but it does speak of God as looking upon all creation as good (Gen. 1:31), as rejoicing in God's works (Ps. 104:31), as delighting in steadfast love, justice, and righteousness in the earth (Jer. 9:24), as delighting in those who act faithfully (Prov. 12:22), as delighting in the prayer of the upright (Prov. 15:8). Most especially is the servant upon whom God's spirit rests, who will bring forth justice to the nations, designated by God in the prophecy of Isaiah as "my chosen, in whom my soul delights" (Isa. 42:1). In the synoptic Gospels God's delight is focused upon Jesus at his baptism in the Jordan when the voice from heaven announces, "This is my Son, the Beloved, with whom I am well pleased" (Matt. 3:17; see also Mark 1:11, Luke 3:22). This announcement of God's good pleasure is later repeated on the mount at the Transfiguration (Matt. 17:5), as recalled also in 2 Peter 1:17. According to the reported teaching of Jesus there is said to be "more joy in heaven over one sinner who repents than over ninety-nine righteous persons who need no repentance" (Luke 15:7). All these instances suggest a uniting of God and human beings in a community of shared delight. *Eucharistia* is a sharing in the body of the life that God finds "well pleasing." The thanksgiving of the body of Christ as a eucharistic community thus may be understood to involve God as well as human beings in that both God's delight and human delight are portrayed as united in a holy communion of rejoicing.

Here we may observe a significant distinction between christological doctrine regarding the person, or life span, of Jesus Christ, and ecclesiological doctrine regarding the church as the body of Jesus Christ. The person of Jesus Christ is confessed, in the language of Chalcedon, to be a "union" of the nature of God and the nature of humanity in one *hypostasis*, or actuality. In chapter 8 this was considered to mean the professed concomitance of eternal life and human life given in the one life span of Jesus Christ. The church as the body of Jesus Christ, in distinction, is confessed to be a "communion" of the delight of God and the delight of humanity in the one life given for all in which God is "well pleased." The language of "communion" derives from Paul: "The cup of blessing that we bless, is it not a sharing [*koinōnia*, 'communion'] in the blood of Christ? The bread that we break, is it not a sharing [*koinōnia*, 'communion'] in the body of Christ?" (1 Cor. 10:16). Thus to refer to the church as a sharing in the body and blood of Christ is not to equate the life span of Jesus Christ with the history of the Christian church, or with the sum total of individual churches. The *communion* of the church is thankfulness for the *union* of human life and eternal life given in Jesus Christ. Just as being loved is not reducible to being thankful for being loved, so the grace of this *union* for all is not reducible to the praise of this *communion* by some. The eucharistic body that delights in the life span of Jesus Christ given for all refuses to believe that the life span of Jesus Christ is limited to those who give thanks for it.

Only as such a eucharistic communion, and only derivatively, does the church discern its life around a common table to be a body not subject finally to corruption. This is a fourth point to be noted in Christian ecclesiological doctrine. Sociology and theology can report this faith conviction, but cannot establish it. Although denied unto death by its own members, the body of Christ becomes manifest to faith as a community — still on the corner and down the road — where good is done and truth is believed and known. From the standpoint of discerning the body in partaking of the cup of blessing and the broken bread both orthodoxy (literally, "right praise as trustworthy confession") and orthopraxy (literally, "right practice as trustworthy service") amount to the same thing, the living out of thankfulness for God's love to all creation in concrete circumstances, "at all times, and in all places," as the traditional words of the *Book of Common Prayer* express it.[31] The "varieties of gifts," so Paul advises the unlikely Corinthians, bring with them "varieties of services" and "varieties of activities" all activated by the same God, to manifest the same Spirit "for the common good," in the one body of Christ, of which there are many members (1 Cor. 12:4–7). That the church's thanksgiving as both orthodoxy and orthopraxy does not prove fruitless in the midst of all denials, betrayals, and corruptions is affirmed by faith that the broken body of Christ exists in the power of the Resurrection. Of the Risen Christ the author of the Ephesian letter writes that God in victorious confrontation with all authorities and powers entrenched in high places "has put all things under his feet and has made him the head over all things for the church, which is his body, the fullness of him who fills all in all" (Eph. 1:22). This claim no social analysis of authorities and powers can confirm. Entailed in the testimony that the corruption of the church is subject to the unfailing power of the Resurrection over all life and death is the refusal to believe that the church in either its living or dying is subject to the failings of its members.

This faithful disbelief serves to explain Melanchthon's statement quoted earlier in the second initial objection. There his words are cited from the Augsburg Confession of 1530, that with regard to "the true unity of the Church, it is sufficient to agree concerning the doctrine of the Gospel and the administration of the Sacraments" even "though they be delivered by evil men." The reference to "evil men" has to do, as the Augsburg Confession goes on to say, with the position of "the Donatists and such like, who denied that it was lawful to use the ministry of evil men [*malorum*, 'of those who are evil'] in the Church, and held that the ministry of evil men is useless and without effect."[32]

From its beginnings the church, as we can see from Paul's Corinthian correspondence, was confronted with the question of what makes a person worthy to participate in the ministry of the Lord's table. Is the power that is conveyed by the sacraments, as somehow the channels of God's grace, negated by the unworthiness of the one who is administering them? The historical occasion in which this issue presented itself with urgency was that of the Donatist controversy in northern Africa in the early part of the fourth century. During a time of persecution under the Roman emperor Diocletian some of the clergy in that area, to protect their lives, handed over (traditioned) their copies of the scriptures for burning when ordered to do so by the civil authorities. By obeying the government they betrayed their faith, and thereafter bore the disgrace of this "handing over" by being signaled out as "the *traditores*." The others who had not succumbed to social pressure, even in the face of persecution and death, came to be represented by one of their number named Donatus. On the principle that whoever betrays grace cannot convey it, Donatus led the cause against the unworthy clergy by contending that any sacraments administered by those who had denied their calling would be of no effect in the body of Christ. In this instance, as in others that resulted in crucial doctrinal conclusions in the history of the church, a number of social variables, political as well as theological, were involved.[33] Yet the decision in 314 of a council called at Arles, in southern Gaul, to consider this controversy has continued to be part of the common teaching of most of the church to this day.

The council at Arles held that the grace of God remains efficacious even when conveyed to others through the hands of an unworthy minister. The Donatist contention was rejected. A minister or priest is such because of the treasure of the grace administered and not because of any excellence or lack thereof in the earthen vessels of its administration. This decision was seen not to sanction moral laxity or human fault but rather to bear witness to the gospel message that worthiness for the ministry of the body of Christ at the Lord's table and elsewhere comes from God and not from ourselves. The earthly existence of the church is found not where there is no sin to be forgiven but, in the words of the Augsburg Confession, wherever "the Gospel is rightly taught [purely preached] and the Sacraments rightly administered [according to the Gospel]."[34] Most of the Reformers agreed that these two indicators were essential to locating the whereabouts of the true church, and they concurred as well in reaffirming the longstanding rejection of Donatism. John Calvin, for example, writes that the "outward communion of the church (where the Word of God is preached and the sacraments are administered)" is not prevented "by the unworthiness of another, whether pastor or layman," nor are the sacraments "less pure and salutary" for the holy and upright "because they are handled by unclean persons."[35] In the background is the testimony of Paul, that confidence for ministry in the body of Christ derives not from any competence "coming from us," but only from that competence which by mercy comes to us "from God" (2 Cor. 3:4–5).

2. The Marks of the Church as Disbeliefs

From this angle of vision provided by the Eucharist, ecclesiological doctrines usually seek to interpret as faith discernments the four ways of designating the existence of the body of Christ affirmed in the Nicene confession of "one holy catholic and apostolic Church." The Apostles' Creed for its part refers to "the holy catholic church, the communion of saints." It is obvious that none of the four marks of the church's unity, holiness, catholicity, and apostolicity represents an empirical, or observable, circumstance. The many social institutions calling themselves churches are clearly not united in organization or even in mutual recognition. Whatever holiness is apparent in them is counteracted by the evidence also in them of corruption. Whatever catholicity, or universality, is professed by some is held by others to be a distortion — the

Roman Catholics being far too Roman, the Anglo-Catholics too Anglo, the Eastern Orthodox too Eastern European, and the Protestants, regardless of whether or not they recite the Apostles' and Nicene creeds, too splintered and individualistic to be representative of any communal universality at all. Whatever the church's apostolicity, disagreements over the signs locating where it belongs have continued to cause division since the members of the body at Corinth broke over who "belonged to Paul" and who "belonged to Apollos," prompting Paul to ask them, "Has Christ been divided?" (1 Cor. 1:13). Looked at as the social institutions they are, observers can only acknowledge the presence of many so-named church bodies and buildings existing in varying degrees of mutual disregard as to who belongs where, and who does not, who is "true," and who is not, and who, if not wholly false, is still only partially ecclesial as "sect," and not fully "church."

Testimony to the effect that the true identity of Christ's body is not observable *kata sarka*, or according to flesh and blood appearances apart from faith, but rather is discerned *en sarki*, or through faithful participation in the flesh and blood of Christ, appears throughout the New Testament. For example, the famous "rock" of confession on which the church is said to be built and to prevail, in the testimony of Matthew's Gospel, is Simon Peter's recognition of who Jesus is that "flesh and blood has not revealed" (Matt. 16:17). Similarly, the incorruptible body given through Christ's resurrection, so Paul writes, is one that "flesh and blood cannot inherit" (1 Cor. 15:50). Yet in John's Gospel eternal life is discerned in Christ's body precisely with reference to communion in Christ's "flesh and blood." To those who question in the synagogue at Capernaum how Jesus, "son of Joseph, whose father and mother we know," can be said to be "bread that came down from heaven," the Johannine testimony gives answer with the words of Jesus: "Those who eat my flesh and drink my blood have eternal life" (John 6:42, 54).

Traditions of gospel testimony such as these lead to the eucharistic teaching that the life of the church as the body of Christ, broken and betrayed though the body is, is finally not subject to corruption because the eternal life of the Resurrection is present in this body. Thus the confession that the church is not subject finally to its own divisiveness, unholiness, exclusiveness, and betrayal rests not upon a denial of such visible corruption and crucifixion of its true life by its members, but upon a discernment of *whose* unity, holiness, catholicity, and apostolicity the church in its Resurrection thanksgiving embodies.

That this discernment of whose body the church is only finds expression in the creeds of the church following the affirmation of faith in the Holy Spirit is consistent with Paul's testimony to the Corinthians that "no one can say 'Jesus is Lord' except by the Holy Spirit" (1 Cor. 12:3).

The distinction without separation between the body of Christ, as a *communion* with God of some of the world in thanksgiving, and the person, or life span, of Christ, as a *union* of God's eternal life and human life given for and extending to all the world, means that any faithful discernment of the four confessed marks of the church will involve a dual reference, distinguishable but inseparable, both to the gathered body and to the wider world. The task of faithful disbelief calls for an inquiry into the dual refusals that are entailed by Christian confession in each of these four instances.

To believe that the church is "one" is to refuse to believe that any part of the body of Christ can truthfully say to any other, "I have no need of you" (1 Cor. 12:21). That churches do say this by their attitudes and actions toward one another is the falsehood of which they are called continually to repent by the gospel message they proclaim. As with the various parts of the anatomy of our physical bodies, so with the body of the church, Paul writes, "If one member suffers, all suffer together with it; if one member is honored, all rejoice together with it" (1 Cor. 12:26). With respect to the wider world spanned by the life, death, and destiny of Jesus Christ, to believe that the church is "one" through variety is equally to refuse to believe that the common good of human society, and indeed all creation, is served by a culture of uniformity and sameness rather than by the full diversity of gifts that come from God's one Spirit.

This faith in a unity opposed to uniformity is given voice in words from the Epistle to the Ephesians which inform so much of the church's ecclesiological doctrine: "There is one body and one Spirit, just as you were called to the one hope of your calling, one Lord, one faith, one baptism, one God and Father of all, who is above all and through all and in all. But each of us was given grace according to the measure of Christ's gift" (Eph. 4:4–7). The grace is given for the various functions of the one body, and is not uniformly measured as if the body could function with only one of its parts. But the diversity in the oneness of Christ's gift is for the good of each and all in promoting "the body's growth in building itself up in love" (Eph. 4:11–16).

In keeping with these disbeliefs the oneness of the church as Christ's body is further confessed not to be limited by death to the visible church militant on earth. Thanksgiving at the Eucharist acknowledges that it is surrounded by a "great cloud of witnesses" who have gone before (Heb. 12:1), "a great multitude that no one could count, from every nation, from all tribes and peoples and languages" (Rev. 7:9). "Therefore with Angels and Archangels, and with all the company of heaven," as the *Book of Common Prayer* expresses the sense of the invisible church triumphant at the Eucharist, "we laud and magnify thy glorious Name." The unity of the churches becomes manifest as they are faithful both to the "varieties of gifts and services" of which Paul writes (1 Cor. 12:4), and to the prayer of Jesus for the disciples and those who follow ever after, "that they may all be one" (John 17:21).

To believe that the church is "holy" is to refuse to believe that the one Spirit of God does not make whole the broken body of Christ. If what it means to be holy is to become a dwelling place of the Spirit of the One "who raised Jesus from the dead" (Rom. 8:11), the denial, betrayal, and crucifixion of this body by its own members cannot prevent its resurrection. This is the church's professed holiness.

Given the decision against Donatism, how visible are the fruits of this holiness? This has been a disputed question in the history of church doctrine. Here the criterion of consequence comes into consideration: "You will know them by their fruits" (Matt. 7:16). In the dogmatic shorthand of the debates over Reformed orthodoxy that followed upon the Reformation the issue is presented as that of the *syllogismus practicus* ("the practical syllogism"). For the Reformed orthodox and their Puritan representatives the question was whether clear evidence of being God's elect could be found in the practices of those who were elect. Adherents of the practical syllogism argued yes: "Whoever truly believes and becomes of a right spirit is elect; But in fact I believe, etc.; Therefore I am elect."[36] Opponents of the syllogism, on the other hand, argued against what they saw to be the misplaced confidence of trusting the perceived gifts of the Holy Spirit, faith as well as any other, rather than the Giver.

With respect to the wider world of Christ's life span, to believe that the church is "holy" is to refuse to believe that any spirit destructive of human wholeness anywhere among the diverse peoples of the earth is God's Holy Spirit. This applies to the practices of all religions and human societies without regard to how "Christian" these may claim to be in their "Lord, Lord" talk (Matt. 7:21). What is disbelieved by the decision against Donatism is that the fruit of holiness in the church is the honor of never having denied or betrayed God's love in Jesus Christ. What is further disbelieved in affirming the gospel testimony that not all are given the same gifts of faith, hope, and love by the Spirit all at once, or in the same measure, is that the members of Christ's body are recognizable by their gifts instead of by the Giver. Disavowed is any claim that the *ekklēsia* is a company of the faithful other than as a company to whom God is faithful. In identifying the Spirit of holiness with the resurrection of the body, the fruits of such holiness anywhere in the earth are identified by what the New Testament writers call *metanoia*, not "repentance" in the false sense of having nothing but regrets, but *metanoia* in the eucharistic sense as a continual turning from the denial and betrayal of life to its resurrection. Only in this continual turning from the denial and betrayal of their true life to its resurrection do members of the body of Christ confess that the life of true communication of one with another is a holy community, a *sanctorum communio*, as the Apostles' Creed expresses it, a "communion of saints."

To believe that the church is "catholic" is to refuse to believe that the love for which the body of Christ gives thanks is not universally God's love to all. The Christ "who descended" is praised as "the same one who ascended far above all the heavens, so that he might fill all things" (Eph. 4:10). Expressed with regard to the wider world, to believe that the church is "catholic" from the perspective of this *eucharistia* is to refuse to believe that being loved by God in the life span of Jesus Christ is not universally the gift of all creation.

The contents of these two disbeliefs have been unpacked historically in several ways. In addition to universality, the term "catholicity" is used to refer to fullness, in the sense of a *communion* of Christ's body that is fully, and not merely partially, receptive to the varieties of the gifts of the Holy Spirit. If, as with Ignatius of Antioch, the catholicity of the church is held to reside "wherever Jesus Christ is,"[37] then the eucharistic *communion* that is always located somewhere is never simply local. If, as with Vincent of Lerins, the catholicity of the church is held to reside in shared beliefs, what is still said to be catholic is something to be taken as trustworthy not simply by one locality but "everywhere, always, and by all."[38] In the theology of the Protestant Reformers such catholicity as universal trustworthiness was said to reside not in compliance with papal authority but in the preaching and the administration of the sacraments that is faithful to the gospel. The point of agreement in these several different ways of defining the content of the term "catholic" is the stipulation that the catholicity of the body of Christ refers to the *sine qua non* of what it takes for the church truly to exist anywhere as a eucharistic *communion*. What is essential for the existence of any such *communion* is that life is received in this body of some that is given for the fulfillment of all. To the extent historically that either the churches allied with Rome or the churches allied with the Protestant Reformers have failed to recognize these two disbeliefs — the refusal to believe that the *communion* of the body of Christ is not a thanksgiving for God's love to all, as well as the refusal to believe that the *union* of the person, or life span, of Christ is not a gift of God's love that encompasses all — they have in practice denied their own professed faith in "the holy catholic church."

To believe that the church is "apostolic" is to refuse to believe that the gathered body of Christ is not sent by the purpose of God. The theme of being sent by God is prominent in the gospel testimonies, especially in the Gospel of John. God's love for the world is depicted as a sending, both of the only-begotten Word made flesh (John 1:14, 3:16), and of the Holy Spirit sent in Christ's name (John 14:26). This sending is said to be for the purpose of saving, and not condemning, the world

(John 3:17), of not leaving those for whom Christ promises to make a home orphaned and comfortless (John 14:18). But not only are Jesus and the Spirit described as being sent, so also are the followers of Jesus. Thus in John's Gospel Jesus prays with regard to the disciples, "As you have sent me into the world, so I have sent them into the world" (John 17:18). With respect to the wider world, therefore, to believe that the church is "apostolic" is to refuse to believe that there are any in the world who are not sent for in the saving purpose of God.

In the writings of Paul we also find references to God's "sending" of Jesus, and the Spirit, and the followers of Jesus who proclaim the gospel in the power of the Spirit. To the Galatians Paul writes both that "God sent his Son, born of a woman" (Gal. 4:4), and that "God has sent the Spirit of his Son into our hearts" (Gal. 4:6). To the Romans he offers the reminder to ask how there can be any proclaimers of the saving name of the Lord "unless they are sent" (Rom. 10:15).

Involved in apostolicity, in being sent where Jesus Christ and the Holy Spirit go, is the idea of God's choosing or electing of a people to convey God's blessing to others in the earth. In the biblical portrayals of both the Old and New Testaments God is not first asked for, sought after, and thus elected to be God by a people. God is first the seeker and the One who elects for a people as God's *ekklēsia* to be. The contrary notion that the readiness of God's grace for us is conditional upon our seeking it, a position usually labeled as "Semi-Pelagianism" (when "Pelagianism" is taken to mean that our own seeking in itself is sufficient for achieving the good), was held by the Council of Orange in 529 to be rebutted by a more faithful testimony of the prophet Isaiah: "I was ready to be sought out by those who did not ask, to be found by those who did not seek me" (Isa. 65:1).

Israel confesses its exodus life as the Lord's people to have been "chosen . . . out of all the peoples on earth" (Deut. 7:6) to be, in the prophet's testimony, "as a light to the nations, that . . . salvation may reach to the end of the earth" (Isa. 49:6). The prophecy of Amos recognizes but refuses to restrict God's exodus purposes to Israel: "Did I not bring Israel up from the land of Egypt, and the Philistines from Caphtor and the Arameans from Kir?" (Amos 9:7). Paul, as a Jewish apostle of the gospel to the Gentiles, is emphatic in Romans 9–11 that Israel's election as those beloved by God for the purpose of salvation in the earth is not abrogated even where there is enmity toward the Gospel, "for the gifts and the calling of God are irrevocable" (Rom. 11:28–29).

In the New Testament all election and predestination is seen in relation to Jesus Christ. To interpret today the confession that the church as the body of Christ is "apostolic," and thus elected and predestined by God for the purposes of salvation, requires once again that we observe the distinction in the gospel testimonies between the person, or life span, of Jesus Christ and the body of Jesus Christ as a eucharistic communion in the Holy Spirit. The sending, to use Johannine terms, of the Word made flesh in Jesus Christ — or in Paul's words, of God's "Son, born of a woman" (Gal. 4:4) — is commonly held in christological doctrine to be "once for all" (Rom. 6:10; Heb. 10:10). "Once for all" (*ephapax*) as applicable to the life span of Jesus as the Christ means final, both in the sense of being at once unrepeatable and irrevocable, and in the sense of at once extending in scope to all: "For the love of Christ urges us on, because we are convinced that one has died for all [*heis hyper pantōn*]" (2 Cor. 5:15). But the sending of the Holy Spirit in Christ's name — or in Paul's words, God's sending of "the Spirit of his Son into our hearts" (Gal. 4:6) — is by contrast not something that occurs as eternal life within every heart all at once, but "in due season [*kairǭ idiǭ*, 'when the time is right']" (Gal. 6:9). That all are elected to being unfailingly loved within the life span of Jesus Christ that is "for all" is the good news for which some in their various times and places are elected by the indwelling of the Holy Spirit in their hearts to render, as the *ekklēsia* in apostleship, faithful thanks. Such faith refuses to believe that all who are elected in the once-for-all *union* of Jesus Christ's life span are also elected all at once for the *communion* of Jesus Christ's body. In short, such faith does not believe that all of God's elect are members of Christian churches.

Failure to recognize this disbelief entailed in the gospel message's distinction between God's sending of Jesus Christ for all, and the sending of the Holy Spirit's witnessing to Jesus Christ in human hearts not all at once, risks equating God's faithfulness with the reputed evidences of human faithfulness. If God's elect consist only of true believers, however defined, then grace, in effect, is limited to its reception. The testimony is ignored that while "not all have faith . . . the Lord is faithful" (2 Thess. 3:2–3). Predestination disputes over this issue have accompanied the doctrine of the church's apostolicity from the time of Augustine. According to the Reformed adherents of the Synod of Dort in Holland in 1619, for example, "not all, but some only, are elected" while the others are "passed by in the eternal decree" in that "saving faith" is not given to them.[39] According to the Lutheran adherents of the Formula of Concord drawn up in Germany in 1577, on the other hand, it is a "false, horrid, and blasphemous" dogma to teach "that God is not willing that all should be saved, but that some are destined to destruction, not on account of their sins, but by the mere counsel, purpose, and will of God, so that they can not in any wise attain to salvation."[40]

Disputed as well, historically and ecumenically, is the question of how, or in what manner, apostolicity in the institutional church is to be recognized. For Episcopalians it is said to belong — in conjunction with the faith standards provided by the Old and New Testaments, the

Apostles' and Nicene creeds, and the two sacraments of Baptism and the Lord's Supper — with the "Historic Episcopate," a recognized succession of bishops.[41] Anglicans, the Eastern Orthodox, some Lutherans, and Roman Catholics as well, affirm a "historic episcopate," without always agreeing on the lines of apostolic succession. For Roman Catholics such apostolicity in the historic episcopate belongs, in addition, to recognition of the papacy.[42] For those Protestants and Evangelicals who do not affirm a historic episcopate, apostolicity may be affirmed in a manner similar to the United Methodist ritual: "Where the Spirit of the Lord is, there is the one true Church, apostolic and universal, whose holy faith let us now declare."[43] Notwithstanding this lack of ecumenical consensus over where and how apostolicity manifests itself, the confession that the church is truly sent by God in the service of God's own purpose and mission in the world remains undisputed in Christian ecclesiological doctrine.

3. Signs, Wonders, and Sacrament

As commonly confessed, the mission of the church is to live out its thanksgiving in trustworthy praise and confession (orthodoxy), and in trustworthy practice and service (orthopraxy), unto the ends of the earth. This lived *eucharistia* is the embodied signification of the gospel of grace. It is said to be "sacramental" in that it is both a material sign in the earth, in the sense of a visible and audible means of God's pledge of trustworthiness, and also an uncircumscribable wonder, in the sense that the material sign only becomes significant and trusted through the mystery of God's grace in making it so. The Latin word *sacramentum*, which originally meant a pledge or oath, comes to be used in early Christianity to translate the Greek term *mystērion*. Ecclesiological doctrine speaks of the sacramentality of the church's eucharistic mission in that this apostolate is said to take place by means of visible and audible signs whose true wonder only the mystery of God's grace can make manifest.

The promise recounted by Luke in Acts 1:8 of the Risen Christ to the chosen apostles, "You will be my witnesses in Jerusalem, in all Judea and Samaria, and to the ends of the earth," reflects a similar testimony from the prophecy of Isaiah to be announced, it is said, before all the nations: "You are my witnesses, says the Lord, and my servant whom I have chosen" (Isa. 43:10). Testimonies to God's witness as involving "signs and wonders" occur throughout the Old and New Testaments. In Hebraic traditions these "signs and wonders" are most commonly associated with the Exodus (Deut. 6:22, 26:8). An example of this appears in the words of Ezra's address to the Lord before all the assembly of Israel, as recorded in the book of Nehemiah: "You performed signs and wonders against Pharaoh. . . . You made a name for yourself, which remains to this day" (Neh. 9:10). The same theme is found in the prayer of Jeremiah where it is extended to include all humankind: "You showed signs and wonders in the land of Egypt, and to this day in Israel and among all humankind, and have made yourself a name that continues to this very day" (Jer. 32:20). Similarly, the God who saved Daniel from the lions is said to work deliverance and rescue with "signs and wonders in heaven and on earth" (Dan. 6:27).

In the New Testament God's signs and wonders in the Exodus are recalled (Acts 7:36) and are said to accompany the apostles as commissioned witnesses. This is especially emphasized in Luke's account of the Acts of the Apostles: "Awe came upon everyone, because many wonders and signs were being done by the apostles" (Acts 2:43); "Now many signs and wonders were done among the people through the apostles" (Acts 5:12). To the fractious Corinthians Paul writes of his ministry, "The signs of a true apostle were performed among you with utmost patience, signs and wonders and mighty works" (2 Cor. 12:12). In the New Testament references the signs and wonders are associated with gospeling (*euangelion*), and those who demand signs are directed, so Paul writes, to the proclaiming of "Christ crucified" (1 Corinthians 1:22–24). "No sign will be given," according to the words of Jesus in Matthew, "except the sign of the prophet Jonah. For just as Jonah was three days and three nights in the belly of the sea monster, so for three days and three nights the Son of Man will be in the heart of the earth" (Matt. 12:39–40; see also, Matt. 16:4 and Luke 11:29–30). The author of the Fourth Gospel refers to the signs Jesus did in the presence of the disciples now "written in this book" so that "through believing you may have life in his name" (John 20:30–31). A consistent point expressed in varying ways by these distinctive New Testament traditions is that any signs and wonders that do not attest to the gospel testimony are held to be deceptive (2 Thess. 2:9), the work of false prophets (Matt. 24:24; Mark 13:22), and not the good news of salvation to which "God added his testimony by signs and wonders and various miracles, and by gifts of the Holy Spirit, distributed according to his will" (Heb. 2:3–4).

The commissioning of these signs is given in the concluding words of the Gospel of Matthew which reflect the significance of the Risen Christ in the memory of the early church:

> And Jesus came and said to them, "All authority in heaven and on earth has been given to me. Go therefore and make disciples of all nations, baptizing them in the name of the Father and of the Son and of the Holy Spirit, and teaching them to obey everything that I have commanded you. And remember, I am with you always, to the end of the age." (Matt. 28:18–20)

Other New Testament expressions of this commission, as noted earlier in the third initial objection, are "Go into all the world and proclaim the good news to the whole creation," from the longer ending of the Gospel of Mark (Mark 16:15); "Repentance and forgiveness of sins is to be proclaimed in his [the Messiah's] name to all nations, beginning from Jerusalem," from the Gospel of Luke (Luke 24:47); and "You will be my witnesses in Jerusalem, in all Judea and Samaria, and to the ends of the earth," from the Acts of the Apostles (Acts 1:8). Ecclesiological doctrines seek to interpret the elements of this so-called Great Commission as signs and wonders and sacrament.

First is the sign of going into all the world. The wonder is that the world into which the apostles are sent is confessed to be one where Jesus Christ has already gone and is expecting them. Christian faith in God's sending of Jesus Christ into the world refuses to believe that there is any "world" of time and space and social circumstance into which the church is commissioned to go that Jesus Christ has not already gone. In this sense there are no "foreign missions." "The true light, which enlightens everyone . . . was in the world" is one way the Gospel of John testifies to this faith; through this Word "the world came into being" so that the Word's coming in flesh in Jesus is a coming "to what was his own" (John 1:9–11). Resurrection testimonies in Matthew and Mark speak, from another angle of vision, of Jesus Christ as being "ahead of" the apostles and already at the very place to which the witnesses are sent. The message to the women at the tomb is, "Go quickly and tell his disciples, 'He has been raised from the dead, and indeed he is going ahead of you to Galilee; there you will see him' " (Matt. 28:7; see Mark 16:7).

In addition, according to the gospel accounts the wonder is not only that Jesus Christ is "ahead of" the apostles and already there in the world to which the witnesses are sent; this Savior is confessed also to be "the One who comes after" the signs that bear witness. Insofar as the church recognizes its own ministry and mission in the figure of John the Baptist preaching in the wilderness, for example, it hears for itself the promise in the narrative, "The one who is more powerful than I is coming after me" (Mark 1:7; see also Matt. 3:11 and Luke 3:16). Equally wondrous for those who hear God's own promise to them in the story (and without such hearing no biblical story for all its academic interest is that wonderful) is Jesus' reported sending of the seventy apostles "on ahead of him in pairs to every town and place where he himself was about to come" (Luke 10:1). The sign to all the world in the apostolic mission is the wonder of the promise, "I will not leave you orphaned, I am coming to you" (John 14:18). Christian faith in this promise refuses to believe that apostles are sent anywhere where the Savior who is mightier than they is not following in merciful judgment the sign of their presence.

Second, along with going into all the world, is the sign of proclamation itself. The wonder is that the unlikely story of the gospel being proclaimed is ever heard by any people as God's own promise of the arrival in their present situation of sufficient grace (2 Cor. 12:9). If by such hearing of proclamation the gift of faith is said to come (Rom. 10:17), this hearing is something of a miracle over which no preacher in the church has control, whatever be the reputed skills in communication, or the rhetorical ability for impressing an audience. Christian faith in the commission to "proclaim the good news to the whole creation" (Mark 16:15) entails the refusal to believe that any preaching is truly of the gospel, whatever its pretensions, if it is opposed to the created good of those to whom it is addressed. That the Word of the Lord comes to the prophet in human words is a biblical understanding that carries over into the importance that is attached to the sermon in Christian worship. Even so, prophetic signs are never limited in biblical tradition to words only. Likewise, proclamation that is faithful to the gospel is understood by the church to involve every form of signification — speech, music, gesture, dance, assistance, public demonstration, or any other art or concerted action — insofar as through such means the grace of God in Jesus Christ finds trustworthy communication in *eucharistia*.

Despite the differences among the branches of Christendom most ecclesiological doctrine regarding the church's proclamation of the Word recognizes its eucharistic context. In this connection the Russian Orthodox theologian Alexander Schmemann writes as follows of "real life [as] 'eucharist,' " a movement "to accept in love, and to move towards what is loved and accepted":

> Western Christians are so accustomed to distinguishing the Word from the sacrament that it may be difficult for them to understand that in the Orthodox perspective the liturgy of the Word is as sacramental as the sacrament is "evangelical." The sacrament is a manifestation of the Word. And unless the false dichotomy between Word and sacrament is overcome, the true meaning of both Word and sacrament, and especially the true meaning of Christian "sacramentalism" cannot be grasped in all their wonderful implications.[44]

Faith that the church's ministry and mission as the eucharistic body of Christ is to signify the gospel in every facet of its life and activity, both within the service of worship and out in the wider world, entails a refusal to believe that the church has any authority for what it says or does in its rituals, policies, pronouncements, or unspoken attitudes if these do not signify the gospel of the One to whom "all authority in heaven and on earth has been given" (Matt. 28:18). Only in keeping with this disbelief does the church that is faithful to the rock of Peter's confession, as recounted in Matthew 16:15–19, come to know "the keys of the kingdom of heaven" in determining what is to be "bound" on earth and what is to be "loosed" (Matt. 18:18). Only by being shown the scars still in the Risen Christ's hands and side, and being sent as Christ was sent, are the apostles portrayed in the Gospel of John as receiving the Holy Spirit for the ministry of the forgiveness of sins (John 20:20–23). What unites all forms of gospeling as they are carried out in the rich variety of the Holy Spirit's gifts and services is the wonder that they ever do become God's own witnesses. But so Christian faith confesses them to become when God's grace is communicated by means of them.

To signify the gospel through preaching, or through what Schmemann refers to in Orthodox tradition as the liturgy of the Word, is denoted in the language of the New Testament as the heralding (*kērygma*), in the sense of a public announcement, to a specific time and place of what is forthcoming from God. As it was noted in chapter 6 on the Word of God, such announcement is understood to author the wondrous gifts of faith, hope, and love when God's Word is enacted through these human words and signs. While biblical perspectives acknowledge that God's Word is not restricted in its means to faithful prophecy alone, that indeed even "human wrath," as the Psalmist puts it, finally serves only to praise God (Ps. 76:10), the ministry of the proclamation of the Word is ordained in the church for no other purpose than to signify the gospel faithfully in the specific times and places to which it is sent. That God's Word is timely in its forthcoming and not timeless means that such kerygmatic signification involves a mutual interrogation of text and context. Thus understood, Christian faith refuses to believe that a sermon in the liturgy of the Word bears trustworthy witness if it does not seek either to question the present situation of its hearers in light of specific scriptural testimonies to the gospel, or to question the scriptural testimonies to the gospel in light of the specific situation of its present hearers. Such is the sign of faithful preaching.

Third is the sign of the sacraments themselves that the church holds to be ordained by Christ for its ministry and mission. While the history of doctrine shows that prior to the twelfth century the word "sacrament" was originally applied more widely than to the two sacraments of Holy Baptism and the Lord's Supper recognized by the three major branches of Christianity, or even than to the seven sacraments recognized by the Roman Catholics and the Eastern Orthodox as Baptism, Confirmation, the Eucharist as the Lord's Supper, Penance, Extreme Unction, Clerical Order, and Matrimony,[45] the understanding of Jesus Christ as *the* Sacrament from which all sacramentality derives has received heightened emphasis in twentieth-century doctrinal interpretation.[46]

To recognize sacramentality with regard to Jesus Christ as the Sacrament requires in this instance as well that the inseparable distinction in the gospel message between the person, or life span, and the body of Jesus Christ be observed. As the Sacrament of the body of Christ, "following, and about to come" where the apostolic ministry and mission is sent, there are signs and wonders of the church's witness *to the world* of grace in the body of those who are received in faith into the waters of baptism and are gathered to be fed from a common table of thanksgiving. But as the Sacrament "already gone before, and ahead" of the apostolic ministry and mission in the person of Christ, there are also confessed to be signs and wonders of grace in the wider world spanned by Jesus Christ's life, death, and destiny that bear witness in turn *to the church.* It is striking to think in this connection how much the dramatic plot and subplots of the gospel accounts, and the Christian liturgies based upon them, are shaped by what Jesus is said to have received, and not simply in a one-sided fashion to have given, to those who are more or less presented as outsiders, even subjects of consternation, within the cultural setting of his ministry. Whether they be depicted as a tax collector with a house for Jesus to visit, a Cyrenean compelled to carry his cross, a rich man with an available tomb for his burial, or more often, as women who show him not only hospitality, but a trust that ventures to touch him in a crowd, to anoint him with the intimacy of tears and costly oil, and at times even dares to risk effrontery, in each circumstance the incident occasions a turn in the gospel narratives toward some unexpected manifestation of grace. As the lilies of the field, the fig trees, the fish of the sea, the birds of the air, and the appearance of the sky provide the necessary occasions for the gospel witness to unfold, even so does the colt waiting tied on the outskirts of Jerusalem: "If anyone asks you, 'Why are you untying it?' just say this, 'The Lord needs it' " (Luke 19:31). The dogmatic point is that faith shaped by such testimony entails a refusal to believe that the sacramental body of Christ in its witness to all the world as a eucharistic community of the baptized does not in turn need and receive from all the world witness of God's grace already there and sent on before in the incarnate, risen, and coming life span of Jesus Christ.

The wonder is that a bath and a meal signal the unfailing grace for all the world as an instantiation of the Sacrament who is confessed to be Emmanuel (Matt. 1:23), "God with us" and for us all as God's own. For churches that baptize infants the sign of baptism signals the wondrous coming once-for-all "at the right time" of grace "while we were still weak" (Rom. 5:6). For churches that await the coming of the Holy Spirit's gift of faith to individuals in their own lifetime before baptizing them the sign of baptism signals the wonder of grace affirmed not all at once as new creation. Both the commissioned bath of baptism that is portrayed in the threefold referentiality of the gospel message as undergone in Jesus Christ (Rom. 6:3) once-for-all but not all-at-once, and the commission to obey what was commanded at the Passover meal, "Do this in remembrance of me" (1 Cor. 11:23–25), are seen to initiate and sustain a communion of saints that gives witness to the union of God's own eternal life and human life in the triune name of the Spirit of the One who raised Jesus from the dead.

Proposed Disbeliefs

In the foregoing interpretation of Christian ecclesiological doctrine these are proposed for recognition as disbeliefs that are entailed in the faith that is affirmed:

1. that what distinguishes church members from others is that they are more loved by God, or possess more goodness.
2. that the life span of Jesus Christ is limited to those who give thanks for it.
3. that the church in either its living or dying is subject to the failings of its members.
4. that any part of the body of Christ can truthfully say to any other, "I have no need of you."
5. that the common good of human society, and indeed all creation, is served by a culture of uniformity and sameness rather than by the full diversity of gifts that come from God's one Spirit.
6. that the one Spirit of God does not make whole the broken body of Christ.
7. that any spirit destructive of human wholeness anywhere among the diverse peoples of the earth is God's Holy Spirit.
8. that the fruit of holiness in the church is the honor of never having denied or betrayed God's love in Jesus Christ.
9. that the members of Christ's body are recognizable by their gifts instead of by the Giver.
10. that the *ekklēsia* is a company of the faithful other than as a company to whom God is faithful.
11. that the love for which the body of Christ gives thanks is not universally God's love to all.
12. that being loved by God in the life span of Jesus Christ is not universally the gift of all creation.

13. that the gathered body of Christ is not sent by the purpose of God.
14. that there are any in the world who are not sent for in the saving purpose of God.
15. that all who are elected in the once-for-all *union* of Jesus Christ's life span are also elected all at once for the *communion* of Jesus Christ's body.
16. that all of God's elect are members of Christian churches.
17. that there is any "world" of time and space and social circumstance into which the church is commissioned to go that Jesus Christ has not already gone.
18. that apostles are sent anywhere where the Savior who is mightier than they is not following in merciful judgment the sign of their presence.
19. that any preaching is truly of the gospel, whatever its pretensions, if it is opposed to the created good of those to whom it is addressed.
20. that the church has any authority for what it says or does in its rituals, policies, pronouncements, or unspoken attitudes if these do not signify the gospel of the One to whom "all authority in heaven and on earth has been given" (Matt. 28:18).
21. that a sermon in the liturgy of the Word bears trustworthy witness if it does not seek either to question the present situation of its hearers in light of specific scriptural testimonies to the gospel, or to question the scriptural testimonies to the gospel in light of the specific situation of its present hearers.
22. that the sacramental body of Christ in its witness to all the world as a eucharistic community of the baptized does not in turn need and receive from all the world witness of God's grace already there and sent on before in the incarnate, risen, and coming life span of Jesus Christ.

In view of these proposed disbeliefs it is clear that any response to the first initial objection, that it would seem to be the case that Christian ecclesiological doctrine acknowledges the earthly presence of the true *ekklēsia* of God only within church institutions of historical Christianity, will depend upon how the word *ekklēsia* is being defined. If it is taken to mean the body of people who give thanks to God in remembrance of Jesus Christ, then like all earthly communities it must be said to be historical, on some corner or down some road, always statistically located somewhere, even if never merely local. But if those "called out" are taken to include all who are elected for grace in the life span of Jesus Christ, once-for-all but not all-at-once, then these cannot be restricted to the membership of church institutions, or to the historical boundaries of Christianity as a world religion. If inclusion within the grace of the life span of Jesus Christ is not limited to those who give thanks for it, in this respect not all of God's elect are members of Christian churches, nor is the institutional body of the modern church the sole locus of the incarnate Christ prolonged on the earth. Further, if the *union* of God's eternal life and human life in the person, or life span, of Jesus Christ is not solely equatable in the gospel message with the *communion* of God's delight and human delight in the eucharistic body of Jesus Christ, then "in Christ" cannot mean only "in the church." The Jews remain God's chosen with an irrevocable call, and as for others there is no "world" of time and space and social circumstance into which the church is commissioned to go that is "outside" where Jesus Christ has already gone.

The second initial objection is that it would seem to be the case that the most commonly held ecclesiologies recognize the true presence of the church more in the manner of right creeds than of right deeds. As a historical observation, asking what the record shows, there is ample evidence for this judgment. As a dogmatic observation, asking what is the faithful position, this objection is addressed first of all by the recognition that what distinguishes the church as such is that it is a body of thanksgiving. Both orthodoxy, as trustworthy praise and confession, and orthopraxy, as trustworthy practice and service, are inseparable ways of living out this thanksgiving. The refusal to believe that there are any in the world who are not sent for in the saving purpose of God denies that creeds, or God-talk, apart from deeds, or God-walk, faithfully characterize the church's apostolic mission. Equally, the refusals to believe that the fruit of holiness in the church is the honor of never having denied or betrayed God's love in Jesus Christ, that the members of Christ's body are recognizable by their gifts instead of by the Giver, and that the *ekklēsia* is a company of the faithful other than as a company to whom God is faithful, rule out as well any culture of moralistic or testimonial uniformity and sameness that denies in either its orthopraxy or its orthodoxy the full diversity of gifts for upbuilding the common good that comes from God's one Spirit.

The third initial objection, that it would seem to be the case that what the church professes its mission to be violates the created integrity of indigenous peoples, also is not lacking in support as a historical judgment. The church's betrayals of its commission are neither to be covered up nor equated with the commission itself. Dogmatically tested, faith's refusals to believe that any spirit destructive of human wholeness anywhere among the diverse peoples of the earth is God's Holy Spirit, and that any preaching is truly of the gospel, whatever its pretensions, if it is opposed to the created good of those to whom it is addressed, serve to uncover this betrayal for what it is. To the perennial question, "But who is to judge?" the call of the gospel remains for all who are affected to test the spirits under the constraint of God's Spirit. To the disciple's complaint, when arguing over who among them was the greatest, "Master, we saw someone casting out demons in your name, and we tried to stop him, because he does not follow with us," Jesus is reported in Luke's Gospel to have replied, "Do not stop him; for whoever is not against you is for you" (Luke 9:49–50). Here "in Jesus' name" suggests more than simply the saying of "Lord, Lord" (Matt. 7:21) within the gathering of the disciples. Rather, here we are told of a witness to the disciples of Jesus' power against the demonic in the wider world outside their company and beyond their bounds. The gospel recognizes a gift of God to be received from the difference of the neighbor. The test of such witness, Paul writes to the Corinthians, is that "no one speaking by the Spirit of God ever says, 'Let Jesus be cursed [*anathema*]!' " (1 Cor. 12:3).

Finally, in repentance of its sins by refusing to believe that the church in either its living or dying is subject to the failings of its members, the eucharistic community on the corner and down the road signals in the midst of the world the wonder of an ultimate hope that is confessed to be not of this world. It is this hope that is the subject of church teaching in the doctrine of the life to come.

Chapter 14

THE LIFE TO COME

Introduction

At no point does the Christian message sound more improbable than in the pronouncement that what is most real about this earth at the present time is heaven. Merely to imply that the only social realism for today which is truly down to earth and actually dealing with "the real world" is a celestial realism surely seems to propel us immediately into the make-believe of a never-never land. In such a realm of fantasy apparently no reports of unidentified flying objects would ever require radar screen confirmation. Hence the initial question of all Christian eschatology, or doctrine of last things, is, Who is kidding whom?

The question arises because accounts of Jesus' preaching in the New Testament highlight the claim first introduced by John the Baptist (Matt. 3:2) that "the *basileia* ['kingdom' or 'dominion'] of heaven is at hand" (Matt. 4:17). Whereas post-Enlightenment thinking tends to view the earth as certain and heaven as mythical, the remnant of an outmoded cosmology, the gospel traditions may be said to assume just the reverse. According to their testimony the dominion of heaven is what is really taking place now, while those unaware of what is happening continue to busy themselves only with "the present form of this world [that] is passing away" (1 Cor. 7:31).

Among the numerous references to "heaven" in the Old and New Testaments a central theme is that heaven is God's "throne" (Isa. 66:1; Acts 7:49), a designation of from where God's will and way is said to come upon the earth. For this reason "the kingdom of heaven" is also referred to as "the kingdom of God" (Mark 1:15). But we lose this sense of direction if we think of heaven as only up in the sky and not down on the ground. To confess that the kingdom or dominion of heaven is "at hand" is to characterize, not the way the sky is, but the way the earth is within the perspective of the gospel's frame of reference. Earth is not simply what is overarched by the sky; earth is what is overarched by an unimpeded dominion of love and freedom, that is, "heaven." Furthermore, earth is confessed to be where this dominion of love and freedom undertakes to come at ground level: "Thy kingdom come, thy will be done on earth as it is in heaven." According to this confession the focus of heaven is directed toward the earth, and what is certain about the earth cannot be understood as it really is except with reference to heaven. To this unconventional way of thinking, heaven, in short, is never unearthly. The question to the disciples at the ascension of Jesus is, "Why do you stand looking up toward heaven? This Jesus, who has been taken from you into heaven, will come in the same way as you saw him go into heaven" (Acts 1:11). Thus, we read, the disciples return to the city, and to a ministry on the earth awaiting them at the day of Pentecost that is depicted as a witness to "every nation under heaven" (Acts 2:5).

Both the Apostles' Creed and the Nicene Creed express the connection of heaven with what is certain about the earth in regard to the coming of Jesus Christ as the future of all things. The Crucified and Risen One is confessed as "ascended into heaven" and seated "on the right hand of God the Father Almighty," and the affirmation is made in the Apostles' Creed that "from thence he shall come to judge the living and the dead." Faith is further affirmed in "the communion of saints; the forgiveness of sins; the resurrection of the body; and the life everlasting." The words of the Nicene Creed for their part express a similar faith affirmation about the one Lord Jesus Christ who "ascended into heaven" and "sits on the right hand of the Father": "And he shall come again with glory to judge both the living and the dead, whose kingdom shall have no end." Following the acknowledgment of "one baptism for the remission of sins," the Nicene Creed concludes, "And I [or, we] look for the resurrection of the dead, and the life of the world to come."

These particular creedal affirmations about the life to come occur in a context of worship that has first spoken of One who was "crucified, dead, and buried." The frame of reference in this instance for speaking about "the life of the world to come" is thus not that of science fiction speculation regarding possible future worlds. Here the currents run deep, for at this point we are brought by the gospel message about the Cross to confront the fact of death in the coming of our own, and every, future. In the approach of death no speculative theory or system of thought, theological as well as any other, has the power to comprehend what lies before us. Church teaching that attests, in Paul's words, to "the power of God" in "the message about the cross" (1 Cor. 1:18) presumes no clairvoyance. Any faithful testing of the spirits about so-called last things offers only "an accounting for the hope" (1 Pet. 3:15) that perseveres in the face of betrayal, crucifixion, and death.

Initial Objections

The question of how to account for hope most faithfully in church teaching today leads to the consideration of three main categories of possible objections.

1. *It would seem that Christian affirmation of the life to come diminishes engagement with life here and now.*

The most widely accepted interpretation among post-Enlightenment scholars of early Christianity is that its expectation about the imminent end of the present world turned out to have been mistaken. The here and now proved not to have been as short as supposed, and the problem for church doctrine ever since has been to accommodate its teaching to this apparent delay of the Parousia.[1] Among twentieth-century interpreters Rudolf Bultmann's emphasis upon this point has been the most influential:

> The early Christian community understands itself not as a historical but as an eschatological phenomenon. It is conscious that it belongs no longer to the present world but to the new Aeon which is at the door. The question then is how long this consciousness can remain vivid, how long the expectation of the imminent end of the world can remain unshaken.[2]

Bultmann himself sees a historical sense already reemerging in the New Testament with Luke's Gospel in a manner that we do not find in the other synoptic Gospels:

> The problem of Eschatology grew out of the fact that the expected end of the world failed to arrive, that the "Son of Man" did not appear in the clouds of heaven, that history went on, and that the eschatological community could not fail to recognize that it had become a historical phenomenon.[3]

The question of the relation of eschatological faith to historical existence was second to no other in much of the theology of the 1940s through the 1970s,[4] but, as Bultmann's statements indicate, the issue of the relation of the life to come with life here and now has been with the church from its beginnings.

In his critique of Christian doctrines as the unconscious projections of disembodied human self-alienation Ludwig Feuerbach's words from more than a century earlier express the broader objection: "Heaven is nothing but the idea of the true, the good, the valid, — of that which ought to be; earth, nothing but the idea of the untrue, the unlawful, of that which ought not to be. The Christian excludes from heaven the life of the species."[5] Feuerbach acknowledges that Christian doctrine does not affirm a resurrection of pure spirit, but of the body, yet this operates to the following effect: "In this world, faith occupies itself with nullifying the body; in the other world, with establishing it."[6] "But as the body in the other world is an incorporeal body, so necessarily the sex there is one without difference, i.e., a sexless sex."[7] That which most occupies life in the here and now — struggle and growth, buying and selling, marriage and giving in marriage, procreating, and all forms of work — are said to have no place in a resurrection of sabbath rest. The image conveyed by such testimony of interminable Sunday afternoon naps with nothing else to do is hard to dislodge.

At any rate, to try to live in the present "as though not" engaged with it (1 Cor. 7:29–31) because of the presumed imminence of its end would seem to amount to placing a moratorium upon life in the meantime. Whether we think of this as akin to a Stoic detachment from any psychological acknowledgment of personal need, or as a more political indifference to the current social conditions within one's environment, the result would appear to be the fostering of a false consciousness and self-alienation.

Christian doctrine would seem at this point to be confounded by the alternative of either having to admit that the eschatological character of the gospel message is simply dispensable for faith today, or that it calls those who seek to be faithful to it to a withholding of judgment in the here and now, a withholding of interest in what is going on in the immediate environment, a withholding of commitment for any really sustained involvement, and finally a withholding of all pleasure and delight in the good gifts of creation. Abstinence becomes the primary Christian virtue. Admittedly, the more dramatic instances of disengagement from the world in expectation of its immediate end are usually associated by mainstream Christianity with so-called cults and fringe groups. More prevalent in many churches, nonetheless, is a sense of "spiritual life," or "being Christian," that tends to view with disdain the realm of current public affairs and to disparage the attempts of those who work within it. Any such holding back, amounting to a deferral of existence, clearly abstracts Jesus' call to deny oneself and take up the cross (Matt. 16:24; Mark 8:34; Luke 9:23) from its context of active engagement in the joys and sufferings of present life as shown in the gospels.

2. *It would seem that church teaching regarding the final judgment renders the situation of much of the world hopeless.*

The question of hopelessness raises a subject about which there appears to be a pervasive ambiguity in Christian eschatological doctrine. On the one hand in the canonical context of biblical usage God may be referred to by the word "hope": "For you, O Lord, are my hope" (Ps. 71:5); "May the God of hope fill you with all joy and peace in believing, so that you may abound in hope by the power of the Holy Spirit" (Rom. 15:13). Similarly, the First Letter of Timothy begins with reference to "Christ Jesus our hope" (1 Tim. 1:1). God's love in Christ is proclaimed by the church to be the hope of all the world. On the other hand, those who in turn do not themselves hope in God would appear to be hopeless: "O hope of Israel! O Lord!," prophesies Jeremiah, "...those who turn away from you shall be recorded in the underworld" (Jer. 17:13). In the testimony of John's Gospel whoever does not believe in the Son whom God has sent to save and not to condemn the world is judged to be "condemned already" (John 3:18). Thus the hope of the world that is in Jesus Christ turns out, it would seem, only to apply to that part of the world that comes to have hope in Jesus Christ. Dante's famous words of inscription above the gateway to hell in Canto III of the *Inferno* make unmistakable the presumed consequence of not having hoped in Christ that will be revealed at the final judgment: "Abandon all hope, you who enter here."

The dilemma posed by the suggestion in Christian teaching of hopelessness for some in the final judgment leads John Calvin to consider point by point a range of objections that were recognized earlier by Augustine and yet continue to be raised today.[8] Obviously not all who have ever lived on earth have heard the gospel, or what Calvin calls "the covenant of life," proclaimed, and of those who have had this opportunity not all have heard in that proclamation the eternal hope for their own lives. Not all hope in the God of the gospel. Either God's will does not encompass their destinies, in which case their fate would be subject to a determination more ultimate than God's own, or else God must be said to have destined for reasons of an eternal goodness we are not given to comprehend that they not enter into this hope. In any case, this is not a matter of moralism because those who do enter into the hope of the gospel cannot rightly be said to be more deserving of it than those who do not. We simply do not know why this difference between those who share the hope and those who do not should be so, but we do know in faith that it is not a differentiation that any human judgment can make. Rather, continuous care must be taken by the church in its mission to all the world to view no one as hopeless but to call all human beings and nations to the hope of God's grace in Jesus Christ for which the promise is that all who truly seek will find. So Calvin argues.

Calvin is here to be commended for facing up to objections that theologians who are less bothered by conflicting evidence, or more faint-hearted, either fail to recognize or attempt to evade. Nevertheless, it is not sufficient even to grant that the failure to hear the gospel as a message of hope when it is proclaimed is something for which the hearer is at fault, like a willful turning of a deaf ear to the truth — which is what most church teaching has historically held regarding the justice of God's condemnations. There is still the fact that the overwhelming majority of the world, if one considers the full sweep of human history, has not even been in a position to hear the gospel proclaimed in any explicit sense, much less to turn a deaf ear to it. Today the most crucial problem in accounting for hope with respect to church teaching regarding the final judgment would appear to be to account for the presumed hopelessness of all those who have, for whatever reason, not hoped in Christ.

3. *It would seem that Christian doctrine concerning the future is incoherent as a confession of hope.*

The faithful coherence of church teaching regarding last things would appear to become questionable in a third respect if the future being affirmed is said to be both conclusive and hoped for. The creedal confession that Jesus Christ "shall come to judge the living and the dead" does not say that "it is a possibility that Jesus Christ shall come to judge the living and the dead." The hope of which Paul writes in Romans is said not to "disappoint" (Rom. 5:5).

The question is the relation of certainty and uncertainty, or the definite and the indefinite, in the church's proclamation of what is yet to come, and whether it is a self-contradiction to speak of hoping in instances of certainty where the outcome is assumed to be definite even if not yet an accomplished fact. In regular discourse we do not speak of hoping for something that is already sure. Anything beyond doubt, it would appear, is not an object of hope. We do not hope that the letter *B* follows the letter *A* in the English alphabet (unless in learning English for the first time we may be unsure and nervous about having to recite the alphabet). We do not hope that tomorrow will be a later date on the calendar than today (although we may hope that we will live to see tomorrow). We may, in short, wish that what is sure were otherwise, but if it is sure then we ordinarily do not say we "hope" that it is, or is not, so.

The recognition that the objects of hope are not within the range of demonstratively certain knowledge is prominent in Western philosophical tradition, most conspicuously in Aristotle and later in Kant. Other philosophers and theologians have appropriated this recognition in varying degree.

In the *Summa Theologiae* Thomas Aquinas, for example, examines the subject of hope, both as a human passion of the order of fear and anger,[9] and as a theological virtue of the order of faith and love.[10] According to Thomas's analysis, hope has to do with that which is "good, future, arduous, and possible."[11] Does not a coherent accounting require the admission that the term "possibility" allows for an eventual outcome other than the one hoped for? Some commentators have explained Thomas's position on the relation of possibility to certainty by saying that hope as a theological virtue does not have the certitude of faith, or of an event that has already happened, but of a tendency which is compatible with that of fear, and which may be said to be absolute, and not merely conditional.[12] Hope springs eternal.

Following Thomas's characterization of hope as having to do with that which is *bonum, futurum, arduum, possibile*, John Macquarrie likewise writes of "Christian hope" as referring to what is difficult but possible to attain.[13] Possibility, in Macquarrie's view, entails vulnerability. Still other analysts of hope have written, not atypically, of "incertitude" and "desire probability": "Some degree of incertitude is a characteristic feature of hope";[14] "Hope is identical with a desire plus a probability estimate"; it is said to involve a desiderative and an estimative component.[15]

The alternative to understanding Christian eschatology as a futurology of prediction based upon possibilities within the present that involve inconclusive outcomes, uncertainty of results, and probability estimates would seem to be an arbitrary speculation about the life to come for which no account of faithful coherence can be given. Church teaching would appear to be faced with the option either of having to acknowledge the incoherence of its account of hope, or of having to acknowledge that its hope is vulnerable to the possibility of ultimate disappointment.

Interpretation

If the biblical depictions of gospeling are not dispensed with, faith that the kingdom, or dominion, of heaven is at hand on the earth allows for no overlooking of what is currently happening on earth. Apostles are depicted as those whose gaze is primarily focused neither backward nor upward. Without claiming the soothsayer's foresight, apostolic hindsight and insight take the form of outlook, what J. Louis Martyn has called "stereoptic vision," in the gospel accounts.[16] In this perspective of looking ahead by focusing attention upon what is at hand, the life to come that is not yet *in* hand is proclaimed to be the only "here and now" there is. We turn now to consider how the "here and now" is confessed in faith to be related to that dominion which is coming, both with respect to the coming of eternal judgment, and with respect to the coming of eternal life. The question is, what faithful disbeliefs does such testimony entail?

1. On Trial for Hope

A single statement from Luke's narrative in Acts regarding Paul before King Agrippa may serve as a prism to illuminate how the coloring of the "here and now" is characteristically shown to be refracted with hope in the light of the gospel. Paul is portrayed as taking a stand concretely before the powers that hold sway in being brought before Agrippa after having been threatened and accused. As Luke records the scene, Paul says, "And now I stand here on trial for hope in the promise made by God to our ancestors" (Acts 26:6). Earlier in the narrative account Paul tells the chief priests and council of his accusers, "I am on trial concerning the hope of the resurrection of the dead" (Acts 23:6).

The words "on trial for hope" in this context aptly serve to sum up more generally how the link between ecclesiology, as the subject of the previous chapter, and eschatology is accounted for in Christian faith. In the first instance, what is seen to be at stake is not a speculative theory of future worlds, but an ethics of hope that derives from God's promise and not from probability estimates based upon what currently appears to be possible within the situation.[17] Theology's classical rationale articulated by Augustine and later Anselm as "faith seeking understanding" (*fides quaerens intellectum*) is lived out in practice at ground level as an ethics of "promise seeking mission" (*promissio quaerens missionem*). Faith "begins, continues, and ends with promise," writes Calvin,[18] and there is no understanding of it without the trials it occasions in being contested — what Luther termed in his Latin and German, *tentatio* or *Anfechtung*, the devil's assault.[19] The accounting for hope as a current "trial process" for the adjudication of rights, a trial initiated by God's promise and not yet concluded, is a theme developed in twentieth-century theology, most notably by Jürgen Moltmann,[20] under the initial influence of both Ernst Bloch's Neomarxist appropriation of biblical apocalyptic, as a philosophy of the "not-yet" in his *Das Prinzip Hoffnung* [The Principle of Hope] (1959),[21] and also the renewed interest among Old and New Testament scholars at midcentury in the eschatological character of scriptural testimonies.[22]

The term "eschatology" did not come into widespread use for a branch of theological study until the nineteenth century, even though a concern for the ultimate future appears to have characterized Christian thinking from the beginning.[23] The Greek work *eschaton* has the rudimentary meaning of something that is "last" in a sequence or rank in contrast to what is held to be *prōtos*, or "first." Thus we read of the reversal of perspective in Jesus' teaching that in view of the *basileia* of heaven "the last [*hoi eschatoi*] will be first, and the first will be last" (Matt. 20:16).[24] This reversal of perspective is reflective of the Old Testament testimony that what is last in time is "the day of the Lord" that is of first importance for life here and now.

Scholars of the Hebrew scriptures emphasize their rich variety and are by no means agreed in all their interpretation of the Hebraic sense, or senses, of the future.[25] The basic motifs around which discussion of eschatology centers are generally held to be the motifs of (1) God's covenant pledge or promise to Israel, (2) the notion of a remnant people, (3) the idea of the coming "day of the Lord" which arises with the prophets, and (4) the so-called apocalyptic literature such as we find in the Book of Daniel.

The covenant pledge or promise motif emerges most graphically in the accounts of Abraham, with Sarah and their child Isaac, as the paradigm of faith. The improbability of the Lord's promise to Abraham and Sarah in their advanced old age, well beyond all possibility of procreation together, that from their union would come the heir of God's covenant blessing to all the peoples of the earth caused them, so the Genesis narrative tells us, to fall on their faces laughing (Gen. 17:17, 18:12–15). To quote the words of Gerhard von Rad, "From Abraham to Malachi, Israel was kept constantly in motion because of what God said and did, and she was always in one way or another in an area of tension constituted by promise and fulfillment," with God's Word ever remaining "pregnant with the future."[26]

In the prophets the future is seen as the direction from which both judgment and hope are coming. For Amos the coming day of the Lord is primarily one of judgment. For Hosea there is the judgment and the more explicit hope: "My people are bent on turning away from me.... How can I give you up, Ephraim? How can I hand you over, O Israel?...for I am God and no mortal, the Holy One in your midst, and I will not come in wrath" (Hosea 11:7–9). In Jeremiah what is said to be "surely coming" is the making of a "new covenant with the house of Israel and the house of Judah" written on the heart (Jer. 31:31–34). In Isaiah (the so-called *Deutero*-Isaiah of chapters 40–55) the promise to the "remnant" of Judah and Israel — "Even when you turn gray I will carry you. I have made, and I will bear; I will carry and will save" — is given a universal scope: "My salvation has gone out and my arms will rule the peoples; the coastlands wait for me, and for my arm they hope" (Isa. 51:5). The particular remnant becomes the bearer of a universal blessing as the inheritance of "Abraham your father" and "Sarah who bore you" is recalled (Isa. 51:2).

Apocalyptic testimonies are generally defined as being similar to prophecy in directing attention to coming events and akin to wisdom sayings as well. But they differ from prophecy and go beyond moral maxims in that the future is portrayed as involving a more cataclysmic break with the present, as we see in the Book of Daniel. There is a distinct separation between the possibilities of the present and the age to come. Judgment and suffering are said to precede the coming age and to be signs of trial signaling its approach. In the period between the Old and New Testaments, from the second century B.C.E. through the first century C.E., apocalyptic ideas flourished and intermingled along with such other convictions, variously held, as those of Sheol, or death's shadowy underworld, of a general resurrection from the dead, and of a final Judgment.

The term "eschatology" when applied to Old Testament traditions of testimony thus may be said to refer broadly speaking to a coming state of affairs when God's glory is expected to fill the earth. There is no uniform belief concerning this ultimate future in the Hebrew scriptures, but there is a prevailing sense of expectation in which God's transcendence and immanence are viewed together as God's *imminence*.

When we turn to the New Testament, scholars do not find a uniform eschatology here either. What is recognized is that all eschatological ideas are interpreted with reference to what happens with Jesus Christ. In some instances the emphasis is more upon the presence of Christ's coming in the community of faith, and in others the stress is more upon the coming of Christ's presence that is yet to become established. But in either case there is both an "already" and a "not yet" frame of reference within the gospel message. The *basileia* of heaven has already come "at hand" in the life and death of Jesus. But this dominion of God has not yet become established over all forms of domination in this present age, and the destiny of Jesus as the crucified and risen Emmanuel, or God-with-us, involves a future for every one of us which has not yet taken place. Faith confesses to know Christ's victory as the *arrabōn*, in Pauline terms, or promissory note (2 Cor. 1:20–22, 5:5; Eph. 1:13–14), issued in the currency of present life in the power of the same Holy Spirit that raised Jesus Christ from the dead, but our own physical death also is still coming due, and "it does not yet appear what we shall be" (1 John 3:2). While the hour of truth is confessed in John's Gospel to be both "coming and now is" (John 4:23), that future which is yet to come is announced in the accounts of Jesus' teaching in the synoptic Gospels to be at a day and an hour that none of us knows or expects (Matt. 24:36, 24:42, 25:13; Mark 13:32–33, 35; Luke 12:40).

Whatever the formal elements ingredient in the traditions of New Testament witness to the future — apocalyptic influences, Gnostic influences, mythical conceptions that do not reduce to literal interpretation — there is the consistent testimony that the promised life to come can be trusted. Faith that is based upon this testimony thus entails a refusal to believe that there is no trustworthy future facing us in coming events wherever and whenever we are. For this reason the Reformers concluded with Paul, "Now we, brothers and sisters, like Isaac are children of promise" (Gal. 4:28).

Such a conclusion is no euphoric utopianism that is blind to the wilderness wandering of betrayal, crucifixion, and the agonizing powers of death. To live by such faith, it is clear from the biblical depictions, is to be on trial as part of a mission in the earth that remains countercultural insofar as the culture embodies the powers of domination opposed to love and freedom that the power of the Resurrection displaces. But the faithful life as a trial in the midst of all social and self-imposed structures of death-dealing, all affliction and infliction of evil, in both its individual and corporate dimensions, is seen to be such precisely because it derives its existence from the hope that comes from a new inbreaking dominion that already is at hand. The New Testament word for a witness, *martys* ("martyr"), in the context of the gospel usage is a witness to life without evasion of death; exactly the opposite is the secular notion of a "martyr complex" as a witnessing to death by the evasion of life. Manna sufficient for each day is only given en route and cannot be stored up ahead of time (Exod. 16:19). The eucharistic bread and cup proclaim the Lord's death "until he comes" (1 Cor. 11:26).

Like Abraham with Sarah, this eschatological reversal of perspective is portrayed in the lyrical rendering of the Letter to the Hebrews as a life of pilgrimage through a wilderness on a journey without evident possibilities that is embarked upon while as yet "not knowing where he was going" (Heb. 11:8). The promise allows for no spiritual bypass of the wilderness at ground level but is given with the call, in short, "Go to the land that I will show you, and I will make your name a blessing" (Gen. 12:1–3). According to this perspective, acts of faith are seen as anticipations of an imminent kingdom that is promised but not yet established. Christian ethicists, mindful of such a vantage point, find equally inadequate both an accounting for hope as a noncontextual prescriptive escapism, and a "situation ethics"[27] that seeks only to maximize the good as a love command within the possibilities the circumstances afford. Rather, the church's eschatological doctrine describes an anticipation ethics that faces what is imminently at hand, and not yet already available in hand, in every situation. By the scandalous practice of Jesus' eating with "tax collectors and sinners" (Matt. 9:10–11; Mark 2:15–16; Luke 5:29–30, 15:1–2) the promise is embodied and enacted contextually at ground level that "many will come from east and west and will eat with Abraham and Isaac and Jacob in the kingdom of heaven" (Matt. 8:11). The promise of the life to come is thus prefigured by anticipatory acts of mission in the concrete circumstances of the present. The investment of the prophet Jeremiah in the field devoid of present possibilities at Anathoth is related as having signaled in practice God's promise that "houses and fields and vineyards shall again be bought in this land" (Jer. 32:15). The practice of *promissio quaerens missionem*, contrary to the stereotypical boundaries imposed by a falsely spiritualized understanding of "missionary activity" as religious proselytization, is actually the day-to-day working out of the ethics of the gospel's anticipation in current situations. Thus the sentence attributed to Paul by Luke in Acts 26:6 provides a rather apt summation of how through the Spirit, as Paul himself writes to the Galatians, *faith* eagerly waits in freedom for the *hope* of righteousness by working through *love* (Gal. 5:5–6): "And now I stand here on trial for hope in the promise made by God to our ancestors." Proscribed is any spirit that claims that the true hope for the life to come does not lead to active engagement in the work of love here and now.

2. The Coming Cloud

How Christian faith's confession of a "world to come" relates to contemporary ways of speaking about "the end of the world" is a question most starkly posed by New Testament sayings regarding the coming of the "Son of Man [*ho huios tou anthrōpou*]." This term, which figures prominently in the gospel accounts, reflects the apocalyptic testimony of Daniel:

> As I watched in the night visions I saw one like a son of man coming with the clouds of heaven. . . . To him was given dominion and glory and kingship, that all peoples, nations, and languages should serve him. His dominion is an everlasting dominion that shall not pass away, and his kingship is one that shall never be destroyed. (Dan. 7:13–14)

The term *ho huios tou anthrōpou* itself simply means a "human being," and not exclusively males, as we see in the words of the Psalmist, "What are human beings that you are mindful of them, mortals [*ben adam*, 'son of man' as 'human offspring'] that you care for them?" (Ps. 8:4; Heb. 2:6). But when used apocalyptically as a way of naming the imminent future, a better translation in this context is "the Coming One." Faith that Jesus Christ is the One who "shall come again with glory to judge both the living and the dead, whose kingdom shall have no end," as the Nicene Creed expresses it, reads Jesus' sayings in the gospels regarding the coming of the Son of Man "at hand" as references to the coming again of Jesus as "the Lord [who] is at hand" (Phil. 4:4) in the "day at hand" (Rom. 13:12). Those today who would discount from further consideration such a personified naming of the future as being too mythical a form of envisagement, and hence too outmoded, for serious reflection would do well to recall the contemporary usage of such personifications in our manner of speaking about Father Time, Mother Nature, Uncle Sam, Lady Liberty, and Infant New Year.

The "end of the world" as a general axiom is hardly a subject that any of us can claim to have knowledge about. Some would reply that theologians tend to specialize in such matters! It is important to make clear that our particular search, here as previously, is for the import of the canonical witness for faith today. The Bible in a number of places speaks of the ultimate future that God is bringing about and the end of all things as they presently are. This topic has surfaced again and again in the history of the church among various groups as different timetables were announced, then readjusted. Since the dawn of the nuclear age such passages have become even more controversial and have received radically conflicting assessment. An example is provided by Luke 21:25–28, 34–36, which has synoptic parallels in Matthew 24:29–31 and Mark 13:24–27:

> There will be signs in the sun, the moon, and the stars, and on the earth distress among nations confused with the roaring of the sea and the waves. People will faint from fear and foreboding of what is coming upon the world, for the powers of the heavens will be shaken. Then they will see "the Son of Man coming in a cloud" with power and great glory. Now when these things begin to take place, stand up and raise your heads because your redemption is drawing near.... Be alert [*agrypneite*, 'Be on watch'] at all times, praying that you may have the strength to escape all these things that will take place, and to stand before the Son of Man.

This passage from Luke's Gospel appears in lectionary readings of the church during the liturgical season of Advent. It proclaims that which is coming in terms of a cosmic upheaval involving the powers of both heaven and earth. In November 1983, before the end of the Cold War, when there was great apprehension regarding the nuclear threat, the American Broadcasting Company produced a television drama entitled "The Day After" on the terrors of nuclear warfare and the projected horrors of its ensuing devastation in the earth. To hear the Advent scripture from Luke 21 read one week later in the churches, after millions had viewed this program with all its attendant publicity, was enough to cause one to wonder if the Bible had been upstaged by network television and co-opted as part of a media event. Watching first a projected vision of terrifying nuclear catastrophe in "The Day After," and then hearing the Lucan passage read when the impact of the television drama upon one's mind was still vivid, made the references in ancient biblical apocalyptic to the shaking of the powers of the heavens "above" and the earth "below" ominously contemporary. It raised the question of whether the Advent scripture from Luke was but a rerun of an already familiar script of prediction concerning the coming cloud and the end of the world.

But the passage from Luke, if we follow it, continues on to take a surprising turn. After referring to the shaking of the heavens and the distress of earth, with people faint from fear and foreboding as they anticipate what is going to happen to the world, we are told, "Then they will see 'the Son of Man coming in a cloud' with power and great glory. Now when these things begin to take place, stand up and raise your heads because your redemption is drawing near" (Luke 21:27–28). To encounter such a testimony leads one to ask if the television script writers and the special effects people have missed something in their end of the world scenarios? Who is kidding whom? Is this apocalyptic way of envisaging reality any longer to be taken seriously, or do we have here only some first-century version of star wars in this depiction of a coming cloud that bears the Son of Man?

Preaching on this gospel text in the sixteenth century, Martin Luther commented that scarcely any other words of God can be so neglected as these, wherein this coming day of judgment is foretold.[28] Christian doctrine today is faced with the question of whether such words perhaps should be neglected if a faithful accounting for the hope of the gospel is to be given at the present time. Do we have in the talk of a coming cloud a text overtaken by current trends and events, or do we have here the current projection of trends and events overtaken by a text? Christian affirmation of the "life of the world to come" confronts dogmatic testing with the question of whether the import for faith of the scripture in Luke 21 is something that the present day has now moved beyond; or whether the import for faith of this scripture is itself beyond the typical understandings of the present day? New Yorkers living through the World Trade Center attacks of September 11, 2001, will not soon forget the cloud that lingered for days over the site.

One reason why there are conscientious and thoughtful people, including many Christians, who think that the church should neglect apocalyptic scriptures today is the way that they are often interpreted. An interpretation that is widely promoted by some Christian groups, and may be latent more often elsewhere than it is spoken, usually contains the following assertions. Apocalyptic testimonies in scripture, such as the Lucan passage in Chapter 21, are — so it is claimed — to be read as predictions. If you are "saved" you can see that these predictions of the end time refer to events taking place today. The predictions tell us that the world is going to be destroyed by fire, and there is nothing we can do about it. There will always be "wars and rumors of wars" (Matt. 24:6; Mark 13:7; Luke 21:9), but conditions are destined to get worse just before the end. The predictions say that we are now living in the final countdown days.

Of course, say those who teach this view, the coming catastrophe does not threaten true believers who have accepted Jesus Christ as their personal Lord and Savior and experienced the Holy Spirit. At the last trumpet Jesus will return to snatch them out of the world before it plunges toward destruction. But everyone else will suffer untold horrors. It is not surprising to find in the conclusion of Hal Lindsey's bestseller, *The Late Great Planet Earth*, which popularized for millions of people in the 1970s the reading of the Bible as prediction, the advice that, since the time is short, Christians should concentrate upon seeing that their families, their friends, and their acquaintances are converted to the gospel — should concentrate upon building, as it were, their private spiritual fallout shelters. In such a scenario no emphasis is given to being peacemakers, working for reconciliation, having regard for the hunger, thirst, exposure, and enslavement of those whom Jesus is reported in Matthew's account as saying that the Coming One will call "the least of these who are members of my family [*ton adelphon mou*]" (Matt. 25:40). Rather, Lindsey writes, "Exactly what happens to those who are in a thermonuclear blast" is what it appears "will be the case at the return of Christ."[29]

Because of interpretations such as this, it is easy to see why many contend today that a faithful accounting for hope requires that the church neglect apocalyptic texts. Using the Bible to predict destruction of people other than your own kind has led in the past to attempts to justify the extermination of Jews, the burning of dissenters, the institutions of racial slavery and segregation, and the dehumanizing of all who are viewed as outsiders and different, whatever the cultural form this discrimination may take.

In addition to such interpretation there are yet two other reasons why objectors have argued historically that "these neglected words" of apocalyptic testimony wherein God foretells unto us God's coming should be neglected. One is the opinion that apocalyptic material in the Bible, such as Luke 21, represents an outmoded way of thinking that makes no sense to the modern mind. Another, more serious objection is that visions of a Coming One in the clouds tend to make people irresponsible about their duties on earth here and now.

The idea that "the coming of the Son of Man" sayings in the gospel accounts lack coherence in the context of modernity was generally assumed by liberal thinkers throughout much of the eighteenth, nineteenth, and early twentieth centuries. Thomas Jefferson, for example, deleted this Lucan section from the condensed version of the New Testament that he pieced together during his first term as president. What Jefferson sought in the scriptures was a reliable code of ethics, and he had no interest, he wrote, in "sophisticating and perverting" the simple ethical teachings of Jesus by "frittering them into subtleties and obscuring them with jargon."[30] For the same reason Jefferson cut out all accounts of the Resurrection and concluded his Bible with the words, "There laid they Jesus, and rolled a great stone to the door of the sepulchre, and departed" (Matt. 27:60).

With the arrival of the nuclear age the assumptions of modernity in this regard were themselves made to appear highly suspect. At the end of the nineteenth century one of the most influential New Testament scholars, Johannes Weiss, wrote that even though the Kingdom of God sayings so central to Jesus' teaching must be said to have an objective cosmic dimension, and are not reducible merely to abstract values or subjective states, any cosmic frame of apocalyptic reference was no longer possible for the informed modern mind. "The real difference between our modern Protestant world-view and that of primitive Christianity," Weiss writes, "is... that we do not share the attitude [that 'the present form of this world is passing away' (1 Cor. 7:31)]..., but we pass our lives in the joyful confidence that *this* world will evermore become the showplace of the people of God."[31] Yet barely more than fifty years later the coming of the nuclear age at Hiroshima on August 6, 1945, caused the so-called modern reader to ask of Weiss and his followers, *Whose* worldview has now become outmoded?

But should not the church neglect the texts that speak of the coming of the Son of Man because they tend to make people irresponsible about their duties on earth here and now? At a time of international peace demonstrations and calls for a halt in the rapidly escalating nuclear arms race, and with the newly emerging ecological awareness that soon followed, this objection confronted church teaching regarding the life to come as never before in all of human history.[32] During this period of the Cold War Jonathan Schell's *The Fate of the Earth* articulated the protest of many. The way that some Christian teaching employs the apocalyptic traditions of scripture to predict what is coming, Schell argues, contributes to "the ultimate evasion of our responsibility as human beings."[33] But what then is our responsibility to one another and to this planet? When confronted with this question, Schell and the ecological experts become hortatory with a list of imperatives insisting, in short, that the human species has got to wake up and have the strength to save the world. We need, Schell concludes, to shake off our lethargy and fatigue and begin to act.[34] We need the passion and the will to save ourselves. We need to awaken to the truth of our peril. But then the discourse of "We need... We need" itself takes a surprising turn: "We need the assurance that there will be a future if we are to take on the burden of mastering the past"; in other words, we are only able to respond to the crises of the present time in a human way if there is, in Schell's words, "promise of a future."

This brings us about face once again to listen for the disbeliefs of faith entailed in the neglected words of God wherein God's coming is foretold. Why? Because the promise of a future is something that no human being can make *and keep* to another. Christian faith refuses to believe that the future is something any of us has the power to guarantee to another, including those whom we love the most. The gospel outlook upon the future at hand obviously is not a product of a nuclear age, but taken in its canonical context it may in certain respects be more hardheadedly realistic than the assumptions of modernity. The simple reason is that a promise of a future, if there is any at all, must come to us and be kept by a power greater than our own. As the prophet Jeremiah envisions it, "The days are surely coming, says the Lord, when *I* will fulfill the promise *I* made to the house of Israel and the house of Judah" (Jer. 33:14).

The early apostolic mission to every nation under heaven apparently trusted that there was a promised future which makes human beings response-able, able to respond in an ethic of hopeful perseverance working through love, before all the terrors overclouding the earth. Here we come to the decisive point of the apostolic outlook: *The difference between seeing eschatological testimony as a promise of the future rather than as a prediction of the future is that in a promise someone has made a commitment to you.* What faith confesses to hear in the gospel testimonies regarding the coming cloud is not a prediction of the inevitability of destruction, but a promise, as only God can make and keep, that even when the worst things come upon us that can possibly happen, they will not be able to prevent Christ's coming to us and to all the world in redemption, an ultimate reclaiming from all harm. Christian eschatological doctrine affirms that the gospel is the promise that the future, whatever threats it holds, can be faced because it bears the face of Jesus. "Then they will see 'the Son of Man coming in a cloud' with power and great glory. Now when these things begin to take place, stand up and raise your heads because your redemption is drawing near" (Luke 21:27–28).

Facing the life to come in this promise, as the Lucan passage portrays it, does not drug people to sleep. It wakes them from the anxiety of escapism and calls them to hold up their heads. And in a very down-to-earth way it also enables them to know what to do in the meantime, how to focus their energies here and now: "Be on watch at all times, praying that you may have the strength ... to stand before the Son of Man" (Luke 21:36). In other words, the call of apocalyptic in the context of Jesus' teaching is to seek to do those things here and now that will endure and "stand" in a day when all opposition to God's promised redemption, or reclaiming of the world from harm, is overcome and destroyed. Christian faith refuses to believe that the coming future, whatever it holds, is not subject to God's own promised commitment to redemption. For this reason, Christian faith equally refuses to believe that the coming future of redemption is subject to human prediction and projection.

In this instance, as in all others, such refusal as an entailment of confessions of faith is not an unwavering psychological state immune to fear and doubt. The promised future conveyed by the apocalyptic testimony of the gospel message allows for no easy optimism or cheap grace, no pretense that there really is no dreadful harm in life from which to be reclaimed by the Coming One. It is instructive to be reminded that the one who wrote the following words of Christian hymnody, so familiar to many Christians, is said to have done so when faced with recurrent torment "as a period of madness approached":

> Ye fearful saints, fresh courage take; The clouds ye so much dread
> Are big with mercy, and shall break In blessings on your head.[35]

3. Hellfire and Damnation

Christian confession affirms the coming of Jesus Christ as a judgment of all the living and the dead. When the Kingdom of God is falsely viewed as "all fulfillment of promise without judgment," the teachings of the church amount to the claim, in H. Richard Niebuhr's memorable words, that "a God without wrath brought men without sin into a kingdom without judgment through the ministrations of a Christ without a cross."[36] Opponents of liberal Protestantism make much of the fact that among liberal Christians all scriptural references to hellfire and damnation tend to be ignored and evaded by a conspiracy of silence. Liberals may offer the rejoinder that some fundamentalist and conservative doctrine for its part mainly reveals that there are those who cannot imagine being happy in heaven unless they are convinced that somebody is forever burning in hell. The more serious dogmatic issue, as indicated in the second initial objection of this chapter, is how most faithfully to account for the hope of the gospel in taking account of the gospel's testimony regarding God's ultimate rejections. This will bring us back to the subject of the individualizing and personalizing of God's judgments in some biblical depictions that was initially raised at the conclusion of chapter 11 on Salvation.

The old-fashioned terms "hellfire" and "damnation" serve to sharpen the issue of God's ultimate rejections. There is no question but that such references figure prominently in a number of scriptural passages regarding the final judgment. Traditionally, "hell" has been the word most often used to translate into English the three biblical terms *Sheol*, *Gehenna*, and *Hades*. Also, in 2 Pet. 2:4, the word *Tartaros* is used. A number of associations arise from this canonical context of usage that go unrecognized when the word is abstracted from this matrix.

According to a testimony of the Psalms, "The dead do not praise the Lord, nor do any that go down into silence [*Sheol*]" (Ps. 115:17). Hell is here associated with that which is silenced before God and not praiseworthy in the shadows of death. A further association of meaning appears in Psalm 9:17–18: "The wicked shall depart to *Sheol*, all the nations that forget God. For the needy shall not always be forgotten, nor the hope of the poor perish forever." In this instance hell is associated with forgetfulness of the God who does not forget the needy and the hope of the poor. The God-forgetfulness of hell is hereby linked to the disregard of the neighbor's need. This linkage is reiterated in the Gospel of Matthew. The demeaning of another's good by insulting the other's worth, "You fool" (Matt. 5:22), or by adulterous regard (Matt. 5:29–30; also 18:8–9), is said to be "liable to the hell of fire [*Gehenna*]." Hell is associated in Matthew with whatever is destructive of both the soul and the body: "Do not fear those who kill the body but cannot kill the soul; rather fear whoever can destroy both soul and body in hell [*Gehenna*]" (Matt. 10:29). Damnation is equated with "being sentenced to hell [*Gehenna*]" (Matt. 23:33).

The association of fire with hell and divine rejection, or damnation, has ancient roots. The brimstone of the Lord's judgment that rained down on Sodom and Gomorrah in the Genesis narrative, the "sulfur and fire from the Lord out of heaven," from which Lot and his household are instructed to turn and flee, is suggestive of a volcanic eruption by which Lot's wife, looking back, becomes petrified, "a pillar of salt" (Gen. 19:24–26). The words of Moses' song in Deuteronomy tell of the Lord's reply to the unfaithful who make provocation with their idols: "For a fire is kindled by my anger, and burns to the depths of *Sheol;* it devours the earth and its increase, and sets on fire the foundations of the mountains" (Deut. 32:22). In Matthew's Gospel the fire "prepared for the devil and his angels" is said to be "eternal" and to mark the rejection in the final judgment of all who have not seen the need, and acted to remedy it, that exists among those considered to be "the least" in their midst (Matt. 25:41). Similarly, the account given in Mark's Gospel of Jesus' excoriating rejection of "any . . . who put a stumbling block before one of these little ones who believe in me" associates the damning judgment with a "hell [*Gehenna*], where . . . the fire is never quenched" (Mark 9:47–48). What is apparent in these examples is that damnation to hell is looked upon as an eternal and unquenchable judgment. Any construal of their import for faith today has this factor of an eternal rejection to take into account.

To these scriptural testimonies must now be added four others that are also part of the matrix of associations that appear in biblical instances of the use of the word "hell."

In one of these, the damning of anyone who is made in the likeness of God is viewed as the work not of God but of hell. The fact that hellfire is not regarded merely in some crudely literalistic manner in the full context of biblical usage may be seen in the reference to it in the Letter of James:

> And the tongue is a fire. The tongue is placed among our members as a world of iniquity; it stains the whole body, sets on fire the cycle of nature, and is itself set on fire by hell [*Gehenna*]. . . . With it we bless the Lord and Father, and with it we curse those who are made in the likeness of God. From the same mouth . . . this ought not to be so. (James 3:6, 9–10)

In yet another reference, hell itself is depicted as sentenced to destruction in the final judgment. According to the apocalyptic vision of the Revelation to John, when "Death and *Hades* gave up their dead that were in them" before the great throne and the opening of the book of life, they themselves were cast away along with all not named in the book of life: "Then Death and *Hades* were thrown into the lake of fire" (Rev. 20:14). Earlier in Revelation "Michael and his angels," those messengers who convey heaven's grace against its opposition, are portrayed as defeating and evicting Satan and his angels, those messengers said to convey accusation and deceit over the whole world, from occupying any place whatsoever in the kingdom of heaven (Rev. 12:7–12).

The most emphatic New Testament witness that the hell which curses and damns those made in the likeness of God is subject to a dominion greater than its own occurs with reference to the recognition of the presence and power of Jesus as the Christ. Against this presence and power the gates of hell are said not to be able to prevail. Two final texts may be cited as evidence. To Simon Peter's confession, "You are the Christ, the Son of the living God," the words of Jesus according to Matthew's Gospel are, "And I tell you, you are Peter [*Petros*], and on this rock [*petra*] I will build my church, and the gates of *Hades* will not prevail against it" (Matt. 16:16–18). In the Revelation of Jesus Christ to John of "one like the Son of Man" the words are given, "Do not be afraid; I am the first and the last, and the living one. I was dead, and see, I am alive forever and ever; and I have the keys of Death and of *Hades*" (Rev. 1:13, 17–18). What is apparent in these examples is that hell is looked upon as subject to eternal life in Jesus Christ. Any construal of their import for faith today has this factor of an eternal subjection to be taken into account.

By being attentive to the diversity of associations that appear with the use of the words "hellfire" and "damnation," or their equivalents, in the Bible, and without seeking any forced harmonization of them, we can see a basis in scriptural testimony for the two primary disbeliefs that are implicit in Christian doctrines of the final judgment: Christian teaching proscribes any claim that God's judgment of damnation to hell is not an eternal rejection; Christian teaching equally proscribes any claim that God's judgment of eternal rejection is not subject to God's gift of eternal life in Jesus Christ. Only by recognizing both of these refusals does the church render today a faithful account of the hope of the gospel.

As it was noted at the conclusion of chapter 11, it is characteristic of much scriptural testimony to refer to both good and evil as personifications. To cite only two examples, that which is good as "wisdom" — where it is viewed in Proverbs as the opposite of the hell which urges, in its abuse of innocent life, "Come with us, let us lie in wait for blood; let us wantonly ambush the innocent; like *Sheol* let us swallow them alive and whole, like those who go down to the Pit" (Prov. 1:11–12) — is personalized and personified as "she": "Wisdom cries out in the street; in the squares she raises her voice. At the busiest corner she cries out; at the entrance of the city gates she speaks" (Prov. 1:20–21). Similarly, that which is antithetical to Christ is personalized as "the antichrist" (2 John 7) and personified as Satan: "And if Satan has risen up against himself and is divided he cannot stand, but his end has come" (Mark 3:26; also Matt. 12:26, Luke 11:18).

In like manner that which God condemns to eternal damnation is also personalized and personified as individuals in a number of biblical passages: "There will be weeping and gnashing of teeth" (Luke 13:23). As mentioned in chapter 11, what is ungodly is often referred to as those who are ungodly. Evil doing is referred to as evil doers. What God eternally rejects is expressed as those whom God eternally rejects. This characteristic of biblical usage is carried over into those church teachings that traditionally have both personified and individualized the "rejected" as a class or group of human beings. Thus the "elect" versus the "rejected," or "the saved" versus the "lost," or "those going to heaven" versus "those going to hell," are presumptively two separate groups of people.

Much controversy in the history of Christian doctrine has resulted from the personalizing, personifying, and individualizing of God's final judgment as an "eternal decree" in which humanity itself is considered to be ultimately divided between those who come to blessing on God's right hand and those who come to condemnation and rejection on God's left.[37] How such an eschatological outlook can be said to be congruent with the import of the gospel message as attested in other doctrines of the church has continually been a subject of intense disagreement. It is significant that in the disputes between strict predestinarians and those who oppose them in the name of allowing for some measure of human choice in the matter of one's eternal destiny, both sides argue with a mutually unquestioned assumption that the import of the gospel message regarding the elect and the rejected is that these are two distinct groups of people. This is apparent whether the predestinarians of the Synod of Dort (1619) are affirming that the grace of election, which is given "not to all, but some only,"[38] is a "reality conferred" and not an offer of faith by God to human beings to be accepted or not at their pleasure,[39] or whether, as the followers of Arminius insisted, such grace is conditional upon the proviso "if only" they accept it.[40]

Evidence for a reading of the canonical testimonies that is more congruent with the recognition that confession of Christ's coming "to judge the living and the dead" includes not only the factor of an eternal rejection, but equally, and indeed more prominently, the factor that this eternal rejection is subject to the eternal life that is in Christ, can also be found within biblical usage. Eternal judgment is said to apply to thrones and dominions, principalities and powers, that cannot be equated simply with flesh and blood individuals (Eph. 6:12). There is, it follows, no rejection of the slavery of sin in a personal and individual sense that is not also a rejection of the sin of slavery in a political and social sense. At this point the inability of existentialist categories, with their emphasis upon discrete individuals and persons, to accommodate the cosmic dimension of the gospel's apocalyptic frame of reference becomes most apparent. Furthermore, "the world God so loved" (John 3:16) and the deniers and betrayers of that love do not compose two groups of humanity in the gospel message, but one and the same. The church ecumenical has consistently proclaimed that "all have sinned and fall short of the glory of God" (Rom. 3:23). But it is also not to be overlooked that this solidarity in sin is confessed by Christian faith only with christological reference, in Paul's words, to the One whom God made "to be sin so that in him we might become the righteousness of God" (2 Cor. 5:21). If that is taken to be the confession of Christian faith, it entails a refusal to believe that there is a human solidarity in sin that is not also a solidarity in grace. This eschatological outlook which views eternal rejection as yet still subject to eternal life in Christ comes to its most all encompassing expression in the following language of Paul:

> But in fact Christ has been raised from the dead, the first fruits of those who have died. For since death came through a human being, the resurrection of the dead has also come through a human being; for as all die in Adam, so all will be made alive in Christ. But each in his own order: Christ the first fruits, then at his coming those who belong to Christ. Then comes the end, when he hands over the kingdom to God the Father, after he has destroyed every rule and every authority and power. For he must reign until he

> has put all his enemies under his feet. The last enemy to be destroyed is death.... When all things are subjected to him, then the Son himself will also be subjected to the one who put all things in subjection under him, so that God may be all in all. (1 Cor. 15:20–26, 28)

From this vantage point what the coming judgment eternally rejects may be said to be not the creature "made in the likeness of God," to recall the words of James 3:9, but the creature as cursed or accursed by all that stands in opposition, including self-opposition, to the creature's own good. Paul's word to the Galatians is that the life in Christ's coming as God's apocalypsed faithfulness is for them a "new creation" (Gal. 6:15). To the Corinthians he writes that no one can be regarded in the old way "according to the flesh" since in Christ there is "a new creation" with everything old having passed off the scene and everything becoming new (2 Cor. 5:17). To the Romans this life in Christ's coming is professed to be extended to "the whole creation in all its suffering, futility, bondage, and decay" which now in the birthpangs of its labor "waits with eager longing" for "the freedom of the glory of the children of God" to take place — literally, "to be apocalypsed" (Rom. 8:19–23).

By identifying the coming judgment as the coming of Jesus Christ, Christian confession entails the refusal to believe that what is ultimately defeated and rejected is ever other than the opposition, in whatever personal and corporate form of denial, betrayal, and crucifixion it takes, to being loved into freedom. The judgment of the One sent not to condemn but to save the world is described in John's Gospel in this way: "And this is the judgment, that the light has come into the world, and people loved darkness rather than light because their deeds were evil" (John 3:19). The eternally "rejected," the "unsaved," and the "lost" is all that is within us and within the world which denies, betrays, and crucifies the love that comes to set us free. But in affirming faith that Jesus Christ "shall come" "whose kingdom shall have no end" Christian faith refuses to believe that the grace of being loved into freedom ultimately stops coming or ceases to be. If the coming of faith (Gal. 3:25) occurs only as the coming of grace, then no time limits of this passing world can be set upon when faith shall arrive in any human destiny. It is only the Devil, or evil, in this sense whose "time is short" (Rev. 12:12). The regret twice expressed in Martha's and Mary's weeping before the tomb of their brother Lazarus, "Lord, if you had been here, my brother would not have died," is answered in the Fourth Gospel by a portrayal of Jesus' power in the face of death and beyond to reveal that grace is never too late (John 11:1–44). When such grace is confessed to have "descended into hell," then hell is acknowledged to have no dominion that can prevail. There is in the proclamation of the gospel no *basileia* of hell that is at hand, but only a *basileia* of heaven. Hell has no eternal dominion. If what God eternally rejects throughout all creation, with the fire of a love that remains unquenchable, is every opposition to our being loved into freedom, including our own, then the hellfire and damnation of Judgment Day is precisely the one true hope of all the earth. The old question of whether or not grace is "irresistible" only becomes a problem when theology forgets Who it is whose judgment is confessed to be coming. What else is the Crucifixion if not the resistance to grace? What finally does a Resurrection faith refuse to believe, if not that the resistance to grace is ever its cessation?

4. Looking Forward: The Resurrection of Body and World

Faith that God's "steadfast love endures forever" (Ps. 118:1) looks forward to what lies ahead in full and open acknowledgment of "the terror of the night, . . . [and] the destruction that wastes at noonday" (Ps. 91:5–6). This is no bravado unmindful of the cry of God-forsakenness at the Cross (Matt. 27:46; Mark 15:34; Ps. 22:1). If it is true that in the gospel's frame of reference the cross indeed casts its shadow only in the light of resurrection morn, it is equally to be recognized that the light of resurrection morn is disclosed only by the shadow of the cross. The historic creeds of the church ecumenical nowhere say, "I believe in death," but they openly acknowledge death in affirming resurrection from the dead. In the language of the Apostles' Creed faith is professed in "the resurrection of the body and the life everlasting." The words of the Nicene Creed are "I [or, we] look for the resurrection of the dead, and the life of the world to come." Any denial or evasion of the fact of suffering unto death, no matter how pious or secular, is not the Christian hope that speaks of being raised from every power of death by the same power of God's Spirit that raised Jesus Christ from the dead.

Affirmation of the "body" in this context is here set against all notions of the immortality of a presumptively disembodied and deathless soul. Although the language of immortality can be found in the New Testament (1 Cor. 15:53–54; 2 Tim. 1:10) and in the history of Christian theology, along with the influence of pre-Christian antiquity where such notions were prevalent, it is the resurrection of the completely dead, and not the immortality of some deathless soul, some presumed spark of divinity that manages to exempt itself from the body's dying, that Christian faith confesses as "a living hope through the resurrection of Jesus Christ from the dead" (1 Pet. 1:3). Entailed in this hope is the refusal of every spirit that claims that the true hope of the life to come rests upon a capacity to avoid dying or to transcend the body. The proclamation of Easter is not the proclamation of out-of-body experiences, whatever their truth in fact. Entailed in this proclamation is the refusal to believe that the resurrection hope for ourselves is somehow in ourselves, or in a part of ourselves that never dies. In the resurrection of the dead all things are said to become new, including the body, and the "spiritual body [*sōma pneumatikon*]" (1 Cor. 15:44) of which Paul writes is not the resuscitation of the physical corpse that remains subject to suffering and death.

New Testament references to the resurrected body provide for no clearly defined understanding. There is a complexity within the scriptural materials that remains subject to differing interpretations by New Testament scholars. A contrast, for example, may be seen in Paul's Corinthian correspondence that suggests a twofold conception in his eschatology. W. D. Davies has argued that in 1 Corinthians 15 we find the view "that the Christian waits for the new body till the Parousia":[41] "At the last trumpet... this perishable body must put on imperishability" (1 Cor. 15:52–53). In 2 Corinthians 5:1, on the other hand, Davies finds the view that "immediately at death [the Christian] acquires the heavenly body": "For we know that if the earthly tent we live in is destroyed, we have a building from God, a house not made with hands, eternal in the heavens." Davies explains this difference by observing that in the Rabbinic thought of Paul's day the so-called Age to Come had two meanings. It stood for both (1) a future aeon of consummation at the end of history, and also (2) a heavenly realm which exists eternally. Thus the life everlasting is believed both to begin at death and also to come in the future at the end of days.

However these contrasting testimonies are assessed as to the background of thinking that has influenced them, affirmation of the resurrection of the body is not simply a reference to the individual who is raised but also to the corporate reality of the one body of many members resurrected as the body of Christ: "For as all die in Adam, so all will be made alive in Christ" (1 Cor. 15:22). In the second century Irenaeus represents this corporate character of Christian hope in its regard for human destiny as summed up, or "recapitulated," in the life span of Christ.[42]

The corporate character of the resurrected life is also to be recognized in the affirmation that this "life everlasting" is professed to be a "world," "the life of the world to come." The cosmic and the personal, the communal and the individual, are never separated in the hope of the gospel's promise of a kingdom, or an unimpeded dominion of love and freedom, that is at hand. Proscribed by the import of this gospel is any claim that the resurrection from the dead is either the disembodiment of human life or its isolation from the community of a world. If the One who is confessed by faith to "go to prepare a place" for us among the many places within God's own dwelling (John 14:1–3) is indeed the One whose love is acknowledged to be that of the Good Shepherd who "calls his own sheep by name" (John 10:3), then corporate identity in this instance can never be said to involve a loss of personal identity. Only when it is forgotten Whose resurrection and life it is (John 11:25) that makes provision of a place for us can eternal life be thought of merely as an objective immortality, a cumulative residue of lingering influence perhaps, but with no individual consciousness or the recalling in glory of one's own irreplaceable life story and name.

The disbeliefs entailed in Christian eschatological doctrine when read as an accounting for hope obviously provide no chronology, or geography, or census of the life of the world to come. When all is said and done faith rests upon the sole promise of God, "My grace is sufficient for you" (2 Cor. 12:9), and perseveres on through this life in the face of death by ever refusing to believe that the One whose love has begun so good a work among us here and now will fail to bring it to fulfillment at the day of Jesus Christ (Phil. 1:6).

Proposed Disbeliefs

The disbeliefs of Christian faith in the life to come, as proposed for recognition in the foregoing interpretation, include the following proscribed claims:

1. that there is no trustworthy future facing us in coming events wherever and whenever we are.
2. that the true hope for the life to come does not lead to active engagement in the work of love here and now.
3. that the future is something any of us have the power to guarantee to another, including those whom we love the most.
4. that the coming future, whatever it holds, is not subject to God's own promised commitment to redemption.
5. that the coming future of redemption is subject to human prediction and projection.
6. that God's judgment of damnation to hell is not an eternal rejection.
7. that God's judgment of eternal rejection is not subject to God's gift of eternal life in Jesus Christ.
8. that there is a human solidarity in sin that is not also a solidarity in grace.
9. that what is ultimately defeated and rejected is ever other than the opposition, in whatever personal and corporate form of denial, betrayal, and crucifixion it takes, to being loved into freedom.

10. that the grace of being loved into freedom ultimately stops coming or ceases to be.

11. that the resistance to grace is ever its cessation.

12. that the true hope of the life to come rests upon a capacity to avoid dying or to transcend the body.

13. that the resurrection hope for ourselves is somehow in ourselves, or in a part of ourselves that never dies.

14. that the resurrection from the dead is either the disembodiment of human life, or its isolation from the community of a world.

15. that the One whose love has begun so good a work among us here and now will fail to bring it to fulfillment at the day of Jesus Christ (Phil. 1:6).

Three of these proposed disbeliefs directly address the first initial objection, that it would seem to be the case that Christian affirmation of the life to come diminishes engagement with life here and now. If the interpretation just given is an acceptable one, the case has been made for the refusal of Christian faith to believe that the true hope for the life to come does not lead to active engagement in the work of love here and now. That work may take as many forms as there are various gifts of the Holy Spirit, and certainly includes a contemplative life of prayer and asceticism that is not merely self-absorbed but concerned with the work of love for others.[43] Further, the disavowal is implicit in Christian confession of the life to come of any spirit or spirituality which claims that the true hope of such life rests upon a capacity to transcend the body. This is reiterated in the recognition that any resurrection from the dead as either the disembodiment of human life, or its isolation from the community of a world, is not credited as trustworthy or given credence in the testimony of Christian faith.

The second initial objection, that it would seem to be the case that church teaching regarding the final judgment renders the situation of much of the world hopeless, finds a response in a number of the proposed disbeliefs, but most particularly in the recognition of faith's refusal to believe that what is ultimately defeated and rejected is ever other than the opposition, in whatever personal and corporate form of denial, betrayal, and crucifixion it takes, to being loved into freedom. The alternative often posed between either affirming an eternal rejection, or affirming that grace comes to all, is shown to be a faithless reading of the gospel message. Both positions are attested in the import of the gospel witness. The rejection by God of all that stands in the way of creation being loved into freedom is eternal, but the denial, betrayal, and crucifixion of grace does not prevent its resurrection, or defeat its coming, even in a descent into hell. Such rejection is forever subject to the eternal life at hand in the coming of Jesus Christ that is confessed as God's own promised commitment to redemption.

The arrival of faith as awareness of and receptivity to the coming of God's grace that is at hand, and when it arrives for some and not for others, is held in the gospel accounts not to be determinable by this world's clocks and calendars, or by our human projections and predictions regarding the limits of any lifetime. There is gospel testimony to a closed door of rejection for all "evildoers" where the doing of evil will try to enter and not be able (Luke 13:22–27), and of the foolish bridesmaids who were not ready with sufficient light in their lamps when the bridegroom arrived to accompany him into the wedding banquet, "and the door was shut" (Matt. 25:1–13). There is also gospel testimony of the Risen Christ coming to breathe the Holy Spirit upon disciples locked in a room with fear, and "although the doors were shut, Jesus came and stood among them and said, 'Peace be with you' " (John 20:19–22, 26). Faith in a steadfast love that endures forever in a dominion of resurrection that is confessed to "have no end" looks upon no situation as hopeless.

The third initial objection, that it would seem to be the case that Christian doctrine concerning the future is incoherent as a confession of hope, is addressed most especially by the refusal of faith to believe either that the coming future, whatever it holds, is not subject to God's own promised commitment to redemption, or that the coming future of redemption is subject to human prediction and projection.

A distinction is to be recognized between the uses of the term "hope" in referring to God and in referring to an anthropological characteristic. The former, as in God or Christ "our hope," is a usage that is held not to entail uncertainty in Christian faith. The latter, our hoping, insofar as it refers to knowing *something* one expects, does entail an element of uncertainty: "What we will be has not yet been revealed" (1 John 3:2). Thomas Aquinas, for his part, explains that hope has a *duplex* object, "one being the future good a person expects to get, the other, the help of someone to make getting it possible."[44] Thus, in Christian hope we have no certainty about the first, what the not yet revealed future holds; but Christian hope does confess to a certainty about the second, that is, Who holds the future: "What we do know is this: when he [Jesus Christ] is revealed, we will be like him, for we will see him as he is. And all who have this hope in him purify themselves, just as he is pure" (1 John 3:2–3). Incoherence arises in accounting for hope, as it is attested in the context of Christian thanksgiving, in terms either of possibility or of probability. In biblical tradition, by contrast with Aristotelian tradition, neither possibility nor probability, but rather promise, is affirmed as the basis of all hope. The confident certainty of hope in God and God's coming kingdom derives not from an estimate of the possibilities or probabilities apparent in things that now appear. But what the promised kingdom will be like, how the vindication of God's righteousness in the Crucified and Risen Christ will manifest itself in the fulfillment of our destinies when Christ comes to meet us in glory, faith is not given to know.

The call of the gospel not to believe every spirit, and to persevere in testing them to see whether they are of God, thus leads to the confessing of eternal hope always within the sound of Rachel's voice. In the end every disbelief we come to recognize of the lurking lie that may seek harbor in what is true in the church's doctrine amounts to the one refusal by God's grace to believe anything that denies that "neither death, nor life, nor angels, nor rulers, nor things present, nor things to come, nor powers, nor height, nor depth, nor anything else in all creation, will be able to separate us from the love of God in Christ Jesus our Lord" (Rom. 8:38–39).

NOTES

Preface to the First Edition

1. As quoted in Mary Bosanquet, *The Life and Death of Dietrich Bonhoeffer* (New York: Harper & Row, 1968), 83. For the original source see Dietrich Bonhoeffer, *Gesammelte Schriften,* 2d ed. (Munich: Chr. Kaiser Verlag, 1960), 1:76–77.

Chapter 1. The Call to Faithful Disbelief

1. M. C. D'Arcy, S.J., *The Nature of Belief* (London: Sheed and Ward, 1931), 15.
2. "Only Believe," copyright 1921 by Paul Rader, assigned to the Rodeheaver Company, in *Hymns for the Family of God* (Nashville: Paragon Assoc., 1976), 585.
3. Alfred, Lord Tennyson, *In Memoriam*, pt. 96, stanza 3, in *The Works of Tennyson*, vol. 3, ed. Hallam, Lord Tennyson (1908; Westport, Conn.: Greenwood Press, 1970), 138.
4. Paul Tillich, *Dynamics of Faith* (New York: Harper and Brothers, 1957), 22.
5. Karl Barth, *Evangelical Theology: An Introduction* (Garden City, N.Y.: Anchor Books, Doubleday, 1963), 117.
6. See Richard H. Popkin, *The History of Skepticism from Erasmus to Spinoza* (Berkeley: University of California Press, 1979).
7. See Van Austin Harvey, *The Historian and the Believer: The Morality of Historical Knowledge and Christian Belief* (New York: Macmillan, 1966). More recently Nicholas Wolterstorff has argued that "our beliefs are rational unless we have reason for refraining; they are not nonrational unless we have reason *for* believing." Wolterstorff, *Faith and Rationality* (Notre Dame: University of Notre Dame Press, 1983), 163.
8. John Locke, *An Essay Concerning Human Understanding* (1690). John Henry Newman, *An Essay in Aid of a Grammar of Assent* (1870; Notre Dame:

University of Notre Dame Press, 1983). Newman clearly favors assent over dissent and sees no necessity within the "grammar" of faith for giving any special attention to the subject of disbelief. "If he [one] disbelieves, or dissents, he [one] is assenting to the contradictory of the thesis" (chap. 1, rubric 1, par. 2, p. 27). Thus in this essay Newman does not consider the significance of not believing precisely as an expression of faith in God. We shall return, however, to look at another side of Newman later.

9. Samuel Taylor Coleridge, *Biographia Literaria* (New York: Leavitt, Lord and Co., 1834), chap. 14, par. 2, p. 174. Coleridge writes of "that willing suspension of disbelief for the moment which constitutes poetic faith."

10. See Raymond E. Brown, S.S., *Anchor Commentary, The Epistles of John* (Garden City, N.Y.: Doubleday, 1982), esp. 486–510.

11. See, for example, E. Garth Moore, *Try the Spirits: Christianity and Psychical Research* (New York: Oxford University Press, 1977).

12. Brown argues that the Pauline testing of spirits as a discernment of charisms (see 1 Cor. 12:10) has "nothing to do" with the Johannine distinguishing between God's Spirit as opposed to the Evil Spirit. See Brown, *Anchor Commentary*, 489 and 503. The differences should be recognized. Notwithstanding, in both the Johannine and Pauline contexts testing and discernment involve a call of faith to some refusal.

13. References to Rachel appear in Genesis 29–31, 33, 35, 46, and 48:7; Ruth 4:11; 1 Sam. 10:2; Jer. 31:15; and Matt. 2:18. An earlier synopsis of my reflections on Rachel appears in Morse, "Celebrating the Incarnation," in *Social Themes of the Christian Year: A Commentary on the Lectionary*, ed. Dieter T. Hessel (Philadelphia: Geneva Press, 1983), 53–55. For the importance of Hebrew midrashic accounts of Rachel see Susan E. Brown-Gutoff, "The Voice of Rachel in Jeremiah 31: A Calling to 'Something New,'" *Union Seminary Quarterly Review* 45 (1991): 177–90. See also Samuel H. Dresney, *Rachel* (Minneapolis: Fortress, 1994).

14. Other traditions place Rachel's tomb north of Jerusalem "in the territory of Benjamin at Zelzah" (1 Sam. 10:2). Matthew's Gospel, however, locates Rachel's voice heard in Ramah with what occurs at Jesus' birth "in and around Bethlehem" (Matt. 2:16–18).

15. I am indebted to my colleague James Cone for first calling my attention to the words of the African American spiritual as adapted in the freedom movement of the 1960s. "Over My Head," *We Shall Overcome! Songs of the Southern Freedom Movement*, compiled by Guy and Candie Carawan (New York: Oak Publications, 1963), 75.

> Over my head, I see freedom in the air.
> Over my head, Oh, Lord, I see freedom in the air.
> Over my head, I see freedom in the air.
> There must be a God somewhere.

16. Any attempt to stereotype so-called female piety as passive suffering is rebutted by the scriptural characterization of Rachel's active refusal. As Dorothy Martyn has reminded me, the poet Emily Dickinson understood: "To relieve the irreparable degrades it." *The Letters of Emily Dickinson*, ed. Thomas H. Johnson (Cambridge: Belknap Press of Harvard University, 1958), 602.

17. For a retelling of the Nativity drawn from Luther's own accounts, see *The Martin Luther Christmas Book*, trans. and arr. Roland H. Bainton (Philadelphia: Westminster, 1948), 74.

18. Leo Tolstoy, *Confession* (orig. published 1885; New York: W. W. Norton, 1983), 88–91.

19. Oscar Cullmann, *The Earliest Confessions* (London: Lutterworth Press, 1949), 27–30.

20. Roland Bainton, *Early Christianity* (Princeton: Van Nostrand, 1960), 21–22.

Chapter 2. Theology as the Task of Faithful Disbelief

1. For the history of the concept of theology as a critical discipline of the church and of the term "dogmatics," consult the following: Yves M.-J. Congar, O.P., *A History of Theology* (Garden City, N.Y.: Doubleday, 1968); Gerhard Ebeling, *The Study of Theology* (Philadelphia: Fortress Press, 1978); also by Ebeling, *Theology and Proclamation: Dialogue with Bultmann* (Philadelphia: Fortress Press, 1966), especially the appendix, "The Meaning of the Word 'Dogmatics,'" 109–13; and *"Theologie,"* in *Die Religion in Geschichte und Gegenwart* (Tübingen: J. C. B. Mohr [Paul Siebeck], 1962), 6:754–69; G. R. Evans, *Old Arts and New Theology: The Beginnings of Theology as an Academic Discipline* (New York: Oxford University Press, 1980); Edward Farley, *Theologia* (Philadelphia: Fortress Press, 1983); F. Kattenbusch, "Die Entstehung einer christlichen Theologie," *Zeitschrift für Theologie und Kirche* (NF) 11 (1930), 161–205; Wolfhart Pannenberg, *Theology and the Philosophy of Science* [*Wissenschaftstheorie und Theologie*] (Philadelphia: Westminster Press, 1976); Karl Rahner, "Theology," and "Dogmatics," *Encyclopedia of Theology: The Concise Sacramentum Mundi* (New York: Seabury Press, 1975), 1686–1701 and 366–370; Gerhard Sauter, ed., *Theologie Als Wissenschaft* (Munich: Chr. Kaiser Verlag, 1971).

2. Tertullian, "Quid ergo Athenis et Hierosolymis? Quid Academiae et Ecclesiae?" See *Liber De Praescriptionibus Adversus Haereticos*, chap. 7, a writing dated c. 200 C.E.

3. Aristotle, *Metaphysics* B 1000a 9.

4. Ibid., E 1026a. 10ff., and K 1064b 3.

5. In book 8 of *The City of God* Augustine looks further at natural theology. Insofar as the philosophers glimpsed the distinction between the creation and the Creator their wisdom may be said to approach that of Christianity. The Platonists come closest. But, Augustine concludes, all true philosophy is subject to the knowledge of God that comes through the one Mediator who is both God and human, Jesus Christ. See Augustine, *The City of God*, bk. 11, chap. 2, in the series The Nicene and Post-Nicene Fathers, 1st ser., ed. Philip Schaff (hereafter NPNF 1), vol. 2 (Grand Rapids, Mich.: Eerdmans, 1886; rpt. 1979): "For this is the Mediator between God and men, the man Christ Jesus. For it is as man that He is the Mediator and the Way... Now the only way that is

infallibly secured against all mistakes, is when the very same person is at once God and man, God our end, man our way."

6. See Augustine, *The City of God*, bk. 6, where he discusses the three types of accounts given of the gods in pagan writings: theology as dramatic fable or mythology, as natural philosophy or metaphysics, and as political ideology.

7. John of Damascus, *De Fide Orthodoxa*, bk. 1, chap. 4, in the series The Nicene and Post-Nicene Fathers, 2d ser., ed. Philip Schaff and Henry Wace (hereafter NPNF 2), vol. 9 (Grand Rapids, Mich.: Eerdmans, 1898; rpt. 1979): "In the case of God . . . it is impossible to explain what He is in His essence, and it befits us the rather to hold discourse about His absolute separation from all things." An alternative translation is given in a footnote: "It is more in accordance with the nature of the case rather to discourse of Him in the way of abstracting from Him all that belongs to us."

8. Thomas Aquinas, *On the Truth of the Catholic Faith: Summa Contra Gentiles*, bk. 1, chap. 14 (Garden City, N.Y.: Image Books, Doubleday, 1955), 96.

9. Ibid., 96–97.

10. See n. 7 above. The articulation of this principle apparently did not lead either John or Aquinas to question their references to God as "He" and "Him."

11. Critics of Augustine have often argued that the Neoplatonist influence upon his theology with respect to his characterization of God's being as impassible and timeless cancels out the incarnational emphasis. See, for example, Daniel Day Williams, *The Spirit and the Forms of Love* (New York: Harper and Row, 1968), chap. 5.

12. The *via negativa* as an aspect of mystical contemplation is a subject not addressed by these brief remarks. Clearly, if the way of negation is taken to mean a mode of spiritual awareness beyond all differentiation it would not be akin to faithful disbelief.

13. Karl Barth, *Church Dogmatics* (hereafter *CD*) I/2, ed. G. W. Bromiley and T. F. Torrance (German orig., 1939; Edinburgh: T. and T. Clark, 1956), 631.

14. Ibid., 630.

15. For the view that the antiheresy factor is the primary one in the way the Creed came to be formulated see Arthur Cushman McGiffert, *The Apostles' Creed: Its Origin, Its Purpose, and Its Historical Interpretation* (New York: Scribner's, 1902). Others have argued that the polemical factor of countering false belief was secondary to the positive setting forth of the faith for catechetical instruction. See Adolf von Harnack, *The Apostles' Creed* (London: Adam and Charles Black, 1901) and J. N. D. Kelly, *Early Christian Creeds* (London: Longmans, Green, 1950). The problem with this position is the omission of uncontested material important for catechesis; for example, the preexistence of Christ, the ministry and teaching of Jesus, ethical instruction, and the Kingdom of God. At any rate, the polemical factor in expressing faithful refusals cannot be denied.

16. This second-century treatise by Irenaeus, Bishop of Lyons, was entitled *Adversus Haereses: Refutation and Overthrow of the Knowledge Falsely So Called*. See the series Ante-Nicene Fathers, ed. Alexander Roberts and James

Donaldson (hereafter ANF) (Grand Rapids, Mich.: Eerdmans, 1885; rpt. 1981), vol. 1.

17. 2 Constantinople (553), 3 Constantinople (680–681), and 2 Nicaea (787).

18. See Paul Tillich, *Systematic Theology*, 3 vols. (Chicago: University of Chicago Press, 1951–63), 1:32.

19. Adolf von Harnack, *History of Dogma* (New York: Dover Publications, 1961), 1:17.

20. Adolf von Harnack, "Fifteen Questions to Those among the Theologians Who Are Contemptuous of the Scientific Theology," in *The Beginnings of Dialectic Theology*, ed. James M. Robinson (1923; Richmond: John Knox Press, 1968), 165–66. The culprit in Harnack's eyes was the early work of Karl Barth, a former student. See their open exchange of letters in this volume.

21. The ecumenical acceptance of this position is not denied by the proviso that in Roman Catholicism the explicit decree when rightly promulgated and rightly elucidated is held to be inerrantly God's decree (*infallibility*), or that in other Christian communions the ultimate or eschatological *indefectability* of the Church's witness to the saving import of the gospel is affirmed.

22. Friedrich Schleiermacher defined the latter task as "Church Statistics," a subject taken less seriously by many of his successors in academic theology than a critical dogmatics requires. See Schleiermacher, *Brief Outline of Theology as a Field of Study*, trans. and ed. Terrence N. Tice (1811; rev. 1830; (Lewiston/Queenston/Lampeter: Edwin Mellen, 1990), rubrics 232–50, pp. 117–26.

23. Thomas Aquinas, *Summa Theologiae* 1a. 1.

24. Martin Luther, "Disputation Held at Heidelberg, April 26th, 1518," rubrics 19–22, in *Luther: Early Theological Works*, Library of Christian Classics (hereafter LCC) (Philadelphia: Westminster Press, 1962), 16:290–92.

25. Immanuel Kant, "What Is Enlightenment?" [1784], in *The Enlightenment: A Comprehensive Anthology*, ed. Peter Gay (New York: Simon and Schuster, 1973), 384–89.

26. Ibid.

27. See Schleiermacher, *Brief Outline of Theology as a Field of Study.* Also, Schleiermacher, *The Christian Faith*, ed. H. R. Mackintosh and J. S. Stewart (orig. published 1830; Edinburgh: T. and T. Clark, 1928), rubrics 1–31.

28. Schleiermacher, *The Christian Faith*, rubrics 32–35.

29. See Friedrich D. E. Schleiermacher, *On the Glaubenslehre: Two Letters to Dr. Lücke*, trans. James Duke and Francis Fiorenza, AAR Texts and Translations 3 (Chico, Calif.: Scholars Press, 1981).

30. Parts of the following paragraphs on Troeltsch and Barth have earlier appeared in journal articles. See Christopher Morse, "The Future of Karl Barth's Theology," *Dialog* 20, no. 1 (Winter 1981): 9–14; and Morse, "Grace in Karl Barth's World and Ours," *Katallagete* 8, no. 2 (Spring 1983): 23–28.

31. Ernst Troeltsch, "Half a Century of Theology: A Review," in *Ernst Troeltsch: Writings on Theology and Religion*, ed. Robert Morgan and Michael Pye (Atlanta: John Knox Press, 1977), 53–81.

32. Ernst Troeltsch, "The Significance of the Historical Existence of Jesus for Faith," in *Ernst Troeltsch*, 199.

33. Ernst Troeltsch, "The Dogmatics of the 'Religionsgeschichtliche Schule,'" *American Journal of Theology* 17, no. 1 (January 1913): 1–21. Another translation appears in *Religion in History*, ed. James Luther Adams (Minneapolis: Fortress Press, 1991), 87–108.

34. Ernst Troeltsch, "The Significance of the Historical Existence of Jesus for Faith," 189.

35. Ibid., 205.

36. Troeltsch, "The Dogmatics of the 'Religionsgeschichtliche Schule,'" 12.

37. Ibid., 10.

38. Karl Barth, *Theology and Church* (New York: Harper and Row, 1962), 61.

39. For an assessment see Sarah Coakley, *Christ without Absolutes: A Study of the Christology of Ernst Troeltsch* (Oxford: Clarendon Press, 1988).

40. Barth, *Theology and Church,* 61.

41. Karl Barth, "The Need and Promise of Christian Preaching" (1922) and "The Word of God and the Task of the Ministry" (1922), in *The Word of God and the Word of Man*, trans. Douglas Horton (New York: Harper Torchbooks, 1957), 101–2, 185–86.

42. See George Hunsinger, ed. and trans., *Karl Barth and Radical Politics* (Philadelphia: Westminster Press, 1976).

43. See Eberhard Busch, *Karl Barth: His Life from Letters and Autobiographical Texts* (Philadelphia: Fortress Press, 1976), 81.

44. Karl Barth, "The Righteousness of God" (1916), in *The Word of God and the Word of Man*, 20.

45. Karl Barth, "The Strange New World within the Bible" (1916), in *The Word of God and the Word of Man*, 28–50.

46. For my own reflections on this particular point see Christopher Morse, "Raising God's Eyebrows: Some Further Thoughts on the Concept of the *Analogia Fidei*," *Union Seminary Quarterly Review* 37, nos. 1–2 (Fall/Winter 1981–82): 39–49.

47. See Barth, *CD* IV/3, first half (German orig., 1959; Edinburgh: T. and T. Clark, 1961), 38–165.

48. See K. C. Abraham, ed., *Third World Theologies* (Maryknoll, N.Y.: Orbis, 1990); Robert McAfee Brown, *Gustavo Gutiérrez: An Introduction to Liberation Theology* (Maryknoll, N.Y.: Orbis, 1990); Curt Cadorette, Marie Giblin, Marilyn J. Legge, and Mary Hembrow Snyder, eds., *Liberation Theology: An Introductory Reader* (Maryknoll, N.Y.: Orbis, 1992); Rebecca C. Chopp, *The Praxis of Suffering* (Maryknoll, N.Y.: Orbis, 1986); Deane William Ferm, *Third World Liberation Theologies: A Reader* (Maryknoll, N.Y.: Orbis, 1986); Alfred T. Hennelly, S.J., *Liberation Theology: A Documentary History* (Maryknoll, N.Y.: Orbis, 1990); Arthur F. McGovern, *Liberation Theology and Its Critics: Toward an Assessment* (Maryknoll, N.Y.: Orbis, 1989); Aloysius Pieris, *An Asian Theology of Liberation* (Maryknoll, N.Y.: Orbis, 1988); Christopher Rowland, ed. *The Cambridge Companion to Liberation Theology,* 2nd ed. (Cambridge, UK: Cambridge University Press, 2007); and Josiah U. Young, *Black and African Theologies* (Maryknoll, N.Y.: Orbis, 1986).

49. See John W. de Gruchy and Charles Villa-Vicencio, eds., *Apartheid Is a Heresy* (Grand Rapids, Mich.: Eerdmans, 1983), 168–73, and Peter Matheson,

ed., *The Third Reich and the Christian Churches* (Grand Rapids, Mich.: Eerdmans, 1981), 45–47. For a full text of the Synod of Barmen see Arthur C. Cochrane, *The Church's Confession under Hitler* (Philadelphia: Westminster Press, 1962), 237–42. We shall look further at the Barmen Confession in chapter 3.

50. Influential in this area has been the work of David Tracy. See, for one example, *The Analogical Imagination: Christian Theology and the Culture of Pluralism* (New York: Crossroad, 1981), 3–46.

51. See, for example, George A. Lindbeck, *The Nature of Doctrine: Religion and Theology in a Postliberal Age* (Philadelphia: Westminster Press, 1984).

52. See, for examples, William C. Placher, *Unapologetic Theology: A Christian Voice in a Pluralistic Conversation* (Louisville, Ky.: Westminster/John Knox Press, 1989); also, Francis Schüssler Fiorenza, *Foundational Theology: Jesus and the Church* (New York: Crossroad, 1984). For still a further perspective, see John Milbank, *Theology and Social Theory: Beyond Secular Reason,* 2nd ed. (Oxford, UK: Blackwell, 2006) and *The Word Made Strange: Theology, Language, Culture* (Oxford, UK: Blackwell, 1997).

Chapter 3. Testing the Spirits Today

1. Dietrich Bonhoeffer, "Was soll der Student der Theologie heute tun?" 1933, *Gesammelte Schriften*, 2d ed., 3:243–47. "Er soll sich durch sein Studium bereit machen, die Geister in der Kirche Christi zu prüfen," 246.

2. See the articles on the Inquisition in the *Encyclopaedia Britannica*, 11th ed. (Cambridge: At the University Press, 1910), and in J. D. Douglas, general ed., *The New International Dictionary of the Christian Church*, (Grand Rapids, Mich.: Zondervan, 1974). Also see the entry under "Congregation for the Doctrine of the Faith" in *New Catholic Encyclopedia* (New York: McGraw-Hill, 1967), 4:944–46.

3. Note especially the strong emphasis on this point in *The Road to Damascus: Kairos and Conversion*, 28 pages, published as "a document signed by Third World Christians from El Salvador, Guatemala, Korea, Namibia, Nicaragua, Philippines, and South Africa" who are "theologians and church leaders belonging to a broad spectrum of Christian traditions" (Washington, D.C.: Center of Concern, 1989).

4. Matheson, ed., *The Third Reich and the Christian Churches*, 4–6.

5. Ibid., 39.

6. See J. S. Conway, *The Nazi Persecution of the Churches, 1933–1945* (London: Weidenfeld and Nicolson, 1968), 364–65.

7. Matheson, ed., *The Third Reich and the Christian Churches*, 24.

8. For the complete text of the Barmen Declaration in English translation see Cochrane, *The Church's Confession under Hitler*, 237–42.

9. The quotations from Barmen cited here are taken from the 1984 fiftieth-anniversary translation by Douglas S. Bax as contained in *Karl Barth: Theologian of Freedom*, ed. Clifford Green (London: Collins, 1989), 148–51.

10. The expression "axial moment" comes from Frederick Herzog; see his article, "Theology of Liberation," *Continuum* 7 (Winter 1970): 515. I have discussed the significance of this moment for American theology in "God's Promise

as Presence," in *Love: The Foundation of Hope*, ed. Frederic B. Burnham, Charles S. McCoy, and M. Douglas Meeks (San Francisco: Harper and Row, 1988), 143–57.

11. See de Gruchy and Villa-Vicencio, eds., *Apartheid Is a Heresy.*

12. Newman, *An Essay in Aid of a Grammar of Assent*, chap. 4, rubric 2, par. 3, p. 78.

13. This is the heresy known as "docetism," from the Greek verb *dokein*, meaning that the humanity of Jesus Christ only "seemed" or "appeared" to be actual.

14. Brown, *Anchor Commentary*, 58–59. Brown notes a similarity between the language of 1 John 4:2 and that of Ignatius with regard to false teachers, but he argues that the docetic positions being opposed in each case are distinguishable. "The issue is not that the secessionists are denying the incarnation or the physical reality of Jesus' humanity; they are denying that what Jesus was or did in the flesh was related to his being the Christ, i.e., was salvific" (p. 505). The distinction would not appear to represent a significant difference, however, as far as Ignatius's own writings are concerned, for his objection to the docetists is precisely on the issue of salvation.

15. See Ignatius, *Epistle to the Trallians*, chap. 10, and *Epistle to the Smyrnaeans*, chaps. 2, 5.

16. Ignatius, *Epistle to the Smyrnaeans*, chap. 5.

17. This is consistent with the canonical writings generally. "Not every one who says to me, 'Lord, Lord,' shall [by so doing] enter the kingdom of heaven" (Matt. 7:21). "Why do you call me 'Lord, Lord,' and not do what I tell you?" (Luke 6:46). "This people honors me with their lips, but their heart is far from me" (Matt. 15:8, see Isa. 29:13). "If you confess with your lips that Jesus is Lord and believe in your heart that God raised him from the dead, you will be saved" (Rom. 10:9).

18. See Martinus C. de Boer, "The Death of Jesus Christ and His Coming in the Flesh (1 John 4:2)," *Novum Testamentum* 33 (October 1991): 326–46. "The use of the term 'flesh' in 1 John 4:2 . . . figuratively emphasizes the *concreteness* or *tangibility* of Jesus Christ's effective saving action, of his 'coming' . . . Discipleship is to be just as concrete or tangible" (p. 345).

19. Martin Luther, *Lectures on the First Epistle of St. John*, Luther's Works, vol. 3, ed. Jaroslav Pelikan, assoc. ed. Walter A. Hansen (St. Louis: Concordia, 1967), 285.

20. John Calvin, *The Gospel according to St. John 11–21 and the First Epistle of John*, Calvin's Commentaries, ed. David W. Torrance and Thomas F. Torrance (Edinburgh: Oliver and Boyd, 1961), 286.

21. *En sarki* ("in the flesh") here is not to be confused with *kata sarka* ("after the flesh," or "according to the flesh") in the Pauline writings. See 2 Cor. 5:16b, "Even though we once regarded Christ *kata sarka*, we regard him thus no longer." See also Rom. 8:3–4, "Sending his own Son in the likeness of sinful flesh [*en homoiōmati sarkos hamartias*] and for sin, [God] condemned sin in the flesh [*en ta sarki*], in order that the just requirement of the law might be fulfilled in us, who walk not *kata sarka* but according to the Spirit." Here where "flesh" is equated with sinfulness Paul writes that "those who are *en sarki* cannot please God" (Rom. 8:8). Paul's reference to "in the cross" is his

nearest equivalent, *mutatis mutandis*, to the positive Johannine sense of "in the flesh." See Gal. 6:14, "But far be it from me to glory except in the cross [*en tǭ staurǭ*] of our Lord Jesus Christ." We shall develop this point in chapter 8. The decisive salvific coming of Jesus Christ into the flesh and blood sufferings of creation is thus equally given primary affirmation, though in quite distinctive ways, in both the Johannine and Pauline traditions. For further discussion of Pauline references to the term *sarx* see Rudolf Bultmann, *Theology of the New Testament* (New York: Scribner's, 1951), 1:232–39. In this connection note the reference to Martin Luther in Paul Althaus, *The So-called Kerygma and the Historical Jesus* (London: Oliver and Boyd, 1959), 36: "Luther says that Christ is indeed known *in carne*, but not *secundum carnem.*" For the documentation cited see *D. Martin Luther's Werke* (hereafter *WA*) (Weimar: Herman Böhlau, 1901), 23:734.

22. This is not to say that Barth, for his part, has solved all the problems of testing the spirits. To claim, as Barth does, that the Word of God as the sole criterion for all such testing in dogmatics is a happening, or an event, continuing to take place apart from all human prediction or control, is to define "criterion" in a way that, as Barth himself readily acknowledges, is not humanly applicable. If such an eventfulness is the only "dogma as such," as Barth maintains, it is, in the view of one critic, "a quite nebulous thing, which the historian of dogma, at any rate, finds of little use." See Bernhard Lohse, *A Short History of Christian Doctrine* (Philadelphia: Fortress Press, 1966), 6. Few, however, have recognized as profoundly the problems involved in dogmatic testing as has Barth.

23. The first recorded use of the anathema in conciliar decrees is generally held to be found in the canons of the Spanish Council of Elvira, c. 306. The apostasy and profligacy of the clergy were made subject to radical condemnation and reprisal. In time the declaration of the anathema as a judgment of rejection came to be invested with ritualistic ceremony. "Acc. to the Pontifical ('*Ordo excommunicandi et absolvendi*'), sentence is pronounced by the Bishop, vested in a purple cope and surrounded by twelve priests who bear lighted candles, which are thrown to the ground when sentence has been uttered," *The Oxford Dictionary of the Christian Church*, 2d ed., ed. F. L. Cross, rev. F. L. Cross and E. A. Livingstone (Oxford: Oxford University Press, 1978), 50. More generally, in the history of doctrine the *anathema sit* is applied to heresy and its representatives.

24. As cited in Hans-Werner Gensichen, *We Condemn: How Luther and Sixteenth-century Lutheranism Condemned False Doctrine* (St. Louis: Concordia, 1967), 65. See also p. 19. The German original is *Damnamus* (Berlin: Lutherisches Verlagshaus, 1955). Quoted from Luther *WA* 33 (1907), 365, 8.

25. The Greek word means both a household and its keeping, from which the English word "economy" is derived.

26. For a contemporary theological reappropriation of this term see M. Douglas Meeks, *God the Economist: The Doctrine of God and Political Economy* (Minneapolis: Fortress Press, 1989). Studies of the history of the term are indicated by Meeks on p. 186, n. 4.

Chapter 4. Tests of Doctrinal Faithfulness

1. See William A. Christian, Sr.'s analysis of "governing doctrines" as the rules by which a community accounts for and regulates the statements of its beliefs and practices ("primary doctrines"), in his *Doctrines of Religious Communities: A Philosophical Study* (New Haven: Yale University Press, 1987).

2. "The Longer Catechism of the Orthodox, Catholic, Eastern Church," promulgated in Moscow in 1839, rubric 275, in *The Creeds of Christendom*, ed. Philip Schaff, rev. David S. Schaff (hereafter *Creeds*) (New York: Harper and Row, 1931; rpt., Grand Rapids, Mich.: Baker Book House, 1983), 2:489.

3. There are no exact English equivalents for the Greek verbal forms, "I traditioned," or "I gospeled," used, for instance, by Paul in 1 Cor. 15:1: "Now I would remind you, brothers and sisters, how I gospeled the gospel to you [*to euangelion ho euengēlisamen hymin*]," and in 1 Cor. 15:3: "For I traditioned [*paredōka*] to you as of first importance what I also received." The English translation of the New Testament verb "to gospel" is usually given as "to proclaim" or "to preach," neither of which suggests the inseparability of the medium and the message, or better, of the mission and the message, that Paul's original redundancy of "I gospeled the gospel" conveys. That the English derivative, "to evangelize," deviates from the original sense is apparent from the fact that in English the Apostle could not have said, "I evangelized the evangel." This alien English sense may help to explain why so-called evangelism in some denominations is so often mistakenly identified with proselytizing and with strategies for denominational expansion.

4. See Barth, *CD* II/2, ed. G. W. Bromiley and T. F. Torrance (German orig., 1942; Edinburgh: T. and T. Clark, 1957), 458–506.

5. In the second century "the tradition which has come down from the apostles" is said, in the words of Irenaeus, to be "guarded by the successions of elders [*presbyteroi*] in the churches." *Against Heresies*, bk. 3, sec. 2, p. 371. The distinction between presbyters and bishops [*episcopoi*] is not clearly drawn, the point being simply that "in this very order and succession the apostolic tradition in the Church and the preaching of the truth has come down even to us" (p. 373). Who counts as the rightful successors, however, and thus as the guardians or, some would say, guarantors of apostolicity has often been disputed in the history of the church.

6. "And he who sat upon the throne said, 'Behold, I make all things new'" (Rev. 21:5). "'I am the Alpha and the Omega,' says the Lord God, who is and who was and who is to come, the Almighty" (Rev. 1:8).

7. The Second Helvetic Confession, issued in 1566 by Heinrich Bullinger, successor of Zwingli in Zurich, at the request of Frederick III, chap. 2, point 5, in *Creeds*, 3:233–306, 831–909. John H. Leith writes, "The Second Helvetic Confession was widely accepted and can justly claim to be the most universal of Reformed creeds." See *Creeds of the Churches*, rev., ed. John H. Leith (Richmond: John Knox Press, 1973), 131.

8. "Epitome of the Articles," the Formula of Concord, in *Creeds*, 3:96.

9. See, for example, Wolfhart Pannenberg, "The Crisis of the Scripture Principle," in *Basic Questions in Theology* (Philadelphia: Fortress Press, 1970),

1:1–14. Pannenberg writes, "For Luther the literal sense of the Scriptures was still identical with their historical content... Luther could still identify his own doctrine with the content of the biblical writings, literally understood" (p. 6). "The gulf between fact and significance, between history and kerygma, between the history of Jesus and the multiplicity of the New Testament witnesses to it, marks one side of the problem of theology today. On the other side is the equally deep gulf between the intellectual milieu of the New Testament texts and that of our own present age" (p. 8).

10. "The Thirty-nine Articles of Religion of the Church of England," 1562, article 6, in *Creeds*, 3:489. See also Christian, *Doctrines of Religious Communities*, 29.

11. The Westminster Confession of Faith, chap. 1, article 6, in *Creeds*, 3:603. See also Christian, *Doctrines of Religious Communities*, 29, 88–89.

12. For the Latin text see *Creeds*, 3:239. A better translation, and the one here quoted, appears in *The Constitution of the Presbyterian Church (U.S.A.)*, pt. 1, *Book of Confessions* (hereafter *Book of Confessions*) (New York: Office of the General Assembly, 1983), rubric 5.010.

13. This academic tendency is challenged by Brevard S. Childs's "canonical approach." See his *Old Testament Theology in a Canonical Context* (Philadelphia: Fortress Press, 1986), *The New Testament as Canon: An Introduction* (Philadelphia: Fortress Press, 1984), esp. 3–53, and *Biblical Theology of the Old and New Testaments* (Minneapolis: Fortress Press, 1992), 70–79.

14. For further discussion of the *analogia fidei* see chap. 7, pp. 122–124.

15. The quote comes from a letter from Harnack to Martin Rade dated January 20, 1929. See Martin Rumscheidt, *Revelation and Theology: An Analysis of the Barth-Harnack Correspondence of 1923* (Cambridge: At the University Press, 1972), 18.

16. Thomas Aquinas, *Summa Theologiae* 1a. 1, 10.

17. See *The Christian Faith in the Doctrinal Documents of the Catholic Church*, rev., ed. J. Neuner, S.J., and J. Dupuis, S.J. (New York: Alba House, 1982), rubrics 1212 and 1913, pp. 343, 549. For discussion see Geoffrey Wainwright, *Doxology: The Praise of God in Worship, Doctrine, and Life* (New York: Oxford University Press, 1980), 224–35.

18. See, for examples, Edmund Schlink, *The Coming Christ and the Coming Church* (Philadelphia: Fortress Press, 1968), 17–45; Pannenberg, *Basic Questions in Theology*, 1:182–238; Wainwright, *Doxology;* Daniel W. Hardy and David F. Ford, *Praising and Knowing God* (Philadelphia: Westminster Press, 1985).

19. The Second Helvetic Confession, chap. 23. Here quoted from *Book of Confessions*, p. 5.219.

20. Ibid., chap. 27, p. 5.241.

21. John Calvin, *Institutes of the Christian Religion* (orig. published 1559; Philadelphia: Westminster Press, 1960) LCC 21, ed. John T. McNeill (hereafter Calvin, *Institutes*), bk. 4, chap. 1, par. 9, p. 1023. See also the earlier Augsburg Confession of 1530, written by Philip Melanchthon and approved by Martin Luther, article 7, where the church is described as "the congregation of saints [the assembly of all believers], in which the Gospel is rightly taught [purely

preached] and the Sacraments rightly administered [according to the Gospel]." *Creeds*, 3:11–12.

22. See Calvin, *Institutes*, bk. 3, chap. 23, pars. 13–14 (LCC 21:461–64).

23. Ibid., par. 7 (LCC 21:955).

24. Ibid., bk. 2, chap. 8, par. 55 (LCC 20:419).

25. Ignatius, *Epistle to the Smyrnaeans*, chap. 8, v. 2. Ignatius, the third bishop of Antioch, was martyred c. 108 C.E.

26. Vincent of Lerins, *Commonitorium*, chap. 2. For an English translation see NPNF 2 (Grand Rapids, Mich.: Eerdmans, 1978), 11:132.

27. Augsburg Confession of 1530, article 22. See *Creeds*, 3:26–27.

28. "Epitome of the Articles," par. 2. See *Creeds*, 3:94–96. As noted earlier, the *Formula* subjects all "symbols and other writings" to the test of Holy Scripture.

29. The Second Helvetic Confession, chap. 2, in *Book of Confessions*, rubric 5.013.

30. Newman, *An Essay in Aid of a Grammar of Assent*, chap. 6, rubric 2, p. 163, and chap. 7, rubric 2, p. 181.

31. Newman was tolerant of superstition and discouraged its theological criticism lest the wheat be rooted up with the weeds.

> Galileo might be right in his conclusion that the earth moves; to consider him a heretic might have been wrong; but there was nothing wrong in censuring abrupt, startling, unsettling, unverified disclosures, if such they were, disclosures at once uncalled for and inopportune, at a time when the limits of revealed truth had not as yet been ascertained. . . . It was safe, not dishonest, to be slow in accepting what nevertheless turned out to be true. Here is an instance in which the Church obliges Scripture expositors, at a given time or place, to be tender of the popular religious sense.

John Henry Newman, *The Via Media of the Anglican Church*, 3d ed. (London, 1877), lv.

32. Augustine at the beginning of the fifth century begins the thirteen books of his *Confessions* with a prayer of praise that contains words which have come to provide the rationale for apologetics in theology: "Thou movest us to delight in praising Thee; for Thou hast formed us for Thyself, and our hearts are restless till they find rest in Thee." Apologists seek to link the gospel proclamation with some prior capacity or incapacity within the individual, in this case with human restlessness. The *cor inquietum* ("restless heart") theme occurs historically and today in numerous variations. Translation quoted from NPNF 1, vol. 1, chap. 1.

33. See Lee Cormie, "The Hermeneutical Privilege of the Oppressed: Liberation Theologies, Biblical Faith, and Marxist Sociology of Knowledge," *Proceedings of the Thirty-third Annual Convention of the Catholic Theological Society of America* 33 (1978), 155–81.

34. See, for example, the essays in *The Future of Empirical Theology*, ed. Bernard E. Meland (Chicago: University of Chicago Press, 1969).

35. Alfred North Whitehead, *Modes of Thought* (New York: Capricorn Books, 1938), lecture 8, p. 232. In this statement we see the precursor of ir-

reconcilable differences in self-styled experiential theological traditions between the metaphysical perspectives of Whitehead on the one hand, and the existential ontology of Heidegger and the phenomenology of Husserl on the other. The latter both emphasize the categorical gulf between the world of natural science and the distinctiveness of human intentionality and being; Whitehead's remark reveals his characteristic instinct to relate them. Heidegger, for his part, never achieved his stated goal in *Being and Time* of moving from an existential account of the distinctiveness of human being to an account of all being, a fundamental ontology. Whitehead, from the other side, has been criticized for allowing scientific models to govern his description of human conscious experience. See the conclusion of an early and appreciative interpreter: "We must ask whether this does justice to the difference introduced by consciousness, the significance of which Whitehead minimizes." Dorothy M. Emmet, *The Nature of Metaphysical Thinking* (London: Macmillan, 1957), 233.

36. See in this connection Richard Rorty, *Philosophy and the Mirror of Nature* (Princeton: Princeton University Press, 1979).

37. Cf. Schleiermacher, *The Christian Faith*, rubric 15, p. 76. See Lindbeck, *The Nature of Doctrine*. The debate continues in that Schleiermacher affirms the role of language and culture in shaping experience. Preaching produces experience, but what is preached is the redemptive experience of Christ's influence.

38. John Macquarrie writes that empiricism "fails when the attempt is made to apply it to personal life." *In Search of Humanity: A Theological and Philosophical Approach* (London: SCM, 1982), 41. See also Macquarrie, "The End of Empiricism?" *Union Seminary Quarterly Review* 37, nos. 1–2 (Fall/Winter 1981–82): 61–68.

39. Jürgen Moltmann, *Theology of Hope: On the Ground and the Implications of a Christian Eschatology* (New York: Harper and Row, 1967). For further discussion see Christopher Morse, *The Logic of Promise in Moltmann's Theology* (Philadelphia: Fortress Press, 1979), esp. 82–108, and "The Resurrection as Myth and as Fable: The Difference After Thirty Years," in Robert Morgan, ed. *In Search of Humanity and Deity: A Celebration of John Macquarrie's Theology* (London: SCM Press, 2006), 254–63.

40. *A Letter To The Author of 'The Enthusiasm of Methodists and Papists Compared,' The Right Reverend The Lord Bishop Lavington of Exeter* (1749), in *The Works of John Wesley*, vol. 9 (Grand Rapids, Mich.: Zondervan, 1958–59; reproduced by photo offset process from the authorized edition published by the Wesleyan Conference Office in London in 1872), 12. Important in this connection as well is Jonathan Edwards, *A Treatise Concerning Religious Affections*, ed. John E. Smith (orig. published 1749; New Haven: Yale University Press, 1959).

41. *The Works of John Wesley*, 5:472–73.

42. Ibid., 478. "The Spirit of God" is not a phrase empty of content for Wesley, as is apparent in words accompanying this statement. "Beware you are not a fiery, persecuting enthusiast. Do not imagine that God has called you (just contrary to the spirit of Him you style your Master) to destroy men's lives, and not to save them. Never dream of forcing men into the ways of God. Think yourself, and let think. Use no constraint in matters of religion. Even those

who are farthest out of the way never compel to come in by any other means than reason, truth, and love."

43. Ibid., 474.

44. Ibid., 417–18

45. Ibid., 421.

46. See n. 27 above.

47. The Westminster Confession of Faith, chap. 20, in *Creeds*, 3:644.

48. See *The Constitution of the Presbyterian Church (U.S.A.)*, pt. 2, *Book of Order* (New York: Office of the General Assembly, 1985), p. G-1.030l.

49. See *Dignitatis Humanae*, sec. 2, in *Christian Faith in the Doctrinal Documents*, ed. Neuner and Dupuis, rubric 2048, p. 604.

50. See *Christian Faith in the Doctrinal Documents*, ed. Neuner and Dupuis, sec. 16, rubric 2052, p. 605.

51. Ibid., 606.

52. See the summary article by Rudolf Hoffman on "Conscience" in the Roman Catholic *Encyclopedia of Theology: The Concise "Sacramentum Mundi,"* ed. Karl Rahner (New York: Seabury Press, 1975), 283–88. "For the overcoming of doubts of conscience there is need above all of prudence" (p. 288). For a critique of theories of conscience that focuses upon "the environment of decision," an environment that includes divine activity and not only anthropological and situational factors, as "the context for the ethical reality of conscience," see the more extensive discussion by Paul Lehmann in *Ethics in a Christian Context* (New York: Harper and Row, 1963), 285–367. The words in quotes are from p. 347. Suspicious of scholastic conceptions of prudence that in his view tend to constrict the prophetic discernment of divine action in the world, Lehmann, acknowledging the influence of Luther and Barth, argues for a "theonomous" conscience that is "immediately sensitive to the freedom of God to do in the always changing human situation what his humanizing aims and purposes require" (p. 358). In Lehmann's theological ethics the appeal to conscience becomes communal as a sensitizing and nurturing art of biblically contextual discernment. For more on Paul Lehmann see Nancy J. Duff, *Humanization and the Politics of God: The "Koinonia" Ethics of Paul Lehmann* (Grand Rapids, Mich.: Eerdmans, 1992).

53. William James, *The Varieties of Religious Experience*, Being the Gifford Lectures on Natural Religion Delivered at Edinburgh in 1901–1902 (New York: The Modern Library, 1936), lecture 1, p. 21.

54. *The Didache, Or Teaching of the Twelve Apostles*, 11:3. See *The Apostolic Fathers*, trans. Kirsopp Lake, Loeb Classical Library (Cambridge: Harvard University Press, 1952), 1:327.

55. Among James H. Cone's numerous writings see on this point especially the early volumes, *Black Theology and Black Power* (New York: Seabury Press, 1969), and *A Black Theology of Liberation* (Philadelphia: Lippincott, 1970), as well as the later writings, *God of the Oppressed* (New York: Seabury Press, 1975), and *Speaking the Truth* (Grand Rapids, Mich.: Eerdmans, 1986).

56. James, *The Varieties of Religious Experience*, 19–20.

57. See the critique of anthropocentrism in James Gustafson, *Ethics in a Theocentric Perspective*, vol. 1 (Chicago: University of Chicago Press, 1981).

With regard to "insight into the purposes of God" Gustafson writes, "One such insight is that fidelity does not lead to what we ordinarily and immediately perceive to be a human good, but that what is of human value must be sacrificed for the sake of the purposes of God" (p. 278).

58. Martin Luther King, Jr., *Letter from Birmingham City Jail* (Philadelphia: American Friends Service Committee, 1963), 11.

59. Three months earlier the white clerical leaders had joined those issuing a statement entitled "An Appeal for Law and Order and Common Sense." See ibid., 15.

60. The significance of this text provides the clue to the dialectical reasoning in Karl Barth's *Epistle to the Romans*, a clue missed by readers who read only as far as the discussion of human impossibility and conclude from this that Barth's interpretation must therefore be hopelessly pessimistic!

61. On this point see Christian, *Doctrines of Religious Communities*, 35–67.

62. See Bultmann's famous position paper and critical responses in *Kerygma and Myth*, ed. Hans Werner Bartsch (London: SPCK, 1960).

63. See Beverly Wildung Harrison, *Our Right to Choose: Toward a New Ethic of Abortion* (Boston: Beacon Press, 1983), 187–230.

64. Augustine, *On Christian Doctrine*, bk. 3, chap. 2, and *On the Profit of Believing [De Utilitate Credendi]*, par. 5, in NPNF 1, vol. 2. For a discussion of the wider application of this principle in regard to Calvin, Barth, and Wittgenstein, see Morse, "Raising God's Eyebrows," 39–49.

Chapter 5. Exploring Doctrines

1. Tolstoy, *Confession*, 91.

2. Schleiermacher, *Brief Outline of Theology as a Field of Study*, rubric 47, p. 28.

3. These "natural heresies" Schleiermacher saw as logical types that have found expression respectively in (1) Pelagianism, (2) Manichaeism, (3) Nazareanism or Ebionitism, and (4) Docetism. Schleiermacher, *The Christian Faith*, rubric 22, p. 97.

4. Ibid., rubric 22, p. 98.

5. See Martin Dibelius and Hans Conzelmann, *The Pastoral Epistles* (Philadelphia: Fortress Press, 1972), 92.

6. *Declaration Mysterium Ecclesiae of the S. Congregation for the Doctrine of the Faith* (May 11, 1973), in *Christian Faith in the Doctrinal Documents*, ed. Neuner and Dupuis, rubric 161, p. 60.

7. The theological use of this term derives from Melanchthon. See Pannenberg, *Theology and the Philosophy of Science*, 240–41.

8. The idea of dogmas as "buoy markers" I first heard as a student in a lecture by Robert Calhoun. See also Barth, *CD* I/1, 2d ed., ed. G. W. Bromiley and T. F. Torrance (German orig., 1932; Edinburgh: T. and T. Clark, 1975), 82, and *Homiletics* [Lectures delivered by Barth in 1932–33, edited for German publication in 1966] (Louisville, Ky.: Westminster/John Knox Press, 1991), 106.

9. To be fair to Schleiermacher, his extended article, often overlooked, showing a detailed analysis of the classical doctrine of the Trinity should be noted here: "On the Discrepancy between the Sabellian and Athanasian Method of Representing the Doctrine of the Trinity," published in English translation in two parts, *The Biblical Repository and Quarterly Observer* 5, no. 18 (April 1835), and 6, no. 19 (July 1835).

10. See appendix "Structure of the *Summa*," in Blackfriars edition of St. Thomas Aquinas, *Summa Theologiae*, 1a. 1, vol. 1 (New York: McGraw-Hill, 1964), 43–46.

11. The current pertinence of "the Thomistic contribution to the recreation of the university as a place of constrained disagreement" is argued by Alasdair MacIntyre, *Three Rival Versions of Moral Enquiry* (Notre Dame: University of Notre Dame Press, 1990), 233. See the Appendix to this book for an adaptation of the form for academic disputation today.

12. Schleiermacher, *The Christian Faith*, rubric 22, p. 99. German text, *Der christliche Glaube*, vol. 1, ed. Martin Redeker (Berlin: de Gruyter, 1960), 131.

13. St. Thomas Aquinas, *Summa Theologiae*, 3a. 16–26, in *The One Mediator*, Blackfriars ed., vol. 50 (New York: McGraw-Hill, 1965), 208–9: *Nihil tamen prohibet aliquos alios secundum quid dici mediatores inter Deum et homines, prout scilicet cooperantur ad unionem hominum cum Deo dispositive vel ministerialiter.*

14. Newman, *An Essay in Aid of a Grammar of Assent*, chap. 4, pt. 2, p. 74.

15. Dietrich Bonhoeffer, *Letters and Papers from Prison*, enl. ed., ed. Eberhard Bethge (New York: Macmillan, 1971), 17. See discussion of this in Robert McAfee Brown, *Theology in a New Key: Responding to Liberation Themes* (Philadelphia: Westminster Press, 1978), 50–74.

16. Carter Heyward, *Touching Our Strength: The Erotic as Power and the Love of God* (San Francisco: Harper and Row, 1989), 67.

17. While earlier than his major dogmatic work, see Friedrich Schleiermacher, *On Religion: Speeches to Its Cultured Despisers* (orig. published 1799; Cambridge University Press, 1996). A similar concern continues to be expressed in his 1829 defense of his dogmatic approach, *On the Glaubenslehre.*

Chapter 6. The Word of God

1. Psalm 100:3. The NRSV rendering of "It is he that made us, *and we are his*" affirms the otherness, although not as memorably as the King James' "*and not we ourselves.*"

2. Since day and night are both portrayed in the Genesis creation accounts as part of God's "good" creation, no inference is to be drawn here that darkness is by mere definition to be associated with evil. Increasing awareness of how the biblical uses of words such as "dark" and "light," and "whiter than snow" (Ps. 51:7), may be heard today with racist overtones requires that dogmatic theology counter any stereotypical assumptions. In Matt. 23:27 Jesus' condemnation of the hypocrisy that serves as a cover-up of "the bones of the dead and of all kinds of filth" is cast in terms of "white-washed tombs." Old Testament references to the plague of deadly leprosy describe it also as "white," even "white

as snow" (Num. 12:10; 2 Kings 5:27). On the other hand, the Lord is said to dwell in "thick darkness" (1 Kings 8:12; 2 Chr. 6:1) and to give "treasures of darkness" (Isa. 45:3). For further study see *Stony the Road We Trod: African American Biblical Interpretation*, ed. Cain Hope Felder (Minneapolis: Fortress Press, 1991).

3. Kant, "What Is Enlightenment?"

4. See Erich Fromm, "An Analysis of Some Types of Religious Experience," *Critiques of God*, ed. Peter Angeles (Buffalo: Prometheus Books, 1976), 155–81. This is the best short statement of objections raised to "authoritarian religion." Similar arguments inform the writings of Dorothee Sölle who acknowledges the influence of Fromm. See her critique of "absolute otherness" in Dorothee Sölle with Shirley A. Cloyes, *To Work and to Love* (Philadelphia: Fortress Press, 1984), esp. 37–52.

5. Tillich, *Systematic Theology*, 1:157.

6. Barth, *CD* II/1, ed. G. W. Bromiley and T. F. Torrance (Edinburgh: T. and T. Clark, 1957), 264–68.

7. The Second Helvetic Confession, chap. 1. in *Book of Confessions*, rubric 5.001.

8. See *The Second Vatican General Council Dogmatic Constitution 'Dei Verbum'* (1965), chap. 2, no. 9, as cited in *Christian Faith in the Doctrinal Documents*, ed. Neuner and Dupuis, rubric 247, p. 89. See also John Meyendorff, *The Orthodox Church* (New York: Pantheon Books, 1960), 18–38; and Timothy Ware, *The Orthodox Church* (Baltimore: Penguin Books, 1963), 203–15.

9. For the development of the scriptural canon and the factors involved in it see Hans von Campenhausen, *The Formation of the Christian Bible* (Philadelphia: Fortress Press, 1972), and, more briefly, Lee Martin McDonald, *The Formation of the Christian Biblical Canon* (Nashville: Abingdon Press, 1988).

10. See J. L. Austin, *How to Do Things with Words*, ed. J. O. Urmson (Cambridge: Harvard University Press, 1962), and Donald D. Evans, *The Logic of Self-Involvement: A Philosophical Study of Everyday Language with Special Reference to the Christian Use of Language about God as Creator* (London: SCM Press, 1963).

11. For a still instructive reminder of the conceptual contradictions that arise in uncritically appropriating biblical language along with the assumptions of contemporary world views see Langdon Gilkey, "Cosmology, Ontology, and the Travail of Biblical Language," *Journal of Religion* (July 1961).

12. The pronounced anti-Idealist tendency in Barth is apparent early in his interpretation of the "spirituality" of the Word: "The Word of God is also natural and physical because in the creaturely realm in which it comes to us men as Word there is nothing spiritual which is not also natural and physical." *CD* I/1, 2d ed., rubric 5, sec. 2, par. 1, p. 134.

13. Augustine, *The City of God*, bk. 21, chap. 8, in NPNF 1, vol. 2.

14. Where the currently popular tendency to portray the Word of God almost exclusively as a matter of data *interpretation*, or "hermeneutics" — whether as textual, social, or psychological construal — veers off course is illustrated by David Tracy's claim in one of his earlier writings that "the present need

becomes that of finding symbolic language which can allow the disclosure of the Christian God to 'happen' for the present actual situation." David Tracy, *Blessed Rage for Order: The New Pluralism in Theology* (New York: Seabury Press, 1975), 189.

15. See Robert W. Jenson, *Visible Words: The Interpretation and Practice of Christian Sacraments* (Philadelphia: Fortress Press, 1978).

16. The Augsburg Confession, article 5, in *Creeds*, 3:11.

17. The Second Helvetic Confession, chap. 1. For the Latin see *Creeds*, 3:238. The translation cited here is in *Book of Confessions*, rubric 5.007. This is not the same as saying that God's Word acts for human knowing without any earthly media or means.

18. Calvin, *Institutes*, bk. 4, chap. 1, sec. 5 (LCC 21:1018).

19. Note the words of one of Paul's earliest passages: "Now I would remind you, brothers and sisters, in what terms I preached to you the gospel. . . . For I delivered to you as of first importance what I also received, that Christ died for our sins in accordance with the scriptures, that he was buried, that he was raised on the third day in accordance with the scriptures, and that he appeared to Cephas, then to the twelve. Then he appeared to more than five hundred brothers and sisters at one time. . . . Then he appeared to James, then to all the apostles. Last of all, as to one untimely born, he appeared also to me" (1 Cor. 15:1–8). See also Richard B. Hays, *The Faith of Jesus Christ: An Investigation of the Narrative Substructure of Galatians 3:1–4:11* (Chico, Calif.: Scholars Press, 1983).

20. See Samuel Terrien, *The Elusive Presence* (San Francisco: Harper and Row, 1978).

21. The expression "memory of the future" is Gabriel Marcel's description of prophetic hope. See *Homo Viator: Introduction to a Metaphysics of Hope*, trans. Emma Craufurd (Chicago: H. Regnery, 1951), 53.

22. *Luther: Lectures on Romans*, LCC 15, trans. and ed. Wilhelm Pauck (Philadelphia: Westminster Press, 1961), marginal gloss on Rom. 4:14, p. 147 [*WA* 56, 45, 15–16].

23. Calvin, *Institutes*, bk. 2, chap. 9, par. 3.

24. Ibid., bk. 3, chap. 2, par. 29.

25. Philip Melanchthon, *Loci Communes* (1555), xi, in *Melanchthon on Christian Doctrine: Loci Communes 1555*, ed. Clyde L. Manschreck (New York: Oxford University Press, 1965), 158.

26. Juan Luis Segundo, S.J., *The Liberation of Theology* (Maryknoll, N.Y.: Orbis, 1976), 37–38, n. 55. On the other hand, a tendency to view anything "new" as nonapostolic finds illustration in Thomas C. Oden's "promise of unoriginality" in *The Word of Life* where the author explicitly "does not focus upon the contributions and critical issues of liberation theology" but — at the seeming risk of not remembering Lot's wife (Luke 17:32) — interprets the catholicity of the Vincentian canon of "everywhere, always, and by all" to mean that in a faithful testing of the spirits "the prime criterion is consensuality," a consensuality assumed to reside somewhere in looking back to a classic past. Thomas C. Oden, *The Word of Life*, vol. 2 of *Systematic Theology* (San Francisco: Harper and Row, 1989), xvi–xxi.

27. This criticism first became prominent in the early 1960s in the writings of Jürgen Moltmann and Wolfhart Pannenberg and was primarily directed against views of Rudolf Bultmann and Karl Barth. For a brief summary see "Transcendental Selfhood or Historical Faithfulness" in Morse, *The Logic of Promise in Moltmann's Theology*, 41–47.

28. See, for example, David H. Kelsey, *The Uses of Scripture in Recent Theology* (Philadelphia: Fortress Press, 1975), 205–16; Gordon D. Kaufman, *An Essay on Theological Method* (Missoula, Mont.: Scholars Press, 1975), and the analysis of Kelsey and Kaufman in Ronald F. Thiemann, *Revelation and Theology: The Gospel as Narrated Promise* (Notre Dame: University of Notre Dame Press, 1985), 47–70. See also Garrett Green, *Imagining God: Theology and the Religious Imagination* (San Francisco: Harper and Row, 1989).

29. Thomas Aquinas, *Summa Theologiae* 1a. 12, 13.

30. Referring to Reformed theologians of the later sixteenth and seventeenth centuries, the period generally characterized as Protestant scholasticism or orthodoxy, Heinrich Heppe writes, "The distinction of the threefold *lumen naturae, gratiae*, and *gloriae* is very frequent with the dogmaticians in treating the doctrine of the knowledge of God." Heinrich Heppe, *Reformed Dogmatics* (1861), rev. and ed. Ernst Bizer, trans. G. T. Thomson (Grand Rapids, Mich.: Baker Book House, 1984), 56.

31. Tillich, *Systematic Theology*, 1:137–44.

32. *On the Truth of the Catholic Faith: Summa Contra Gentiles*, bk. 1, chap. 3, par. 2, ed. Anton C. Pegis (Garden City, N.Y.: Image Books, 1955), 63. See also Thomas Aquinas's *Summa Theologiae* 1a.12, 12.

33. See Calvin's *Institutes*, bk. 1, chaps. 1–5. Such primal knowledge from the natural order is subject to the proviso, "if Adam had not fallen" [Latin ed., *si integer stetisset Adam;* French ed., *si Adam eust persiste en son integrite*] (bk. 1, chap. 2, par. 1).

34. Barth, *CD* IV/3, first half, pp. 38–165. "We must now answer . . . whether there really are other words which in this sense are true in relation to the one Word of God" (p. 113). "Our thesis is simply that the capacity of Jesus Christ to create these human witnesses is not restricted to His working on and in prophets and apostles and what is thus made possible and actual in His community. His capacity transcends the limits of this sphere" (p. 118). "To be sure, what is seen and heard must be tested. This is a duty which is not to be evaded" (p. 125).

35. Aloys Grillmeier, S.J., *Christ in Christian Tradition: From the Apostolic Age to Chalcedon (451)* (New York: Sheed and Ward, 1965), 27.

36. My use of the term "christomorphic" differs from that of Richard R. Niebuhr in his account of Schleiermacher's interpretation of the Word made flesh. I am not thinking of the *morphē* of Christ in psychological terms, as a reforming or reconfiguration of a prior consciousness of dependency upon God, but in more historical and social terms, as an eventful shaping of human affairs in relation to Christ's vindication in all of reality. See Richard R. Niebuhr, *Schleiermacher on Christ and Religion* (New York: Scribner's, 1964), 210–14.

37. Justin Martyr, *First Apology* (c. 155 C.E.).

38. Calvin, *Institutes*, bk. 2, chap. 13, par. 4 (LCC 1:481).

39. Martin Luther, *Lectures on Galatians, Chapters 1–4*, Luther's Works, ed. Jaroslav Pelikan, assoc. ed. Walter A. Hansen (St. Louis: Concordia, 1963), 26:4–12.

Chapter 7. The Being of God

1. Thomas Aquinas, *Summa Theologiae* 1a. 3, 5.

2. Robert Jenson writes, "God, we may therefore identify, is what happens with Jesus." *The Triune Identity: God According to the Gospel* (Philadelphia: Fortress Press, 1982), 22. The idea of God as "act," "happening," "occurrence," or "event" is found throughout the history of Christian theology.

3. Dietrich Bonhoeffer, *Christ the Center*, 1933 (New York: Harper and Row, 1966), 27.

4. Ignatius, *Epistle to the Ephesians*, chap. 15, vv. 1–2.

5. Karl Barth, "The shadow would not fall if the cross of Christ did not stand in the light of His resurrection." *CD* II/1, 406.

6. See in this connection, Eberhard Jüngel, *The Doctrine of the Trinity: God's Being Is in Becoming* (Grand Rapids, Mich.: Eerdmans, 1976); Jürgen Moltmann, *The Crucified God* (New York: Harper and Row, 1974), chap. 6, and *The Trinity and the Kingdom* (New York: Harper and Row, 1981); and Jenson, *The Triune Identity.*

7. Friedrich Nietzsche, preface to *Beyond Good and Evil* (1885), *"Christentum ist Platonismus fürs volk," Gesammelte Werke* XV.

8. See, as one example, Thorleif Boman, *Hebrew Thought Compared with Greek* (Philadelphia: Westminster Press, 1960). Criticism of juxtaposing unduly the differences based upon word etymologies appears in James Barr, *Semantics of Biblical Language* (London: Oxford University Press, 1962). Albert Schweitzer writes of the critical investigation of the life of Jesus in Germany in the eighteenth and nineteenth centuries that "it turned to the Jesus of history as an ally in the struggle against the tyranny of dogma." Read today, the rest of his statement unwittingly reminds us of the new tyranny as well that only later became apparent in this insufficiently self-critical criticism of dogma: "Thus each successive epoch of theology found its own thoughts in Jesus; that was, indeed, the only way in which it could make Him live." *The Quest of the Historical Jesus* (orig. published 1906; New York: Macmillan, 1959), 4.

9. Thomas Aquinas, *Summa Theologiae*, 1a. 2, 2.

10. Melanchthon, *Loci Communes* (1521), in *Melanchthon and Bucer*, LCC 19, ed. Wilhelm Pauck (Philadelphia: Westminster Press, 1969), 21–22.

11. Schleiermacher, *The Christian Faith*, rubric 50.

12. In this connection, for one example, see the fourteenth-century writings of Julian of Norwich, *Showings* (New York: Paulist Press, 1978), 290–305, where the three persons of the Trinity are characterized as our Father, Christ Jesus our Mother, and the Holy Spirit, one God as "truly Mother" as Father since "the Trinity is comprehended in Christ."

13. See Sally Noland MacNichol and Mary Elizabeth Walsh, "Feminist Theology and Spirituality: An Annotated Bibliography," *Women's Studies Quarterly* 21 (1993): 177–96.

14. See Elizabeth A. Johnson, *She Who Is: The Mystery of God in Feminist Theological Discourse* (New York: Crossroad, 1992).

15. This paragraph draws upon my essay "Raising God's Eyebrows," 39–49.

16. Thomas Aquinas, *Summa Theologiae* 1a. 13, 5.

17. Contemporary discussion of proportionate meaning tends to speak more of metaphor than of analogy, but the central question of the appropriateness of attributing predicates to the subject "God" remains. On this point see especially Janet Martin Soskice, *Metaphor and Religious Language* (Oxford: Clarendon Press, 1985), 64–66.

18. Thomas Aquinas, *Summa Theologiae* 1a. 13.

19. Barth, *CD* I/1, 2d ed., rubric 6, sec. 4, par. 2, pp. 237–44, and II/1, pp. 81–84.

20. Pannenberg, *Basic Questions in Theology*, 1:237–38.

21. The Hebrew tetragrammaton YHWH is translated both ways.

22. The author of 1 John writes that "love is *of* God" (4:7).

23. Barth, *CD* I/1, 2d ed., p. xiii.

24. Thomas Aquinas, *Summa Theologiae* 1a. 13, 5.

25. Ibid., 1a. 13, 6.

26. One of the first to level this criticism was Donald Evans, "Barth on Talk about God," *Canadian Journal of Theology* 16, nos. 3–4 (1970): 175–92. For my own further discussion see my *Logic of Promise in Moltmann's Theology*, 61–63.

27. See Barth, *CD* II/1, pp. 257–677.

28. The so-called Pseudo-Athanasian Creed, or the *Quicumque Vult*, is generally held to date from the fifth century. See *Creeds*, 2:68, line 28: "*Qui vult ergo salvus esse, ita de Trinitate sentiat.*" While officially sanctioned by some ecclesiastical bodies for occasional liturgical purposes, the creed is mainly recognized as a dogmatic statement, and one unexcelled for its succinct summation of the classic trinitarian affirmations. For analysis see J. N. D. Kelly, *The Athanasian Creed* (London: Adam and Charles Black, 1964).

29. Heinrich Bullinger, *Compendium Christianae Religionis decem libris comprehensum* (1559), 2, 2, as quoted in Heppe, *Reformed Dogmatics*, 105.

30. To the simple statement of Nicaea in 325, "and [we believe] in the Holy Spirit," that followed the more developed affirmation of faith in "one God, the Father" and "one Lord Jesus Christ, the Son of God," Constantinople in 381 added "and [we believe] in the Holy Spirit, the Lord and giver of life; who proceeds from the Father; who with the Father and the Son together is worshiped and glorified; who spoke by the prophets." In the West the modified clause "who proceeds from the Father *and the Son [Filioque]*" came to be adopted officially in the sixth century, creating a creedal and dogmatic dispute between the Eastern and Western branches of Christianity that continues to this day. See NPNF 2, vol. 14 (Grand Rapids, Mich.: Eerdmans, 1977), 163–69. We shall return to this dispute in chapter 9. For analysis, see T. Herbert Bindley, *The*

Oecumenical Documents of the Faith (London: Metheun and Co., Ltd., 1899; rev. by F. W. Green, 1950).

31. Augustine, *On the Trinity*, bk. 15, chap. 2, in NPNF 1, vol. 3 (Grand Rapids, Mich.: Eerdmans, 1887; rpt. 1978).

32. Tertullian, *Against Praxeas*, no. 3. See A. D. Galloway, ed., *Basic Readings in Theology* (Cleveland: World Publishing, 1964), 27.

33. Basil of Caesarea, *On the Holy Spirit*, chap. 1, rubric 3, in NPNF 2, 8:3.

34. Ibid., chap. 18, rubric 45, p. 28.

35. In the Eastern Orthodox rite this gospel account of the epiphany, or manifestation, of the relation of Father, Son, and Holy Spirit at the baptism of Jesus is read on the Feast of the Epiphany as a testimony to the triunity of God.

36. Athanasius *Discourse IV against the Arians*, rubric 15, par. 21, in NPNF 1, vol. 4, and Basil of Caesarea, *On the Holy Spirit*, chap. 10, in NPNF 2, vol. 8.

37. Calvin, *Institutes*, bk. 1, chap. 13, par. 16 (LCC 20:141).

38. Basil of Caesarea, *On the Holy Spirit*, chap. 18, rubric 44, in NPNF 2, 8:28.

39. The Latin translation of *perichōrēsis* is less edifying. From *circumincessio* we derive the term *incest*.

40. The expression "and the Son" [*et Filio* or *Filioque*] with respect to the procession of the Holy Spirit is, as noted above, a Western addition not accepted by the Eastern Church. We shall postpone consideration of this until we take up the doctrine of the Holy Spirit.

41. Moltmann, *Theology of Hope*, 116–17.

42. This theme is prominently articulated by Moltmann in *The Crucified God* and *The Trinity and the Kingdom.* For further discussion see my chapter on Moltmann in *A Handbook of Christian Theologians*, enl. ed., ed. Martin E. Marty and Dean G. Peerman (Nashville: Abingdon Press, 1984), esp. 669–72.

43. Karl Rahner, *Foundations of Christian Faith* (New York: Seabury Press, 1978), 133–37.

44. Calvin, *Institutes*, bk. 3, chap. 20, par. 49 (LCC 21:917).

45. Drawing upon Julian of Norwich, James F. Kay has proposed as a supplemented trinitarian baptismal formula: N, I baptize you "in the name of the Father and of the Son and of the Holy Spirit, One God, Mother of us all." James F. Kay, "In Whose Name? Feminism and the Trinitarian Baptismal Formula," *Theology Today* 49, no. 4 (January 1993): 524–33. In this connection see also Ruth C. Duck, *Gender and the Name of God: The Trinitarian Baptismal Formula* (New York: Pilgrim Press, 1991).

46. See Johnson, *She Who Is*, 191–223, and Duck, *Gender and the Name of God.*

47. Julian of Norwich, "The Long Text," chap. 59, in *Showings*, Classics of Western Spirituality (New York: Paulist Press, 1978), 297.

48. This ascription alludes to the NRSV's somewhat expanded rendering of 1 Cor. 1:30 [*ex autou de hymeis este en Christǭ Jēsou*] as, "He is the source of your life in Christ Jesus." By denoting the First Person as "the Source" it also retains the classical designation of the First Person as the underived *fons et origo* (font and origin) within the triunity.

49. I am indebted to Richard Norris for this ascription. That the one equally full perichoretic activity or *energeia* of God dances "from" the Father, and "through" the Son, and "in" the Spirit is affirmed by classical Eastern theologians (although the application of the prepositions "through" and "in" may vary). See, as examples, Athanasius, *Epistle to Serapion*, Epistle 1, pars. 14, 30–33. *The Letters of Saint Athanasius Concerning the Holy Spirit*, ed. C. R. B. Shapland (London: Epworth Press, 1951), 92–95, 139–49; and Basil of Caesarea, *On the Holy Spirit*, chap. 18, par. 47.

Chapter 8. Jesus Christ

1. Wolfhart Pannenberg writes, "Fate [*das Schicksal*] designates what is sent, what happens to Jesus, in distinction from his work and activity." *Jesus — God and Man* (Philadelphia: Westminster Press, 1968), 32. See also 245ff.

2. The expression "Jesus as the Christ" is familiar to readers of Paul Tillich. See his *Systematic Theology*, 2:97ff.

3. The theme of Jesus as "earthworm" and as cradled in a "cow stall, a manger with an ox and an ass" is characteristic of the earthiness of grace in Luther's Christmas sermons. See vol. 52 of Luther's Works, ed. Hans J. Hillerbrand and Helmut T. Lehmann (Philadelphia: Fortress Press 1974), 22–23, and vol. 22, ed. Jaroslav Pelikan (St. Louis: Concordia, 1957), 24. See also *The Martin Luther Christmas Book*, trans. and arr. Bainton, 45–48.

4. For one author's reminder to readers of "persons and beings who have been rendered weak, invisible, or ashamed by the church's affirmation of Jesus Christ as center of all things" see Tom F. Driver, *Christ in a Changing World: Toward an Ethical Christology* (New York: Crossroad, 1981), 44ff. Driver stresses a "present-future" Christ and maintains, "The Christ who has *already* come provides little hope for 'outsiders' " (p. 45).

5. Søren Kierkegaard, *Philosophical Fragments or a Fragment of Philosophy*, trans. David F. Swenson (Princeton: Princeton University Press, 1936), 87, 48.

6. The term *enhypostasia* is earliest associated in the sixth century with Leontius of Byzantium and John of Damascus. See "Enhypostasia," *Oxford Dictionary of the Christian Church*, 458.

7. Schweitzer, *The Quest of the Historical Jesus*, 3.

8. Ibid., 401.

9. Ibid.

10. Ibid.

11. John 1:14, 1:18, 3:16, 3:18, and 1 John 4:9.

12. See Robert M. Grant, *Jesus after the Gospels: The Christ of the Second Century* (Louisville, Ky.: Westminster/John Knox Press, 1990). In this condensed but illuminating account Grant points out "the startling diversity in Christological doctrines even toward the end of the second century" (p. 82). For an anthology of lesser known selections from the first- and second-century period of Christian origins see *The Other Gospels: Non-Canonical Gospel Texts*, ed. Ron Cameron (Philadelphia: Westminster Press, 1982).

13. Justin Martyr, *The Second Apology*, chap. 13, and *Dialogue with Trypho*, chap. 128, in ANF, vol. 1.

14. John Hick, "Jesus and the World Religions," in *The Myth of God Incarnate*, ed. John Hick (Philadelphia: Westminster Press, 1977), 181.

15. See Driver, *Christ in a Changing World.*

16. Maurice Wiles, "Christianity without Incarnation?" in *The Myth of God Incarnate*, ed. Hick, 8–9.

17. See Richard A. Norris, Jr., *The Christological Controversy* (Philadelphia: Fortress Press, 1980), 159.

18. See J. Louis Martyn, "Epistemology at the Turn of the Ages: 2 Corinthians 5:16," in *Christian History and Interpretation: Studies Presented to John Knox*, ed. W. R. Farmer, C. F. D. Moule, and R. R. Niebuhr (Cambridge: At the University Press, 1967), 269–87. In summarizing his discussion of Paul, Martyn writes that until the parousia the opposite of knowing *kata sarka* in the logic of Paul's teaching is not knowing *kata pneuma* ("according to the spirit") but knowing *kata stauron* ("according to the cross"). Put another way, to live in the spirit is at present to live not "before the cross," or "after the cross," but "in the cross." The cross is seen by Paul as the "juncture" between the old irreconcilable state of affairs that he refers to with the word *sarx* ("the flesh"), a state that has been defeated in the crucifixion but is not yet fully vanquished on the human scene until the parousia, and the coming reconciled state of affairs that he refers to with the word *pneuma* ("the spirit"), a state that faith now knows only by living "in the cross" and not in its final establishment yet to come over all opposition. Martyn in this essay does not himself make the dogmatic connection that I am suggesting between the Pauline knowing *kata stauron* and the import of the *en sarki* language of 1 John 4:2.

19. *Narrative of Sojourner Truth* (New York: Arno Press and The New York Times, 1968), 134–35. This is a reprint of Olive Gilbert, *Narrative of Sojourner Truth; A Bondswoman of Olden Time, Emancipated by the New York Legislature in the Early Part of the Present Century; with a History of Her Labors and Correspondence Drawn from Her "Book of Life"* (Battle Creek, Mich.: Published for the Author, 1878).

20. Martin Luther, "The Magnificat," in vol. 21 of Luther's Works, ed. Jaroslav Pelikan (St. Louis: Concordia, 1956), 314.

21. Ibid., 352.

22. I have discussed this further in *The Logic of Promise in Moltmann's Theology*, 92–108.

23. The words are from the American revival song "Jesus Is Always There," by Bertha Mae Lillenas, copyright 1934, The Rodeheaver Co.

24. See in this connection Raymond E. Brown, *The Virginal Conception and Bodily Resurrection of Jesus* (New York: Paulist Press, 1973).

25. This is not to deny that such theories appear at times in the history of Christian theology.

26. See, for example, Reginald H. Fuller, *The Formation of the Resurrection Narratives* (New York: Macmillan, 1971), 179–80.

27. Matt. 28:1–10, Mark 16:1–8, Luke 24:1–12, John 20:1–18.

28. This is the first verse of John Updike's "Seven Stanzas at Easter," in Updike, *Telephone Poles and Other Poems* (New York: Knopf, 1964), 72–73.

29. See Brown, *The Virginal Conception and Bodily Resurrection of Jesus.* "Our earliest ancestors in the faith proclaimed a bodily resurrection in the sense that they did not think that Jesus' body had corrupted in the tomb. However, and this is equally important, Jesus' risen body was no longer a body as we know bodies, bound by the dimensions of space and time" (127–28).

30. Updike, "Seven Stanzas at Easter."

31. Rudolf Bultmann, "New Testament and Mythology," in *Kerygma and Myth*, ed. Bartsch, 1–44.

32. See, for examples, Gen. 19:13, Exod. 19:9 and 34:5, Num. 9:15, Matt. 17:5, Mark 9:7, and Luke 9:35.

33. The faith and history question occupied center stage in Protestant theology throughout much of the nineteenth and twentieth centuries up until the 1970s and produced a formidable literature of terminological refinements and debate. See, for example, Martin Kähler, *The So-Called Historical Jesus and the Historic, Biblical Christ* (Philadelphia: Fortress Press, 1964), originally published in German in 1896 as *Der sogenannte historische Jesus und der geschichtliche, biblische Christus.* Also, for a useful summary of positions, see C. F. D. Moule, ed., *The Significance of the Message of the Resurrection for Faith in Jesus Christ*, Studies in Biblical Theology, 2d ser., no. 8 (London: SCM Press, 1968). My debt to the contribution of Jürgen Moltmann on this subject may be seen in my attempt to think through the issues in my *Logic of Promise in Moltmann's Theology*, 82–108.

34. See Paul M. Van Buren, *The Secular Meaning of the Gospel* (New York: Macmillan, 1963), 39–40: "*Hypostasis* may be translated as *actuality.*"

35. Leopold von Ranke, *Geschichten der romanischen und germanischen Völker*, preface to the first edition, as cited in R. G. Collingwood, *The Idea of History* (New York: Oxford University Press, 1956), 130.

36. See Morse, "When does a narrative qualify as history, in distinction from merely fiction or myth?" in *The Logic of Promise in Moltmann's Theology*, 102–8.

37. Here my translation of Heb. 11:1 differs from that of the NRSV and renders *elegchos* as "the proving true," rather than as merely "the conviction."

38. See, for example, Wolfhart Pannenberg, "Redemptive Event and History," in *Basic Questions in Theology*, 1:15–80.

39. See, for examples, Moltmann, *The Crucified God*, 160–99, and Paul Lehmann, *The Transfiguration of Politics* (New York: Harper and Row, 1975), 229–37.

40. See Pannenberg, "Redemptive Event and History."

41. Schweitzer writes: "The historical investigation of the life of Jesus did not take its rise from a purely historical interest; it turned to the Jesus of history as an ally in the struggle against the tyranny of dogma." *The Quest of the Historical Jesus*, 4.

42. See disbeliefs 8 and 9 in chapter 6.

43. Ernst Käsemann, "Blind Alleys in the 'Jesus of History' Controversy," *New Testament Questions of Today* (Philadelphia: Fortress Press, 1969), 64.

While Käsemann in this instructive essay argues against looking for the history of Jesus "as it *must have* happened" (a tendency he attributes to systematic theologians) rather than "as it *actually* happened," his statement in effect suggests that there *must* be some historical link between Jesus and the gospel testimonies or else that testimony is only "docetic." That such a claim itself asserts a theological and not a historical-critical necessity is not surprising. What, by later definition, counts as nonhistoricality was disbelieved with respect to the person of Jesus Christ in the dogmatic refusal of docetism from the beginning, long before the introduction of historical-critical methods.

Chapter 9. The Holy Spirit

1. Carol Christ and Judith Plaskow, eds., *Womanspirit Rising: A Feminist Reader in Religion* (San Francisco: Harper and Row, 1979). For a more recent compilation, see Susan Frank Parsons, ed., *The Cambridge Companion to Feminist Theology* (Cambridge, UK: Cambridge University Press, 2002).

2. The phrase "from the Father, through the Son, in the Spirit" is emphasized by Athanasius in his *Letters to Serapion* 1.28 and 1.30. See Athanasius, *Letters Concerning the Holy Spirit* (London: Epworth Press, 1951), 133–36, 139–42. The author of the Ephesian letter writes that "access to the Father" is "through" Christ Jesus "in one Spirit" (Eph. 2:18). Basil of Caesarea in his treatise *On the Holy Spirit* discusses the theological insights afforded by reflecting upon the complementary use of such prepositions as "through" and "in" in testimonies of faith but warns against the "vain philosophy" of thinking of such prepositional expressions as if they were scripturally invariant rules. NPNF 2, 8:2–50.

3. See, for example, Cyril C. Richardson, *The Doctrine of the Trinity* (New York: Abingdon Press, 1958).

4. Athanasius, *Letters to Serapion,* 1, 27.

5. Augustine, *On the Trinity*, bk. 15, chap. 19, par. 37.

6. Ronald Knox, *Enthusiasm* (New York: Oxford University Press, 1950).

7. Max Weber's term is the "routinization of charisma," *Economy and Society*, ed. Guenther Roth and Claus Wittich (Berkeley: University of California Press, 1978), 2:1121–23.

8. Karl Barth, whose own theology opposes nontrinitarian pneumatologies and is usually cited as a leading proponent of "christocentrism," recommended in his later years that new thought be given to rethinking a fully trinitarian theology focused upon the third article: "What I have already intimated here and there to good friends, would be the possibility of a theology of the third article, in other words, a theology predominantly and decisively of the Holy Spirit." *Karl Barth: The Theology of Schleiermacher, Lectures at Göttingen, Winter Semester of 1923/24*, ed. Dietrich Ritschl (Grand Rapids, Mich.: Eerdmans, 1982), 278. (The quotation is from "Concluding Unscientific Postscript on Schleiermacher" [1968], an "Afterword" added to the much earlier lectures published in this volume.) For work along these lines see especially Jürgen Moltmann, *God in Creation: A New Theology of Creation and the Spirit of God* (San Francisco: Harper and Row, 1985).

9. Ludwig Feuerbach, *The Essence of Christianity* (1841; New York: Harper Torchbooks, 1957), 14. Translation slightly altered.

10. Recipients of the gift of the Holy Spirit are described in Acts as those "who belonged to the Way" (Acts 9:2).

11. "The Divinity School Address, 1838," in *The Collected Works of Ralph Waldo Emerson*, ed. Alfred R. Ferguson (Cambridge, Mass.: The Belknap Press of Harvard University Press, 1971), 1:85–86.

12. Note the interpretative shift in emphasis at Gen. 1:2 between the first RSV translation of 1952 and that of the NRSV of 1989.

> and the Spirit of God was moving over the face of the waters.
> (RSV, 1952)
>
> while a wind from God swept over the face of the waters. (NRSV, 1989)

13. It is inexact to say, as does Helmut Thielicke, that "the *historical Jesus of Nazareth*, through the Holy Spirit, makes himself contemporary with us." *The Evangelical Faith* (Grand Rapids, Mich.: Eerdmans, 1974), 1:131 (italics mine).

14. In this connection Alasdair I. C. Heron writes, "The Spirit is specifically associated with such cardinal moments as Jesus' conception, baptism, defeat of demons, crucifixion and rising from the dead. Most of this evades any straightforward translation in terms of his psychological experience." *The Holy Spirit* (Philadelphia: Westminster Press, 1983), 128. Friedrich Schleiermacher, whose theological insights often prove to be more profound than the conventional criticisms of his detractors, does appear, notwithstanding, to err insofar as "the existence of God in Christ" is construed solely as the "constant potency of His God-consciousness." *The Christian Faith*, rubric 94, p. 385. From this it follows that, in Schleiermacher's words, "the facts of the Resurrection and the Ascension of Christ, and the prediction of His Return to Judgment, cannot be laid down as properly constituent parts of the doctrine of His Person" (rubric 99, p. 417).

15. With reference to the First and Second Persons of the Trinity Augustine writes of the Holy Spirit, "Nor is He less than they because they give, and He is given. For He is given as a gift of God in such way that He Himself also gives Himself as being God. . . . We have not here the creating of Him that is given, and the rule of them that give, but the concord of the given and the givers." *On the Trinity*, bk. 15, chap. 19, in NPNF 1, 3:219.

16. Thomas Aquinas, *Summa Theologiae* 1a. 38, 2, "Whether 'Gift' is a name proper to the Holy Spirit."

17. Thomas Aquinas, *Summa Theologiae* 1a. 37, 1, "Whether 'Love' is a name proper to the Holy Spirit." See also, 1a. 36, 1, "Whether this name 'Holy Spirit' is proper to any divine person."

18. Cyril of Jerusalem (c. 315–386), *Catechetical Lectures*, lecture 16.2, in NPNF 2, vol. 7 (Grand Rapids, Mich.: Eerdmans, 1893; rpt. 1978).

19. Heron, *The Holy Spirit*, 75. For the primary source see Cyril of Jerusalem, *Catechetical Lectures*, 1–157.

20. An alleged exception is Prov. 8:22, cited by the Arians at Nicaea in their attempted equating of begetting with a "first born" form of creation: "The Lord created me at the beginning of his work, the first of his acts of long ago." The text itself refers to "wisdom" as being created, a term sometimes identified with the Word and sometimes with the Spirit. The interpretation, however, was

rejected at Nicaea as applicable to the Son with the phrase "begotten, not created," and again rejected at Constantinople as applicable to the Holy Spirit in confessing the Spirit as "Lord."

21. See J. N. D. Kelly, *The Athanasian Creed* (London: Adam and Charles Black, 1964), 85.

22. See Yves M. J. Congar, *I Believe in the Holy Spirit* (New York: Seabury Press, 1983), 3:49–50.

23. John of Damascus, *On the Orthodox Faith*, bk. 1, chap. 12, in NPNF 2, vol. 9. See Congar, *I Believe in the Holy Spirit*, 3:36–48, where this statement is quoted on p. 39. See also the essays in *Spirit of God, Spirit of Christ: Ecumenical Reflections on the Filioque Controversy*, World Council of Churches, Faith and Order Paper no. 103 (London: SPCK, 1981).

24. This point will be discussed in chapter 12.

25. Translators disagree as to the precise sense of the Greek *eis apolytrōsin tēs peripoiēseōs* of this verse. Literally, "to (or until) the redemption of the possession (of that which has been saved, put into savings)." I have chosen to render the phrase with a more fiscal connotation than either the RSV or the NRSV (which themselves differ markedly). The *arrabōn* is the guaranty that what has been saved up for us by Christ's death and resurrection will have the full value promised when it comes due.

26. Quoted from Congar, *I Believe in the Holy Spirit*, 2:134. In the original Hebrew text "piety" and "fear" are not distinguished, and the famous "sevenfold gifts" familiar in Christian hymnody reduce to six-fold.

27. For an informative discussion set in the broader context of Roman Catholic renewal movements see Congar, "The Renewal in the Spirit: Promises and Questions," in *I Believe in the Holy Spirit*, 2:145–212.

28. See Congar, "The Motherhood in God and the Femininity of the Holy Spirit," in *I Believe in the Holy Spirit*, 3:155–64, and Virginia Ramey Mollenkott, *Divine Feminine: The Biblical Imagery of God as Female* (New York: Crossroad, 1983).

Chapter 10. Creation

1. Thomas Aquinas, *Summa Theologiae* 1a. 1, 2–3.

2. Ernest Nagel, "Philosophical Concepts of Atheism," in *Critiques of God*, ed. Angeles, 4.

3. Calvin, *Institutes*, bk. 1, chap. 5, par. 14 (LCC 20:68).

4. See James Nash, *Loving Nature: Ecological Integrity and Christian Responsibility* (Nashville: Abingdon Press, 1992).

5. See Matthew Fox, *Original Blessing* (Sante Fe, N.M.: Bear and Company, 1983).

6. For Whitehead's own account of a "consequent nature" in God as well as a "primordial nature" see his *Process and Reality* (New York: Harper and Row, 1929), pt. 5, chap. 2, pp. 519–33. Also influential in this regard has been the work of Charles Hartshorne. See, for example, *The Divine Relativity* (New Haven: Yale University Press, 1948).

7. Calvin, *Institutes*, bk. 1, chap. 16, par. 8 (LCC 20:207).

8. See in this regard the account attributed to Pseudo-Dionysius the Areopagite, *On the Celestial Hierarchy.* This teaching and that of Thomas Aquinas, who was influenced by it, is discussed by Barth in his *CD* III/3, ed. G. W. Bromiley and T. F. Torrance (German orig., 1950; Edinburgh: T. and T. Clark, 1960), 380–401.

9. Augustine, *The City of God*, bk. 11, chap. 16, in NPNF 1, 2:214.

10. Rosemary Radford Ruether, *Sexism and God-Talk* (Boston: Beacon Press, 1983), 79.

11. Julian H. Hartt, "Creation and Providence," in *Christian Theology: An Introduction to Its Traditions and Tasks*, rev. ed., ed. Peter C. Hodgson and Robert H. King (Philadelphia: Fortress Press, 1985), 146.

12. James M. Gustafson, *Ethics from a Theocentric Perspective* (Chicago: University of Chicago Press, 1981), 1:41.

13. Ibid., 271.

14. See esp. Moltmann, *God in Creation.*

15. See Elisabeth Schüssler Fiorenza, *In Memory of Her: A Feminist Theological Reconstruction of Christian Origins* (New York: Crossroad, 1983), 41–95, and the references in Ruether, *Sexism and God-Talk*, and Phyllis Trible, *God and the Rhetoric of Sexuality* (Philadelphia: Fortress Press, 1978).

16. See Louis Bouyer, *The Seat of Wisdom* (New York: Pantheon Books, 1962), 189: "Its [the Spirit's] role in creation, as described in Genesis, suggests the image of a bird brooding over the world as over an egg." For opposition to such interpretation see Gerhard von Rad, *Genesis: A Commentary* (Philadelphia: Westminster Press, 1961), 47–48.

17. The hallmark text in this regard is Mary Daly's *Beyond God the Father* (Boston: Beacon Press, 1973).

18. Augustine, *On the Trinity*, bk. 1, chap. 5.

19. The Second Helvetic Confession, chap. 7.

20. Bonhoeffer, *Letters and Papers from Prison*, 219–20.

21. Here, as in chapter 8, I depart from the NRSV's more psychological and less apocalyptic translation of this verse: "Now faith is the assurance of things hoped for, the conviction of things not seen."

22. Irenaeus, *Against Heresies*, bk. 1, chap. 10, in ANF, 1:330.

23. *Rufinus: A Commentary on the Apostles' Creed*, trans. and ann. J. N. D. Kelly (Westminster, Md.: Newman Press, 1955), 36.

24. Ibid., 36–37. Heb. 1:2 is also cited.

25. Augustine, *Confessions*, bk. 7, chap. 12.

26. von Rad, *Genesis*, 44.

27. For reference to God's self-limitation as "contraction" in Jewish and Christian sources see Moltmann, *God in Creation*, 86–93.

28. For examples of twentieth-century treatments of this ancient question see Karl Barth on "God and Nothingness [*das Nichtige*]" in *CD* III/3, pp. 289–368; Paul Ricoeur, *The Symbolism of Evil* (New York: Harper and Row, 1967); and the essay by Robert P. Scharlemann, "The No to Nothing and the Nothing to Know: Barth and Tillich and the Possibility of Theological Science," *Journal of the American Academy of Religion* 55, no. 1 (Spring 1987): 57–72.

29. The allusion is to a bestseller of the 1980s by Harold S. Kushner, *When Bad Things Happen to Good People* (New York: Avon, 1983).
30. Heppe, *Reformed Dogmatics*, 256ff.
31. Calvin, *Institutes*, chap. 16, par. 8 (LCC 1:207–8).
32. Barth, *CD* III/3, p. 90.
33. Thomas Aquinas, *Summa Theologiae*, 1a. 22, 4. "On whether it is the case that Providence imposes a necessity on the things provided for?"
34. The Second Helvetic Confession, chap. 6, par. 4.
35. The Westminster Confession of Faith, chap. 5, par. 3.

Chapter 11. Salvation

1. John Hick, *Evil and the God of Love*, rev. ed. (San Francisco: Harper and Row, 1977), 12–14.
2. Augustine, *The City of God*, bk. 22, chap. 30.
3. See Irenaeus, *Against Heresies*, bk. 5, chap. 1, par. 2, in ANF, 1:527; Luther, *Lectures on Galatians*, 26:4–12; Schleiermacher, *The Christian Faith*, rubric 4, p. 12.
4. Calvin, *Institutes*, bk. 3, chap. 23, rubric 7 (LCC 21:955).
5. José Míguez Bonino, *Doing Theology in a Revolutionary Situation* (Philadelphia: Fortress Press, 1975), 140.
6. Augustine, *The City of God*, bk. 21, chap. 12.
7. Thomas Aquinas, *Summa Theologiae* 1a. 23, 3–4.
8. Melanchthon, *Loci Communes* (LCC 19:21).
9. See, as one characteristic example, Augustine, *On Grace and Free Will*, in NPNF 1, vol. 5 (Grand Rapids, Mich.: Eerdmans, 1887; rpt. 1987).
10. Thomas Aquinas, *Summa Theologiae*, 1a.2ae. 113, 3.
11. Barth, *CD* III/3, 138.
12. D. M. Baillie, *God Was in Christ* (New York: Scribner's, 1948), 114.
13. Tillich, *Systematic Theology*, 2:44–59.
14. For still the best treatment of this subject in relation to the development of Christian doctrine see Bultmann, *Theology of the New Testament*, 2:119–54.
15. Here I cite the RSV's rendering as preferable for purposes of illustration to the NRSV's "promoting self-imposed piety, humility, and severe treatment of the body" (Col. 2:23). The word translated "humility" here [*tapeinophrosynē*] is the same as that translated "self-abasement" in Col. 2:18. It is used in Phil. 2:3 to denote "humility," but in that context explicitly in an unselfish and not a self-demeaning sense.
16. In the older scholastic terminology dating back to the second century, *acedia* as the denial of hope leading to self-demeaning abasement and inertia is said to involve the sin of "sluggishness" or "sloth." See *The Shepherd of Hermas*, bk. 3, chap. 11, v. 3 (second century); John Cassian, *Institutes*, bk. 10, chap. 2 (fifth century); Thomas Aquinas, *Summa Theologiae* 2a2ae. 35 (thirteenth century); and Barth, *CD* IV/2, ed. G. W. Bromiley and T. F. Torrance (German orig., 1955; Edinburgh: T. and T. Clark, 1958), 403–83 (twentieth century). Barth sums up the matter by writing that the sinner who in *superbia* defies

God's incarnate humbling and thus "stands bitterly in need of humiliation" also in the "sloth" of *acedia* that defies the Resurrection "stands no less bitterly in need of exaltation" (p. 404). Feminist theology has also objected to thinking of sin exclusively as "pride" and neglecting the sense of low self-esteem.

17. The words are familiar to Christian worship from the twelfth-century anonymous Latin hymn of the Passion translated by Paul Gerhardt, 1656, and James W. Alexander, 1830.

18. As previously cited in chapter 2. Martin Luther, "Disputation Held at Heidelberg, April 26th, 1518."

19. Ernst Käsemann, *Commentary on Romans* (Grand Rapids, Mich.: Eerdmans, 1980), 28. See also Käsemann's earlier essay, " 'The Righteousness of God' in Paul," in *New Testament Questions of Today* (Philadelphia: Fortress Press, 1969), 168–82.

20. See, for example, Gustaf Aulén, *Christus Victor* (New York: Macmillan, 1969); Delores Williams, *Sisters in the Wilderness: The Challenge of Womanist God-talk* (Maryknoll, N.Y.: Orbis, 1993), 161–67, and "Black Women's Surrogacy Experience and the Christian Notion of Redemption," in *After Patriarchy: Feminist Transformations of the World Religions*, ed. Paula M. Cooey, William R. Eakin, and Jay B. McDaniel (Maryknoll, N.Y.: Orbis, 1991), 1–14.

21. The idea of Christ offering his flesh as bait to catch the Devil is most developed in Gregory of Nyssa, *Catechetical Orations* 21–26, but the image is a familiar one in Patristic writings. See *Documents of the Christian Church*, 2d ed., ed. Henry Bettenson (New York: Oxford University Press, 1963), 34–35. See also Luther, vol. 22 of Luther's Works, ed. Jaroslav Pelikan (St. Louis: Concordia, 1957), 24: "For the hook, which is the divinity of Christ, was concealed under the earthworm. The devil swallowed it with his jaws when Christ died and was buried. But it ripped his belly so that he could not retain it but had to disgorge it. . . . This affords us the greatest solace; for just as the devil could not hold Christ in death, so he cannot hold us who believe in Christ."

22. See Anselm in *A Scholastic Miscellany: Anselm to Ockham*, LCC 10, ed. Eugene R. Fairweather (Philadelphia: Westminster Press, 1961), 100–183.

23. Peter Abelard, *Commentary on the Epistle to the Romans.* See selections in *Basic Readings in Theology*, ed. A. D. Galloway (Cleveland: Meridian Books, World Publishing, 1964), 102.

24. Gregory of Nazianzus, *Orations*, bk. 45, chap. 22, in *Documents of the Christian Church*, 34.

25. No true reconciliation without the honoring of justice as God's liberating action in history is a theme emphasized by James H. Cone. See, for example, *God of the Oppressed*, 228–32.

26. Dietrich Bonhoeffer, *The Cost of Discipleship* (German orig., 1937; New York: Macmillan, 1963), 45–60.

27. Anathema xiv, "The Anathemas Against Origen," p. 319 in *The Seven Ecumenical Councils*, NPNF 2, vol. 14.

28. For examples of references characteristic of Origen's teaching that all things shall be restored to their original state see Origen, *On First Principles* bk. 1, chap. 6, bk. 2, chap. 1, and bk. 3, chap. 6.

29. Augustine, *The City of God*, bk. 21, chaps. 17 and 23.

30. Calvin, *Institutes*, bk. 3, chap. 21, par. 1 (LCC 22:920–21).

31. Augustine, *The Confessions*, bk. 10, chap. 29.

32. Karl Barth has developed this point in criticizing Calvin's doctrine of the "horrible decree." Both election and rejection occur as God's free decision of predestination "in Christ" and refer not to two eternally separate groups of people but to all people as those for whom Christ is elected both to rejection with us in the far country of homelessness and to resurrection with us in the glory of an ultimate welcome home. See "The Election of the Individual," in *CD* II/2, pp. 306–506, and the entire structure of *CD* IV/1–4, which comprise Barth's treatment of the doctrine of reconciliation.

Chapter 12. Humanity

1. Karl Barth, *Ethics*, 1928–29 (New York: Seabury Press, 1981), 128.

2. The same Greek term, *eikōn*, may be translated as "image" or as "likeness." For later theological efforts to distinguish these meanings see, for example, Thomas Aquinas, *Summa Theologiae* 1a. 93, 9. In 2 Cor. 3:18 *eikōn* denotes not some original imprint upon human existence but that reflected glory of the Lord into which humans are being transformed.

3. Augustine, *The City of God*, bk. 12, chap. 23.

4. Augustine, *The Confessions* 13.32. See also Thomas Aquinas, *Summa Theologiae*, 1a. 93, 6.

5. Barth, *CD* III/2, ed. G. W. Bromiley and T. F. Torrance (German orig., 1945; Edinburgh: T. and T. Clark, 1960), 287.

6. Susannah Herzel, "Correspondence between Henrietta Visser't Hooft and Karl Barth, 1934," *A Voice for Woman*, Women in Church and Society (Geneva: World Council of Churches, 1981), Appendix 1, 165.

7. *The Gospel according to Thomas* (New York: Harper and Brothers, 1959), logion 114.

8. Ruether, *Sexism and God-Talk*, 116–38.

9. See, for example, Schleiermacher, *The Christian Faith*, rubric 12, pp. 60–62.

10. Calvin, *Institutes*, bk. 3, chap. 7, sec. 1 (LCC 20:690).

11. The Heidelberg Catechism, in *Creeds*, 3:307.

12. The embryos from miscarriages, for example, are not traditionally baptized by Christian churches that baptize human infants.

13. See Beverly Wildung Harrison, *Our Right to Choose: Toward a New Ethic of Abortion* (Boston: Beacon Press, 1983): "As the gestating fetus matures biologically, moving toward the point of functional maturation, the pregnant woman has good reason to impute claims to the fetus, grounded in intrinsic value, that weigh against her own. But from a moral point of view there can be no 'demand' that she take her own moral claim to life and wellbeing less seriously or as something readily to be discarded. What she — and the rest of us — need to understand is that it is best, when possible, to avoid living into [a] situation where such conflicting claims arise" (p. 229).

14. Calvin, *Institutes*, bk. 1, chap. 15, par. 4 (LCC 20:189).

15. The following synopsis relies primarily though not exclusively upon Karl Holl, "A History of the Word Vocation (*Beruf*)," 1928, trans. H. F. Peacock. Mimeograph copy in U.T.S. Library, catalogued as XC, H733. The original is "Die Geschichte des Wortes Beruf," *Gesammelte Aufsätze* 3 (1928).

16. See Matt. 19:16–30, Mark 10:17–31, and Luke 18:18–30.

17. Raymond Bernard Blakney, ed., sermon on "The Love of God," 1 John 4:9, in *Meister Eckhart: A Modern Translation* (New York: Harper, 1941), 127.

18. Proposals have been made to find cognates by translating the noun *dikaiosyne* not as "righteousness" but as either "justice" or "rectitude" to conform more with the verb *dikaioō* as either "justify" or "rectify," and the noun *dikaiosis* as either "justification" or "rectification." See Leander E. Keck, *Paul and His Letters*, 2d ed. (Philadelphia: Fortress Press, 1988), 111–12. Also the old English verb "right-wising" has been suggested for use in place of "justifying" by Kendrick Grobel, translator of Rudolf Bultmann's *Theology of the New Testament*, vol. 1 (New York: Scribner's, 1951), 253.

19. *Book of Common Prayer* (New York: Seabury, 1979), Holy Eucharist, Rite 1.

20. Augustine, *The City of God*, bk. 22, chap. 17. Unacceptable references appear in Augustine as well. See Rosemary Radford Ruether, "Misogynism and Virginal Feminism in the Fathers of the Church," in *Religion and Sexism: Images of Women in the Jewish and Christian Traditions*, ed. Ruether (New York: Simon and Schuster, 1974), 150–83.

21. From "Crown Him with Many Crowns," words by Matthew Bridges, 1851, and Godfrey Thring, 1874, with music by George J. Elvey, 1868. Note also the allusion to the vision of the heavens opened in Rev. 19:13 where the One whose "name is called the Word of God" is seen as "clothed in a robe dipped in blood."

22. Thomas Aquinas, *Summa Theologiae*, 3a. 1, 3. See Hick, *Evil and the God of Love*, 97–98.

23. For a convenient guide to recent authors and texts addressing this subject, see the *Anglican Theological Review* 90, no. 3 (Summer 2008), in which I also have an article.

24. *The Book of Discipline of the United Methodist Church 2008* (Nashville: United Methodist Publishing House, 2008). For "Official Statements from Religious Bodies and Ecumenical Organizations" see J. Gordon Melton, ed., with Nicholas Piediscalzi, contributing ed., *The Churches Speak On: Sex and Family Life* (Detroit: Gale Research Inc., 1991), and J. Gordon Melton, ed., *The Churches Speak On: Homosexuality* (Detroit: Gale Research Inc., 1991). The most current information may be found on denominational websites.

25. See John Witter, Jr., and Eliza Ellison, eds., *Covenant Marriage in Comparative Perspective* (Grand Rapids, Mich.: Eerdmans, 2005.

26. See, e.g., Eph. 5:22, Col. 3:18, 1 Tim. 2:11–15, and 1 Peter 3:1–2.

27. The Second Helvetic Confession of 1566, chap. 2, par. 1, *De Interpretandis Scripturis Sanctis, Et De Patribus, Conciliis, Et Traditionibus.*

28. George S. Hendry, *Theology of Nature* (Philadelphia: Westminster Press, 1980), 218. The Bonhoeffer quote is cited in *Letters and Papers from Prison*, letter of December 18, 1943.

29. For examples of studies by Roman Catholics reflecting this recognition see Donald Goergen, O.P., *The Sexual Celibate* (New York: Seabury Press, 1974),

and Keith Clark, Capuchin, *Being Sexual... and Celibate* (Notre Dame, Ind.: Ave Maria Press, 1986).

30. Calvin, *Institutes*, bk. 4, chap. 13, sec. 3 (LCC 21:1257).

31. A number of studies make a similar point. See James B. Nelson, *Embodiment: An Approach to Sexuality and Christian Theology* (Minneapolis: Augsburg, 1978), 180–210, and Robin Scroggs, *The New Testament and Homosexuality* (Philadelphia: Fortress Press, 1983).

32. Following the testimony of Ephesians 5:31–32 that the "great mystery" of the union of "man and wife" referred to in Genesis 2:24 signifies to faith the relation of Christ to the church — a church where according to the Apostle "each has a particular gift from God, one having one kind and another a different kind" (1 Cor. 7:7) — Christian tradition has not restricted the term "marriage" solely to the covenant fidelity of heterosexual couples, as some recent advocates of so-called "Defense of Marriage" legislation mistakenly contend, but has historically applied the import of marital language of the church as the "bride of Christ" to other faithful unions "in Christ" as well, as, for example, in the case of those taking the vows of religious orders.

33. While secular usage and legal statutes largely restrict the biblical sin of "Sodom" to sexual practices deemed to be unnatural, the import of the biblical testimonies allows for no such restriction. Clear evidence of how the real sin of "sodomy" is seen in faith to occur in the violation of covenant fidelity appears in the prophecy of Ezekiel: "This was the guilt of your sister Sodom: she and her daughters had pride, excess of food, and prosperous ease, but did not aid the poor and needy. They were haughty, and did abominable things before me; therefore I removed them when I saw it... Yes, thus says the Lord God: I will deal with you as you have done, you who have despised the oath, breaking the covenant; yet I will remember my covenant with you in the days of your youth, and I will establish with you an everlasting covenant" (Ezek. 16:49–50, 59–60).

34. Barth, *CD* III/2, p. 324.

35. Barth, *CD* I/1, 2d ed., rubric 10, par. 2, p. 393; III/1, ed. G. W. Bromiley and T. F. Torrance (German orig., 1945; Edinburgh: T. and T. Clark, 1958), 16; and III/2, p. 219.

36. Barth, *CD* I/1, 2d ed., rubric 10, par. 2, p. 393.

37. Barth, *CD* III/2, p. 286.

38. Ibid., 287.

39. Ibid., 250–65, 274.

40. Barth himself characteristically returns again and again to this focal point. See, for example, ibid., 219–20, 323–24.

Chapter 13. The Church

1. See Martin Luther, "Explanations of the Ninety-five Theses," rubric 58, in vol. 31 of Luther's Works, ed. Harold J. Grimm and Helmut T. Lehmann (Philadelphia: Muhlenberg Press, 1957).

2. Basil of Caesarea, *On the Holy Spirit*, chap. 30, in NPNF 2, 8:48–49.

3. See, for examples, especially Rom. 12:4, 1 Cor. 12:27, and also Eph. 1:22–23, which is thought by many scholars to have been authored most likely by a follower of Paul.

4. Paul S. Minear, *Images of the Church in the New Testament* (Philadelphia: Westminster Press, 1960), 173, 280.

5. Ignatius of Antioch, *Epistle to the Smyrnaeans*, chap. 8, v. 2, in *The Apostolic Fathers*, ed. Kirsopp Lake (Cambridge: Harvard University Press, 1952), 1:261.

6. Ignatius of Antioch, *Epistle to the Philadelphians*, 3.2, in *The Apostolic Fathers*, ed. Lake, 1:241.

7. See Hans Küng, *The Church* (New York: Sheed and Ward, 1968), 404ff.

8. Cyprian, *On the Unity of the Catholic Church* in ANF, vol. 5, ed. Alexander Roberts and James Donaldson (New York: Christian Literature, 1886–97), 423.

9. Tillich, *Systematic Theology*, 3:152–55.

10. Karl Rahner, *Theological Investigations*, vol. 6 (Baltimore: Helicon Press, 1969), 390–98; vol. 12 (New York: Seabury Press, 1974), 161–78; vol. 14 (New York: Seabury Press, 1976), 280–94.

11. The Canons and Decrees of the Council of Trent (1563), in *Creeds*, 2:91. A reaffirmation of this position may be found in the "Letter of the Holy Office to the Archbishop of Boston (1949)" where the teaching of *extra ecclesiam nulla salus* is upheld with the interpretation that "to gain eternal salvation it is not always required that a person be incorporated in reality (*reapse*) as a member of the Church, but it is required that he belong to it at least in desire and longing (*voto et desiderio*)." See *Christian Faith in the Doctrinal Documents*, ed. Neuner and Dupuis, rubric 855, p. 241.

12. Vincent of Lerins, *Commonitorium* 2.3.

13. Another exception is the Scots Confession of Faith (1560), which in Article XIV enumerates what works are good before God, and in Article XVIII makes "*Ecclesiastical discipline uprightlie ministred, as Goddis Worde prescribes, whereby vice is repressed, and vertew nurished*" the third note of "*the trew Kirk of God.*" *Creeds*, 3:454–56, 460–64.

14. The Augsburg Confession, articles VII and VIII, in *Creeds*, 3:12.

15. See the Dordrecht Confession (1632), Article VIII, a Mennonite document, in *Creeds of the Churches*, ed. Leith, 299.

16. Immanuel Kant, *Religion within the Limits of Reason Alone* (orig. published 1793; New York: Harper and Row, 1960), 92.

17. Frederick Herzog, *Justice Church* (Maryknoll, N.Y.: Orbis, 1980), 51. See also Herzog, *God-Walk: Liberation Shaping Dogmatics* (Maryknoll, N.Y.: Orbis, 1988), 17.

18. Gustavo Gutiérrez, *A Theology of Liberation* (Maryknoll, N.Y.: Orbis, 1973), 10.

19. James H. Cone, "What is the Church?" in *Speaking the Truth*, 112.

20. Martin Luther King, Jr., *Letter from Birmingham City Jail*, 1963, reprinted in *A Testament of Hope: The Essential Writings of Martin Luther King, Jr.*, ed. James Melvin Washington (San Francisco: Harper and Row, 1986), 289–302.

21. Matt. 10:16; Luke 10:3.

22. Matt. 10:1–5; Mark 6:7; Luke 9:1–2.

23. See Matt. 28:7 and Mark 16:7–8. John 20:1–4 and following emphasizes the role of Mary Magdalene as the first who "runs" with news from the tomb.

24. Fiorenza, *In Memory of Her*, 332.

25. "Commonalities, Divergences, and Cross-fertilization among Third World Theologies: A Document Based on the Seventh International Conference of the Ecumenical Association of Third World Theologians, Oaxtepec, Mexico, December 7–14, 1986," in *Third World Theologies*, ed. K. C. Abraham (Maryknoll, N.Y.: Orbis, 1990), 209.

26. Ibid., 204.

27. Ibid., 209.

28. Calvin, *Institutes*, bk. 4, chap. 1, par. 2 (LCC 21:1014).

29. Schleiermacher, *Brief Outline of Theology as a Field of Study*, rubric 249, p. 125.

30. Matt. 26:27; Mark 14:23; Luke 22:17; Luke 22:19; and 1 Cor. 11:23.

31. *The Book of Common Prayer*, Holy Eucharist, Rite 1: "It is very meet, right, and our bounden duty, that we should at all times, and in all places, give thanks unto thee, O Lord, holy Father, almighty, everlasting God." In Rite Two the revised wording is "always and everywhere."

32. See the Augsburg Confession, Article VIII, in *Creeds*, 3:12–13.

33. Whether the historical individual whose name is used to label a theological position actually held to it, or had some other aim in mind, is often a debatable matter in the history of doctrine. This is especially the case when the position is a discredited one, known mainly through the polemic directed against it by its opponents — in this instance (as also in the later instance of Pelagius), the influential Augustine (354–430). Some, for example, have viewed the ecclesiastical politics of the Donatist movement more as a regional rivalry in opposition to an unwelcome domination by Rome. The theological issue, nevertheless, remains to be tested, whether or not Donatus was a Donatist (or Pelagius a Pelagian). For suggestions of further reading see the entry on "Donatism" in *Oxford Dictionary of the Christian Church*, 419.

34. The Augsburg Confession, Article VII, in *Creeds*, 3:11–12.

35. Calvin, *Institutes*, bk. 4, chap. 1, sec. 19 (LCC 21:1033).

36. Francis Turretin, *Institutio theologiae* (1688 and 1701), IV, xiii.4, as quoted in Richard A. Muller, *Dictionary of Latin and Greek Theological Terms* (Grand Rapids, Mich.: Baker Book House, 1985), 293.

37. Ignatius, *Epistle to the Smyrnaeans* 8.2.

38. Vincent of Lerins, *Commonitorium* 2.3.

39. The Canons of the Synod of Dort, Article XV, "Of Divine Predestination," in *Creeds*, 3:584.

40. The Formula of Concord, Article XI, Negative III, in *Creeds*, 3:171–72.

41. See Resolution 11 of the Lambeth Conference of 1888 on the Protestant Episcopal Church's basis for approaching church reunion, *The Book of Common Prayer*, 877–78.

42. See "The Church and the Churches," in *Christian Faith in the Doctrinal Documents*, ed. Neuner and Dupuis, 253–72.

43. *The United Methodist Hymnal: Book of United Methodist Worship* (Nashville: United Methodist Publishing House, 1989), rubric 885.

44. Alexander Schmemann, *The World as Sacrament* (London: Darton, Longman and Todd, 1966), selection from pp. 29–55 reprinted in *Readings in Christian Theology*, ed. Hodgson and King, 284–85.

45. For further reference see "The Sacraments," in *St. Thomas Aquinas: Theological Texts*, selected and translated with notes by Thomas Gilby (Durham, N.C.: Labyrinth Press, 1982), 349–400; and the General Council of Florence, Decree for the Armenians (1439), based upon Thomas, in *Christian Faith in the Doctrinal Documents*, ed. Neuner and Dupuis, 368–70.

46. See references to the Roman Catholic teaching of the Second Vatican General Council in *Christian Faith in Doctrinal Documents*, ed. Neuner and Dupuis, 378–80. Among twentieth-century Orthodox interpretations see Alexander Schmemann's discussion of "Christ Our Eucharist" in *The World as Sacrament*, 29–55, and Christos Yannaras's reflections on the ethics of eucharistic ontology in *The Freedom of Morality* (Crestwood, N.Y.: St. Vladimir's Seminary Press, 1984). As for a Protestant view, Karl Barth's final rebellious chapters on baptism restrict the New Testament meaning of *mysterion*, as opposed to that of "the Greek and Hellenistic mystery religions," to "the sacrament of the history [*Geschichte*] of Jesus Christ, of His resurrection, of the outpouring of the Holy Spirit," refusing to call either baptism or the Lord's Supper themselves sacraments: Barth, *CD* IV/4, ed. G. W. Bromiley and T. F. Torrance (fragment) (German orig., 1968; Edinburgh: T. and T. Clark, 1969), 102, 108–9.

Chapter 14. The Life to Come

1. See Martin Werner, *The Formation of Christian Dogma* (London: Adam and Charles Black, 1957).

2. Rudolf Bultmann, *History and Eschatology* (Edinburgh: The University Press, 1957), 37.

3. Ibid., 38. For an assessment of Bultmann in the context of late twentieth-century theological discussion see James F. Kay, *Christus Praesens: A Reconsideration of Rudolf Bultmann's Christology* (Grand Rapids, Mich.: Eerdmans, 1994).

4. The preeminent example is Reinhold Niebuhr's *The Nature and Destiny of Man* (New York: Scribner's, 1955).

5. Ludwig Feuerbach, *The Essence of Christianity* (orig. published 1841; New York: Harper Torchbooks, 1957), 168.

6. Ibid., 316.

7. Ibid., 169.

8. Calvin, *Institutes*, bk. 3, chaps. 21–25 (LCC 21:920–1008).

9. Thomas Aquinas, *Summa Theologiae*, 1a2ae. 40:1–8.

10. Ibid., 2a2ae. 17–22.

11. Ibid., 2a2ae. 17:7, 18:2, 20:4.

12. Ibid., appendix to Vol. 33 in the Blackfriars edition, 162–166.

13. John Macquarrie, *Christian Hope* (New York: Seabury Press, 1978), 9.

14. H. H. Price, *Belief* (London: Allen and Unwin, 1969), 269.

15. J. P. Day, "Hope," *American Philosophical Quarterly* 6, no. 2 (April 1969): 89.

16. J. Louis Martyn writes, "The dicta most basic to the apocalyptic thinker are these: God created both heaven and earth. There are dramas taking place both on the heavenly stage and on the earthly stage. Yet these dramas are not really two, but rather one drama.... What transpires on the heavenly stage is often called 'things to come'... Stereoptic vision is necessary." "Apocalyptic thought therefore carries with itself profound epistemological implications." In the case of the Fourth Gospel, Martyn argues, the earthly stage of Jesus' life-story, "which on the face of it is about the past," is seen to define the drama of present life rather than, in the usual apocalyptic sense, the heavenly or future stage. Yet Jesus is said to be "from above." The present drama of the "above" and the "below" thus is viewed to be taking place "on an earthly, present stage" and has to do with "events in the world." "[John] presents his two-level drama in a way which is obviously intended to say with emphasis: 'This is *the* drama of life.'" Martyn, *History and Theology in the Fourth Gospel*, rev. and enl. (Nashville: Abingdon Press, 1979), 135–37.

17. See Hans G. Ulrich, *Eschatologie und Ethik* (Munich: Chr. Kaiser Verlag, 1988).

18. Calvin, *Institutes*, bk. 3, chap. 2, par. 29 (LCC 20:575).

19. Martin Luther, "Preface to the Wittenberg Edition of Luther's German Writings," 1539, Luther's Works, vol. 34, ed. Helmut Lehmann (Philadelphia: Fortress Press, 1960), 285–88.

20. See Moltmann, *The Crucified God*, chaps. 4 and 5. For my further comment see *The Logic of Promise in Moltmann's Theology*, 3–16, and "Jürgen Moltmann," in *A Handbook of Christian Theologians*, ed. Marty and Peerman, 660–76.

21. Ernst Bloch, *The Principle of Hope*, 3 vols. (Cambridge: MIT Press, 1986).

22. See *Apocalypticism*, ed. Robert W. Funk, Journal for Theology and the Church, no. 6 (New York: Herder and Herder, 1969); Klaus Koch, *The Rediscovery of Apocalyptic*, Studies in Biblical Theology, 2d ser., no. 22 (Naperville, Ill.: Alec R. Allenson, 1970); and W. G. Kümmel, *Promise and Fulfilment: The Eschatological Message of Jesus*, Studies in Biblical Theology, no. 23 (London: SCM Press, 1957.

23. R. H. Charles's classic work first published in 1899 is still of interest, *Eschatology: The Doctrine of a Future Life in Israel, Judaism, and Christianity* (New York: Schocken Books, 1963).

24. See also Matt. 19:30, Mark 10:31, and Luke 13:30.

25. See, for example, Paul D. Hanson, *The Dawn of Apocalyptic*, rev. ed. (Philadelphia: Fortress Press, 1979).

26. Gerhard von Rad, *Old Testament Theology* (New York: Harper and Row, 1965), 2:371–72.

27. The reference is to a label much discussed in the 1960s. See Joseph Fletcher, *Situation Ethics: The New Morality* (Philadelphia: Westminster Press,

1966); also, for analysis, *Norm and Context in Christian Ethics*, ed. Gene H. Outka and Paul Ramsey (New York: Scribner's, 1968).

28. Martin Luther, *WA* 10, I, 2, 115.

29. Hal Lindsey, with C. C. Carlson, *The Late Great Planet Earth* (Grand Rapids, Mich.: Zondervan, 1970), 164. See also the bestselling *Left Behind* series by Tim LaHaye and Jerry B. Jenkins, beginning with *Left Behind: A Novel of the Earth's Last Days* (Wheaton, Ill.: Tyndale House, 1996) and proceeding (at present) through twelve more books, the most recent of which appeared in September 2007.

30. Thomas Jefferson, *The Jefferson Bible: The Life And Morals of Jesus of Nazareth*, c. 1804, with an introduction by F. Forrester Church and an afterword by Jaroslav Pelikan (Boston: Beacon Press, 1989), 12.

31. Johannes Weiss, *Jesus' Proclamation of the Kingdom of God* (orig. published 1892; Philadelphia: Fortress Press, 1971), 135.

32. See Gordon D. Kaufman, *Theology for a Nuclear Age* (Philadelphia: Westminster Press, 1985).

33. Jonathan Schell, *The Fate of the Earth* (New York: Avon Books, 1982), 127.

34. Ibid., 230 and 165.

35. See the entry on William Cowper (1731–1800) in *Oxford Dictionary of the Christian Church*, 355. The verse is from the hymn "God Moves in a Mysterious Way," first published in England in 1774.

36. H. Richard Niebuhr, *The Kingdom of God in America* (New York: Harper Torchbooks, 1937), 193.

37. The foremost critique in the history of dogmatics of the tendency to think of God's rejection as having to do with a separate group of individuals occurring outside of the grace of Jesus Christ is to be found in Karl Barth's treatment of election as God's "grace choice" in Barth, *CD* II/2, 3–506.

38. The Canons of the Synod of Dort, 1619, Article XV, "Of Divine Predestination," in *Creeds*, 3:584.

39. Ibid., Article XIV

40. The Five Arminian Articles, 1610, Article V, in *Creeds*, 3:548.

41. See W. D. Davies, *Paul and Rabbinic Judaism*, 4th ed. (Philadelphia: Fortress Press, 1980), 311.

42. Irenaeus, *Against Heresies*, bk. 5, chap. 1, par. 2, in ANF, 1:527.

43. See Vincent L. Wimbush, *Paul, the Worldly Ascetic: Response to the World and Self-Understanding according to 1 Corinthians 7* (Macon, Ga.: Mercer University Press, 1987), 96: "Thus, the relativizing argument (*hōs mē* = *amerimnos*) is used not for debunking, but for accepting involvement in the structures of the world, with the proviso that concern for 'the things of the Lord' take priority."

44. Thomas Aquinas, *Summa Theologiae*, 2a2ae. 19:1.

Appendix A

GUIDELINES FOR *UTRUM* PAPERS

(LENGTH: 5 OR 6 TYPED PAGES)

The purpose of this exercise is to develop the complementary skills in addition to doing scriptural exegesis and historical exposition required for what is called "dialectic," meaning here the pros and cons of argument involved in adjudicating disputed issues, a task of dogmatic theology as a "testing of the spirits." The steps set forth in the articles of the *Summa Theologiae* of Thomas Aquinas provide the pattern adapted in the points below. See chapter 5, note 10 on page 362.

1. The *Utrum* ("whether") — 1 clause or 1 sentence

Here at the beginning of the paper in a clause or sentence state precisely your exact issue with the words, "Whether it is the case that . . . " An *utrum* issue is one question that has plausible alternative answers. If either of the alternative answers to the question is not plausible, that is, if it is already obvious that one or the other answers put forth cannot be so, then the question is not a real *utrum*.

2. The *Videtur* ("it seems") — approx. 1½ to 2 pages

First, on the one hand, give an answer to the *utrum* that seems on the face of it to be legitimate but that, upon further reflection, in your judgment will prove to be indefensible. One should argue this first answer as convincingly as possible as if presenting a legal case in court to a judge or jury. Give the evidence you consider most authoritative (i.e., appeals to scripture, church tradition, ethical impact, scientific data, logic, personal experiences — whatever you deem most valid to make the case). Check the tests of doctrinal faithfulness suggested in chapter 4. The *vide-*

tur presentation will demonstrate your ability to recognize and articulate accurately and fairly a plausible position with which you do not agree.

3. The *Sed Contra* ("but on the other hand") — approx. 1½ to 2 pages

Here give an alternative answer to your *utrum* question with your best supporting reasons and evidence. In both the *videtur* and *sed contra* arguments avoid constructing "straw" positions that anyone could easily dismiss or recognize as "bearing false witness." Try to anticipate the arguments against each of the alternative answers in order to make each of your two cases as strong and persuasive as possible.

4. The *Responsio* ("reply") — only 1 or 2 sentences

In no more than a sentence or two give now your own answer or reply to the *utrum* as definitely as possible. Be sure to address the exact issue and not get off the subject as you have raised it. Your view may be essentially the position elaborated in the *sed contra* or, more likely, a third position drawing something and rejecting something from both the *videtur* and the *sed contra* arguments you have just presented. Here you take a stand. Leave all explanation of your reply for the *ergo* section.

5. The *Ergo* ("hence") — approx. 2½ pages

This conclusion forms a major section of the paper. Here you demonstrate accountability by recalling the reasons offered in the *videtur* (and, if applicable in your case, in the *sed contra*) that you then rejected and found unacceptable in your *responsio*. Tell as convincingly as you can why these arguments you made and then rejected cannot in your judgment be considered defensible when examined more closely.

Appendix B

CREEDS

The Niceno-Constantinopolitan Creed

Dating from the Second Ecumenical Council, Constantinople I in 381, this creed contains, with significant additions, affirmations similar to those from the First Ecumenical Council, Nicaea, in 325, and is commonly referred to in both the East and West in worship services as "The Nicene Creed."

We believe in one God the Father Almighty, Maker of heaven and earth, and of all things visible and invisible;

And in one Lord Jesus Christ, the only-begotten Son of God, begotten of the Father before all worlds, God of God, Light of Light, true God of true God, begotten, not made; being of one substance with the Father [*homoousion tō patri*] by whom all things were made; who for us humans, and for our salvation, came down from heaven, and was incarnate by the Holy Spirit of the Virgin Mary, and was made human, and was crucified also for us under Pontius Pilate. He suffered and was buried, and the third day he rose again according to the Scriptures, and ascended into heaven, and sits on the right hand of the Father. And he shall come again with glory to judge both the living and the dead, whose kingdom [*basileias*] shall have no end.

And we believe in the Holy Spirit, the Lord and Giver of Life, who proceeds from the Father [and the Son (*et Filio or Filioque*)],* who with the Father and the Son together is worshipped and glorified, who spoke by the prophets. And we believe one holy catholic and apostolic Church. We acknowledge one baptism for the remission of sins. And we look for the resurrection of the dead, and the life of the world to come. Amen.

*A later addition only in the Latin West.

For this creed in Greek, Latin, and English see Creeds and Confessions of Faith in the Christian Tradition, *vol. 1, ed. Jaroslav Pelikan and Valerie Hotchkiss (New Haven and London: Yale University Press, 2003), pp. 162–63, 672, and* The Creeds of Christendom: With a History and Critical Notes, *vol. 2, ed. Philip Schaff and David S. Schaff (Grand Rapids: Baker Book House, 1931 and 1983), pp. 57–61. See also references to "N-CP" in Jaroslav Pelikan,* Credo: Historical and Theological Guide to Creeds and Confessions of Faith in the Christian Tradition *(New Haven and London: Yale University Press, 2003).*

The Apostles' Creed

Originating in the second century from baptismal services in the church at Rome, The Roman Symbol, *the fully developed form of this creed used in the West dates from the eighth century.*

I believe in God the Father Almighty, Maker of heaven and earth.

And in Jesus Christ his only Son our Lord; who was conceived by the Holy Spirit, born of the Virgin Mary, suffered under Pontius Pilate, was crucified, dead, and buried; he descended into hell (*ad inferna* or *ad inferos*); the third day he rose again from the dead; he ascended into heaven, and sits on the right hand of God the Father Almighty; from thence he shall come to judge the living and the dead.

I believe in the Holy Spirit; the holy catholic Church; the communion of saints; the forgiveness of sins; the resurrection of the body; and the life everlasting. Amen.

For this Western creed in Latin and English see Creeds and Confessions of Faith in the Christian Tradition, *vol. 1, ed. Jaroslav Pelikan and Valerie Hotchkiss (New Haven and London: Yale University Press, 2003), p. 669, and* The Creeds of Christendom: With a History and Critical Notes, *vol. 2, ed. Philip Schaff and David S. Schaff (Grand Rapids: Baker Book House, 1931 and 1983), pp. 45–55. See also references to "Ap" in Jaroslav Pelikan,* Credo: Historical and Theological Guide to Creeds and Confessions of Faith in the Christian Tradition *(New Haven and London: Yale University Press, 2003).*

INDEX OF SCRIPTURAL REFERENCES

OLD TESTAMENT

Genesis

APOCRYPHA

NEW TESTAMENT

INDEX OF NAMES

INDEX OF SUBJECTS